Management and Organisational Behaviour

CONTEMPORARY CHALLENGES AND FUTURE DIRECTIONS

EDITED BY
RETHA WIESNER
AND
BRUCE MILLETT

John Wiley & Sons Australia, Ltd

BRISBANE • NEW YORK • CHICHESTER • WEINHEIM • SINGAPORE • TORONTO

First published 2001 by
John Wiley & Sons Australia, Ltd
33 Park Road, Milton, Qld 4064

Offices also in Sydney and Melbourne

Typeset in 10.5 Garamond Book

© R. Wiesner, B. Millett 2001

National Library of Australia
Cataloguing-in-Publication data

Management and organisational behaviour:
    contemporary challenges and future directions

    ISBN 0 471 34302 1

    1. Management   2. Organisational behaviour.
    I. Millett, Bruce.   II. Wiesner, Retha.

302.35

All rights reserved. No part of this publication
may be reproduced, stored in a retrieval system,
or transmitted in any form or by any means,
electronic, mechanical, photocopying, recording,
or otherwise, without the prior permission of
the publisher.

Illustrated by Brent Hagen

Cover image © 2000 PhotoDisc, Inc.

Printed in Singapore

10 9 8 7 6 5 4 3 2 1

contents

About the editors iv
About the contributors v
Preface ix
Acknowledgements x
Introduction xi

PART 1 Organisational behaviour and the contemporary environment

1. James Hunt: The future of work 3
2. Kerr Inkson: Rewriting career development principles for the new millennium 11

PART 2 Managing individuals in organisations

3. Margaret Patrickson: Stimulating high-performance outcomes through non-financial incentives 25
4. Richard McKenna: Identity, not motivation: the key to effective employee–organisation relations 35
5. Teresa Marchant: Organisational commitment in an era of restructuring 46

PART 3 Managing groups in organisations

6. Robin Kramar: Managing diversity: challenges and future directions 61
7. Ron Cacioppe: Using individual and team reward–recognition strategies to achieve organisational success 73
8. Abraham Ninan and Greg Hearn: New communication technologies in organisations: issues and impacts 86
9. Susan Long: Cooperation and conflict: two sides of the same coin 95

PART 4 Managing organisations

10. Bruce Millett: Understanding organisations: the basis of managerial action 111
11. Dianne Lewis: Organisational culture — theory, fad or managerial control? 121
12. David E. Morgan and Ian Hampson: The professionalising of management? Functional imperatives and moral order in societal context 135

PART 5 Managing the processes of organisational behaviour

13. Terry F. Waters-Marsh: Exploiting differences: the exercise of power and politics in organisations 153
14. Ken W. Parry: Could leadership theory be generalised? 161
15. Greg Latemore: The heroic archetype for leaders: integrating the old with the new 174
16. Bruce Millett and Chris Marsh: The dynamics of strategic learning in an era of industry restructuring 185
17. Mara Olekalns: Layers of meaning: understanding organisational communication 197

PART 6 Managing organisational dynamics

18. Patrick Dawson: Organisational change 211
19. Ronel Erwee: Business networks: spanning boundaries and incorporating teams 224

Index 238

about the editors

Retha Wiesner

Dr Retha Wiesner is currently Associate Professor and Associate Dean (Academic) of the Faculty of Business at the University of Southern Queensland. Before entering academia in 1989, she gained extensive management and organisational behaviour experience as a human resource manager and an industrial psychologist. Her current research interests include a major national and international study on employee management practices and organisational change in small and medium size enterprises and a large international study on downsizing and restructuring. Retha has published articles and book chapters on organisational change, employee management practices and organisational restructuring in Australia and overseas. She has taught management and organisational behaviour courses in Australia and overseas. She is still actively involved as a consultant to many Australian organisations.

Bruce Robert Millett

Dr Bruce Millett is currently head of the Human Resource Management and Employment Relations Department, Faculty of Business, at the University of Southern Queensland. He earned his PhD in the management of organisational change at Griffith University. He is co-author of a popular textbook on organisational behaviour and has published articles and book chapters on organisational change, performance management and the learning organisation. He has taught management courses in Australia and overseas. His current research interests include the learning organisation, organisational change, and the work of consultants.

about the contributors

James Hunt

James Hunt (BA (Hons), MA Mngt, Kent, UK) is a lecturer in human resources management and organisational behaviour at the University of Newcastle's School of Business on the Central Coast Campus. His research interests include the psychological determinants of leadership style, management competencies, and organisational forms of the twenty-first century. He has lived and worked in Bahrain, Spain, England, Hong Kong, Malaysia, the Philippines, Indonesia, South Africa and Australia.

Kerr Inkson

Kerr Inkson is Professor of Management at the Albany (Auckland) campus of Massey University. Kerr has held positions at the University of Aston (UK), the University of San Diego (USA), and the universities of Otago and Auckland (New Zealand). His publications include eight books and over 40 refereed journal articles. He was first author of *Theory K: The key to Excellence in New Zealand Management* (Auckland: David Bateman, 1986), the best-selling management book in New Zealand's history, and of *Management: New Zealand Perspectives* (Auckland: Addison Wesley Longman, 1998), currently New Zealand's leading management textbook. His most recent research has focused on careers in the contemporary work environment, and his latest book, with Michael B. Arthur and Judith K. Pringle, is *The New Careers*, published by Sage, London, in 1999.

Margaret Patrickson

Margaret Patrickson is Associate Professor in Human Resource Management in the International Graduate School of Management at the University of South Australia. Her research interests include the management of older workers and the management of international diversity. She is the author of four books and many articles in the field of human resource management.

Richard McKenna

Richard J. McKenna is a senior lecturer in the School of Management, Faculty of Business and Public Management at Edith Cowan University, Western Australia. He teaches management, decision making and strategic management. His research interests include business ethics, the identity of individuals in organisations, learning and management education. He is the author of *New Management*, published by McGraw-Hill Australia in 1999, and of articles in recent editions of *Journal of Business Ethics* and *Journal of the Australian and New Zealand Academy of Management*. He has presented papers at national and international conferences. Richard completed his BEcon and MBA at the University of Western Australia and worked in the public sector and banking before turning to academia.

Teresa Marchant

Teresa Marchant is a lecturer in the department of Human Resource Management and Employment Relations at the University of Southern Queensland. She lectures in organisational behaviour and management, and in human resource research and practice. She recently completed her PhD on the effects of organisational restructuring and redundancy on the careers of Australian managers. She has written about careers in marketing, and about the changing nature of work. Her consulting activities involve the use of large-scale surveys, her most recent project being an evaluation of the change influences faced by the National Print Managers Association. Before taking up her academic career, Teresa spent 10 years in business, with roles in marketing and management, including nearly 5 years with IBM.

Robin Kramar

Robin Jana Kramar (BCom (Hons), MCom (Hons), PhD) is an associate professor in management in the Macquarie Graduate School of Management at Macquarie University in Sydney. She has more than 20 years' experience lecturing in Australian universities. Robin has lectured, researched and published internationally and in Australia in a range of areas including human resource management, strategic human resource management, industrial relations, management strategy and labour market economics. She has received funding for a number of projects, including a study of youth unemployment and labour market programs, the development of work and family policies, the management of professionals and managers, and labour flexibility. Her most recent project involves an international study of developments in strategic human resource management policies and practices. This study is part of an international study of human resource practices in more than 30 countries. In addition, she is Director of the Centre for Australasian Human Resource Management, Associate Editor and Book Review Editor of *Asia–Pacific Journal of Human Resources*, is on the editorial board of two journals and is Director of the Master of Management at the Macquarie Graduate School of Management.

Ron Cacioppe

Ron Cacioppe is an associate professor in the Graduate School of Business at Curtin University. He is director of the Master's program in leadership and management. Ron is also a partner, director and active member of Integra Pty Ltd, a consulting company providing services and advice to both government and the private sector firms regarding organisational change strategies, leadership development and the implementation of effective business solutions. Ron has an engineering background, with 15 years' experience at a senior level in industry. He has written and published many articles and books in these areas.

Abraham Ninan

Abraham Ninan teaches organisational communication at the Department of Communication, Purdue University, West Lafayette, IN, USA, while pursuing a PhD (Organisational Communication) with the school. His research concentrates on the adoption of innovative communication technologies, network analysis and change management. He earned his Master's in Business (Communication Management) from Queensland University of Technology, Brisbane, after double bachelor degrees in commerce and English literature. Abraham also consults for Sigma Research Management Group, Cincinnati, Ohio, on quantitative and qualitative marketing research and strategic planning projects. He draws from over 4 years of international consulting experience in marketing research and teaching organisational communication, communication technology and research methods in academe, across the Asia–Pacific region and the US. He has published articles in the *Australian Journal of Communication*, *Prometheus*, *Economics Conference Monograph*, *Asia Pacific Journal of Marketing and Logistics* and *Journal for Research in Higher Education*.

Greg Hearn

Dr Greg Hearn is Associate Professor in the School of Communication at the Queensland University of Technology. Over the last 8 years, his consulting and research activities have targeted the impact of global communication networks on organisations. He was a consultant to the Broadband Services Expert Group, the national policy group which formulated Australia's foundation framework for the information superhighway in 1994. He has been involved in high-level consultancy and applied research with many organisations including Telstra, Austa Energy, Stanwell Corporation, Thiess, many Australian and Queensland government agencies, and British Airways, focusing on organisational adaptation to new communication technologies. He has published research articles in *Human Relations*, *Psychological Record*, *Australian Psychologist*, *Australian Journal of Communication*, *Asia–Pacific Journal of Human Resources* and *Prometheus, Futures and Foresight*. He has co-written two editions of the text *Organisational Behaviour*, published by Harcourt Brace in 1992 and 1996. His latest book, published by Allen & Unwin in 1998, is *The communication superhighway: Social and economic change in the digital age*.

Susan Long

Dr Susan Long is Professor of Organisation Dynamics in the Graduate School of Management at Swinburne University in Melbourne, Australia. Originally a psychologist and psychotherapist, she has worked with groups and organisations as a consultant and action researcher for the past 25 years. She has been a member of the board of the Australian and New Zealand Academy of Management (1995–97), is a Fellow of the Australian Institute of Socio-Analysis and Chair of their Fellowship Board and is President Elect of the International Society for the Psychoanalytic Study of Organizations. She has worked in the field of group and organisational relations in Australia, England, USA, Holland and Germany, and has articles published in English, Hebrew and German. She is currently coeditor of a new journal, *Socio-Analysis* published by the Australian Institute of Socio-Analysis.

Bruce Millett

Dr Bruce Millett is coeditor of this book and is currently head of the Human Resource Management and Employment Relations Department, Faculty of Business at the University of Southern Queensland. He earned his PhD in the management of organisational change at Griffith University. He is co-author of a popular textbook on organisational behaviour and has published articles and book chapters on organisational change, performance management and the learning organisation. He has taught management courses in Australia and overseas. His current research interests include the learning organisation, organisational change, and the work of consultants.

Dianne Lewis

Dr Dianne Lewis, BA, AEd (University of Queensland), PhD (Griffith University), AIMM, is a senior lecturer in management at the Queensland University of Technology, Queensland, Australia. Her research interests are organisational culture, change, power, politics and leadership and she has published widely in these areas. Both in her research and in her consultancy she has had experience in analysing organisations structurally, culturally and strategically with the aim of helping them plan for the future.

David E. Morgan

David Morgan lectures in industrial relations and human resource management in the School of Industrial Relations and Organisational Behaviour at the University of New South Wales. He previously taught sociology, organisation studies, industrial relations and human resource management at a number of institutions. He has published on workplace industrial relations, enterprise bargaining and management studies, and has completed a PhD thesis in labour studies. His current research topics include organisational policy and procedures for management education and development.

Ian Hampson

Ian Hampson lectures in human resource management and industrial relations in the School of Industrial Relations and Organisational Behaviour at the University of New South Wales. He has completed his PhD at Wollongong. Previously he taught Australian politics, and technology and society studies at the University of Wollongong. He has published on the Prices and Incomes Accord and union strategy, technological change and work reorganisation, and industrial relations macroregulation. His current research interests include management education and training.

Terry F. Waters-Marsh

Terry Francis Waters-Marsh (BBus (Charles Sturt University), MBus (Mngt) (Queensland University of Technology) is a Senior Lecturer in Organisational Studies and Human Resources Management in the Faculty of Business and Law at Central Queensland University in Rockhampton, Queensland. He has had more than 12 years' experience lecturing in Australian Universities. Terry has lectured, researched and published in a range of areas, including human resources management, strategic human resources management, contemporary organisational studies, organisational change, performance management and organisational behaviour. He is co-author of the highly successful textbook *Organisational behaviour: leading and managing in Australia and New Zealand* (with Robbins, Cacioppe and Millett), which is going into its third edition shortly. Before entering academia, he worked for 15 years in the construction industry.

Ken W. Parry

Ken Parry is an associate professor of management and Director of the Centre for Leadership Studies at Victoria University in Wellington, New Zealand. He gained his PhD from Monash University. His research interests include the qualitative case study analysis of leadership, the operationalisation of social process theory, managerial reputation, and the auditing of social capital outcomes within organisations.

Greg Latemore

Greg Latemore is Director of Latemore & Associates Pty Ltd, Organisation and Management Consultants at 23 Real Avenue, Norman Park, Qld 4170. Greg began his adult career by studying for the Catholic priesthood. He has held senior management consulting positions at the Australian Institute of Management, Coopers & Lybrand and Price Waterhouse Urwick. Since 1981, he has specialised in management development, strategic thinking and organisational transformation. He also provides executive coaching, team building and counselling in midlife transition. Greg has clients throughout Australia and New Zealand and regularly presents papers at conferences on leadership, change and personal growth. He lectures part-time in the subject 'Organisational Behaviour', at the Graduate School of Management at the University of Queensland. He holds a Bachelor of Arts (1979) and the inaugural Master of Management (1988), both from the University of Queensland, Brisbane, Australia. He is married to Roslyn and has one daughter, Monique. This chapter was drafted during a mini-sabbatical at the CG Jung Institute, Zurich, Switzerland, in October 1997.

Chris March

Chris is a director of nursing at the Peninsula Private Hospital, Redcliffe. Previously, she was Director of Nursing at St Andrew's Hospital, Toowoomba. She has a wealth of clinical and managerial experience in both the private and public health services in Australia and New Zealand. Throughout her career, Chris has maintained an interest in quality management, management education and organisational development. She has served on numerous organisational committees and participated in various groups dealing with strategic planning issues, team-building agendas and continuous quality improvement strategies.

Mara Olekalns

Mara Olekalns is a senior associate at the Melbourne Business School, University of Melbourne, where she teaches negotiation and organisation behaviour. She has previously been employed at the University of Adelaide, the University of Otago and in the Department of Management at the University of Melbourne. In 1999, Dr Olekalns held a Universitas 21 Teaching Fellowship awarded by the University of Melbourne. Her research focuses on communication processes in negotiation. She has examined how the timing and sequencing of strategies link to high joint gain and, more recently, has investigated how a range of situational and personality factors shape the choice and sequencing of negotiators' strategies. Dr Olekalns' current research focuses on the relationship between language use, social judgements, negotiators' strategy choices and negotiation outcomes.

Patrick Dawson

Professor Patrick Dawson is holder of the Salvesen Chair of Management in the Department of Management Studies at the University of Aberdeen and Guest Professor on the Danish research program 'Working Environment and Technological Development'. He has held positions at the universities of Adelaide, Wollongong, Surrey, Southampton, Edinburgh and Roskilde, and at the Danish Technical University. His main research interest centres on various aspects of organisational change, and he has published numerous articles in scholarly books and refereed journals.

Ronel Erwee

Ronel is Professor in Human Resource Management at the University of Southern Queensland and she teaches postgraduate courses in international human resource management, leadership and contemporary issues in business. Her research interests include managing diversity, developing business networks, the internationalisation of companies and organisational change. Recent consultation projects have included diversity management in the Department of Education, Victoria, and management development programs in Queensland Health. She is an associate fellow of the Australian Institute of Management, a member of the Academy of International Business and the Australian Institute of Human Resource Management, and the Academy of Management (USA). She was a professor in the Graduate School of Management, University of Pretoria, South Africa, after completing her Master's and DPhil degrees. She served on the national boards of directors of the Small Business Development Corporation, the Women's Bureau and Denel Informatics, and was Technical Adviser to the Subtheme Committee in the Constitutional Assembly, Parliament, South Africa.

preface

This book is dedicated to all students who are on their way to becoming managers and all managers who strive to 'manage' and not 'just manage'.

The management process of the next decade will be geared to the non-stop search for competitive advantage, which in turn is dedicated to providing customers with the best in quality and service. Managers will have to concentrate on unleashing potential all around them and all the way down. If they do not, they will find their organisations drowning in the competitive tide. The pathway to success is pictured in every management and organisational textbook. The picture looks something like this: Manager 2000 will manage conflict effectively and practise cooperation and collaboration with everybody, inside and outside the firm, from colleagues and subordinates to customers and suppliers. He or she will be a tolerant team worker, tolerant of different and new ideas, forgiving of errors made in the cause of progress, putting the objects of the team above the ambitions of the person. The environment will encourage this by devolution of power and delegation of duties — right down to the empowered, self-managing worker near the top of the inverted pyramid. Everybody knows about the manager of the future. Every guru has been painting much the same portrait for years. Whether the path to the vision leads through quality, or business process re-engineering, or the search for competitive advantage, or leadership, or anything else, the final picture remains the same: an undeniable formula for twenty-first century success.

However, practice very seldom equals theory. This book does not replicate those success formulas provided in organisational behaviour textbooks. This book goes one step further. This book brings together a group of foremost academics and practitioners to outline emerging trends and issues in their respective areas of expertise. They discuss the challenging issues, future directions and controversies related to various organisational behaviour topics found in most organisational behaviour textbooks and identify the implications for organisations, managers and employees. This book is meant to provide scholars and managers with an authoritative reference source for their work in managing individuals, teams and organisations.

Retha Wiesner
Bruce Millett

acknowledgements

I wish to thank my husband, Johan, and daughter, Anchen, for their enthusiastic support, which made the completion of this project possible. I also wish to thank my dear friends, Belinda de Villiers, Pat Boshoff, Marlene Potgieter and Aletta Viljoen for the 'how can I help?' questions, the 'it's no bother' favours and the 'you can do it' cheers. Thank you to Sheree Schott, Betty Cooper and Amanda Web, who took many other tasks off my shoulders during the duration of this project.
Retha Wiesner

I wish to thank my family, Jennifer, Rachael, Scott and Jessica for their patience, which has extended well past my PhD.
Bruce Millett

Together, we gratefully acknowledge all the authors who made this book possible. We would like to thank them for their outstanding cooperation and professionalism. We wish to thank Judith Fox whose encouragement and comments proved invaluable in producing this book. Also, thank you to Maggy Saldais for her valuable comments, Chris O'Reilly for her valuable assistance, and Joy Window for tying the loose ends together during the final stages of this book.

The authors and the publisher would also like to thank the following copyright holders, organisationas and individuals for their permission to reproduce copyright material in this book. The acknowledgements listed are in addition to those that appear on particular pages in the text.

Images
Figure 11.2: from 'Communicating Organisational Culture' by Dianne Lewis, in *Australian Journal of Communication, 1992*, reprinted with permission; figure 19.1: from *The New Organisation* by Colin Hastings; Radar Screen Model, © Colin Hastings, New Organisation Consulting; figure 19.3: from 'Forming and maintaining cross-cultural interorganisational ties' by Ron Erwee, Chad Perry and Paula Tidwell, reproduced by permission.

Text
Page 174: extract reprinted by permission of *Harvard Businesss Review*, from 'The Sound of the Forest' by W. C. Kim and R. Mauborgne, July–August 1992, p. 124, © 1992 by the President and Fellows of Harvard College, all rights reserved; p. 180: extract from *Leadership: Australia's Top CEOs: Finding out what makes them the best*, by James C. Sarros and Oleh Butchatsky, © 1996, reprinted with permission of HarperCollins Publishers Australia; p. 180: extract from *Leadership, Research and Practice* by Ken Parry, © 1996, Pitman Publishing, reprinted by permission of Woodslane; p. 228, table 19.1: G. Batonda, 1995, 'Developmental processes in Australian/Chinese business networks', paper presented to the Doctoral Colloquium of Australian Services Marketing Research Academy, QUT, Brisbane.

Every effort has been made to trace the ownership of copyright material. Information that will enable the publisher to rectify any error or omission in subsequent editions will be welcome. In such cases, please contact the Publisher's Permissions Section which will arrange for the payment of the usual fee.

introduction

The twentieth century was heralded as a period of great achievements and great changes. From a managerial perspective, we were concerned with the 'isms' — Fordism, Taylorism, humanism and post modernism. We know from the new sciences investigating complexity and chaos that much of the new millennium is unknowable at this point in time. However, there is general agreement that technological innovation, globalisation, deregulation and changing consumer preferences will continue to have an impact on the way we manage our organisations and do business. There is also agreement that we have entered a knowledge-based era where the emphasis is increasingly on human capital rather than financial and physical assets.

Management and organisational behaviour have been serious topics of study and discussion for the past 50 years and there is nothing to suggest that this will not be the case for the next 50 years. Why? Because, more than ever, we need to learn how people can work together more constructively to achieve a desirable and sustainable future.

While there is a lot of optimism and excitement about e-commerce and the many opportunities that emerge from new product developments and knowledge creation, there is still a small sense of despair at the gaps in our understanding about dealing with people in an organisational context. The twenty-first century will bring new challenges for managers and students of management. But the old questions of productivity, workplace satisfaction, effective leadership, cultural diversity, motivation, teamwork, structure and change will still be embedded in organisational life. More than ever, we need to identify and discuss the current practices and theories of human behaviour in the workplace if we are to take advantage of the opportunities that abound.

Management and organisational behaviour: contemporary challenges and future directions is a book of invited chapters about aspects of management and organisational behaviour, a book that poses particular challenges and offers advice to managers of contemporary organisations. The purpose of this book is fourfold. First, it provides valuable insights into managing people. Second, it addresses contemporary challenges that managers face every day. Third, it outlines the practical implications of these issues for organisations, managers and employees. Fourth, it identifies future directions for managers to consider in their quest to develop high-performance workplaces.

Overall, we feel the book fulfils a real need for managers and students of management alike. It supports current texts on management and organisational behaviour with alternative views and perspectives. It is unique in that it provides up-to-date commentary from a group of noted authors on significant issues relating to workplace management.

The chapters have been grouped into six parts: Organisational Behaviour and the Contemporary Environment, Managing Individuals in Organisations, Managing Groups in Organisations, Managing Organisations, Managing the Processes of Organisational Behaviour, and Managing Organisational Dynamics. The details of each part are described below.

Part 1 | Organisational behaviour and the contemporary environment

What does the contemporary environment look like? What will the future environment look like? What does it take for organisations, managers and employees to succeed in these environments? *Part 1* provides answers to these questions. In *chapter 1*, James Hunt emphasises that the world of work is currently being transformed at an unprecedented rate, placing increasing pressure on us to adapt to the changes going on around us and to cope with the challenges that emerge from these changes. Instead of pointing out all the negatives associated with these changes, he asserts that we are actually in a better position than were our counterparts of the early 1990s. We are less likely to be taken by surprise, as permanent employment prospects continue to diminish. James also provides us with some future scenarios. He argues that the leaner organisational models of the present era make it virtually impossible for us to operate according to the old hierarchical paradigms with their emphasis on command-and-control.

The relationship between modern managers and their employees has changed towards a mutual and reciprocal interdependency. He argues that in the information age the 'symbolic analyst' will reign supreme, replacing the traditional 'organisational man' of the industrial era. He stresses that future generations will probably wonder in disbelief at the constraints organisations placed on employees in the industrial age, just as they will take the flexibility that is now emerging in the world of work for granted. He sets the scene for fundamentally altered workplaces and individual careers, which are further explored in the rest of the book.

Kerr Inkson writes a delightful *chapter 2*, mainly targeted at anyone who is trying to build a career. With his colleagues Michael Arthur and Judith Pringle, he has completed an in-depth study of the 75 careers of a representative sample of members of the New Zealand workforce. He begins the chapter by stating: 'this chapter is for **YOU**!' He uses this very personal approach to help us think about and find ways to develop. He emphasises that our careers are ours to hold and ours to develop. Kerr argues that academics and theorists have contributed to a false picture of career stability. He provides us with alternative contemporary and future scenarios. He emphasises that knowledge is a key to the 'new careers' and, if we are pursuing a career in tomorrow's society, we are actually 'knowledge capitalists' or 'career capitalists'. He provides us with very practical tools to become 'knowledge capitalists' and not 'just manage', but to 'manage' our careers in the twenty-first century.

Part 2 | Managing individuals in organisations

What does it take to effectively manage individuals in organisations? The answers to this question could be found in *part 2* of this book. Margaret Patrickson, well-known author and researcher, argues in *chapter 3* that money and its corollaries are not the only, nor even the most powerful, source of potentially motivating enticements.

She outlines the non-financial outcomes, such as intrinsic rewards which staff can receive as a consequence of their employment, in a unique way. She asserts that, given their low cost, or, in some cases, even nil cost, they should form part of the infinitely expandable package of rewards available to all of us who wish to energise, sustain and reward those who contribute to team efforts.

Why are intrinsic rewards so important? She argues that intrinsic rewards are inexhaustible. Everyone is eligible. There are no constraints on making them visible. They can be reversed at any time. Their consequences are not permanent. However, their effects can be longlasting. They operate whenever an individual's effort is noticed and acknowledged, and receives a positively valued response. However, there is much more to non-financial incentives than meets the eye. Margaret demonstrates this to us and provides us with some very valuable insights and practical guidelines for using the power of non-financial incentives.

Talk about new insights! Richard McKenna has made 'new insights' an art during his professional career. In *chapter 4* he makes it very clear that managers do not and cannot motivate their employees. Motivation is an individual trait — emerging from our identities. It is, therefore, an aspect of the manager's own personality, as well as a part of each manager's environment in so far as managers interact with other people. Why is an understanding of human motivation important? It informs our self-awareness and contributes to improving the organisation-employee relationship. Richard stresses that even more important is awareness that organisations and managers can and do shape and promote individual identities. He introduces a new way of understanding the relationship between individual employees and their work organisation.

Building on the previous two chapters, Teresa Marchant illustrates in *chapter 5* how to bridge career 'capitalism' on the one hand and organisational commitment on the other. She argues that, in the era of downsizing during the 1980s and 1990s, job security and opportunities for upward career progression have been eroded. The consequence? Organisational commitment has declined, and personnel turnover has increased. Despite planned reductions in workforce numbers, what can organisations do to avoid losing skilled or high-performing employees? Teresa provides us with the answers to this question, by outlining new strategies to retain the employees organisations wish to keep. She goes one step further and addresses the question of whether organisational commitment is really a good thing for employees.

Part 3 | Managing groups in organisations

Teams, in contrast to the individuals and their jobs, have been promoted in recent times as the most appropriate means around which to build organisations. *Part 3* of this book analyses the use of teams, as important building blocks of organisations, in order to create the desired synergies to meet future challenges in organisations. This synergy could result from the integrated and flexible application of specialised competencies and knowledge about the management of diversity, team-reward strategies, new communication technologies and conflict. Why are these competencies and knowledge so important? Because contemporary organisations have no choice other than to strive to continuously improve, so that the performance of the whole is greater than the sum of its parts.

In *chapter 6*, Robin Kramar, one of Australia's experts in diversity management, argues that managing diversity has not become a high priority management initiative in Australian organisations. She acknowledges that diversity management in the future will continue to be influenced by legislation; however, it will also be influenced by the changing nature of the workforce and the nature of the relationships that people doing the work have with the organisation. She encourages an understanding of identities in organisations at the group/inter-group, individual, organisational and societal level. Why is this so important? She argues that, just as the proponents of human resource initiatives are increasingly being required to demonstrate their benefits to the organisation, it will become increasingly important for managers to demonstrate the value of diversity initiatives in terms of outcomes that benefit the organisation as well as the individual. If you want to find out how to build a creative and productive work environment, to improve service delivery and provide a better working environment for employees through managing diversity, this is the chapter to read.

Ron Cacioppe addresses a very important gap in the literature on teams, in *chapter 7*. There are numerous books and articles available on how to build high-performance teams, but there is a paucity of literature which addresses the question, 'how can individual and team-based reward strategies be used to achieve organisational success?' Ron argues that the use of team-based rewards has interested managers, but many hesitate to implement a team-based system, since team rewards appear more complex and may have adverse affects on individual performance. In this chapter, Ron provides very practical 'rewards' guidelines and tools which can be used for individual or team incentives. He puts forward a comprehensive matrix that could be used to determine what tools should be used at various stages of a team's development, and with what type of team. He encourages a thorough rethinking and restructuring of reward and recognition practices, to align them with new organisational goals and culture.

Abraham Ninan and Greg Hearn argue that, with the increasing development and application of technology to communicate locally and globally, it has become essential to investigate and analyse the role technology plays in communication within and between organisations. They succeed in doing this in *chapter 8*. E-mail communication, as well as other forms such as video-conferencing and computer conferencing, have steadily extended to allow and accommodate the crucial need to communicate globally as well as locally. They clarify in this chapter the reasons why organisations implement certain technologies, and address the common focus of teams and organisations on whether or not to implement a certain technology. They then move beyond these issues and consider how organisational culture affects the adoption of technology and how this adoption affects organisational culture, specifically addressing the adoption of electronic mail as part of an organisational culture.

Chapter 9 is essential reading if we wish to understand and manage conflict between individuals, within ourselves, within our groups, within the organisation-as-a-whole, and at an institutional level. In *chapter 9*, Susan Long draws on her extensive knowledge and experience in the field of group and organisational relations, to explain how conflict might be contained, managed and worked through. She explains that conflicts do not simply dissolve when they are avoided — they become displaced. Sometimes conflicts may be what they seem and can be dealt with directly. At other times, conflicts may appear as an overt problem, but mask an issue 'somewhere else' in the system. Susan argues that conflicts may be suppressed or repressed and appear as problems in another guise — workplace accidents or poor performance, for example. Susan also explains how we are affected by our own internal conflicts — say, about change, or the nature of the task we are asked to perform. She makes it clear that to understand the cost of chronic workplace conflicts, we must first recognise their symptoms.

Part 4 | Managing organisations

Part 4 examines what organisational theories say about organisations and how managers view organisations. It then seeks to explore the impact of organisational culture on organisational functioning and, finally, examines the professionalising of management.

In *chapter 10*, Bruce Millett succeeds in making sense of the 'management theory jungle' and argues that, if managers are to respond effectively to the challenges they confront, they need to continually clarify the underlying assumptions they hold about the organisations they manage. He asserts that this is not only what learning is about, but is also a basic component of the way organisations are able to adapt to the challenges and changes in their environments. He takes us through a very interesting journey in his attempt to bridge the gap between the theories of organisations and what actually happens.

Bruce challenges the notion that management and organisational behaviour texts generally define organisations in simplistic terms, and provide limited models that indicate what the basic attributes of organisations are, and how they function. He encourages us and shows us how to actively and continuously seek out alternative explanations about the nature of the organisations we are involved with. He stresses that this is important to expand our understanding of our own arenas of influence and accountability.

In *chapter 11*, Dianne Lewis demonstrates her extensive experience in analysing organisations structurally, culturally and strategically, with the aim of helping them plan for the future. She covers the main trends in the literature on organisational culture, highlights the nature of culture, and those aspects of it that researchers have been interested in studying and that managers have been interested in finding out about. Some of these aspects include what effects culture has on an organisation, how it might be changed to achieve better organisational performance, and how one might measure culture and culture change. She outlines some of the challenging questions and controversies that surround organisational culture, where culture theory appears to be headed, and some implications of culture for managers and employees alike.

She identifies the controversies that remain, including debates on whether it is the prerogative of management to attempt to change culture and to try to control people's feelings, beliefs and values; and argues the strengths and weaknesses of culture as a *useful* management tool. In addressing the question, 'is culture a genuine theory or just a passing fad?', she argues that the idea of organisational culture has been around for long enough not to be considered as just another fad. However, she encourages a critical perspective and warns against accepting *any* theory at face value, because most management theories are value-laden, unitarist and prescriptive. They tell people what to do and they usually take a particular point of view (or bias). They are therefore open to interpretation and analysis.

In *chapter 12*, David Morgan and Ian Hampson discuss the professionalising of management. In doing so, they fill an important gap in the management literature. They argue that while business management as an identified occupational group emerged from a functional role in organisations over a period of time, there are no direct antecedents to which we can point to understand the essential features of management, or the manner in which such features have changed in content or social role. They assert that this is particularly the case if management is seen as a professional activity.

David and Ian explore the range of demands made on management at a number of levels. These demands range from understanding individual behaviour and competence as it is shaped by the practical imperatives of managerial work to forming a collective identity and acknowledging social responsibility and societal leadership. They discuss the broad literature of professionalism, drawing out the key features of the prevailing concepts of professionalism. They also discuss managerialist and neo-managerialist conceptions of the nature and role of management, and they argue that the professionalisation of management suffers from tensions between the profit-making and 'ethical' roles of management. They sketch what they see as the path towards the professionalisation of management in general, and professionalisation in management in particular, and identify problems and constraints.

Part 5 | Managing the processes of organisational behaviour

Part 5 explores the challenging issues and future directions associated with the processes of organisational behaviour, such as power and politics, leadership, organisational learning and organisational communication.

In *chapter 13*, Terry Waters-Marsh engages the reader in a journey of discovery and reflection on power and political behaviour by offering some divergent views on the topic. Some emerging themes in the study of power and political behaviours are also presented. In doing so, he hopes that readers will question their own conceptualisations of power and political behaviour and that they will seek to find new approaches and understandings appropriate to the emerging organisational forms. He notes that, if the chapter stimulates reflective thought and reflection on power, what power may involve and the resultant political behaviours that attend power, then it will have achieved its stated aims.

In *chapter 14*, Ken Parry, a well-known researcher on leadership, puts a new face on some traditional leadership perspectives. He argues that the recurring theme in leadership is the extent to which 'leadership' is something that we can learn and apply readily to the leadership challenges we face. He questions the resolution of the leadership/management debate, and argues that we need to rethink the nature of the relationship between leadership and management. He proposes a style of management called 'managership', which is a style of management that contrasts with the leadership style. Ken also argues the case for auditing the social capital of organisations. These audit outcomes could be used as a basis for developing the capability of managers to improve the social capital of their organisations for the good of the individuals, of society and of the organisational bottom-line.

In *chapter 15*, Greg Latemore builds on the leadership theme introduced in chapter 14. Greg supports the argument that the constructs of management and leadership are often misconstrued: each is necessary but not sufficient to produce organisational effectiveness. He uses metaphors to describe the fact that, while leaders must to some extent blaze their own path, they stand upon the shoulders of their predecessors. He encourages a critical openness to the past by discussing the power and types of archetypes and integrates certain older viewpoints on leadership with more contemporary approaches. He draws upon the 'heroic journey' as an action metaphor for courageous leadership and then addresses more recent understandings of leadership. The approach in this chapter draws upon the best of current thinking and practice in the realms of leadership, while acknowledging the lessons of the past. Finally, he attempts to equip the modern leader with a range of strategies which draw upon the wisdom of both the past and the present.

Bruce Millett and Chris Marsh illustrate the tensions of managing continuity and change in *chapter 16*. They use a case study to demonstrate the importance of an organisation's identity as a strategic focal point for action. They effectively demonstrate the tremendous impact executive leaders could have on an organisation during a time of crisis and major restructuring. They do this by describing the change in the case study firm's identity over a 10-year period of major restructuring, and the phases of identity change that were apparent in this period. Bruce and Chris identified three phases of identity: crisis, doubt and shared vision. Although this chapter is written around a particular case study, theoretical issues and practical implications are outlined. This enhances our understanding about leadership and organisational learning, by relating them to the context, content and processes of organisational experiences.

Mara Olekalns addresses the theme of organisational communication in *chapter 17*. She identifies several models of communication and, for each model, she also identifies the challenges that organisations must address in order to ensure high-quality communication. She argues that traditional models, which emphasise the accuracy with which messages are sent, must meet the challenge of electronic communication. However, new electronic communication media must guard against a reduction in the informal social contact between individuals in organisations. She asserts that newer perspectives on communication highlight the context within which messages are sent and received. Mara stresses that the changing nature of work and organisation structures are increasing the complexity of organisational communication. She provides guidelines to foster a positive communication climate and increase employees' communication satisfaction. She concludes that one of the principal criteria for achieving this is a willingness to view communication as a means for building better relationships, rather than as a tool for gaining power and control.

Part 6 | Managing organisational dynamics

We live in an era where effective and positive approaches to change are essential in order to manage organisational dynamics. *Part 6* addresses the themes of organisation change and building networks.

In *chapter 18*, Patrick Dawson, well-known for his work in the organisational change arena, presents conceptual and practical issues which surround discussions on change management. He informs and educates us by presenting new material which should promote further discussion and debate. He proposes a process-oriented framework of organisational change that is concerned with understanding the political arenas in which decisions are made; histories re-created and strategies rationalised (politics); the enabling and constraining characteristics of change programs; the scale and type of change (substance); and the conditions under which change is taking place in relation to external elements, such as the business market environment and internal elements, including the history and culture of an organisation (context). Patrick acknowledges that it would be neither appropriate nor feasible to produce 'tablets of stone' or exhaustive lists of the key ingredients for successful change. Nevertheless, he succeeds in providing us with some very practical guidelines, which can be drawn from his process-oriented perspective.

In *chapter 19*, Ronel Erwee fills a gap in the management and organisational behaviour literature by exploring the link between two streams of research, namely networks and teams. She argues that, despite the fact that team leaders and managers build systems and networks in all directions across levels and boundaries in organisations, management and organisational behaviour textbooks pay insufficient attention to themes such as building networks and the role of teams within these networks.

She argues that we cannot assume that teams in an organisation will spontaneously form networks that span boundaries or, conversely, that people belonging to a broad business network will evolve into teams. She discusses issues such as how to map networks, as well as discerning the stage of development of a network. She identifies specific dilemmas in managing networks such as dealing with interdependence; cooperation and competition in a network; and the development of trust between members. This chapter also enhances our understanding of the practical implications for organisations, managers and employees in building competencies in managing networks. She provides new insights into cultural diversity in networks and how key actors in a network manage knowledge.

PART 1 | Organisational behaviour and the contemporary environment

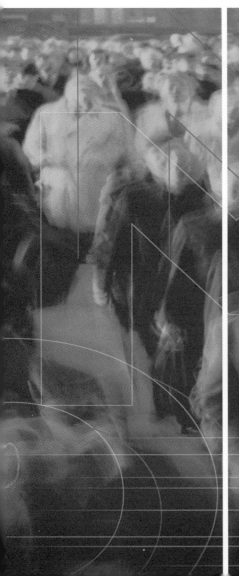

CHAPTER 1

The future of work

by James Hunt

School of Business, University of Newcastle, Central Coast Campus, NSW

MGJBH@cc.newcastle.edu.au

Introduction

The world of work is currently being transformed at an unprecedented rate, placing increasing pressure on individuals to adapt to the changes around them and to cope with the challenges that emerge from these changes. It has been fashionable for management writers to portray the current climate of organisational change as a white-hot cauldron of turbulence driven by the juggernaut of globalisation, and fuelled by a tidal wave of technological innovation. While these kinds of descriptions help to dramatise the magnitude of change in today's organisational world, they also tend to convey the misleading impression that today's changes are spontaneous, and that individuals are strapped into a roller-coaster ride beyond their control.

It is certainly true that the 20-year period between 1980 and 2000 has proven to be very much a transitional one — a period where the industrial age progressively gave way to the economic imperatives of the information era. The first 80 years of the twentieth century belonged largely to the industrial age, with its mass-production factories, its hierarchical organisational structures, its relatively stable employment patterns, and its clear career paths providing lifetime job security for blue- and white-collar workers alike. The world's wealthiest individuals throughout this period derived their profits from the oil industry, beginning with J.D. Rockefeller at the turn of the century, and culminating with the Sultan of Brunei 80 years later. By the mid-1990s, however, Microsoft CEO William H. Gates had become the world's richest person, effectively symbolising the transition from the industrial age to the information era.

Time magazine's choices for 'person of the year' have also reflected this change. Between the 1920s and 1990, just two individuals from the commercial world made the grade: Walter Chrysler in 1928 and Harlow Curtice, CEO of General Motors, in 1955. Both men were captains of an industrial age that is now in the throes of deep transformation. In the short period between 1990 and 1999, however, *Time*'s editors featured a business representative as the magazine's 'person of the year' on three separate occasions. Their selections were Ted Turner of CNN, whose television news empire helped to form the world's 'global village' status, in 1991; Andrew Grove of Intel whose computer chips helped to change the world and its economy, in 1997; and Jeff Bezos of Amazon.com, who began to change the way the world shops, in 1999. Turner, Grove and Bezos all represent the dawning of the 'information age', along with its profound impact on the global economy and the world of work.

This chapter outlines the forces that have fuelled organisational changes over the past 20 years. It begins with an assessment of the importance of the Japanese ascendancy in the global business landscape of the early 1980s, and traces the escalation of international competitiveness through to the present day, demonstrating its role as a catalyst for the profound changes that are now occurring in organisations and in individual patterns of work. The emergence of portfolio workers, career lattices and flexible working arrangements such as 'hotdesking' are noted as recent manifestations of the shift from the industrial era to the information age. These changes have produced a world of work that is characterised by continuous innovation as well as by a high level of volatility.

The origins of change

It is important to realise that the current climate of change facing individuals and organisations today is effectively a product of the shifting that is still under way between the old imperatives of the industrial age and the new rules of the information economy. This shift can be traced back to the early 1980s when a number of large Japanese manufacturing firms first seriously challenged their US rivals at the international level. Before the 1980s, Japanese products were considered to be cheap and often of poor quality. The international corporate arena at this time was dominated by US organisations, and the United States had few serious commercial rivals, with the exception of a handful of German, British and French companies. By 1980, Japanese car manufacturers had begun to penetrate the US automotive market, while Japanese consumer electronics started to capture the world. This provoked western manufacturers to focus increasingly on lifting their levels of productivity, in order to remain competitive at the international level. What followed was a lengthy boom period for western economies that lasted until 1990. Japan's economic ascendancy also provided impetus for growth amongst several smaller economies in the Asia Pacific region, notably the 'tiger' economies: Hong Kong, Singapore, Taiwan, and South Korea.

This 1980s boom period produced significant technological improvements to working arenas everywhere. By the end of the decade, most professional workers had become reliant on a desktop computer to process information. Waste and incompetence were no longer ignored in assembly plants. Zero-defects and just-in-time procedures combined to produce a world of work that had become increasingly concerned with competitiveness at the global level. Advances in computing and data management systems during this decade meant that it had now become easier than ever to compare productivity rates across teams, plants, companies, industries and nations. These years of economic prosperity and technological ascendancy helped to mask the significance of the transitions that had been set in motion. The Japanese wake-up call of 1980 had effectively set in train a decade of profound organisational change on a worldwide scale that few people seemed to notice, at least until the deep recession of the early 1990s.

The 1990s: the age of corporate restructuring

Australia led the world into the recession of the early 1990s, and was closely followed by the United States, then Britain, and later Germany and Japan. Both Australian and US corporations immediately responded to the new economic climate by embarking on unprecedented downsizing initiatives, slashing employee numbers and reducing their organisations to a small core of permanent employees. Britain also followed this restructuring pattern, while Germany and Japan opted to pursue production-based cost-saving initiatives instead. The result was that the German and Japanese economies took considerably longer to recover. Indeed, Japan's steadfast refusal to abandon its cultural ties with lifelong employment meant that the nation spent almost the entire decade of the 1990s in the grip of a serious economic downturn.

This period of organisational reshaping took many people by surprise, particularly the large group of middle managers in Australia, New Zealand, the United States and Britain who found themselves joining the ranks of the unemployed, many for the first time in their lives. Mostly males in their forties, these individuals had begun their professional careers in the early 1970s at a time when lifelong employment prospects were still very real. Previous downsizing initiatives in organisations had been largely restricted to blue-collar workers, leading many of these managers to mistakenly assume that they would remain immune from periodic organisational contractions.

The large-scale downsizings swept through the corporate landscapes of the United States and Australia between 1990 and 1994 at a rate so relentless that it sent shock waves through large parts of modern society. In Australia alone, Westpac, the Commonwealth Bank and IBM all laid off employees by the thousands. Corporate CEOs aggressively pursued one-off productivity gains by slashing total expenditure on salaries. By dispensing with non-essential permanent staff positions and resolutely holding total productivity levels constant, organisational productivity rates rose dramatically on a per capita basis. In many cases, however, the downsizing initiatives went too far, creating understaffed organisations where workloads had become excessive. Stress levels climbed to new heights as individual employees were finally feeling the pressure of the new world of work. Performance expectations had risen dramatically. There no longer seemed to be any room for those who were unable to perform at the highest level.

By 1995, much of the world had emerged from the recession of the early 1990s, and had now entered a prolonged period of growth, led by the US-based technology industries. Firms such as Intel and Microsoft came to symbolise the rapid progress in information technology, while global giants such as Rupert Murdoch's News Corporation demonstrated the commercial advantages of leveraging the rapidly converging multimedia industry. This period presented CEOs with the opportunity to rehire many of those employees who were made redundant several years earlier. Rather than revert to the stable hierarchical organisational structures of the past, however, most firms began rehiring expert talent on a temporary basis to undertake specialist tasks. This trend has continued steadily to the present day, so that we now have a world of work consisting of at least three types of workers. Firms today typically consist of a small core of organisational specialists who enjoy some permanency, a growing supplement of expert contractors and consultants who charge fees for hours worked, and an expanded periphery of contingency workers who perform less essential tasks in times of demand.

By 1999, even Japan was no longer able to ignore the ascendancy of what could appropriately be called the 'North American model of management'. This is the lean corporate model with a small permanent staff profile, and where excess workload is routinely outsourced to specialist providers, or taken up by short-term contractors. In March 1999, 8 years after the United States and Australia had first begun reshaping their organisations for the information era, Sony announced that it would be shedding 17 000 jobs over the next 4 years, while Oji Paper, Japan's largest paper manufacturer, announced plans to cut its workforce by 8 per cent. In April of the same year, the electronics giant Mitsubishi Electric declared that it would eliminate 14 500 jobs over a 3-year period, in order to regain profitability. By October 1999, Nissan had announced its corporate restructuring plan to cut 21 000 jobs from its workforce. Yasuyuki Nambu is a Japanese entrepreneur who anticipated his country's emerging temporary jobs market by establishing the now highly successful Pasona Group, a job placement and retraining business. As early as 1995, the Pasona Group had 120 000 employees on its books. Nambu predicts that unemployment in Japan will climb from 3.1 million in 2000 to almost 5 million in the next few years, as large corporations continue to adopt more flexible organisational forms (Hiscock 1999).

The new world of work

Our increasingly wired world has effectively been evolving progressively over the past two decades. This dramatic evolution has been driven by two key factors. The first is the widespread commitment on the part of organisations everywhere to accelerate and maximise their levels of competitiveness. The second is the digital revolution, which has resulted in technological developments that have helped to transform the way in which work is carried out. As a result of these forces, our markets and our organisations are now much more interconnected than they have ever been in the past. This is the process of globalisation, and it has brought with it the opportunity for competitors to forge strategic alliances in order to leverage economies of scale while sharing markets and technology.

A series of mega-mergers swept through the world's corporate landscape in 1998–99. The largest of these was the merger between Exxon and Mobil Oil, who joined forces to create a company valued at US$86 billion, while Daimler-Benz merged with Chrysler in a US$40 billion partnership. In Europe there was a trillion dollars worth of mergers-and-acquisitions activity in 1999 alone. In 2000, large-scale mergers continued to dominate global business initiatives. The merger between AOL, the world's largest Internet company, and Time-Warner, the world's biggest media conglomerate, created a multimedia empire valued at US$350 billion. These strategic changes have inevitably resulted in triggered organisational structural adjustments, whereby unnecessary duplication of effort has been steadily eliminated. Jeremy Rifkin, in his book *The end of work*, has painted a bleak picture for many employees in the future:

> Today all three traditional sectors of the economy — agriculture, manufacturing and services — are experiencing technical displacement, forcing millions on to the unemployment rolls. The only expanding sector is the knowledge sector, made up of a small elite of entrepreneurs, scientists, technicians, computer programmers, professionals, educators and consultants. (Rifkin 1995, p. xvi)

While this assessment of the world's transition from the relative security of the industrial age to the volatility of the information era may appear unnecessarily alarmist, it would be wrong to deny the global growth rates in part-time and temporary working options which have come at the expense of more permanent and stable career opportunities. As far back as 1993, *Time* magazine observed this trend in the employment pattern, with the following bold proclamation:

> America has entered the age of the contingent or temporary worker, of the consultant and subcontractor, of the just-in-time workforce, fluid, flexible, disposable. This is the future. Its message is: You Are on Your Own. (*Time* 1993, p. 212)

William Bridges was one of the first management writers to take this message seriously, and to provide individuals with constructive advice on how to prosper in a world without traditional long-term employment opportunities. His 1995 bestseller, *Jobshift*, pointed to the growing trend towards temporary and part-time employment models. Bridges noted that Manpower, the US-based temporary employment agency, had more employees on its books than corporate giants like IBM or General Motors (Bridges 1995). In the same year, Britain's Institute of Management reported that nine out of ten British firms used part-time or temporary workers to fill positions that were formerly designated as permanent (Micklethwait & Wooldridge 1996). By 1999, the international employment agency, Adecco, was operating across 49 countries with an annual revenue of $12 billion. Adecco now places over 14 000 people in positions with client organisations each year across Australia alone (Carmichael 1999).

Bridges observes 'today's organisation is rapidly being transformed from a structure built out of jobs, to a field of "work needing to be done"' (Bridges 1995). His advice to the contemporary professional worker is to search for customers and clients, rather than seeking out permanent jobs. Peter Renfrew, the director of Drake Executive Consulting, confirms the necessity of this approach, noting that flexible staffing rates are currently growing at a rate of 20 per cent per year in Australia. Renfrew advises workers not to attach themselves too closely to a single organisation, because in today's volatile employment market it is important to be alert to a wide range of career opportunities. Bridges echoes this sentiment, emphasising the need for individuals to constantly market their skills and services to potential employers, and to maintain an active network of contacts throughout the world of work. There are clear signs in both Australia and New Zealand that today's workers have understood these messages. A 1999 study by the University of Melbourne found that a mere 56 per cent of employees felt secure in their current jobs, compared with 73 per cent in 1989 (Bullock & Potts 1999).

Career implications for 2000 and beyond

Despite the apparent upheaval in the world of work over the past few years, today's professionally minded individual is far from the passive subject of uncontrollable forces, as some of the management literature tends to imply. Indeed, today's managers and employees are actually in a better position than their counterparts of the early 1990s, because they are less likely to be taken by surprise as permanent employment prospects continue to diminish. It is now widely accepted that the single-company career is an artefact of the industrial age. Predictable career ladders, along with slow and steady promotions based on seniority, have given way to the more challenging opportunities thrown up by project-based and team-centred organisations. There has been a surge in outsourcing, subcontracting, and consultancy-style engagements, all of which represent the move towards the introduction of more flexible working arrangements.

Individuals today are more likely to progress through *career lattices* than career ladders. The career lattice captures the pattern of career movement typified by a series of lateral and diagonal shifts, often into areas where an individual has little or no prior experience. Career lattices can develop in multiple directions, and are increasingly viewed as effective ways to gain valuable learning experiences which help to boost personal competence levels and enhance expertise.

Those who have mastered the fast-paced learning skills of the information age are now likely to actively pursue *portfolio careers*, drawing upon a whole series of work-related experiences, enabling them to move freely between positions as diverse as market analysis and professional training, for example. These individuals tend to view single-career professionals as narrow risk-avoiders, and normally relish the transient nature of their own diverse working assignments. In particular, they value the considerable flexibility which they enjoy, along with the capacity to shape their own careers through a series of portfolio assignments extending beyond the confines of a single organisation.

Robert Reich, a political economist at Harvard, refers to this emerging class of intelligence based workers as 'symbolic analysts'. Their essential skills consist of manipulating data to add value to products or services. Most of them are university graduates and tend to gravitate towards careers in information-based industries such as advertising, public relations, the media, management consulting, education, or professional development. In his landmark book, *The work of nations: preparing ourselves for twenty-first century capitalism*, Reich outlines the four fundamental skills of the successful new-generation worker, the symbolic analyst. These are:

- the capacity for abstract thinking and conceptualisation
- systems thinking
- experimentation
- collaboration (Reich 1991).

These skills are vital in today's working arena because they combine to determine an individual's capacity for complex problem solving.

Reich suggests that individuals in the future who fail to develop these sorts of skills will find themselves redundant in a world where information drives our economies, and where routine tasks are rapidly being mechanised. Car manufacturers and other assembly plants are fast approaching the point where these processes will be fully automated, while banks no longer require people to count or dispense money. Even the 'pickers' at Amazon.com — who roam the aisles at their Seattle distribution centre, filling their trolleys with customer orders received on-line — are expected to execute a multitude of tasks requiring intelligent responses to the company's data-processing systems. They have to remain alert and highly motivated, a now universal requirement of professionals in the information era (Zeff 1999).

Changing work arrangements

In a recent article in *HR Monthly*, the question was posed: 'Are we creating the unmanageable organisation?' (Fleming 1995). There is little doubt that successive waves of downsizing initiatives and the drive towards outsourcing key corporate functions have placed greater pressures on managers to ensure that their organisations remain cohesive and integrated, while preserving the capacity for innovation and adaptability. The leaner organisational models of the present era make it virtually impossible for managers to operate according to the old hierarchical paradigms with their emphasis on command-and-control administrative measures. New job titles such as project managers, process leaders, boundary spanners, employee coaches, facilitators, professional mentors and knowledge brokers have begun to emerge in today's organisations. These titles reflect the new imperatives facing modern managers.

The revolutionary developments in information technology have not only empowered employees at all levels by enabling them to make faster and more informed decisions for themselves — they have also added to the demands and expectations placed upon managers. Today's managers are expected to share information to a far greater degree than ever before, because it has become evident that their capacity to do so impacts upon the performance levels of many individuals around them. The relationship between the modern manager and her or his subordinates is now far more fluid than in the past. It is characterised by mutual and reciprocal interdependency, rather than the old superior–subordinate relationships that were typical of the hierarchical organisations that once existed.

Managers are also increasingly letting go of some of the status symbols that once went hand-in-hand with executive positions. Ken Thomas is a regional manager for BMW Australia, whose area of responsibility spans the state of NSW (Scott 1997). He has no luxurious office suite, and no cadre of secretaries, assistants, or office advisers. Instead he operates out of his home office or his car, using a laptop, a fax machine and a mobile phone to remain in touch with dealers, business partners and his colleagues at head office in Melbourne. He is one of a growing army of telecommuters capitalising on recent advances in technology to free himself from the physical confines of the corporate office. In 1997 there were more than 300 000 telecommuters throughout Australia, a number which has continued to grow rapidly (Kramar 1997).

Ann Heyden, the corporate vice president of Metropolitan Life Insurance, refers to telecommuting as a strategic staffing asset, due to its capacity to significantly boost productivity levels amongst workers while maintaining the flexibility required in today's information age. As long ago as 1990, Bell Atlantic trialled telecommuting arrangements on two separate groups of managers, finding no discernible decline in weekly productivity levels (Weiss 1997). Several managers in the trial achieved a 200 per cent productivity increase, and many others demonstrated a 20 per cent time-saving in the completion of sales reports.

Along with the growth of telecommuting has come a reassessment of the utilisation of office space, particularly at corporate headquarters where real estate is often a significant ongoing organisational expense. A number of firms around the world have begun to introduce the concept of *hotdesking*, where multipurpose workstations are established at organisational headquarters. These workstations are booked in advance by employees to accommodate them on specific days and at specific times according to their individual schedules. This arrangement enables professionals to travel domestically and internationally without unnecessarily tying up office space, but it also provides them with vital office infrastructure and services when they are needed. This means that 'hotdeskers' need not forgo face-to-face secretarial assistance or person-to-person software training and support. It also enables them to maintain access to corporate meeting rooms along with satellite technology videoconferencing facilities, for example. In the United Kingdom, Digital Equipment Corporation successfully introduced hotdesking at its headquarters in 1996, and its person-to-desk ratio immediately leapt from two:one to twelve:one, saving the company £3.5 million a year in office expenses (Micklethwait & Wooldridge 1996).

So what does the future hold?

All these developments have fundamentally altered the pace of work in organisations today, and have begun to reshape and redefine the very concept of 'an organisation'. The changes have also placed increasing stresses on managers charged with the responsibility of synchronising collective effort. This in turn has impacted upon the way managers today approach the whole responsibility of 'managing'. More and more individual workers are now being drawn into the sphere of responsibility that was once the exclusive territory of the traditional manager. The concept of cooperative effort has become even more vital than ever before. The sharing of responsibilities for the coordination of effort is central to organisational effectiveness in the information era. Team leadership has become less formally defined than in the past, and coordination duties are normally either dispersed evenly throughout the team, or they tend to gravitate towards the individuals with the highest levels of task-centred experience and problem-solving expertise.

More is being asked of professional workers at all levels in today's organisations. Above all, organisations have finally begun to require individuals at every level to think for themselves, to exercise initiative, to innovate, and to solve problems at the source as quickly as possible. In order to achieve these things, employees are becoming increasingly reliant on the power of modern technology. Many of the signs of this shift are already apparent today. The mobile telephone, the quintessential instant communications tool for the modern world of work, is enjoying explosive growth around the globe. In January 2000, France had 20 million mobile phone users, while the Czech Republic had 2 million — out of a population of just 10 million. In the United Kingdom there were 4.4 million mobile phones sold in the fourth quarter of 1999 alone. Even more revealing is the phenomenal growth of the Internet. The whole rewiring of the planet's central nervous system is producing the kinds of business-to-business linkages that have already begun to radically alter our organisational worlds. Even China — which is still very much in transition from a centrally planned economy to a market economy — is estimated to have 18 million Internet users by December 2000.

In the information age, the symbolic analyst will reign supreme, replacing the traditional 'organisational man' of the industrial era. Future generations will probably wonder in disbelief at the constraints organisations placed on employees in the industrial age, just as they will take the flexibility that is now emerging in the world of work for granted. Many of us will probably work fewer hours than our parents, for example, because we will need to be fully alert 100 per cent of the time. Our working lives are likely to consist of intense periods of creativity and project-based work characterised by high levels of performance and output. But these will be interspersed with lengthy periods of rest and relaxation where there will be opportunities to enjoy life in a way that was much more limited throughout the 9 to 5 industrial age. Each of us is faced with a horizon that will be shaped by our own desire to succeed in the world of work. At least in that respect, very little has changed since the beginning of the Industrial Revolution.

Conclusion

The current 'wave of change' sweeping through organisations around the globe today is not a phenomenon that has materialised without warning. It has been building momentum for at least 20 years, and can be traced back to the Japanese ascendancy in the manufacturing industry during the early 1980s. The surge in business and organisational competitiveness accelerated noticeably throughout the 1980s to the point where hierarchical structures began to noticeably impede future growth prospects. As a consequence, the 1990s unfolded as a decade of profound structural adjustment for large organisations around the world. The rise of outsourcing and subcontracting arrangements over this period has enabled organisations to develop much greater levels of flexibility. These changes have, in turn, had far-reaching effects on individual careers. The emergence of symbolic analysts, knowledge brokers, and portfolio workers has given rise to a new information-based economy that is increasingly reliant on continuous technological innovation. Perhaps above all else, the world of work has become the domain of the technologically literate.

References

Bridges, W (1995) *Jobshift: how to prosper in a workplace without jobs*. London: Nicholas Brealey Publishing.

Bullock, G & Potts, D (1999) Jobs slump legacy of downsizing. *The Sun Herald*, 13 June, p. 62.

Carmichael, M (1999) The key to success is in flexibility. *The Sunday Telegraph*, 29 August, p. 78.

Fleming, D (1995) Are we creating the unmanageable organisation? *HR Monthly*, October, pp. 16–8.

Hiscock, G (1999) It's on for young, but not old, in fad-crazy Japan. *The Australian*, 24 December, p. 42.

Kramar, R (1997) *Human resource management in Australia*. Melbourne: Addison Wesley Longman, p. 79.

Micklethwait, J & Wooldridge, A (1996) *The witch doctors*. London: Random House, pp. 212, 226.

Reich, R (1991) *The work of nations: preparing ourselves for twenty-first century capitalism*. Simon & Schuster.

Rifkin, J (1995) *The end of work*. New York: Putnam, pp. xvi–xvii.

Scott, R (1997) Tele-guerilla armed with modem, laptop. In R Kramar (1997), *Human resource management in Australia*, Melbourne: Addison Wesley Longman, pp. 78–80.

Time (1993) The temping of America. 29 March edition. In J Micklethwait and A Wooldridge (1996) *The witch doctors*. London: Random House, p. 212.

Weiss, J (1997) Telecommuting boosts employee output. In R Kramar (1997), *Human resource management in Australia*. Melbourne: Addison Wesley Longman, p. 144.

Zeff, J (1999) From your mouse to your house. *Time*, 27 December, pp. 38–9.

CHAPTER 2

Rewriting career development principles for the new millennium

by Kerr Inkson

Department of Management and International Business, Massey University, New Zealand

k.inkson@massey.ac.nz

 ## Introduction

Are you going to have a career? Yes? When? Soon! Or perhaps you have already started one.

Will that career be important to you? You bet! It will most likely be the main factor determining your financial welfare until you are 55 or 60. It has the potential to provide you with great fulfilment or considerable unhappiness. Together with your personal relationships and family, it will be the key feature determining your long-term future welfare.

What have you learned so far, to prepare you for your career? Most likely, you know a bit about topics such as motivation, communication, groups, and leadership. Does that help you with your career? It tells you about the world of work, particularly the human side. But typically it does so from a *managerial* perspective — for example, how to motivate others, how to use teams, to lead, and so on, rather than taking the *worker* perspective of how to achieve one's goals through work. A managerial perspective may help you if and when you become a manager, but it may be of limited assistance with the here-and-now task of functioning properly in your first jobs and commencing your career. Information about career development — although it is needed more than management development, and sooner, by most students — tends to be limited in textbooks.

So this chapter is for *you*! It is here to help you think about, and find ways to develop, your career. The study of management, organisational behaviour and careers has taught us plenty that you can turn to your advantage — you just have to think about it the right way. Think about yourself, and what you want out of life. For this chapter, become ruthlessly self-centred.

In the first half of the chapter, I urge you to take responsibility for your own career, regardless of the activities of employers who think your career really belongs to them. Then I warn you about some of the myths that currently exist about careers, and how they are embedded in much of our academic theory about careers, as well as in our everyday ways of thinking about the world. After that, I look at some of the business realities, such as restructuring, that are nowadays affecting careers, and at the new forms of career they are creating. In the second half of the chapter, I consider the issue of how to build a worthwhile career in the contemporary and future environment. I provide some conventional lists of rules, and try to show how they are out-of-date. I present 10 'career principles' based on my own research, representing potential action strategies for you and other career builders. I show how they work in people's lives, and provide a case study example of each. After that, I leave the 'individual' focus for a few moments to show how management must change to adjust to the new career realities. Finally, I introduce the concept of 'career capitalism' as a handy way of summarising the new principles of career action.

Taking responsibility for your own career

Who will your career belong to? Who will be responsible for it? You!

This is not as obvious as it sounds. Many management books seem to be saying that careers are for employers to manage. They tell you that organisations have 'career development schemes' (Robbins, Millett, Cacioppe & Waters-Marsh 1997, pp. 634–7), through which managers provide employees with career pathways, career-relevant training, and career counselling. Career development schemes, they say, enable companies to increase the value of their human resources, reduce labour turnover and provide their people with satisfaction and advancement in their company careers. Sounds good? Think again. What is the long-term value to *you* in your company's lowered labour turnover? As for satisfaction in your company career, what is the advantage to *you* in having a company career rather than an intercompany (or self-employed) career? Lastly, why would you want to entrust your career, which is *your* property, to the faceless Human Resources Department of a company whose objectives are simply not the same as yours?

Your career is yours to hold and yours to develop. Your employer may provide worthwhile assistance and development opportunities for you. This will hopefully be to mutual advantage. But your employer is encouraged to think of you as a 'human resource', whose contribution to the organisation can be maximised by 'human resource management'. The phrase 'human resource' is, I believe, insulting to your status as an autonomous, self-determining person. In the long-term this kind of thinking puts *your* career under *the organisation's* management. Is this not a bit one-sided? Suppose we turn it on its head. Think of the organisation as a resource — a resource for your career. How can you practise 'organisational resource management'? How can you utilise your organisational experiences to maximise your long-term benefits? This may sound selfish, but it is simply applying the same thinking to your employer as your employer applies to you.

Discarding career mythologies

Part of the problem may be the mass mythology about careers. Many of the messages we receive from the world about careers lead us to believe that careers are stable and predictable. At home and at school, you may have been told it is wrong to want just a job, and right to want a career, because it is longer term, and more secure. Consult 'career' in the dictionary and you will find terms such as 'profession', 'advancement', and 'lifetime'. The best careers, you are told, are in particular occupations, usually those with extensive educational requirements. A trade or professional qualification is thought to be a 'ticket for life'. But recently I met a highly qualified accountant who had gained his qualifications as a young man 35 years ago. At age 45 he lost his job in a 1988 stock market crash. He has not worked since. He bought into the myth. He thought his qualifications would last for life. They failed to do so. Do not repeat his mistake. Careers are a lot less stable than most people think. In my own career study, nearly 60 per cent of the participants had moved to a totally different occupation at the end of the 10-year study period (Arthur, Inkson, & Pringle 1999).

Academics and theorists have also contributed to our false picture of career stability. This is understandable for two reasons. First, the theorist's job is to try to determine what order exists in an apparently disorderly world. Second, these theorists have been able to look at careers only from a standpoint of looking backwards over them, even as they have changed.

For example, Schein (1978) developed his well-known theory of 'career anchors' based on a sample of business graduates whom he assessed in the 1950s and then followed up in the early 1970s. The theory has much to contribute to our understanding of careers, but we also need to consider the dramatic changes since then (not to mention the atypicality of US business graduates). A 'career anchor' is a cluster of individual values and interests which Schein said remain relatively stable for most of us and which provide a focus for our career behaviour over time. For example, some people have a strong 'technical/functional competence' anchor, and seek always to achieve good results in specific areas such as engineering or marketing. Other anchors include 'managerial competence', 'security', 'creativity', 'autonomy', and 'lifestyle'. The term 'anchor' indicates that individuals have sources of stability even in turbulent conditions. It is of value to understand one's own anchor. But it is also good to understand how to adapt anchors in a changing world.

Other career theories are likewise incomplete because they overemphasise predictability. For example, *age-stage theories* (e.g. Super 1980) consider careers as predictable sequences that individuals go through, such as:
- the exploration stage (age 14–25 approximately)
- the establishment stage (age 25–45)
- the maintenance stage (age 45–65).

Age-stage theorists tend nowadays to emphasise that some careers may develop right outside these parameters. Nevertheless, age-stage theories do have a tendency to produce age-related stereotypes, and to make career developments seem inevitable. They are not — for example, attempting to maintain the same career with little change from age 45 to age 65 is a risky business in today's environment.

Vocational fit theories, exemplified in the work of Holland (1992), emphasise identifying and measuring the unique but enduring characteristics of each individual and the complementary characteristics of occupations. The objective is to bring about effective job and career performance by matching people against the occupations for which they possess the right characteristics. If you become skilled at assessing your own characteristics and knowledgeable about them, and also at seeing what different types of work have to offer, you have a basis for effective decision making about your career. But again, the theory tends to emphasise stability, in the form of *ongoing* characteristics of both people and jobs, and encourages a rather static view of career processes.

Lastly, consider *human resource theories* of careers, based around the idea of the 'organisational career'. In early work on organisation structure, Weber (1947) indicated that a key characteristic of an effective formal organisation is a 'career system' that enables people to be progressively promoted in the organisational hierarchy as their expertise increases. The idea of building an organisation around stable, loyal staff who can be upwardly mobile in their organisational careers retains its appeal, not least in the famous 'lifetime employment' practices of big Japanese companies. In return for loyalty to the company, the individual is assured a worthwhile, progressive, and secure career. This is the 'commitment' model of human resource management proposed by Beer et al. (1985) and many others. Again, the assurances of career security promised by the model may prove illusory, and the large Japanese companies, following several years of stagnation, are now beginning to lay off staff who thought they had employment for life (*Time* 1999).

In short, much of our career theorising offers some understanding of how careers work, yet is based on assumptions of stability of people, organisations and economic infrastructure which are increasingly questionable in today's — not to mention tomorrow's — dynamic environment. Of course, these theories are not just part of academic theory, but are the basis of many of our most basic ideas and stereotypes about careers. For example, 'older people who have established themselves can have a more settled way of life', 'find a good occupation and stick to it', 'the company will look after my future' and so on are dangerous myths.

Seeing the future

Can you see your own future? Probably not. Can you forecast the world of work in which you will conduct your career? Even that is difficult. However, you can look at trends. You can consider current developments — for example, in organisation restructuring, globalisation, and information technology — and ask the question, 'Where will these take us tomorrow?' Think of the world of work as a jungle through which you have to find your way. You are unable to see far into the jungle, but if you pay attention you can notice how it changes. As you find your way through it, you see further into it as it changes about you. You can get some idea of the kind of person a jungle traveller ought to be, the skills he/she needs, and the tools to be taken along or fashioned as you go.

One problem of careers, unlike other areas of organisational behaviour, is that they take a long time. The careers that are finishing today started in the 1950s and 1960s. That makes it difficult to use them as guides to your own career. Your parents may want to help you from their experience, but their experience may be obsolete. The principles on which they built their careers probably no longer apply.

Consider some of the trends that have taken place since 1980 affecting careers and those that are continuing to alter the ground on which you will walk your career even as you go.

- *Restructuring and downsizing*: Under competitive pressures, organisations in both the private and public sectors have in recent years restructured substantially — for example, merging, changing ownership, downsizing (reducing, sometimes dramatically, the number of employees) and delayering (reducing the number of hierarchical levels). Frequently, careers are disrupted by the requirement to transfer to another job, or by voluntary and involuntary redundancy.
- *Flexible forms of work*: As organisations strive to maximise the flexibility of their workforces in changing conditions, employees become multiskilled and are expected to work across traditional occupational and job boundaries. One effect is 'de-jobbing' (Bridges 1995) whereby 'jobs' — in the form of those nice, convenient, 40-hours-a-week bundles of work which suit us so well — are replaced by contracts, projects, part-time assignments and so on.
- *Outsourcing*: Many organisations nowadays seek to focus on their core business and to contract out subsidiary functions to specialist organisations, to individual contractors and to consultants.
- *Extending the periphery*: As organisations restructure, the 'core' (permanent) workforce shrinks, and the periphery grows, including temporary, part-time and casual workers, all of whom can be employed on a short-term basis and then dispensed with when circumstances change.
- *Globalisation*: The fact that organisations can nowadays shift activities internationally to secure competitive advantage means that the work relied on by local employees may suddenly disappear. Globalisation also results in more career moves taking place across international boundaries.
- *Information technology*: Technological changes result in whole occupations disappearing. Other occupations requiring different skills take their place, and the character of work in most other occupations alters dramatically. E-commerce is dramatically shifting the balance of job opportunities.
- *Feminisation of the workforce*: Women are entering the full-time workforce in ever-increasing numbers. Their careers, and those of men too, must change to take account of the child-rearing commitments in their families. In dual-career marriages, each partner's career must take account of the other's.
- *Education and development*: As unskilled work is automated out of existence, it is replaced by work requiring interpersonal and information processing skills, technical qualifications and so on. Employees are increasingly expected to have acquired requisite technical qualifications, often relatively recently, so that they are up-to-date.

The net effect of all this is to make careers less secure and predictable. Career paths are harder to plan. Hierarchical or occupational progress is more likely to be interrupted. New learning becomes more necessary. Conventional career forms such as the organisational career and the occupational career become harder to sustain.

Instead, for the future, Handy (1989) talks of 'portfolio careers' in which the individual carries around, and develops, a portfolio of skills and a portfolio of current projects. He/she may be involved in several projects at a time. The portfolio is a means of spreading risk and developing new opportunities, much like an investment portfolio, and yields investment returns in the same way. Miles and Snow (1996) predict 'fourth-wave organisations' which will essentially be loosely connected networks of relatively autonomous professionals interacting in overlapping teams to complete projects based on their complementary skills, thereby developing 'fourth-wave careers'. Arthur and Rousseau (1996) posit 'boundaryless careers' which take place between, rather than within, organisations. The career is a 'repository of knowledge' (Bird 1996), and the individual develops knowledge both as a career resource and as a means of enriching and cross-fertilising the organisations in which he/she works.

It is this world — of shifting organisational structures and new, more ambiguous, career opportunities and forms — that you will have to cope with in the years ahead How should you fashion your career? Unfortunately, because of the mythology mentioned earlier, there is plenty of bad advice about. Let us look at some of that first — it is handy to know the convincing, but wrong, ideas you should be wary of.

How not to build a successful career

One of the world's more popular management textbooks, Robbins, Bergman and Stagg (1997, pp. 787–90) offers 11 'keys to a successful management career'. These keys are:
- Select your first job judiciously.
- Do good work.
- Present the right image in terms of what the organisation wants.
- Learn the power structure of the organisation.
- Gain control of organisational resources.
- Stay visible to those in power in the organisation.
- Do not stay too long in your job before transferring to a new assignment.
- Find a mentor higher up in the organisation.
- Support your boss.
- Stay mobile within the organisation.
- Think laterally — if you are not getting ahead in your organisation, consider moving sideways or out.

What is striking about this list is its staggering irrelevance to the organisational world of today and tomorrow. Note the repeated emphasis on 'the organisation'. It is as if none of the restructuring trends mentioned in the section above existed. The fact that managers moving between jobs most frequently move outside the organisation, rather than within it (Nicholson & West 1988; Inkson 1995), is ignored. Note the 'grease ball' aspect of the successful career builder — status-seeking, sucking up to the bosses, presenting image as much as substance and gathering power as you go. Note the clear implication that the only networking worth considering is the network of powerful high-status people in your organisation. Overall, it is hard to imagine a more bankrupt set of guidelines for the new, dynamic, careers environment.

To be fair to Robbins, Bergman and Stagg (1997), they do present, elsewhere in their chapter (pp. 774–5), an alternative list of recommendations for career success. These recommendations are:
- Demonstrate competence, in order to achieve recognition and advancement.
- Actively seek new responsibilities that will stretch your capabilities.
- Make meaningful contributions, treat your superior and coworkers as customers.
- Learn to adapt to organisational expectations.
- Make a commitment to give the job your best shot.
- Continue to learn through formal education, participation in external activities, networking and self-development.
- Prioritise your loyalties, particularly between your loyalty to the organisation and to your own career objectives.

This list is better, because of the implicit acknowledgement that career development is not just about progression in your current organisation. But even this list is limited by the view that *most* of your career development takes place through your current job in your current organisation.

Clearly, a new organisational world calls for dramatically different principles for today's and tomorrow's career builders, such as the readers of this book.

Preparing for your career

Like some readers of this book, you may currently be in 'pre-career'. That is, you have not yet made a full-time, permanent commitment to the world of work, but you are limbering up to do so, through your studies and in other ways. For example, you may be choosing subjects for study according to their apparent relevance to your career. You may be involved in part-time work, or learning about a family business, or looking for vacation work opportunities, or considering postgraduate study or professional qualifications, with career opportunities in mind. What can you do now, to optimally prepare? Lots.

For example, consider your approach to study. If I ask you what you most want out of your courses, do you — like many students — say, 'relevance', meaning relevance to what you may call the 'real world' of work? Fine. But are you also one of the many students who fret about structure in your academic work? What is the precise course content? What is the lecturer *really* looking for in *his/her* essay? Which precise *pages* of the prescribed book chapter should you read? Can you have a 3-day extension, because a lot of assignments have come at the same time? And, of course, what is going to be in the exam? Students taking this approach seek certainty and protection. They want 'relevance', yet they try to prepare themselves for an ambiguous, unstructured world by seeking to reduce ambiguity and increase structure at every opportunity! This is understandable, but it does not make sense.

Out there in what students call 'the real world' (I don't like the term: is the university, somehow, not 'real'?) everything is more ambiguous. There is no clear structure of jobs constituting success. You may have a job description. You may not. If you do, you will most likely be expected to innovate around it. Even if you are not expected to innovate, you should do so, for the sake of your own development. No boss will have time to tell you which pages of which reports you should read in your research. Unfair deadlines will be sprung on you at short notice. If you ask for an 'extension' because of your own poor self-management the boss may either laugh at you or begin to wonder if you have what it takes. You may even be fired or laid off at short notice for something that is not your fault. You need to learn to be resilient. You will not do so by whining at your lecturers for more structure.

If I were to create a course relevant to career development in tomorrow's organisations, it would be of indefinite duration. Classes would be held when people requested them, around topics they needed. If the course was not going well, I'd stop and give students a couple of 'redundancy credits'. I would not set course objectives or prescribed reading or methods of assessment — students would set their own and submit them to me for agreement, or possibly even submit a portfolio of work at the end of the course and hope for the best. I might drop in for a class and say, unexpectedly, 'I've decided to examine you today.' If you weren't ready to be examined or hadn't come to that class, you would probably fail. Could you cope with a course run like that? If not, maybe you should learn to — that is what you'll face in your career!

I do not run my courses like that, because it would be against university principles of quality assurance and equity. But if you want *real* preparation for your career, there is no reason you should not practise similar principles in your own behaviour. For example, resist any temptation to ask for more structure. Choose project courses where you can invent your own assignments. Ask lecturers if you can substitute topics of special interest to you for those set. Try the most ambiguous, unstructured, difficult-looking assignment and exam topics. Set yourself the challenge of submitting assignments *before* they are due. Take subjects outside your usual range — subjects that do not look 'safe'. Change to another university midway through your degree. These ways of doing things may be better career preparation than more conventional ones.

It is the same in your other activities — part-time and vacation work, home and leisure pursuits. In my careers class, I have some students who are really clued up: they are thinking about business opportunities, developing their initiative and entrepreneurial abilities, learning about industries they might like to work in, capitalising on family connections, seeking work that extends their capabilities, taking risks, and networking furiously in search of future possibilities. Others are behaving in a dangerously naïve way. They assume that their degree is all they need to get their first job, and that the first job will inevitably lead to the second and the third. They go for the easy options; they avoid extending themselves in work or leisure.

How are *you* playing it? The choice is yours.

Career principles for the twenty-first century

In this section, I use my own recent research on careers to develop a series of principles which I believe are more appropriate than those from Robbins, Bergman and Stagg (1997) which I criticised earlier, and which look at methods to build careers in the new environment I have described. I will focus particularly on the early career — up to, say, age 35.

With my colleagues, Michael Arthur and Judith Pringle, I have completed an in-depth study of 75 careers of a representative sample of members of the New Zealand workforce (Arthur, Inkson & Pringle 1999). Our sample included approximately equal numbers of men and women, all aged over 25, from all occupational groups, from managing directors and professionals to retail sales workers and manual labourers. We interviewed each one in depth, asking them to tell us particularly about their careers since 1985 — a time of dramatic change in New Zealand and elsewhere. Although the study was conducted in New Zealand, the trends underlying it are international and there is no reason to believe the same general results would not have been obtained through similar investigation in Australia, UK, USA, or other developed countries.

As a start, 10 worthwhile principles will be outlined.

Be open to discontinuity

The conventional view of careers urges you to undertake continuous development within your organisation or occupation. Some do well this way. But many find fulfilment and success only when they move outside familiar parameters. The more discontinuous experiences you have, the greater the likelihood of finding a type of experience that really works for you. In our study, most of the young people who had attempted or completed education or qualifications in a specific occupation were already working in something else. A food technology graduate was a marketing manager. An accounting trainee had become an oyster farmer. A civil engineer was a bar manager. A welder was making good progress as a nurse aide. And so on. In some cases those concerned had not felt fulfilled in their chosen occupation; in others they had not been able to find jobs. In nearly all cases the discontinuity had brought them major benefits.

Example: Brett, a business student, dropped out of university after getting only half a degree in 3 years. He tried factory work, but found it boring. He tried business, but found it constraining. These experiments were valuable in teaching him what he did *not* want. Just to maintain his income, he helped a friend to plaster a house — and found he loved it and had a talent for it. In 4 days he learned enough to get plastering jobs on his own. He taught himself to do ornamental plastering, using books from the public library as a guide. Seven years on, he has his own plastering business, with friends contracted to do the routine plastering while he does the fancier work. He has even finished his business degree in his spare time.

The self-designed apprenticeship

In a formal apprenticeship, you undertake an approved course of training and development to qualify you in a chosen occupation, such as welding or hairdressing. Typically, you work for low wages, attend classes and receive instruction from experienced workers. In a self-designed apprenticeship, you organise the same kind of deal yourself. If you are smart, you will know what you want to know more than any external certification authority or technical college. You may have to make temporary financial sacrifices, putting learning ahead of earning. Most of the more successful young people in our sample had done a self-designed apprenticeship, though none of them called it that.

Example: Jeff, a qualified draughtsman, wanted to get away from what he saw as a boring, dead-end career. He was interested in gardening and landscaping, but had no formal training. So he offered his services as a gardener, at half the going rate. That enabled him to choose his clients. He chose those with the best and most interesting gardens, from which he could learn the most. He networked extensively with knowledgeable garden owners, head gardeners and landscapers. When he felt he knew enough, he started to offer his services at above the going rate. Now he runs his own successful landscaping business.

Self-reliance through travel

The traditional Australian/New Zealand OE (overseas experience) embarked on by thousands of young people every year is a wonderful career development institution (Inkson et al. 1997). In the classic OE, there is no 'career plan'. You are motivated by a desire to 'see the world' or 'have new experiences'. You travel spontaneously. You get whatever temporary jobs you can, often below your level of skill and outside your area of expertise. You learn self-confidence in an alien environment. You learn networking skills. You learn to be versatile and to improvise. In other words, you replicate, in microcosm, some of the key conditions and skills of twenty-first century careers. Do it!

Example: Wendy's early career decisions were taken by her parents. After dropping out of university and having a few dead-end clerical jobs, she got on a plane to London. It was OE which unstuck her career. She found a job, on low wages, working for a small entrepreneurial company, where she controlled its whole sales administration function. Helped by trips to the rest of Europe, she acquired a new self-confidence, a new range of skills, and a special interest in the pharmaceutical industry. On her return to New Zealand, she opened the 'situations vacant' column of the newspaper and was struck by an advertisement for a marketing assistant in a pharmaceutical company which 'fitted me exactly'. Despite having no formal qualifications, she was able to talk her way into the job.

Conduct experiments

If you do what you want to do early, and stick to it, you give yourself only one chance to find out what you really enjoy and are good at. Many people have 'moments of truth' when a new experience helps them to see a new, positive direction for their careers. The more career experiments you conduct, especially when you are young, the greater are your chances of a 'moment of truth'. Experiments may involve seeking new duties, moving to a temporary job to see what it is like, taking on a second job, or taking new educational courses.

Example: Owen's early career involved training as an accountant, fairground work, charter boat work, taking a BSc degree, laboratory research, and scientific work on fishing boats. Some experiments were productive in telling him that he didn't want, for example, office work (accountancy), indoors work (laboratory research). Owen then travelled extensively overseas with his girlfriend (see 'self-reliance through travel' above). They toured Europe in a van, picking up jobs as best they could. At one stage Owen found work on a scallop farm. His moment of truth came when he realised the special appeal of rearing molluscs. He returned to New Zealand and bought a share in an oyster farm, supporting it financially with a combination of contract computer programming and tree pruning!

Treat your employer as a temporary partner

In the new environment, your psychological contract with your employer is less likely to be a promise of a long-term relationship, and more likely to be a transaction of performance for rewards (Rousseau 1995). In this context, you should ensure that you give of your best to your employer, but retain control over your own career. Pursue employability, rather than long-term employment. Consider how relevant the skills you are learning in the organisation are to your employability elsewhere. To repeat: you may be a human resource for your company, but your company is also an organisational resource for your career. Maximum benefit for each party is likely when both recognise the mutuality of benefits, but also that these may be temporary.

Example: Catherine was an accounting graduate who wanted to develop a career in marketing. At the age of 27, she joined the marketing department of a large company. She stayed 5 years with the company, but had four different jobs. In each job she learned a new facet of marketing work — market analysis in the first, strategic marketing in the second, advertising and promotion in the third, and product management in the fourth. In each case, she campaigned for a transfer when she felt she had learned enough. At the end of her time, she was sufficiently experienced as an all-round marketing specialist to obtain work as the marketing manager of a smaller company. She had given good service to the large company, in a variety of roles, but had refused to become part of its 'career track'. Instead, she had customised its learning opportunities to her own career needs.

Learn, learn, learn

Within a few years of your graduation from university, half of what you know may be obsolete. The time taken for knowledge gained at university to become obsolete is probably declining with each passing year. Successful career builders tend to be compulsive learners. Their learning has general, rather than specific, relevance — it goes beyond simply being able to do the current job better. They also constantly replenish their stock of knowledge and expertise, by means of reading, further education, taking on projects with built-in learning opportunities, volunteering for transfer to leading-edge work and so on.

Example: Damien was apprenticed as a chef in a local hotel. While he respected his organisation, he soon realised that the scope for learning was limited. So, three times during his first few years of work, he absented himself from the hotel for several months, instead taking temporary work with other hotels from which he could learn different styles of service, buffet work, specialities of other chefs, and so on. He also studied the management methods of each chef and hotel manager under whom he worked. As a result, he developed special versatility and expertise. By the time he was 30, Damien was head chef in a major restaurant.

Build your own networks and reputation widely

In our study, nearly two-thirds of the transfers by study participants to new jobs were mediated by personal contacts. In over half the cases, personal contacts were the *main* means of finding the new job. If you have limited contacts, you may be badly handicapped in your career development. Organisational contacts are valuable mainly if you seek an organisational career. Career building is mediated by 'career communities' — for example, through industry groups, professional associations, clients and suppliers met through work, social and family contacts and so on. You need to network to develop a 'reputation', so that employers tend to look for you — rather than you having to look for employers.

Example: Martin is a qualified engineer who at an early stage in his career worked in industrial research, but later started his own company, specialising in making equipment for yachts. This was related to Martin's personal interest in yachting as a hobby: over the years he has become well known in competitive yachting circles and has also represented his country competitively. The success of Martin's business is based on his reputation both as a manufacturer of high-quality equipment and as a skilled yachtsman who is at the centre of the yachting community and understands his clients' needs.

Consider self-employment

Self-employment is not for everyone, but in recent years self-employment has increased as more organisations have contracted out work previously done by employees. Many former employees now have careers as consultants and contractors, often to the same organisations that once employed them. Self-employment typically requires you to have knowledge or skills you can sell on the open market. Many of the people in our sample had developed small businesses on the basis of their accumulated career expertise.

Example: Gina's career as a child-care worker took her through a number of positions until, in her mid-twenties, she had a position as supervisor in a commercial child-care centre. When she was dismissed without a reference for insubordination, her career seemed to be in serious trouble. But nine of the parents who were clients of the centre sided with Gina in the dispute with her employer, and suggested that Gina open her own child-care centre for which they would be willing customers and advocates. Their enthusiasm was, of course, based on their perception of Gina's professionalism. Gina used her savings and some borrowings to finance the new venture, which was very successful.

Leverage your experience

Everything you do and are interested in is a potential career asset. If you understand enough about yourself, you can use your assets to get what you want. The assets are not just the obvious things you have like qualifications, aptitudes and work experience, but also things like self-confidence, sense of direction and motivation. Some people even find apparently peripheral things, like hobbies and social contacts, are potential career assets.

Example: Susan qualified in food technology but knew, even before she graduated, that she was really more interested in marketing. Initially, however, the only jobs she could get were those utilising her food technology background. So she looked for marketing applications in her work. Eventually, she applied for a marketing position in the food company she worked for as a technologist, and talked her way into it. Then she used her marketing experience in the food company to get a marketing job in another company outside the food business whose marketing professionalism she really admired and knew she could learn from.

Keep your options open

If careers are becoming 'portfolio' careers, everyone should have more than one folder in their portfolio. You never know when disaster may strike your main career track. Do you have anywhere else to go? Successful career builders cultivate versatility through hobbies, second jobs, small businesses on the side and network connections held 'in reserve'.

Example: Albert graduated as a civil engineer at a time when there was a severe recession in the construction industry. After being made redundant three times in a year, he had had enough. He walked into a bar and offered to work as a barman for nothing ('self-designed apprenticeship', see above) in return for being taught the job and the business. Of course, he did so well that he was eventually offered a full-time bar job. Later on, the construction industry picked up and he got a job as a technical sales representative using his qualifications. But he kept on working as a barman in the evenings and banked his earnings. He was promoted to bar manager and when we interviewed him he had been offered a partnership in a new bar business. Was he an engineer or a barman? He didn't know. He did have a choice.

Implications for management

At the beginning of this chapter, I urged you to be ruthlessly self-centred in your appreciation of it. My consideration of the issues has been very much from the perspective of the individual. As a result, managers reading this material from the perspective of their organisations may be a little horrified. After all, am I not urging loyalty to the self, above loyalty to the organisation? If people act as I advocate, won't they create impossible labour turnover problems for their employers? Won't their experiments, their constant seeking for new learning, their focus outside rather than inside the organisation make them unstable, uncommitted, and rather unmanageable organisation members?

There are a number of answers to this. First of all, modern organisations and their managers have themselves contributed to many of these problems, in their cavalier disruption of employees' careers in the interests of competitiveness and restructuring and their assumption that it is their prerogative to utilise employees in their own interests. What I advocate is simply redressing the balance.

Secondly, insightful organisations may be able to see that there is much in the new career behaviour of individuals that managers of tomorrow's more flexible organisations can capitalise on if they organise themselves sensibly. For example, compulsive learning by employees can become organisational as well as individual learning in an organisation that frames good partnerships and focuses on encouraging the sharing and institutionalising of knowledge. (Note the word 'partnership' — part of the agenda for companies is to reframe their thinking about employees, from 'human resources' to 'human partners').

Most fundamentally, managers must reconceptualise their understanding of the organisation. The organisation of the future will *not* be a monolithic structure through which fortunate and loyal people can have long-term careers by following company objectives, job descriptions, and succession plans. Rather, it can be thought of as a dynamic, ever-changing nexus of employment relationships where individual career aspirations and knowledge combine with corporate plans and resources to create worthwhile 'joint ventures'. In their free-spirited career self-development, individuals develop a natural energy which becomes the wellspring of wider, coordinated enterprise. The manager becomes a 'matchmaker', developing opportunities for individuals to capitalise on their motivation and knowledge by investing them in projects utilising the resources of capital, finance and wider competencies to which the company has access. In organisational forms of the future — to which the modern professional service organisation has some similarities (Brock, Powell & Hinings 1999) — work will be organised less around the blueprint of a large bureaucracy to whose aims the individual must always subordinate his or her own wishes and more around the complementary interests of mobile groups of knowledge workers (Miles & Snow 1996).

As for practical, 'here-and-now' advice to managers, I have dealt with that in a paper based on the input of a high-quality group of 'human resource' managers who faced the 'new careers' issues in their own organisations (Parker & Inkson 1999). Increasingly, managers must become aware of the external labour market in which they operate. This may actually mean outsourcing much of the human resources function to agencies with a greater sensitivity to the external knowledge environment. They must also try to cultivate authentic career understandings with their staff, so that discussions in which the idea that the individual might choose to leave become an acknowledged part of the dialogue. Once managers can acknowledge that the individual's priority is external employability, rather than internal employment, they may be able to work with them to provide experiences and development *within the organisation* which enhance employability. Paradoxically, the more people's organisations help them to stay employable elsewhere, the less likely they are to want to leave where they are (Waterman, Waterman & Collard 1994).

Conclusion

How do we summarise all this? The world in which we must frame our careers is changing fast. Careers are taking on new, more ambiguous, more flexible forms. Yet much of our thinking about careers is rooted in the past, derived from a world which no longer exists, or framed to meet the interests of large business organisations, rather than those of ordinary people trying to live a worthwhile life. To be fulfilled and happy in our careers, we must think about them in new ways and develop new career skills. The principles of the 'new careers' are based not around security, the acquisition of status, and organisational politics, but around autonomy, flexibility, learning, and networking beyond the employing organisation. In the new careers environment, management needs to cultivate a new appreciation of the nature of human organisation, and of the growing need to develop organisations which respond to knowledge workers' energies, rather than attempting to constrain and contain them.

The new world of careers is not a very benign place. Security of employment, and of progression, has gone. There is growing career inequality. Those without the qualifications, the skills, and the willingness to learn are likely to be casualties. So are those who stick to the old myths. So are many in the older generation, whose aspirations are frequently for a quieter, less mobile life than the new careers environment can provide. So are organisations trying to build stability through loyalty, for they find that employees have unlearned what it means to be loyal.

One way of understanding this is to think about a phrase which is heard with increasing frequency: 'the knowledge economy'. Knowledge resources, we are told, are the key to the future. Knowledge is also the key to the 'new careers' (Arthur, Inkson, & Pringle 1999). It follows that if you are pursuing a career in tomorrow's society, you are a kind of 'knowledge capitalist' or 'career capitalist' (Arthur, Inkson & Pringle 1999, pp.168–70). Your knowledge capital is made up of such things as your qualifications, your motivation and your experience, which you constantly invest in jobs, occupations and organisations. You hope that the investment will yield a dividend in the money and other satisfactions you get from the job. But you also hope the capital increases through your involvement, so that the market value of your knowledge (in currencies of value on future markets) is enhanced. Investing in a dead-end company or in a job in which you gets lots of pay, but no learning, is dangerous.

In the twentieth century, the key 'career' words have been 'security', 'advancement', 'specialisation', 'status', 'lifetime', 'qualifications', 'loyalty' and 'planning'. In the twenty-first, they may be 'flexibility', 'versatility', 'mobility', 'multiskilling', 'satisfaction', 'temporary', 'learning', 'entrepreneurship' and 'improvisation'. These words call for a totally new type of career self-development. Do you have what it takes?

References

Arthur, MB, Inkson, K & Pringle, JK (1999) *The new careers: individual action and economic change*. London: Sage Publications.

Arthur, MB & Rousseau, DM (eds) (1996) *The boundaryless career: a new employment principle for a new organizational era*. New York: Oxford University Press.

Beer, HR, Spector, B, Lawrence, PR, Mills, DQ & Walton, E (1985) *Human resource management*. New York: Free Press.

Bird, A (1996) Careers as repositories of knowledge: considerations for boundaryless careers. In MB Arthur & DM Rousseau (eds) *The boundaryless career: a new employment principle for a new organizational era*. New York: Oxford University Press.

Bridges, W (1995) *Jobshift: how to prosper in a world without jobs*. London: Allen & Unwin.

Brock, DM, Powell, MJ & Hinings, CR (eds) (1999) *Restructuring the professional organisation*. London: Routledge.

Great news: no more jobs for life. *Time*, November 1999.

Handy, C (1989) *The age of unreason*. Boston: Harvard University Press.

Holland, JL (1992) *Making vocational choices* (2nd ed.) Odessa, FL: Psychological Assessment Resources.

Inkson, K (1995) The effects of economic recession on managerial job change and careers. *British Journal of Management*, 6: 183–94.

Inkson, K, Arthur, MB, Pringle, JK & Barry, S (1997) Expatriate assignment versus overseas experience: contrasting models of human resource development. *Journal of World Business*, 32(4): 151–68.

Miles, RE & Snow CC (1996) Twenty-first century careers. In MB Arthur and DM Rousseau (eds) *The boundaryless career: a new employment principle for a new organizational era*. New York: Oxford University Press.

Nicholson, N & West, M (1988) *Managerial job change: men and women in transition*. Cambridge: Cambridge University Press.

Parker, P & Inkson K (1999) New forms of career: the challenge to human resource management. *Asia-Pacific Journal of Human Resources*, 37(1): 67–76.

Robbins, SR, Bergman, R & Stagg, I (1997) *Management*. Sydney: Prentice Hall.

Robbins, SP, Millett, B, Cacioppe, R & Waters-Marsh, T (1997) *Organisational behaviour: leading and managing in Australia and New Zealand* (2nd ed.) Sydney: Prentice Hall.

Rousseau, DM (1995) *Psychological contracts in organizations*. Thousand Oaks, CA: Sage Publications.

Schein, EH (1978) *Career dynamics: matching individual and organizational needs*. Reading, MA: Addison-Wesley.

Super, DE (1980) A life-span, life-space approach to career development. *Journal of Vocational Behavior*, 16: 282–298.

Waterman, RH, Waterman, J & Collard, J (1994) Toward a career-resilient workforce. *Harvard Business Review*, July-August, pp. 87–95.

Weber, M (1947) *The theory of social and economic organization*. New York: Free Press.

PART 2 Managing individuals in organisations

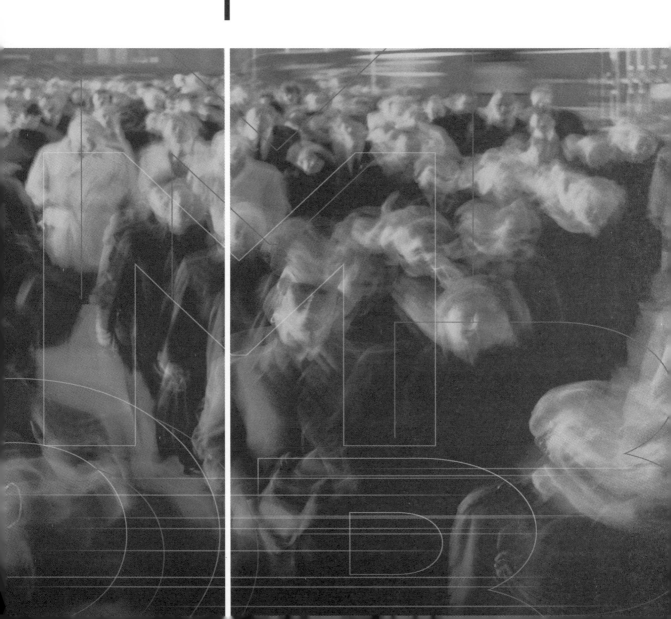

Stimulating high-performance outcomes through non-financial incentives

CHAPTER 3

by Margaret Patrickson

The International Graduate School, University of South Australia, Adelaide

margaret.patrickson@unisa.edu.au

Introduction

Motivation is an integral component of what most managers perceive to be their role. Some believe it is simply a matter of offering good pay, good conditions and the occasional opportunity. Yet knowing what to offer, how to offer it, when to offer it, distinguishing between monetary and other benefits, and how to evaluate whether your offer has been effective can be far from simple. Individuals receive a vast array of outcomes from working. Some of these are financial, such as salary and fringe benefits, and others non-financial, such as exciting challenges, career opportunities and feeling part of the action. Both types of outcome are important to people and both are necessary. Pay and associated benefits, for example, can play a critical role in the recruitment or retention of key staff. Yet money and its corollaries are not the only, nor maybe even the most powerful, sources of potentially motivating enticements. This chapter is concerned with the non-financial outcomes, such as intrinsic rewards, which staff can receive as a consequence of their employment. Given their low cost or in some cases even nil cost, they should form part of the infinitely expandable package of rewards available to all leaders who wish to energise, sustain and reward those who contribute to team efforts.

Intrinsic rewards are inexhaustible. Everyone is eligible. There are no constraints on making them visible. They can be reversed at any time. Their consequences are not permanent. However, their effects can be longlasting. They encompass all those inner experiences that improve our sense of well-being as a consequence of working. Intrinsic rewards can include all of the good feelings that result from recognition of effort, increased responsibility, participation in decision making, challenge, excitement, creativity and power — in fact, any experience that improves our concept of who we are and what we can do. Most are mediated, either internally or through interpersonal interaction, rather than through organisational policy. They operate whenever an individual's effort is noticed, acknowledged, and receives a positively valued response.

This chapter will address the topic by considering a number of issues in order to understand which activities fall within the ambit of intrinsic motivation, how intrinsic motivation works and how leaders can harness its power to stimulate high performance and emotional commitment.

What activities can be intrinsic motivators?

Intrinsic motivators at work are stimulated whenever individuals seek to improve their sense of competence, achievement, skill, knowledge or general well-being. Any outcome that makes individuals feel better about what they are doing and raises their level of effort can be thought of as a potential intrinsic motivator. Such motivators can be understood as valued outcomes that have positive effects on well-being and raise effort levels. Examples include the factors mentioned above — recognition, challenge, work that is sufficiently interesting to stimulate involvement, learning new skills and the ability to influence others. Whether originating in the nature of the component tasks of the job itself, dispensed through interpersonal interaction with colleagues, or administered by the individual to him- or herself, they are experienced as internally satisfying. They act on the emotions to raise the level of energy, thus increasing effort, involvement and commitment.

Some intrinsic motivators have their origins in the human condition and are regarded as being innate (Eisenberger 1972). These include curiosity, discovery and sensory stimulation. However, the majority are learned through the socialisation process and include:

- the need for recognition
- achievement
- power
- mastery
- self-determination
- reduction of uncertainty
- excitement
- challenge
- influence
- parity.

In fact, the list of learned motives can be endless, since individuals vary strongly on what they perceive to be an energising stimulus.

These learned motives can be acquired at any stage in the developmental process. By the time most individuals join the workforce, they are already adults with their intrinsic needs active. As such, they are likely to seek jobs with the potential to continue to satisfy these needs by providing opportunities to exhibit skills acquired in the pre-work training process. Once employed, they will continue the quest, seeking jobs which allow them to express their individuality and exhibit their competencies, and seeking to work with supervisors who recognise their contribution. Once these conditions are present, they are likely to work harder, longer and more consistently.

How does intrinsic motivation work?

Intrinsic motivators make up only one component of the total motivation package. Extrinsic externally administered incentives may also act to energise behaviour. There are almost as many theories of how motivation works as there are theorists. In spite of massive research and numerous publications, no theory of work motivation that can explain and predict behaviour exists. Luthans has identified four major approaches (Luthans 1992). Content models (e.g. Taylor 1911; Maslow 1943; Herzberg, Mausner & Synderman 1959) form one approach: a second set can be grouped under the heading of process models that are cognitively based. These include expectancy-based models (e.g. Vroom 1964; Porter & Lawler 1968), attribution models (e.g. Kelley 1973) and equity-based models (e.g. Adams 1965). None of these approaches specifically separates extrinsic and intrinsic aspects of the motivation process.

Intrinsic motivation is primarily a psychological phenomenon. The individual experiences a boost in emotional well-being, either as a consequence of receiving a positive appreciation response from others or, alternatively, the boost can be entirely self-administered as a consequence of meeting some personal challenge. The critical component is that well-being is enhanced and this can, in turn, lead to improved attachment, improved commitment and improved involvement.

Intrinsic rewards make the recipient feel good, confident, competent, successful, powerful, appreciated, essential, worthwhile — in fact all the potential positive impacts on self-esteem. Conversely, their lack can lead to people feeling unappreciated and taken for granted. Intrinsic rewards are an essential ingredient to the establishment of an emotional tie to another person or to a group — less frequently to a task. Without them an individual feels part of a machine. With them he or she can feel a valued part of a team.

Models of intrinsic motivation

Deci and Ryan (1985) trace the origin of intrinsic motivation back to William James, whose 1890 assertion was that personal interest is an important influence in directing a person's attention to his or her own valued pursuits. Intrinsic motivation was different from the concurrent emergent drive theories in that it did not reduce physiological needs but rather was aimed at establishing conditions which are experienced as rewarding — an aspect first suggested by DeCharms (1968), who conceptualised intrinsic motivation as energised by an internal cause based on the need for competence and self-determination.

DeCharms' work drew on the earlier efforts of Ginzberg, Ginzberg, Axelrad and Herma (1951) who had categorised three types of motivation — intrinsic, extrinsic and concomitant. Intrinsic satisfactions were derived from the job itself, extrinsic ones from the returns that the job provided and concomitant ones from the job environment. However, this tripartite distinction later became blurred. Herzberg and colleagues (1957) reduced the motivational categories to two, specifying a distinction between intrinsic and extrinsic, which dominated theory building for many years. Intrinsic motives became understood as the internal energisers of behaviour as Deci and Ryan (1985) assert (p. 34):

> When people are intrinsically motivated, they experience interest and enjoyment, they feel competent and self–determining, they perceive the locus of causality for their behaviour to be internal, and, in some instances, they experience flow...

In their opinion intrinsic motivation could be inferred whenever an individual performed an activity in the absence of external reward, contingency or control and appeared to be emotionally engaged in the effort.

In a later publication Deci and Ryan (1987) assert intrinsic motivation is one of the most powerful initiators of behaviour. They claim intrinsic motivators are associated with enhanced performance, improved conceptual and creative thinking, superior memory recall, positive affect, higher subsequent willingness to engage in other tasks, and better psychological and physical health.

Thus, intrinsic motivation can be understood as behaviour initiated by the individual in order to experience something which is interesting, exciting, satisfying or personally challenging. Its locus is both in the stimulus of the environment and the inner desires of individuals who may experience differential response to the same stimuli. Intrinsically motivated individuals feel more in control, experience more challenges, and have higher levels of commitment (Maddi & Kobasa 1981). Arnabile (1997) describes the distinction between intrinsic and extrinsic motivation clearly and succinctly as follows:

> Motivation can be either intrinsic (driven by deep interest and involvement in the work, by curiosity, enjoyment or a personal sense of a challenge) or extrinsic (driven by the desire to attain some goal that is apart from the work itself — such as achieving a promised reward, meeting a deadline or winning a competition). (Arnabile 1997, p. 43)

In a recent meta-analysis aimed at reconciling the distinction between intrinsically motivated individuals and intrinsically motivating tasks, Leonard, Beauvais and Scholl (1999) suggest five basic sources of work motivation — intrinsic process, extrinsic/instrumental rewards, external self-concept, internal self-concept and goal internalisation. According to this model, thinking of intrinsic motivation as a single concept may obscure its complexity; intrinsic motivation could in fact emanate from three separate sources. It could be self-initiated in response to deep-seated needs to affirm one's concept of self, arise from internalised goals taken originally from others and later adopted as one's own or from a need to repeat an enjoyable experience. Intrinsic process motivation can also include activities in which individuals engage because they are perceived as fun. This type of motivation includes Bandura's (1986) notion of personal standards and a sense of mastery such that behaviour is driven by the need to contribute personally to the success of the outcome. Goal internalisation motivation occurs whenever internalised values and goals become the driving force to initiate and maintain effort. Leonard et al. caution against the assumption that all intrinsically motivated individuals are likely to behave in similar ways or likely to react similarly to the same incentive. Individual differences will always occur in the direction, level and persistence of effort.

Such emergent conceptualisations can alert managers to the need to design non-financial rewards with the same level of individual choice as in the salary packaging available in traditional monetary reward systems.

Challenging issues in harnessing intrinsic motivation

If intrinsic motivation is so powerful and if it can only be initiated internally (by individuals themselves seeking situations which have the potential to maintain and improve their wellbeing), it makes little sense for managers to think of motivating staff intrinsically through the provision of externally administered rewards. Rather, experience has shown (Deci & Ryan 1987) that to do so may lead to a drop in energised effort under circumstances where the monetary reward is thought to be inappropriate. Intrinsic motivation can be stimulated only if the individuals perceive that their environment has the potential to supply valued self-administered rewards. Self-administered rewards can include the successful solution of problems and puzzles, being absorbed in an activity with inherent interest and challenge, feeling in control, meeting personal goals and experiencing mastery of the task. Investigating the use of non-financial rewards and generating that perception are the keys to harnessing the power of intrinsic motivation.

Potentially intrinsically motivating environments need:
- interpersonal relations between individuals and within teams that are supportive
- information flows which provide feedback that is regularly updated
- jobs designed to be interesting, challenging, exciting, responsible and, to some degree autonomous
- lifelong learning that is encouraged.

Interpersonal relationships play an important role in reinforcing our concept of our competencies and ourselves. Recognition lets us know our efforts have been appreciated, having our opinion sought after confirms its worth, being regarded as an expert affirms our competency, and seeing our ideas taken up by others reinforces our sense of self as contributing value. Information flows that supply data on the consequences of actions, initiatives and behaviours become essential to the process of receiving feedback on behaviour.

However, the area that has received the greatest attention in research into intrinsic motivation has been that of job design and work organisation. Examining the consequences of variations in work content for productivity and job satisfaction led to over 4000 publications in the area by the end of the 1980s (O'Reilly 1991). Early work by Herzberg et al. in the 1950s separated task factors from contextual influences and alerted managers to the need to ensure that jobs were designed to provide opportunities for achievement, recognition, responsibility, advancement and growth. A later job characteristics model developed by Hackman and Oldham (1976) further expanded the job redesign concept to incorporate the calculation of a motivating potential score for each job based on a diagnostic survey which measured job variety, task identity, task significance, autonomy and feedback. Their work led to a set of guidelines for job redesign that, even today (Robbins et al. 1998), incorporates its main themes as an integral part of best practice in designing stimulating jobs.

The encouragement of lifelong learning, the fourth feature, emerged as a goal that forward-looking organisations might sponsor during the period of dramatic change that characterised the last decade of the twentieth century. Senge's publication in 1990, *The fifth discipline*, helped stimulate the popularity of the concept and spawned a number of subsequent efforts, summarised by Marquardt in 1996, which were designed to show how continued skill development raised staff involvement and commitment. Clearly, the opportunity to maintain and develop skill levels provided many individuals with a boost; it raised their commitment and improved their motivation.

Intrinsic rewards thus encompass a wide variety of options, many of which are of low to minimal cost. Perth's Burswood casino, for example, has implemented a program called 'Investors in People', sponsored by the Australian Institute of Management, in an effort to set up comparable assessment standards of efficiency levels between staff (James 1997a). Whirlpool has set up a retailer support program in an effort to grow sales through establishing its sales staff in business development roles (Shoebridge 1997). A more experienced change strategist, Telstra, attempted to drive decision-making autonomy down the structure by empowering regional staff to change work practices (James 1997b). They report that these initiatives resulted in workers demonstrating new enthusiasms and a more rapid installation of new procedures than previous experience had led them to expect. In a more detailed publication, Curtain and Ormond (1994) report on a competency training program implemented by the Rural Water Corporation in Victoria which succeeded in raising the level of staff skills and broadening career opportunities and led to a greater sense of staff ownership. Similar results were reported by Mundy (1998) for the SGS group, which introduced a reward and recognition strategy designed to improve productivity following a period of restructuring. SGS's program provided for flexibility according to differing personal needs by offering a range of rewards that could be varied with changing the individual circumstances of staff.

New initiative programs such as those described represent only one type of usage. However, the more frequent impact of non-financial rewards is likely to be on routine work throughput. Given the almost infinite capacity of humans to receive ego-enhancing outcomes as a consequence of their activities, four important questions must be addressed if non-financial rewards are to be used realistically, efficaciously and equitably in the work environment. These questions are:
- the relationship between intrinsic rewards and non-financial rewards (are these terms interchangeable?)
- the relationship between financial and non-financial rewards
- the choice between motivational strategies open to managers
- the choice between work outcomes open to staff.

The relationship between intrinsic and non-financial rewards

While all theorists agree that intrinsic rewards are non-financial, the reverse (that non-financial rewards are necessarily intrinsic) is not as straightforward. Key to the debate has been the nature of the reward supplier. Some theorists (for example, Deci & Ryan (1985)) see intrinsic rewards as accruing to the individual only as a consequence of self-initiated activity. The reward is thus given to the individuals by themselves and does not require the existence of any third party. This approach underlies the development of the intrinsic motivation inventory by Ryan, Mims and Koestner (1983) and its subsequent use in sports motivation (McCauley, Duncan & Tammen 1989; McCauley, Wraith & Duncan 1991). The inventory separates individuals in terms of their propensity to initiate their own involvement and maintain their engagement.

Others, however, believe the source of the reward to be less important than the individual's experience of internal satisfaction following its receipt. This group is more likely to use the terms more or less interchangeably. An individual is considered to be intrinsically motivated whenever he or she experiences and subsequently seeks an ego boost regardless of whether the activity that preceded the reward was initiated by the individual in response to his or her own internal need or whether the boost resulted from the actions of another. The key factor is that its receipt is a positive internal experience. Katz and Kahn (1978), for example, distinguish between external rewards and internal motivation.

External rewards exist outside the individual and can be used by a third party to stimulate behaviour that would not exist in their absence. Internal motivation can initiate individual behaviour in the absence of any externally administered outcome. Internal motivation is always self-initiated and aimed at the satisfaction of internal needs. It can be satisfied by either internal or external sources. External rewards are always administered by others and predominantly include the attainment of resources controlled by others. Non-financial rewards include everything the individual receives which has no monetary equivalent. Most often, these include intrinsic satisfiers but it is possible for some non-financial rewards to be externally administered (for example, parking space or office space), which can have elements of both an external source and an internal experience.

The relationship between financial and non-financial rewards

Financial rewards include pay, fringe benefits, share options, superannuation entitlements — anything that has a monetary equivalent and is regarded as part of the remuneration package a job occupant receives as a component of the employment contract.

Given that organisational objectives are most often expressed as financial goals, the attraction of financial reward systems lies in their ability to be closely aligned to these outcomes and to direct financial rewards to those who most clearly contribute to organisational achievement. Stone (1998) lists the conditions for financial rewards to be effective as staff attaching high valence to pay; believing that good performance leads to high pay; believing that good performance is a consequence of strong effort; believing that the overall benefits of receiving more money outweigh the costs of not receiving more money; and believing that good performance is a valued behaviour. One would anticipate, therefore, that performance-based pay that attempts to make explicit the linkages between effort, performance and income would be effective when both the culture of the organisation and the staff place high value on income as a measure of contribution and worth.

Research, however, has failed to establish such a clear-cut link between financial incentives and performance for all staff (Kohn 1993). O'Neill (1998) claims that almost all reviews of performance-based pay point to the lack of empirical data on which to base firm conclusions; he highlights the difficulties associated with gathering robust evidence in organisational settings. The only firm conclusion is that while financial rewards can be effective with many staff, they are not effective for all staff, in all types of jobs, in all types of organisations. They are more likely to be part of executive remuneration, given the greater ease with which the linkages can be established between individual contribution and organisational achievement at this level and the necessity to recruit scarce executive talent through the marketplace.

Non-financial rewards include all work outcomes without monetary value for the recipient. These include all the intrinsic rewards mentioned earlier in the chapter plus any extrinsic rewards that make little or no difference to the recipient's income, like workspace, equipment and tools, safe working practices, or work location. However, unlike intrinsic rewards whose cost to the organisation is minimal, these non-financial rewards may involve some financial outlay even though they provide no financial benefit to the receiver.

Choosing between motivational strategies

Repeated evidence confirms that managers hold stronger beliefs in the efficacy of monetary rewards than do staff and there is little doubt that insufficient financial rewards can be demotivating (Lawler 1971). Yet their supply, in terms of an organisation's capacity to pay, is finite. Remuneration should be set at a level high enough to attract the needed talent, but not so high as to become a cost blow-out and threaten the organisation's capacity to survive in a competitive environment. It is a specialised area requiring expert advice to ensure parity, encourage effort, reward achievement and enhance competitiveness. Most organisations, claims Stone, do not achieve optimum value for the dollars they spend (1998, p. 431). Compensation administration is such an important part of staff management that the board most often determines executive remuneration, and non-executive salaries are set with narrow bands. Managers thus have only limited power to vary their staff salaries within restricted parameters.

Nonetheless, financial rewards do have one common factor which enhances their motivating potential. They can be exchanged. Staff can elect to spend their income in their own way. Thus, they are capable of choices which enable each individual to pursue his or her preferred action.

By comparison, the supply of non-financial rewards is infinite, their cost is low, and few are able to be exchanged. Their motivating potential can be released by attention to the goals which individuals consider important, attention to ensuring that valued outcomes are achieved as a consequence of desired levels of performance, and ensuring that these relationships are constantly revisited to maintain their efficacy. Unfortunately, this is a situation whose potential for volatility is high. Managers have other demands on them that shift their focus, staff performance levels are difficult to measure, and individuals can change their preferences for particular rewards. Only constant monitoring of the situation will ensure that it is effective and this takes time and commitment to maintaining relationships. Managers need to be genuinely interested in their staff as individuals and to value differences. At the same time, they have other priorities (like reaching their profit goals efficiently) which may override such personal issues.

Preferences for non-financial rewards

Differences in preferences can result from a myriad of causes. Innate differences between individuals can account for some variation in intellectual functioning and, thus, for some of the desire for continuous stimulation. Yet by far the greatest contribution to establishing and maintaining preference must be attributed to life experiences and the socialisation process. Early work by Lewin (1938), Porter and Lawler (1968), Vroom (1964) and others highlighted the connection between individual needs for intrinsic satisfaction and the characteristics of jobs which were potentially able to satisfy these needs.

What influences particular intrinsic needs to become dominant has received less attention, however. Based on earlier work by Locke (1976, 1984), Reed (1997) suggests that both individual backgrounds and social characteristics produce variations in what people want from their jobs. Strong international variations have been reported (Mead 1995), indicating strong input from national cultures. Gender differences have been reported by Gutek and Cohen (1992), income and job differences by Kovach (1987), age differences by Encel (1998) and variations in family upbringing by Nicholson (1997).

Furthermore, preferences are unlikely to remain totally stable during a lifetime. Changing circumstances mean changing preferences. Checklists may provide managers with examples of possible intrinsic motivators, but they only indicate potential options to explore. One popular book by Firth (1995) offers suggestions associated with each letter of the alphabet. Each possibility needs to be checked out. There is no substitute for finding out through conversation and observation what it is that individuals are seeking and ensuring that this information remains current during their tenure.

Individuals, in turn, need to regularly examine their preferences. Do they still seek and value the same outcomes as before? If not, what has changed? How will this impact on their jobs?

Non-financial motivators are most likely to be effective when they allow for and foster individual variation in the outcomes received. Learners need encouragement that focuses on specific effort, high achievers need acknowledgement of their success, teams need recognition of their ability to work successfully together — the list is endless. The key is to offer what is sought and valued, to offer something not available at the same quality or in the same quantity as elsewhere, to ensure that this information is well distributed and to ensure that the system is monitored consistently. Selecting staff who place high value on intrinsic rewards, socialising them to work in ways that reinforce these preferences and fostering a culture of rewarding contribution encourage a more effective use of non-financial rewards.

An overall motivation strategy

Where do non-financial motivators fit in the overall package? Should they be an explicit component of staff management practice? Are they simply another form of charismatic leadership? None would doubt these questions are important but there are few definite answers.

Ever since Maslow (1943) proposed his hierarchy of needs and Herzberg, Mausner and Synderman (1959) published their motivation–hygiene theory, the perception has existed that intrinsic needs are only initiated and operate more strongly once basic needs have been met. Furthermore, once lower level needs have been more or less satisfied, they lose their motivating power. Such beliefs, however, oversimplify the issue as they deal with the distinction between needs and do not directly confront the distinction between financial and non-financial outcomes.

Each working individual receives a combination of outcomes as a consequence of his or her employment. Financial outcomes can be translated into the achievement of a desired standard of living. Non-financial outcomes can be translated into well-being. But even these categories are not mutually exclusive, given that well-being can also be influenced by the size of one's income.

Both financial and non-financial rewards can be used in response to individual and team achievements. Critical to using non-financial rewards is the fact that these can be used to recognise and differentiate between job occupants in ways that respond to their emotional involvement in their jobs. Non-financial rewards are more likely to be adopted by managers who see themselves as mentors, coaches or leaders who have already discovered that rewards have differential impacts on different staff. Paying such attention to individual differences takes time. Katzenbach's (1996) conceptualisation of 'real change leaders' describes such people as creating excitement and momentum in others by providing opportunities for those around them to follow their example and take personal responsibility for their activities. A similar viewpoint is expressed by Kotter (1999), who advocates a variety of motivational approaches, such as involving people in deciding how to achieve, providing coaching, feedback and role modelling, helping people grow professionally and enhancing self-esteem. He states:

> Good leaders recognise and reward success, which not only gives people a sense of accomplishment but also makes them feel they belong to an organisation which cares for them. (1999, p. 61)

There are few short cuts. Simply raising the level of alertness is a beginning. Conducting a job analysis to understand what potential intrinsic motivators are available in different jobs, making these explicit to potential recruits, selecting staff who value these task outcomes, and rewarding their input is a further step. The next steps are to learn more about the differences between individual staff and to strive to match the desired outcomes to their efforts and achievements.

Explicit reference to intrinsic rewards is becoming a more frequent practice in recruitment, as evidenced by a recent perusal of job vacancy advertisements. But there is less evidence that specific attention is being paid to identifying intrinsic motivators as an activity to be pursued at organisational level. Rather, it appears to be left to the discretion of individual managers to know their staff well, manage them in ways which stimulate the desired effort and reward them in terms which are individually valued.

Future directions for intrinsic motivation

Will tomorrow's workers be different? If so, how? The jobs dominating the world of work in the twenty-first century are significantly more likely to require skills in information processing and problem solving. Restructuring of many industries in the last decade has led to many jobs being more intensified, staff working more cooperatively, and greater attention being paid to customers. Establishing and maintaining mutually agreeable relationships between managers and staff, between staff and customers and among staff members themselves are becoming the key effective operations. To stimulate effort in this climate is going to require that even greater attention is paid to both team efforts and to individual differences than is the case today.

New work measurement systems provide regular measurement of progress. Both individuals and teams will be seeking feedback, and striving to obtain the rewards tied to their achievements. While some of these may be explicitly financial and contain achievement bonuses, there is also likely to be a strong demand for intrinsic outcomes. Recent pressure on executive remuneration has significantly widened the differential between executive and non-executive salaries (O'Neill 1995, 1998) and increased the visibility of high salaries for senior managers. For other levels, the broadening gap means their salaries are now relatively lower and further increases are likely to be elusive without promotion. In such a climate, becoming noticed and acquiring the necessary competencies to advance to a higher office have definite financial implications. Simultaneously, developments in work assessment mean that work performance is significantly more likely to be measurable. With the increasing pervasiveness of new developments in information technology, almost all jobs have been developed to significantly upgrade their knowledge and skill requirements. Tomorrow's workers will turn toward emerging new values that place a higher importance on trust, caring, meaning, self-knowledge and dignity (Maccoby 1988), placing more importance on the intangible than on the non-financial outcomes.

Conclusion

Future managers need to be sensitised to the necessity to constantly question what outcomes accrue to their staff as a consequence of their work performances. What is the relative balance between financial and non-financial outcomes? How does this line up for each individual and within each team? How does it compare with the desired outcomes? When an imbalance occurs, how is this best addressed? What can be done to best suit the configuration of the stakeholders? Remember that, while the supply of financial rewards is limited, the supply of non-financial is infinite. All that is needed is to pay constant attention to the kaleidoscope of changing needs.

There are no easy answers, but there are rich rewards for those prepared to put in the necessary effort to understand each different situation. Having an inquiring approach to each individual and being constantly attuned to the similarities and differences in individual preferences can assist in creating the appropriate environment for intrinsic motivation to flourish. High output levels, high commitment and retention of key staff are all potential rewards. Their value cannot be overestimated.

References

Adams, JS (1965) Injustice in social exchange. In L Berkowitz (ed.) *Advances in Experimental Social Psychology*, 2: 276–99.

Arnabile, TM (1997) Motivating creativity in organizations: on doing what you love and loving what you do. *California Management Review*, 40(1): 39–58.

Bandura, A (1986) *Social foundations of thought and action: a social cognitive theory.* Englewood Cliffs, NJ: Prentice Hall.

Curtain, R & Ormond, H (1994) Implementing competency based training in the workplace: a case study of workforce participation. *Asia-Pacific Journal of Human Resources*, 2, (2): 133–43.

DeCharms, R (1968) *Personal causation: the internal affective determinants of behaviour.* New York: Academic Press.

Deci, EL & Ryan, RM (1985) *Intrinsic motivation and self-determination in human behaviour.* New York: Plenum Press.

Deci, EL and Ryan, RM (1987) The support of autonomy and the control of behaviour. *Journal of Personal and Social Psychology*, 53: 1024–37.

Eisenberger, R (1972) Explanations of rewards that do not reduce tissue needs. *Psychological Bulletin*, 77: 319–39.

Encel, S (1998) Age discrimination. In M Patrickson and L Hartmann (eds) (1998) *managing an ageing workforce.* Warriewood, Australia: Woodslane.

Firth, D (1995) *How to make work fun.* Gower, Aldershot, UK.

Ginzberg, E, Ginzberg, SW, Axelrad, S & Herma, JL (1951) *Occupational choice: an approach to a general theory.* New York: Columbia University Press.

Gutek, B & Cohen, A (1992) Sex ratios, sex role spillover and sex at work: a comparison of men's and women's experiences. In Mills and P Tancred (eds)

(1992) *Gendering organisational analysis*. Newbury Park, California: Sage.

Hackman, JR & Oldham, GR (1976) Motivation through the design of work test of theory. *Organisational Behaviour and Human Performance*. August.

Herzberg, F, Mausner, B, Peterson, RO & Capwell, DF (1957) *Job attitudes: review of research and opinion*. Pittsburgh, USA: Psychological Service of Pittsburgh.

Herzberg, F, Mausner, B & Synderman B (1959) *The motivation to work*. New York, USA: Wiley.

James, D (1997a) Trying to take the gamble out of managing a casino, *Business Review Weekly*, 21 April, pp. 64–6.

James, D (1997b) An outsider who switched on the power and got Telstra moving, *Business Review Weekly*, 12 May, pp. 70–2.

Katz, D & Kahn RL (1978) *The social psychology of organisations* (2nd ed.). New York: Wiley.

Katzenbach, J (1996) *Real change leaders*. London, UK: Nicholas Brealey.

Kelley, HH (1973) The process of causal attribution. *American Psychologist*, February: 107–28.

Kohn, A (1993) Why incentive plans cannot work. *Harvard Business Review*, September–October, pp. 54–63.

Kotter, JP (1999) *What leaders really do*. Mass, USA: Harvard Business School.

Kovach, KA (1987) What motivates employees? Workers and supervisors give different answers. *Business Horizons*, September–October: 58–65.

Lawler, EE (1971) *Pay and organisational effectiveness*. New York: McGraw-Hill.

Leonard, NH, Beauvais, LL & Scholl, RW (1999) Work motivation: the incorporation of self-concept based processes. *Human relations*, 52(8): 969–98.

Lewin, K (1938) *The conceptual representation of the measurement of psychological force*. USA: Duke University Press.

Locke, EA (1976) The nature and causes of job satisfaction. In M Dunnette (ed.) *Handbook of industrial psychology*. Chicago: Rand McNally.

Locke, EA (1984) Job satisfaction. In M Gruenberg and T Wall (eds) *Social psychology and organisational behaviour*. London, UK: Wiley.

Luthans, F (1992) *Organizational behaviour* (6th ed.). New York: McGraw-Hill.

Maccoby, M (1988) *Why work? Motivating and leading the new generation*. New York: Simon and Schuster.

Maddi, SR and Kobasa, SC (1981) Intrinsic motivation and health. In HI Day (ed.) *Advances in intrinsic motivation and aesthetics*. New York: Plenum Press.

Marquardt, M (1996) *Building the learning organization*. New York: McGraw-Hill.

Maslow, AH (1943) *Motivation and personality*. New York: Harper.

McCauley, E, Duncan, TE & Tammen, VV (1989) Psychometric properties of the intrinsic motivation inventory in a competitive sport setting: a confirmatory factor analysis. *Research quarterly for exercise and sport*, 60: 48–58.

McCauley, E, Wraith, S & Duncan, TE (1991) Self-efficacy, perceptions of success, and intrinsic motivation for exercise. *Journal of Applied Social Psychology*, 21: 139–55.

Mead, R (1995) *International management: cross-cultural dimensions*. Oxford, UK: Blackwell.

Mundy, C (1998) Changing reward and recognition practices at SGS Australia. In G O'Neill and R Kramar (eds) *Australian human resources management*, Melbourne, Australia: Pitman Publishing, pp. 171–80.

Nicholson, N (1997) Evolutionary psychology: toward a new view of human nature and organisational society. *Human Relations*, 50(9): 1053–78.

O'Neill, G (1995) Trends and issues in pay design and management. In G O'Neill and R Kramar, (eds) *Australian human resources management, current trends in management practice*. Melbourne, Australia: Pitman Publishing.

O'Neill, G (1998) Linking pay to performance: conflicting views and conflicting evidence. In RJ Stone, *Readings in human resource management*, 3, pp. 191–201, Milton, Queensland: Jacaranda Wiley.

O'Reilly, CA (1991) Organisational behaviour: where we've been, where we're going. *Annual Review of Psychology*, 42: 427–58.

Porter, LW & Lawler, EE (1968) *Managerial attitudes and performance*. Homewood, USA: Irwin.

Reed, K (1997) *International differences in job satisfaction: an 11-nation comparison*. Working Paper No. 27/97, Department of Management, Monash University, Melbourne, Australia.

Robbins, SP, Millett, B, Cacioppe, R & Waters-Marsh T (1998) *Organisational behaviour* (2nd ed.). Sydney, Australia: Prentice Hall.

Ryan, RM, Mims, V & Koestner, R (1983) Relation of reward contingency and interpersonal context to intrinsic motivation: a review and test using cognitive evaluation theory. *Journal of Personality and Social Psychology*, 45: 736–50.

Senge, P (1990) *The fifth discipline*. New York: Doubleday.

Shoebridge, N (1997) Whirlpool's smaller ripples are turning the tide, *Business Review Weekly*, 9 June, pp. 76–7.

Stone, RJ (1998) *Human resource management* (3rd ed.) Milton, Australia: Jacaranda Wiley.

Taylor, FW (1911) *Scientific management*. New York: Harper and Bros.

Vroom, VH (1964) *Work and motivation*. New York: Wiley.

Identity, not motivation: the key to employee–organisation relations

CHAPTER 4

by Richard McKenna

Edith Cowan University, WA

r.mckenna@cowan.edu.au

 ## Introduction

Management is generally defined as the art of getting things done through and with people in formally organised groups. For the past century in the western world, this has implied that managing involves motivation of self and of others. However, managers do not and cannot motivate their employees. Motivation is an individual trait emerging from the person's identity. It is, therefore, an aspect of the manager's own personality as well as a part of each manager's environment in so far as managers interact with other people. Understanding human motivation is important for managers as it informs their self-awareness and contributes to improving the organisation–employee relationship. More important is the awareness that organisations and managers can and do shape and promote individual identities.

This chapter introduces a new way of understanding the relationship between individual employees and their work organisation. The new understanding is based on the concept of identity. After a brief introduction of this concept, an explanation is given of why motivation theories are imperfect. Then, several theories and models of individual identity are introduced as background to the main argument of the chapter — that the complex and dynamic identities of organisational members are central to achieving congruence between individual and organisational goals. That is, managing requires understanding of identity and helping individuals in their search for and development of identities. Within organisational settings each individual is both an organisational actor and a natural person, and this duality adds complexity to the identity. Also, identity in an organisation has both situational identification and deep structure identification elements. The latter leads to congruence between the self-at-work and one's broader self-concept.

What is identity? Identity is 'composed of numerous, often conflicting elements which coexist in an individual's unconscious' (Gabriel 1999). Identity exists in relation to others, and comes from both action and words, and the way these are perceived by others. It is something the individual must claim for himself or herself (Casey 1995, p. 58). Every individual, including all managers, has an identity-set relevant to various social situations — family, social groups and the work organisation — and is seeking to move to some new variant of this identity. Identity can be both dynamic and stable, responding to relationship changes that can be conceptualised as historical dynamic systems (Fogel & Lyra 1997). Most individuals belong to a range of organisations and institutions, each with a particular relationship or psychological contract, through which various identity requirements are able to be satisfied. The work organisation competes with other organisations and institutions as the source of outcomes that satisfy relational expectations. Similarly, a work organisation is able to select employees from a large pool and the individual must compete with others to receive the desired outcomes, including a preferred identity.

The introduction of new organisational structures and technology in response to environmental forces, or managerial whim, will have an effect on the people within that organisation, both individually and as members of groups. Coincidentally, there are also environmental pressures directly affecting the people employed within the organisation. It is possible for managers to respond to the environmental forces by making technological and organisational changes while ignoring the identities of members and using leadership behaviour based on inappropriate assumptions and perceptions of the organisation and its people. Such behaviour privileges those who currently own and manage organisations and is expressed as a concern with 'motivating' employees to be more productive in pursuit of owner interests. Increasingly, it is being recognised that not only owners but many other stakeholders, including individual employees and work groups, have legitimate rights in organisations. In the future, it will be recognised that effective managing includes recognition of the importance of individual identity as a replacement for concern with motivation. Both theory and practice will recognise that motivation is not a tool of management.

Motivation as part of identity

The endeavour to understand work, and the commitment to the purpose of an organisation, raise the underlying question of the nature of a useful life. The theories of motivation have neither changed the relation between work and life nor contributed to a better understanding of its relatedness. 'Work can only have meaning in its fundamental sense when it is regarded not just as a dimension of the employing [organisation] but also as part of an individual life and of our collective lives' (Sievers 1986, pp. 346–7).

As long ago as the mid-1950s, Douglas McGregor recognised that human behaviour in industrial organisations was approximately as managers perceived it to be. He argued that this was a result of the nature of organisations and of a management philosophy based on incorrect assumptions about human nature (McGregor 1957, p. 431). McGregor described this philosophy as Theory X and advocated its replacement by a new philosophy — Theory Y. He saw the essential task of management as arranging 'organisational conditions and methods of operation so that people can achieve their own goals best by directing their own efforts toward organisational objectives (McGregor 1957, p. 435).

This viewpoint is further developed by Eccles and Nohria, who state that people are *always* motivated, and that the manager's task is to simply recognise *who* someone wants to be (Eccles & Nohria 1992, p. 63). A manager can try to influence the identity being sought within the organisation, but in doing so he or she must take into account the identities that already exist and where they are going (Eccles & Nohria 1992, p. 64). Motivation is one part only of this identity. By attempting to motivate employees, managers exclude from their cognition the awareness of the many complex interests and processes of a person's identity.

The concept of 'sensemaking' suggests that an individual will or will not persist in a behaviour in accordance with whether or not it helps him or her to make sense of the environment and events. Continued performance of a task at a required level is determined internally, not in response to inducements offered by others. Weick (1995) suggests that sensemaking processes are elusive. They include the beliefs and actions through which people impose frames and link frames with cues to achieve meaning. Beliefs are embedded in ideologies or paradigms that influence what people notice and how events unfold: to believe is to notice selectively. The search for explanation involves interpretation focused on explaining behaviours for which the individual is responsible and simplification of the perceived world by actions on the real world, rather than on the perceiver (Weick 1995, pp. 133–5). Weick's sensemaking concept helps us to understand why the motivation theories are less than completely successful. The relevance of the concept is strengthened through understanding of the 'self', or individual identity.

Conceptual models of identity

All identities are social identities because identity is about meaning, and meanings are always the outcome of agreement or disagreement, always to some extent shared, to some extent negotiable (Jenkins 1996, p. 4). The definition of the *self* and others is relational. That is, people tend to classify themselves and others (Ashforth & Mael 1989, p. 20) as students, parents, basketball players, shop assistants, computer programmers, energetic, loyal and so forth. Such categorisation helps individuals to locate others and to define themselves in the social environment. Identity is never a final matter; it is a process of *being* or *becoming* that requires constant comparison with others (du Gay 1996, pp. 47, 51; Eccles & Nohria 1992, p. 64; Jenkins 1996, p. 4).

Each person may have different identities in different social groups and circumstances, and throughout life there is an expansion of the self to include larger and larger sets of social objects (Coleman 1990, p. 517). A psychological perspective sees the *self* as a set of innate interests and processes that develops as a person interacts with his or her environment (Casey 1995, p. 61). Casey (1995, pp. 64–5) also notes that, while social psychology recognises the importance of the family and immediate social group on the development of identity, it fails to recognise the broader social dimensions, such as work organisations and other groups.

Concern about identity is a reflection of the uncertainty brought about by rapid change and cultural contact. Each individual exists with produced identities in a meaningful world (Deetz 1992, p. 27). However, as individuals are exposed to new situations and new people they become uncertain about who they are (Jenkins 1996, p. 10). They grasp for clarity in their relationships with other individuals, with groups, organisations and institutions. They have choice. In the past, this was not a significant issue. People were born into a class or societal group and trained to accept a preformed pre-existing model (Friedman 1990, cited in Eccles & Nohria 1992, p. 77). Today, however, an individual's identity is something that can be cultivated out of a range of possibilities.

Identification of self is a psychological or cognitive state wherein an individual perceives himself or herself as part of a human aggregate (Ashforth & Mael 1989; Rousseau 1998). It is not necessarily associated with a particular behaviour or affective response. Several researchers suggest that insight from psychoanalytic theory can be used to understand identity (e.g. Brown 1997; Carr 1998). Carr uses the development of Freud's theory of narcissism to argue that 'it is through identification that narcissism is transformed into a "dependence", not necessarily centred upon self, but an ego ideal, satisfaction of which may come from other objects (Carr 1998, p. 86). Carr cites Freud's theory that the individual may substitute a group ideal for the current ego ideal, consequentially identifying self with others in the ego (ibid, p. 87). Brown reviews the development of the theory of narcissism and its role in the identification of individuals with groups and argues (p. 665) that 'in acknowledging the legitimacy of the groups and organisations with which they identify, individuals are tacitly reaffirming their sense of self.'

Both sociologists and psychologists have recognised that individual identity has meaning only in the context of the social world. Because the self is a metaphysical construct, it cannot be readily broken down into constituent parts and measured using positivist methods (Casey 1995, p. 87). Thus, it is unlike motivation and other traits that can be observed, measured and compared. This abstractness of the concept largely explains why managers and researchers have focused on motivation, rather than identity, in seeking to understand and modify the behaviours of people at work. The sociological viewpoint is that 'self' is an ongoing and simultaneous synthesis of self-definition and definitions of oneself offered by others. Finding out how others see you depends on your ability to listen and to understand the nature of the perceived identity to which they are responding (Eccles & Nohria 1992, pp. 206–7). An identity seeks to be validated, or not, by others with whom we interact (Jenkins 1996, pp. 20–1).

Development psychologists focus on the mother–infant relationship (Fogel & Lyra 1997). Fogel and Lyra (1997, p. 76) extend their analysis to interactions between adult dyads, and suggest that the principles can be applied to groups of any size. Relationship systems (between two or more individuals) develop stable patterns of co-action called 'frames' (ibid., p. 77). These recur as recognisable forms in a relationship, but are slightly different each time. Change in a frame arises through the amplification of fluctuations, including the dynamics of communication processes. Identity comes from both action and words, and the way these are perceived by others. A dialogue involves discrete packages of each individual's action alternating with discrete acts of the partner, or mutual coordination of participants' simultaneous co-action. Communication is, therefore, more than the sum of the partners' input: either partner can interpret or make a reflection about the other partner, or about the relationship itself (Fogel & Lyra 1997, pp. 79-83). Such interpretations are both evaluative and reflexive: partners assess each other and notice changes in the relationship process.

From a sociological perspective 'identities are to be found and negotiated at their boundaries, where the internal and external meet' (Jenkins 1996, p. 24). Change and stability in an individual's frames are inherent tensions in identity shaping. 'Sameness (through time) is not a required feature of identity, rather what is required is a sense of continuity' (Rousseau 1998, p. 227). The pattern of shifting frames enables this sense of continuity as a relationship develops (or degenerates). Sociological theorists have extended these concepts to groups: group identity is constructed in interaction with others across the group boundary. Jenkins (1996, p. 23) defines a collectivity which is identified and defined by others as a 'category *in* itself', and a collectivity which identifies and defines itself as a 'group *for* itself'. Most theorisation about identity, he says, has undervalued, or ignored, the former. Yet, in political contexts (organisations), the collective identities are 'asserted, defended, imposed or resisted' (ibid.).

Identity in work organisations: challenging issues

Membership of an organisation requires affiliation which has to be recognised or proven. This occurs through a selection process — the individual must want, and demonstrate, qualification for membership and, more importantly, has to be admitted (Ahrne 1994, p. 6). An individual's identity within an organisation is shaped partially by the organisational setting and may vary from the identity of the individual in other settings. An individual's identity, therefore, is an amalgam that may include identities that impose inconsistent demands upon the person (Ashforth & Mael 1989, p. 29). Similarly, an organisation is made up of persons, but not whole persons — they are 'organisational centaurs' (Ahrne 1994, pp. 28-9; Casey 1995, p. 180; Coleman 1990, p. 543). That is, in organisational settings there are two kinds of actors: corporate actors and natural persons. Ahrne quotes Goffman (1968, p. 280): 'Our sense of being a person can come from being drawn into a wider social unit, our sense of selfhood can arise through the little ways in which we resist the pull.' Casey sees a 'strategic self, successful in the corporate environment, but still constantly under disciplinary siege, [who] lives in defended privacy and defended out-of-work life.'

From the perspective of the organisation the human part of the centaur is often a nuisance (Ahrne 1994, p. 45). The organisation prefers malleable beings moulded to its own needs. Formal organisations structured according to classical principles, in particular, tend to create an environment requiring the characteristics of the individual that are incongruent with the adult identity (Argyris 1957, p. 66).

Contemporary organisations endeavour to develop strong cultures replicating family relations and bonds and promising the psychic rewards of primary narcissism (Casey 1995, p. 181). These bonds to the corporation offer a distinct identity that replaces the identification with class and occupation prevalent in manufacturing industries earlier in this century. The new corporate self displays devotion to the company through active participation in ritualised practices and reciting the official discourse. It revives the old monolithic Protestant work ethic (Casey 1995, pp. 193-4). Excellent companies, in the Peters and Waterman (1982) sense, seek to cultivate *enterprising subjects* who are self-regulating productive individuals (du Gay 1996, p. 60) working in teams.

Every manager is in the position of having multiple perceived identities, and shaping the perceived identities of others. The actions and rhetoric used by a manager help others to formulate a perceived identity for that manager, to respond to that identity as followers or non-followers and to perceive their own identities. Rousseau (1998) notes that sociologists maintain that individuals expand the way they think about themselves to include larger and larger sets of objects. This cognitive process includes both situational identification and deep structure identification. Situational identification is a perception of a discrete work setting based on situational cues and remains as long as the cues persist. Deep structure identification refers to 'the cognitive schema formed in work settings across roles, over time, and across situations that leads to congruence between self-at-work and one's broader self concept' (Turner 1978, cited in Rousseau 1998, p. 218).

Working in a group (e.g. a project team) can change perceptions though situational identification — a shift from a view of self as an individual to a view of self as part of a group. If the situational cues cease, the collective identity can erode quickly (Rousseau 1998, pp. 219-22). Deep structure identification originates under specific organisational conditions — a psychological contract in which 'employee and employer act to benefit each other and when the locus of control shifts from individual to firm' (Rousseau 1998, p. 222). Rousseau suggests that the relinquishing of control to the firm by individuals makes a strong normative culture possible, reducing the need for performance monitoring and in many cases enhancing the members' sense of accomplishment and belonging (ibid., p. 226). The degree to which this occurs depends on the relative strength of each individual's projective (displaying) and introjective (perceiving and absorbing) identification (Carr 1998, p. 88). The psychodynamics in this relationship help the comprehension of compliance and dissent in organisations. Where introjective identification is strongest, the reified organisation and/or its leaders can be raised to the level of an ego-ideal, and the narcissistic needs may be satisfied so well that the individual views his or her identity in terms of the work context (ibid.).

The pragmatic (economic utility) and psychological (moral and cognitive) rewards offered by organisations to their members are the vehicles through which self-esteem is reinforced narcissistically (Brown 1997, p. 665). If, however, the locus of control in the exchange whereby employee and employer act to benefit each other is with the organisation/supervisor, then the idea of mutual choice appears absurd and the exchange may be better described as seduction by the employer (Carr 1998, p. 94).

Employment process and identity

The processes whereby employees are managed in modern organisations are often described as inhuman (Legge 1999; Schneider 1990) and instrumental. Labour processes have fragmented and atomised a 'working class', turning workers into competitive individuals rather than members of a community (Knights 1990, p. 311). Further, the dominance of the machine in imagery and in actuality gives rise to a view of employees as depersonalised labour input (Legge 1999, p. 248). Both image and practice reinforce the individual's preoccupation with control and the reduction of uncertainty. Knights argues that the processes (targets and bonus schemes, wage differentials and career systems) separate individuals from one another, causing comparative social isolation. With reduced community, the sense of identity cannot be taken for granted. 'As competition for material rewards increases, so identity, self-worth or confirmation of our own significance also become more problematic and precarious' (Knights 1990, p. 321). The technology, structure and processes of work organisations that have developed during this century have fragmented and displaced the class-based deep structure identification which was of concern to Karl Marx. This has not been replaced by an alternative object for deep structure identification by individual employees.

Senior management acting as the agent of the organisation's owners may believe that an appropriate object is the goal of profit maximisation. Both Mayo and Maslow contributed to a fundamental belief that, for effective organisational functioning, the members must identify with the organisation's goal (O'Connor 1990).

O'Connor notes that Mayo recognised that the Industrial Revolution removed man's (sic) sense of meaningful work, leading to a sense of alienation. If there is conflict in the workplace, it is the employee's problem, and the manager's job to fix it by listening and counselling. Maslow perceived that, in organisations, individuals could be encouraged to be synergic with others so that the goals of the individual merge with those of the organisation (ibid., p. 238).

These visions have not eventuated. Instead, both market and communitarian images of employees have emerged. The market imagery of the past 50 years identifies employees as internal customers, commodities or assets. An alternative communitarian metaphor of family or team member has also emerged (Legge 1999, pp. 249–52). The customer metaphor has two aspects. First, each employee is expected to identify with and be responsive to external customers to ensure customer needs are met. Internally, there is an obligation to satisfy the needs of the next 'customer' in the organisation's value chain. Second, the employer, as customer, buys cooperation and effort (Legge 1999, pp. 249–50). Employees are also consumers: work is re-imagined through the language of the consumer culture (du Gay 1996, p. 78). This modified perception changes the self-image of individuals and enables a process of autosurveillance and self-discipline. Identification by individual employees may then attach to the quality of products/services and the satisfaction of external customer requirements.

The conception of labour as a commodity to be bought and sold is evidenced in the use of outsourcing and insourcing and the growth of the contingent workforce (Legge 1999, p. 250). Under these arrangements, the organisation has no responsibilities to its contractual labour, leaving the employee further isolated from sources of deep structure identification.

The organisational asset metaphor presents the employee as a source of the organisation's 'value added', an asset to be cherished and developed (ibid., p. 252). In return, the employee offers attitudinal commitment — a deep structure identification.

An alternative paradigm uses images of community to represent the employee as a member of a social organisation where the bonds are those of socially embedded reciprocity (Legge 1999, p. 252). Legge suggests that the family metaphor has a paternalistic element which is less relevant in today's society than it was in the past. The metaphor of a sporting team is more appropriate. There exists 'the implication of reciprocal obligations supported by affective bonds of comradeship, shared interests and even mutual enjoyment' (ibid., p. 254). And the demand for attitudinal correctness and high performance and the insecurity of tenure are recognised. Teamwork practices can disempower employees by strengthening management control and intensifying work activity.

All these metaphors throw light on individual identity in the work organisation. Only the organisational assets metaphor provides a base for deep-seated identification with the organisation. For the employee, there is a reciprocity in being valued and nurtured. All of the other metaphors highlight situational identification with customers, products, projects, tasks and team members. Further, both the commodity and teamwork metaphors may lead to in-groups identifying management and the organisation as an out-group (see below).

Exchange between organisation/manager and subordinate

Employees develop exchange relationships with both organisations and immediate superiors. Such exchanges have a political face (Deetz 1992, p. 27), and occur between an employee and the employing organisation, and between an employee and the immediate superior (Wayne, 1997, p. 82). Deetz emphasises the importance of language in the way individuals engage with the world and produce objects with particular characteristics. He follows Althausser (1971) and de Saussure (1974) in seeing language as a system of distinction, rather than of representation (Deetz 1992, p. 29). Language as an ideological practice transforms the individual into subject (Althausser 1971, cited in Deetz 1992, p. 31) and 'the "subject" is always an image or constructed self, rather than an individual in a full set of relations to the world.' In an organisational setting, consideration of alternative meanings and alternate subjectivities poses a threat to the claimed identity and the individual rejects the possibility of freedom. Through sharing an ideology, the individual identifies with those in power. And institutional artefacts, routines and practices reinforce the positioning of a subject and direct the construction of particular experiences (Deetz 1992, pp. 32-3). Dominant group definitions of reality, norms and standards appear as normal, rather than as political and contestable. In this way, modern organisational power is seen to be a web of arbitrary asymmetrical relations which provide personal identity and from which certain (high-status) groups benefit (ibid, pp. 35-7).

Employees seek a balance in their exchange relationships with organisations. They develop global beliefs about the extent to which the organisation values their contributions and cares about their well-being (Wayne, Shore & Liden 1997, p. 83). Such exchanges have been called 'perceived organisational support' (POS). Exchanges between the employee and the supervisor are referred to as 'leader-member exchange' (LMX). Wayne, Shore and Liden (1997, pp. 106-7) conclude that POS and LMX have different antecedents, and similar effects on some employees and not on others. POS is influenced by treatment of employees during the history of their employment. In exchange for support, employees become affectively committed to the organisation. Antecedents to high LMX include characteristics of the interpersonal relationship and future expectations of the employee. In exchange for high LMX, employees perform well. Both POS and LMX may result in organisationally desired attitudes and behaviours in return for benefits.

Both of these approaches allow scope for the recognition that employees can identify with the holistic organisation and/or a particular division or work group, including identification with and loyalty to an immediate superior.

Subgroups, identity and conflicts

The employing organisation is only one possible potential source/object of identification in the workplace (Eccles & Nohria 1992, p. 67). Each individual may identify primarily with the organisation, a particular division or department, a work group or project team, or a profession. Situational identification is most likely in work groups and project teams; deep structure identification with the organisation or profession. These are not exclusive identity sets — each individual has multiple identities, even within one organisation. These multiple identities can be a source of conflict, embedded in or additional to the conflict of being an organisational centaur. Social identities are maintained primarily by intergroup comparisons, and much intergroup conflict stems from the very fact that groups exist (Ashforth & Mael 1989, p. 31).

Two forces work towards pluralism and complexity of identities in the organisation: technology (acting through structure) and people. Technological changes, especially those related to information, have allowed organisations to become more holistic and less differentiated internally. Organisational structure is transitory, and the *virtual* organisation is a reality, not merely a theoretical construct. That is, organisation structure can be shaped and reshaped according to the needs of people and changing tasks. A process of periodically changing situational identity is nourished, and the development of deep structure identification can be endangered.

Eccles and Nohria (1992, p. 78) refer to strong empirical evidence over the preceding 20 years that shows there has been a strong decline in 'employees' commitment to and identification with management and the firm as a whole.' Subcultures undoubtedly develop more readily than organisation-wide cultures. However, management's (and theory's) attachment to the managerial prerogative blinds it to the existence of multiple cultures within the organisation (Hocking & Carr 1996, p. 78). They note that people's occupations are the most distinctive and pervasive sources of subcultures. Increased demographic diversity within the work organisation is also a contributing cause: as diversity increases, the number of possible identities multiplies (Eccles & Nohria 1992, p. 80). Consequently, the real challenge for managers is to cope with the greatly expanded complexity of the identities with which they are confronted on a daily basis.

Where groups are clearly differentiated and bounded, there can be a tendency towards biased intergroup comparisons. Ashforth and

Mael (1989, p. 32) suggest four interconnected effects of this bias:

1. An in-group might develop negative stereotypes of the out-group and de-individuate and depersonalise its members.
2. The in-group is seen as deserving its successes and not its failures, while the opposite applies to the out-group.
3. Emerging biases may soon become a contagion so that an organisation may polarise into rival camps.
4. Such competition exacerbates the above tendencies because it threatens the group and its identity.

Conflict may be mitigated if groups compare themselves on different dimensions. Furthermore, the authors state, the relative status of groups modifies the dynamics of intergroup comparisons. A low-status group is implicitly threatened by a high-status group, but a high-status group is less likely to feel threatened and is less in need of affirmation. Therefore, while a low-status group may direct a lot of effort into differentiating itself, the high-status group may not form any impression about the low-status group, expressing indifference to it. This indifference is the greatest threat to the low-status group because its identity remains unvalidated (Ashforth & Mael 1989, p. 33).

The psychological contract and identity: challenging issues

The employment contract between an organisation and its individual employees comprises both a (usually) written legal–economic contract and an unwritten psychological contract. In the context of an Anglo-Saxon legalistic culture, managers and management theorists have favoured the legal–economic component, neglecting, until recently, the psychological contract. This concept is based on the sociological principle of reciprocity and was probably introduced into management literature by Argyris (1960) and Levinson (Levinson et al. 1962). Psychological contracts are not unique to work organisations; they exist in families, schools, churches, political parties and other institutions. In a work organisation context, a psychological contract is an open-ended agreement concerned with the social and emotional aspects of exchange between the employer and the employee (Sparrow 1998, p. 30) Above all, a psychological contract is founded on trust.

A psychological contract is based on perceived promises — the communication of future intents as perceived by an individual employee (Morrison & Robinson 1997, p. 228). The contract represents an employee's beliefs about obligations between himself/herself and 'the organisation', rather than any specific agent of the organisation. Each individual has a set of expectations that can be satisfied by the work organisation and is willing to commit attitudes and effort in exchange for receiving these expected internal outcomes. Similarly, the organisation is perceived by the employee to have a set of expectations about the contributions from individuals and to promise payments and other outcomes in return for these contributions. Such promises may be communicated in written form in mission statements and internal publications. Agents (e.g. supervisors) may have their own understanding of psychological contracts, but are not party to them (ibid, pp. 228–9).

The psychological contract is revised throughout an employee's tenure with the organisation, building repeated cycles of contributions and reciprocity onto an initial contract (Robinson & Rousseau 1994, p. 246). An initial contract is shaped by 'anticipatory socialisation' — the specific promises made by recruiters, human relations staff and supervisors to recruits. Revisions occur as a consequence of the perception of the organisation's culture(s) and standard operating procedures and social cues from peers (Turnley & Feldman 1999, p. 898).

Change and the psychological contract

Major change in organisations is often initiated in response to external pressures such as the availability of, or threat from, new technology; shareholder and financial sector disaffection with economic performance; actions by competitors; or a change in economic conditions. It can also accompany a change in the strategic direction followed by top management, or a redesign of the organisation brought about by change in the composition of the top management team. Such change is pervasive (involving multiple aspects of the organisation) and deep (involving change in such fundamental aspects as values) (Mohrman & Associates 1989). Such changes are important in explaining the dynamics of psychological contracts (Martin, Staines & Pate 1998, p. 21).

Traditionally, the psychological contract has been based on job security — careers and a job for life offered by the organisation, reciprocated by trust and loyalty from the employee. The competitive conditions of the past 20 years and the managerialism ideology have led to employers seeking flexible organisational structures, downsizing, centralised control and decision making, and cultural change (Martin, Staines & Pate 1998, p. 21). These changes are perceived by the employee, who has continued to contribute loyalty and effort, as violations of the psychological contract. The employee will then reciprocate by offering decreases in the full range of employee contributions to the organisation (Robinson 1996, p. 592), or through the mechanisms of exit, voice, reduced loyalty and neglect (Turnley & Feldman 1999, p. 917).

Superficially, an individual's responses to violation of the psychological contract may appear similar to the responses to perceived inequity in rewards for performance as explained by one theory of motivation. Equity theory (Adams 1963), when used as an explanation of motivation in organisational behaviour, is focused on comparisons that individuals make between themselves and another (Mullins 1996, pp. 170–2). In this application, the focus is on extrinsic rewards, especially pay, relative to another and does not represent the effect of organisational decisions and behaviours on the sense of self. The comparison with others, however, is integral to the individual's development of an identity.

The impact of change and the psychological contract on identity

The mechanisms of change and psychological contract violation affect, simultaneously, the individual's identity and identity development.

Strong deep structure identification with the organisation as a whole promotes rapid adjustment to change and blurs the boundary between the employee's concept of self and the organisation (Rousseau 1998, pp. 227–8). Because an individual's mental models of self are adaptable, continuity in the midst of change, not sameness, is required. Therefore, organisations undergoing change should signal continuity, particularly by reinforcing the valued role that the individual plays within the community of the organisation. This can be achieved through what Tsui et al. (1997) call a *mutual investment* employee–organisation relationship approach. In this approach, the employer achieves a balanced exchange relationship wherein both the employee and employer have some degree of open-ended and long-term investment in each other. Tsui notes that under competitive pressure many organisations have moved from an *overinvestment* approach to either an *underinvestment* or a *quasi-spot-contract* approach. Both favour performance of closed-ended tasks and immediate monetary rewards for that performance. The absence of open-ended, long-term promises from the organisation reduces the ability of the employee to identify with the organisation, thereby severely affecting the 'sense of self'. Under such circumstances, individuals will seek identity outside the work organisation. When psychological contract violation is high, employees are more likely to attempt to exit their current organisation, to voice their displeasure with organisational practices to upper management, to neglect task performance, and to be less loyal in representing the organisation to outsiders (Turnley & Feldman 1999, p. 908).

Conclusion

Management theory has long been concerned with the task of motivating people. It has been claimed that a manager must allocate attention to the level of motivation of organisational members, and encourage those members to direct their efforts towards the successful achievement of organisational goals (Mullins 1996, p. 480). This approach assumes that some people (managers) have the right to control the behaviour of others, either on the basis of their social class or because they are acting as the agents of another group — the owners. Such a notion suggests acceptance of the principle of control as a fundamental component of organisational life (Golding 1996, p. 8). This acceptance leads to the institutionalisation of *control* as a feature of society. Modern society may have perceived this arrangement as acceptable, but post-modern society does not: 'people are *always already* motivated to become who they want to be' (Eccles & Nohria 1992, p. 63). Managers must recognise, therefore, that people need to be accepted for what they are and what they want to be. They cannot be motivated through managerial action.

Management's objective to have all organisational members working towards the organisation's goals (in the broadest sense of satisfying, in some way, the conflicting needs of all stakeholders) is best met by encouraging and assisting all individuals to seek an identity that coincides with serving the organisation's purpose. That is, managers, as the agents of the organisation, should see their managing activity as serving a mutual investment employee-organisation relationship. In exchange for support, employees become affectively committed to the organisation.

Effective managing in the future will include recognition of the importance of individual identity and the psychological contract as a replacement for the concern with motivation. Motivation is a characteristic of individuals, and is of only indirect concern for managers. The most that managers can hope to accomplish is to recognise the plurality of groups and cultures within the organisation, and to help individuals to find an identity within the organisational context so that their personal motivation will cause their efforts to coincide with both their primary group and the organisation as a whole. As indicated above, this can be achieved best by using a mutual investment approach in shaping the perceived psychological contracts — by offering the opportunity for open-ended, long-term outcomes for each employee.

References

Adams, JS (1963) Towards an understanding of inequity. *Journal of Abnormal and Social Psychology*, 67, pp. 422–36.

Ahrne, G (1994) *Social organisations: interaction inside, outside and between organisations.* London: Sage.

Althausser, L (1971) Ideology and ideological state apparatuses. In *Lenin and philosophy and other essays*, trans. Ben Brewster, London: New Left Books.

Argyris, C (1957) *Personality and organization: the conflict between systems and the individual.* New York: Harper & Row.

Argyris, C (1960) *Understanding organizational behaviour.* Homewood, Il: Dorsey.

Ashforth, BE & Mael, F (1989) Social identity theory and the organisation. *Academy of Management Review*, 14(1): 20–39.

Brown, AD (1997) Narcissism, identity and legitimacy. *Academy of Management Review*, 22(3): 643–86.

Carr, A (1998) Identity, compliance and dissent in organizations: a psychoanalytic perspective. *Organization*, 5(1): 81–99.

Casey, C (1995) *Work, self and society: after industrialism.* London: Routledge.

Coleman, JS (1990) *Foundations of social theory.* Cambridge, Mass: Harvard University Press.

Deetz, S (1992) Disciplinary power in the modern corporation. In M Alvesson & H Willmott (eds) *Critical management studies.* London: Sage.

de Saussure, F (1974) *Course in general linguistics.* London: Fontana.

du Gay, P (1996) *Consumption and identity at work.* London: Sage.

Eccles, RG & Nohria, N (1992) *Beyond the hype: rediscovering the essence of management.* Harvard: Harvard Business School Press.

Fogel, A and Lyra, CDP (1997) Dynamics of development in relationships. In F Masterpasqua and PA Perna (eds) *The psychological meaning of chaos: translating theory into practise.* Washington, DC: American Psychological Association.

Friedman, L (1990) *The republic of choice: law, authority and culture.* Cambridge, Mass: Harvard University Press.

Gabriel, Y (1999) Beyond happy families: a critical reevaluation of the control–resistance–identity triangle. *Human relations*, 52(2): 179–202.

Golding, D (1996) Producing clarity — depoliticising control. In S Linstead, RM Small & P Jeffcutt (eds) *Understanding management.* London: Sage.

Hocking, J & Carr, A (1996) Culture: the search for a better organisational metaphor. In C Oswick and D Grant (eds) *Organisation development: metaphorical explorations.* London: Pitman.

Jenkins, R (1996) *Social identity.* London: Routledge.

Knights, D (1990) Subjectivity, power and the labour process. In D Knights and H Willmott (eds) *Labour process theory.* London: Macmillan.

Legge, K (1999) Representing people at work. *Organization*, 6(2): 247–84.

Levinson, H, Price, CR, Munden, KJ, Mandl, HJ & Solley, CM (1962) *Men, management and mental health.* Cambridge, Mass: Harvard University Press.

Martin, G, Staines, H, Pate, J (1998) Linking job security and career development in a new psychological contract. *Human Resources Management Journal*, 8(3): 20–40.

McGregor, D (1957) The human side of enterprise. *Management Review*, 6(11): 22–8, 88–92. In MT Matteson and JM Ivancevich (eds) (1991) *Management and organizational behaviour classics*, (6th ed.) Chicago: Irwin.

Mohrman, AN & Associates (1989) *Large-scale organizational change.* San Francisco: Jossey-Bass.

Morrison, EW & Robinson, SL (1997) When employees feel betrayed: a model of how psychological contract violation develops. *Academy of Management Review*, 22(1): 226–56.

Mullins, LJ (1996) *Management and organisational behaviour* (4th ed.) London: Pitman Publishing.

O'Connor, E (1990) Minding the workers: the meaning of 'human' and 'human relations'. In Elton Mayo, *Organization*, 6(2): 223–46.

Peters, TJ & Waterman, RH (1982) *In search of excellence.* New York: Harper & Row.

Robinson, SL (1996) Trust and breach of the psychological contract. *Administrative Science Quarterly*, 41(4): 574–99.

Robinson, SL & Rousseau, DM (1994) Violating the psychological contract: not the exception but the norm. *Journal of Organizational Behaviour*, 15: 245–59.

Rousseau, DM (1998) Why workers still identify with organizations. *Journal of Organizational Behaviour*, 19: 217–33.

Schneider, SC (1990) Human and inhuman resource management: sense and nonsense. *Organization*, 6(2): 277–84.

Sievers, B (1986) Beyond the surrogate of motivation. *Organization studies*, 7(4): 335–51.

Sparrow, PR (1998) Reappraising psychological contracting. *International Studies of Management and Organization*, 28(1): 30–63.

Tsui, AI, Pearce, JL, Porter, LW & Tripoli, AM (1997) Alternative approaches to the employee–organization relationship: does investment in employees pay off? *Academy of Management Journal*, 40(5): 1089–121.

Turnley, WH & Feldman, DC (1999) The impact of psychological contract violations on exit, voice, loyalty and neglect. *Human Relations*, 52(7): 895–922.

Wayne, SJ, Shore, LM & Liden, RC (1997) Perceived organizational support and leader-member exchange: a social exchange perspective. *Academy of Management Journal*, 40(1): 82–111.

Weick, KE (1995) *Sensemaking in organizations.* Thousand Oaks, CA: Sage.

Organisational commitment in an era of restructuring

CHAPTER 5

by Teresa Marchant

Dept of Human Resource Management and Employment Relations, Faculty of Business, USQ, Toowoomba

marchant@usq.edu.au

Introduction

Loyalty or commitment to organisations has declined, partly as a consequence of organisational downsizing. Expectations of having a 'job for life' with one company are no longer realistic. Such rewards originally formed the employees' side of the psychological contract, in return for which they committed to the organisation. Unlike loyalty to the organisation, employees' commitment to their fellow workers or to their own development may have strengthened. Other important desires, such as that for job satisfaction and meaningful work, are just as important today. Employers can capitalise on these other needs with alternative strategies for engendering commitment, including job design.

The material discussed in this chapter is significant for several reasons. The downsizing era in large organisations during the 1980s and 1990s eroded job security and opportunities for upward career progression. As a consequence, organisational commitment declined and turnover increased. However, despite planned reductions in workforce numbers, organisations still need to avoid losing skilled or high-performing employees. Therefore, new strategies are needed to retain those they do wish to keep.

In terms of the practice of management, this chapter will point out that life-long learning can replace the old notion of life-long employment. Job rotation or sideways moves may also encourage commitment to the organisation. Managers can implement strategies based on the job characteristics model that meet individual needs for growth.

There are a number of challenges facing organisations in relation to organisational commitment. These include the way the concept of organisational commitment is understood; utilising the benefits that organisations derive from high organisational commitment; whether different jobs attract different levels of organisational commitment; whether organisations can identify the characteristics of employees that guarantee high commitment; whether commitment is simply a western concept that is not transferable to other cultures; whether organisational commitment is really a good thing for employees; and whether organisational commitment can be maintained in an era of downsizing and, consequently, the way it informs organisational and individual action.

Defining organisational commitment

Although it is rarely explained in these terms, the concept of organisational commitment can be understood using ideas that describe personal relationships between individuals — for example marriage. Organisational commitment includes an idea of dedication, with a judgmental component. In marriage, this translates into fidelity. There is an emotional element in terms of positive feelings and attraction between the two parties. Then there is the intention to stay in the relationship. In some wedding ceremonies, this intent is conveyed by the words 'until death us do part'.

Organisational commitment is similar in that there are normative or prescriptive components. That is, it includes ideas about what should be done, as well as affective or feeling components, including emotional attachment. The final element is a continuance or 'not leaving' component.

Mowday, Steers and Porter (1979, p. 226) define organisational commitment as the 'relative strength of an individual's identification with and involvement in an organisation.' Their definition distinguishes between *normative*, *affective* and *continuance* commitment. The differences between these types of organisational commitment within this general definition are shown in table 5.1. Views from other authors have been included to give more depth to this definition.

The definitions in table 5.1 suggest that a range of positive behaviours should be exhibited by committed employees, as will be discussed later in this chapter. For example, when individuals are highly committed, their job becomes part of their identity, and 'invisible T-shirts inscribed with Kodak, DEC, or AT&T are sometimes impossible icons to wash off' (Hakim, cited in Brown 1995, p. 16).

Table 5.1: Three elements of organisational commitment

Element	Definition	Some authors
Normative	Obligation and loyalty towards the organisation. Duty and responsibility. Motivation to act on the organisation's behalf, or work hard on its part. Action that transcends self-interest. Implementation of new ideas in the interests of the organisation.	Awamleh (1996); Robbins et al. (1998); Mowday, Steers and Porter (1979); Brewer (1996)
Affective	Represents the 'feeling' aspect of the attitude. Employees feel emotionally attached to, identify with and are highly involved with the organisation. Employees adopt management's values, or believe that their values and goals are compatible.	O'Reilly and Chatman (1986); Mowday, Steers and Porter (1979).
Continuance	Highly committed individuals want to, and intend to, stay with the organisation. Employees put a high price on the cost of leaving the organisation.	Brewer (1996); Mowday, Steers and Porter (1979); Robbins. Millett, Cacioppe and Waters-Marsh (1998)

Benefits of organisational commitment

Organisational commitment is important because it can result in lower attrition or turnover, lower absenteeism and greater work effort (Randall 1990, in Tan & Akhtar 1998; Robbins et al. 1998; and DeConinck & Bachmann 1994). The evidence for these outcomes is consistent, although the relationship is not always particularly strong (Randall 1990, in Tan & Akhtar 1998). The main evidence seems to link high commitment with lower turnover.

Turnover has negative consequences for organisations in terms of general instability, the cost of replacing those who leave and specific disruption to the workplace, including damage to relationships with customers, for example. For the employees, there can also be costs in terms of losing friendships (Meadows-Taylor 1999). Nevertheless, even the link between commitment and turnover is not necessarily simple or straightforward, as Cohen (1991) found that it is stronger in the early stages of employees' careers.

Another organisational advantage associated with high commitment is citizenship behaviour, which is unofficial or informal behaviour that is good for the organisation (Schappe 1998). In a related study, Knoop (1995) also showed that organisational commitment is related to turning up to work on time. This idea of 'tardiness' does not receive much attention in the literature, but it is desirable employee behaviour. This is particularly the case in customer-service-orientated industries such as retail and hospitality (Hawk & Sheridan 1999), or where shift-changeover operations are critical, such as in nursing.

Does organisational commitment improve productivity? It is hard to find strong and consistent evidence for a relationship between high organisational commitment and good work performance, in terms of productivity, quality and other indicators. Nevertheless, some evidence has been found amongst a group of 213 women working in clothing manufacturing in New Zealand (Putterill & Rohrer 1995). This was a piece-work operation, where each worker's output could be measured objectively. Therefore, it may have been easier to demonstrate that workers with higher commitment also produced more work than it would be in other types of jobs (Taylor & Pierce 1999). In another context, organisational commitment has been linked to better service quality amongst insurance salespeople (Boshoff and Mels 1995).

In summary, the benefits of high organisational commitment for organisations include lower turnover and, to a lesser extent, lower absenteeism, more effort, punctuality and good citizenship. Despite one component of commitment being willingness to exert effort on behalf of the organisation, there seems to be little real evidence of a link between high organisational commitment and productivity. This may be because the link does not actually exist, because productivity is harder to measure in some jobs, or because one of the most popular tests for measuring organisational commitment may not address the effort component very well (White & Parks 1995). Nonetheless, organisational commitment is desirable for organisations, at least in terms of retaining key employees.

Organisational commitment: challenging issues

The reader may be interested in the different types of occupations and what is known about their organisational commitment. Some details have been summarised in table 5.2, which shows that organisational commitment has been of interest to researchers throughout the 1990s. Commitment has been measured in a broad range of occupations and employment settings, and varies quite widely across these different settings.

Table 5.2: Different jobs and different levels of organisational commitment

Type of job (number of employees studied)	Comments on organisational commitment	Source
Pharmacists in Western Australian hospitals ($n = 83$)	Commitment was lower than for the average worker. This was due to high stress and under-staffing.	Savery and Syme (1996)
Graduate engineers early in their careers in the UK ($n = 853$)	Dissatisfaction with promotion opportunities was related to low commitment.	Cramer (1993)
Nurses in Canada ($n = 171$)	High commitment was related to satisfaction with promotion opportunities.	Knoop (1995)
Marketing managers in the United States ($n = 336$)	Commitment depended on the availability of promotion opportunities.	DeConinck and Bachmann (1994)
Secondary teachers in the United States ($n = 116$)	Teachers tended to be committed to their profession rather than to their school.	Burrows and Munday (1996)
Public accountants in the United States, large chartered accounting firms ($n = 100$)	Commitment was moderate. This was attributed to negative views of change, and to low perceived job security.	Pasewark and Strawser (1996)
Information systems personnel in the US ($n = 464$)	Job design was useful for increasing commitment, but not for all individuals. It had more effect on those with stronger growth needs.	Igbaria and Parasuraman (1994)
Professionals in the New Zealand public service ($n = 129$)	Implementation of a performance management system had some positive effects on commitment.	Taylor and Pierce (1999)
Bus drivers in Sydney ($n = 179$)	Commitment was considered to be quite high.	Brewer (1996)
Engineers in the United States ($n = 40$)	Commitment was relatively high.	Ofori-Dankwa, Kanthi and Arora (1999)
Public servants in Jordan ($n = 293$)	Commitment was higher than expected.	Awamleh (1996)
Military personnel in Canada ($n = 473$)	Commitment was high for this group.	Leiter and Clark (1994)
Bank employees in Papua New Guinea ($n = 63$)	Commitment was very high for this group.	Ramos (1999)

One point that emerges from these research studies is that organisational commitment seems to be related to satisfaction with perceived promotion opportunities. Interestingly, the studies mostly focus on white-collar or professional jobs. Is organisational commitment relevant to blue-collar workers? This seems to be the case according to a study by Loscocco (1990). Over 3500 blue-collar workers were surveyed in this research and the results showed that their organisational commitment was in the standard range compared to most other workers.

Determinants of organisational commitment

Given the benefits that may accrue to organisations from a workforce that is highly committed, is it possible to identify such employees? What determines employees' levels of organisational commitment? By amalgamating findings from nine different studies, McClurg (1999, p. 18) concluded that employees who are more likely to demonstrate high organisational commitment are:

- females
- older workers
- those who are less well-educated
- those who have been with the organisation for a longer time
- those who believe they have fewer opportunities to change jobs
- those whose jobs have a lot of rules and procedures
- those who believe their organisation offers a lot of support
- those who are paid more.

In addition, there is some evidence that employees who come from single income families may be more likely to have higher commitment than those from dual-income families (Elloy & Flynn 1998). There are also some gender differences in the causes of organisational commitment. For women, social cohesion with their work colleagues is associated with higher organisational commitment, whereas this is not the case for males (Leiter & Clark 1994).

It might be tempting to think that all employers need to do is recruit female workers or older workers in the hope that they will be more highly committed. However, most readers would be aware that such a strategy would be in breach of the principles of equal opportunity and affirmative action (Norris 1998). Relying on such simple demographic characteristics is not necessarily advisable. Instead, this chapter will look at other processes that organisations can focus on to engender commitment amongst existing employees.

Caldwell and Chatman (1990) looked more closely at the organisational processes adopted in recruitment and selection, and at socialisation. They were able to show that positive organisational commitment can be generated by certain HR practices. These practices were providing opportunities for new employees to learn and accept the values of the company, exposing employees to core functions and using training and rewards to promote desired behaviours. Further, the folklore of the firm and role models should reinforce key values. Thus, their findings suggest that the organisation's culture and how it is transmitted can engender strong organisational commitment. This point, however, was not made frequently in the literature reviewed for this chapter.

Is organisational commitment a western concept?

The applicability of organisational commitment in different cultures should be considered for at least two reasons. Firstly, globalisation has now brought together employees and management from many different cultures in new ways and in situations where new understanding is necessary (Pearson & Chong 1997; Jolley 1997; Kheaomareun 1999). Secondly, it is important to question whether cultural values influence the usefulness of different management concepts such as organisational commitment (Geiger & Robertson 1998). Consequently, this issue will be addressed here.

There is an argument that many of the concepts taught in management and organisational behaviour texts are culture-bound or ethnocentric. They may be applicable only in western business cultures such as those enjoyed in the

United States, United Kingdom or Australia. This argument is well summarised by Pearson and Chong (1997, p. 357) as follows: 'One emergent dominant belief is that management is a set of universal principles that can be transferred from one country to another as if there is global relevance.' For example, job design has emerged as a key position in the literature as a way of increasing organisational commitment and job satisfaction (Glisson & Durick 1988; Johns, Xie & Fang 1992). Job design involves considering how parts of a job can be organised to form a more meaningful whole. It concentrates on improving jobs so that they are less routine, more varied in terms of the skills they utilise, and more challenging or enriched (Robbins et al. 1998). However, job design is based on western assumptions about autonomy and self-achievement. Such assumptions may not be relevant where collectivism is valued (in Singapore, for example), or where other cultural values such as the Confucian ethic are adhered to (in Chinese-owned organisations, for example) (Pearson & Chong 1997).

The argument that key management concepts are culture-specific has been extended to organisational commitment (Tan & Akhtar 1998). In the western view, the relationship between employer and employee is based on rational, logical and calculated contract-based understandings. The individual is the focus and essentially pursues self-interest. In contrast, the Confucian culture values self-in-relation-to-others, trust, harmony and the avoidance of conflict. These values lead to different types of employer–employee relationships in organisations that are Chinese-owned and based on Confucian values. The relationship between the superior and subordinate is one of paternalism and loyalty, where avoiding conflict and maintaining face is important.

Tan and Akhtar (1998) support their argument with evidence that normative commitment was higher than affective commitment amongst employees of a Chinese-owned bank in Hong Kong. They attributed this difference to the stronger influence of obligation and duty in the Confucian tradition. Their research also accorded with Hofstede's (1980) finding that commitment has stronger moral or prescriptive overtones in other cultures than it does in the west.

A second example of the need to take cultural differences into account comes from a study of 286 Malaysian nurses. Pearson and Chong (1997) found that, in Malaysia, relationship-orientated job design may have more impact on satisfaction and commitment than does western-style task-orientated job design. Such relationship-orientated design includes feedback from others, whereas feedback from the job itself is prescribed in the well-known job characteristics model of Hackman and Oldham (1980), which is based on western job design principles. Two other aspects of the relationship focus are dealing with others and building relationships at work that are predictable and harmonious.

As in Malaysia, Korean workers have values that are aligned with the Confucian ethic, although the cultural and political economy also shape some differences in workers' attitudes within each country. Korean organisational commitment was relatively high compared to United States and Japanese workers (Bae & Chung 1997).

In a fourth example, organisational commitment has been shown to be a relevant concept in the Japanese business culture (White & Parks 1995). In fact, Japanese workers have high organisational commitment because of a strong national tradition of lifetime employment, job security and seniority-based promotion. These unique features of Japanese work even carry over to Japanese firms based in the United States. United States engineers in a Japanese firm (that was also located in the United States) had higher organisational commitment than United States engineers in a United States firm (Ofori-Dankwa, Kanthi & Arora 1999). However, the instrument used to measure organisational commitment in western firms does not completely tap into the 'willingness to work hard' dimension of commitment, when applied to Japanese workers (White & Parks 1995).

The final example in this section comes from Mexico. With the expansion of United States firms into Mexico, there is now more focus on understanding the attitudes and behaviours of Mexican workers, including their levels of organisational commitment. The way that cultural factors affect the validity of western management concepts can be seen in Mexican workers' views of management initiatives to expand employee involvement. These are generally valued and are labelled as empowerment or participation in western thinking. However, Mexican workers see them as signifying managerial incompetence. As a consequence, Mexican workers can be reluctant to participate in such activities (Harrison & Hubbard 1998).

Since different countries have different cultures, not all principles of organisational commitment can be translated directly across cultures. For example, the Confucian tradition emphasises loyalty to superiors, to senior employees and to the workplace. Thus it might be expected that employees in countries where the Confucian tradition is strong would have higher organisational commitment. This has proven to be the case with nurses in Malaysia (Pearson & Chong 1997) and both blue-collar and white-collar workers in Korea (Bae & Chung 1997). Similarly, there are subtle differences between the meaning of this concept and its application in Japanese and United States firms, even within the same country. Experience gleaned from a new focus on employees in Mexico also supports this argument. Therefore, care needs to be taken when western management ideas, such as organisational commitment, are exported to different countries.

Sheridan (1999) argue that this growth is mediated by excellent customer service, which can be achieved only with a committed workforce. There may be a 'commitment gap' in so far as employees perceive that they are substantially more committed to organisations than organisations are to them (Sales and Marketing Management, April 1999). There is even a question as to whether strong organisational commitment is actually desirable in the current business environment.

There are alternative views, which argue that high levels of organisational commitment are not desirable because they can stifle creativity, engender conformity and generate the sort of strain that results in burnout (Tan & Akhtar 1998). For example, employees may be reluctant to suggest new or radical ideas, or to engage in diverse thinking. They may be so involved with the organisation and its fortunes that they suffer from stress. These criticisms suggest that increasingly high levels of organisational commitment should not be seen as an unending source of positive benefits to organisations and employees. Rather, commitment is one of several aspects of the employer–employee relationship that organisations should strive to improve, in balance with other factors.

Organisational commitment and employees

What about employees? Much of this discussion has focused on what organisations may extract from the exchange, but what do employees gain from their commitment? Owing to the changing nature of organisations and of employees, both of which have influenced the nature of the employer–employee relationship, this is a complex question.

Very little discussion takes place concerning the reverse relationship between employers and employees in the debate about organisation commitment — concerning the commitment of organisations to employees. This is despite quite compelling United States evidence that organisations who are committed to their workers exhibited much higher share price growth than did other organisations. Hawk and

Organisational commitment in an era of restructuring?

Organisational commitment can be said to develop on the basis of social exchange. That is, organisational commitment is given in return for pay, promotions and job security (Mattaz 1989, in Brewer 1996). Satisfaction with the organisation's career structure is associated with higher commitment (Cramer 1993). Therefore, another organisational factor of interest in this chapter is career structures, or opportunities for progression based on promotion. Career opportunities fulfil status needs according to Maslow's (1954) hierarchy. Such career structures have a role in engendering commitment and effort and in encouraging long tenure (Stinchcombe 1974).

Thus the traditional psychological contract traded lifelong employment and job security for employee loyalty and commitment. Recent events in organisations, as well as changes in the demographics and values of employees, have resulted in a situation where the traditional contract may no longer apply. As a consequence, it appears that organisational commitment has declined. However, organisations may now be facing a dilemma, in that they do wish to attract and keep high-performing employees, even if they cannot offer the job security that formerly contributed to commitment.

This dilemma can be further illustrated as follows. Attempting to achieve 'the objectives of effectiveness and cost reduction means organisations tend to undermine the welfare and well-being of their employees' (Baruch 1998, p.141). However, in terms of downsizing, the 'slash-and-burn regime' of the early 1990s has not contributed to long-term productivity (Littler 1998). Similarly, other organisational changes such as relocation may have negative effects on employees, including on their commitment (Lawson & Angle 1998).

Recent feedback from nearly 500 companies suggests that Australian organisations are experiencing a backlash from a decade of downsizing. The backlash is being felt in the form of unacceptably high turnover rates. The workforce is now much more mobile and much less loyal than in earlier times. Up to 66 per cent of Australian employees have little or no understanding of, or commitment to, organisational values. Companies are finding it difficult to retain the employees that they want to keep (Meadows-Taylor 1999). In another study of 1000 Australian managers, just over half indicated that their loyalty to employers had decreased (Marchant 1998). Thus, reports from both organisations and individuals suggest that downsizing has negative consequences for organisational commitment.

To describe this situation in other words, the 'death of corporate paternalism' (Davidson 1991, p.34) means that it is no longer realistic to expect strong loyalty from employees in exchange for lifelong job security. In fact, research shows that organisational commitment has declined in most industries, age groups, income groups and job types (Stum 1999). Further, the relationships between organisational commitment and the two important outcomes of turnover and absenteeism have declined throughout the 1980s and 1990s (Randall 1990; and Cohen 1993, in Baruch 1998). This is not to say that all employees no longer have any loyalty to their employers. On the contrary, it is still possible to find evidence of commitment (Hawk & Sheridan 1999). However, this commitment may not be based on the same reasons or factors as in earlier times.

As we begin the new millennium, there are several factors that make it less likely that organisational commitment can be maintained, or even that it is a realistic goal of management. These factors include employees being subject to frequent change, sometimes on a 'like it or not' basis, and explicit contracts replacing the old psychological contract. As a consequence, some argue that today's employees are more likely to be committed to their profession, to their workmates or colleagues and to other activities outside of work such as family and leisure (Robbins et al. 1998). This idea of commitment to the work group is elaborated by Poole and Jenkins (1997). They distinguish between commitment to fellow workers, which is much more specific and focused, and commitment to the organisation as a whole, which is a more abstract concept. Interestingly, the majority of Australian managers did not feel that their loyalty to colleagues had decreased (Marchant 1998).

There have been other changes besides downsizing that might also affect organisational commitment, as businesses begin the new millennium. One of these is the increase in 'peripheral' roles in organisations. There has been a substantial increase in the incidence of temporary employment in Australia (Bramble, Littler & O'Brien 1996). Temporary positions are referred to as 'the periphery' in the core-versus-ring model of new organisations (Robbins et al. 1998). There is at least one organisational commitment issue that arises with this newer, increasingly prevalent group of workers: whether they are committed to the organisation, to their own careers, or to the employment agency that organises the temporary position (where one is involved). Research has suggested that these employees are loyal to both the employing organisation and the agency, although in many cases their primary aim is to obtain a permanent position (McClurg 1999). Thus, organisational commitment or lack of it may not be an issue in dealing with 'peripheral' workers. These issues, however, have not been extensively investigated.

Future directions — alternative strategies for organisations and managers

Regarding the provision by management of facilities and practices which might foster commitment, Putterill and Rohrer (1995, p. 61) observe that 'grudgingly, ignorantly or lavishly, the common root of the problem is the lack of understanding of the factors and processes which promote organisational commitment.' That is, it would seem that organisations do not know how to, or do not want to, take action to enhance the commitment of their employees. This is particularly true in relation to the negative consequences of organisational downsizing discussed in the previous section.

What can be done to combat downsizing's negative consequences for organisational commitment? One way that management can ensure less drastic fallout is to make sure that downsizing is done properly. This means with due attention to supporting those employees to be retrenched and to following equitable procedures. Consequently, the remaining employees receive a more positive message about management's concern for them. The damage to organisational commitment arising from downsizing may therefore be contained (Naumann, Bennett, Bies & Martin 1998). Unfortunately, in Australia management has not been particularly effective in properly executing downsizing, particularly with regards to the procedural justice elements of the process. Loyalty to the organisation appears to have declined as a result (Marchant 1998).

More general actions that management can take to increase organisational commitment include:
- better communication
- improved person–job fit
- effective induction
- clear and available promotion opportunities
- positive mentoring (Robbins et al. 1998).

However, promotion (and job security) as the core elements of the old psychological contract are not as available as they were in the pre-downsizing era (Marchant, Critchley & Littler 1997). Organisations need to develop a 'new deal' or exchange between employers and employees (Baruch 1998; Meadows-Taylor 1999). Some of the conditions that Australian employees would like as part of the new exchange are:
- better work–family balance
- opportunities for personal development
- being fairly rewarded for their efforts (Meadows-Taylor 1999).

Other useful suggestions on what management can do to increase commitment are also available. For example, Stum (1999) lists the following 'actions drivers', based on his large-scale, current research in the United States:
- Address work–life balance
- Provide compensation that is seen to be equitable and adopt a 'cafeteria benefits' approach that recognises individual differences
- Attend to the organisational culture and provide leadership which exhibits a clear sense of direction
- Anticipate and implement change programs that are effective and well managed
- Ensure that employees are recruited and developed based on sound, high-level skills, as employees feel more committed to an organisation if they believe that their work colleagues' skills are up to scratch.

There is some overlap between these lists of suggestions, particularly work–life balance, pay equity and a skills development focus. These suggestions for improving organisational commitment also appear to reflect ideas that are advanced in the HR professional literature as constituting good practice, given the current nature of organisations and employees.

Organisations may be advised to focus on providing opportunities for development and employability. The advice is well described by Doherty and Horsted (1995, p. 29) as follows.

> Organisations are buying only half of the new psychological contract. They cannot offer job security, but at the same time they do not want to lose the traditional commitment and loyalty of their employees. If organisations move to employability rather than employment as a conceptual model, they must find alternative ways to develop skills, and to retain and motivate employees.

Looking at alternatives to the traditional notion of advancement or promotion, Igbaria and Parasuraman (1994) suggest the idea of capitalising on employees' satisfaction with their developmental prospects. While not representing promotions, these prospects are still career-enhancing. They allow for challenge and the acquisition of new skills by moving to new positions or new projects. Igbaria and Parasuraman (1994) found that employees' perceptions of their developmental prospects positively influenced organisational commitment. This finding concurs with Meadows-Taylor (1999) since opportunity for personal development is one current employee desire.

One developmental opportunity that may lead to increased organisational commitment is an involvement program, which draws on the psychological underpinnings of job design (Hackman 1977). Involving employees more frequently in decisions about how their work is done, and other aspects of their work, may lead to greater commitment (Juravich 1996). There is some evidence that such programs also lead to lower absenteeism and increased job satisfaction. For example, a participatory management style allows employees to experience responsibility for work outcomes (Hackman 1977). This style has been linked to higher organisational commitment (Boshoff & Mels 1995).

Yet there is little consistent evidence that such programs actually improve the performance of individuals, or that of the firm as a whole (Juravich 1996). Similarly, as noted above, organisational commitment, while having several benefits for employers, does not in itself seem to be strongly linked to actual improvements in performance or productivity.

Still on the negative side, Juravich (1996) also points out that such programs add responsibility to employees' roles, and may actually lead to adverse consequences such as increased work stress. The value of job redesign also depends on how strong employee growth needs are (Igbaria & Parasuraman 1994). In summary, there is some evidence that participation or involvement can in some instances generate advantages, particularly if the right employees, with the right expectations, are involved. This discussion suggests that job redesign may not be a universal panacea to organisational ills including low commitment. Rather, successful implementation depends on understanding the diverse needs of employees, amongst other factors.

One example of the necessary leadership and top management commitment is given by Mescon and Mescon (1996) in a study of a United States pest control company. The managers of this organisation were all expected to spend 3 days in the field with customers and employees every week. CEO Gary Rollins travelled the country, meeting frequently with his managers. He believed that by communicating often, sharing his visions and 'putting his money where his mouth is', he could generate enthusiasm and commitment amongst his employees. This example also supports the emphasis put on communication above.

Future directions — alternative strategies for employees

Instead of encouraging employees to be dependent on the organisation for their identity, and thus committed to the employer, perhaps a philosophy of continuous learning should be adopted. Here the idea is that employees should be committed to their own continuous improvement, through learning and development (Webber 1997). This will free them from being dependent on their employer. From the organisational viewpoint, such workers are less likely to have strong organisational commitment, which may mean greater turnover. However, that turnover may be less costly than having low-performing or unproductive employees and is certainly less traumatic than being forced into downsizing.

This encouragement for employees to take responsibility for their own learning, and thus ensure their employability, is consistent with observations that employees are demanding more interesting work. Further, lack of learning has been implicated as a cause of retrenchment for Australian managers (Marchant & Littler 1998). Retrenchment is the ultimate expression of an organisation's lack of commitment to employees.

In summary, employees should focus on their own employability. They should commit to their own development and learning rather than to the rapidly vanishing benevolence of any one employer. Some authors even urge employees to 'sever the corporate umbilical cord' (Garcia 1997, p. 23).

Conclusion

The following main points have been made in this chapter. Although definitions of organisational commitment vary, there are common elements of loyalty or obligation, aligning employee values with those of the organisation, and retaining membership in the organisation.

Organisational commitment is desirable because it is associated with lower attrition and possibly other advantages, although any link to productivity is not clearly established. Organisational commitment has been measured and analysed amongst white-collar workers and blue-collar workers. The level varies quite markedly, depending on several factors including promotion opportunities and job security.

There are also certain characteristics of employees that may signal stronger commitment, including gender, age and perceptions of fewer outside opportunities. Further, one of the key factors associated with commitment is satisfaction with promotion opportunities and job security. However, given the extent of downsizing in western nations throughout the 1980s and 1990s, this form of the psychological contract has been severed, or at least weakened.

Culturally, there are variations between countries and organisations, but organisational commitment is still a relevant concern in both western and eastern cultures. Again, types, levels and causes vary and therefore so do appropriate strategies for harnessing this employee attribute.

New strategies for organisations and management include capitalising on employee growth needs through rotation, involvement, participation and relationships with colleagues. Organisations can also add other benefits to the employer–employee exchange. These benefits should take into account a more diverse range of employee desires, such as that for work–life balance. Finally, employees are strongly advised to keep learning and take responsibility for their own development.

References

Awamleh, NAHK (1996) Organisational commitment of civil service managers in Jordan: a field study. *Journal of Management Development*, 15(5): 65–75.

Bae, K and Chung, C (1997) Cultural values and work attitudes of Korean industrial workers in comparison with those of the United States and Japan. *Work and Occupations*, 24(1): 80–97.

Baruch, Y (1998) The rise and fall of organisational commitment. *Human Systems Management*, 17(2): 135–44.

Boshoff, C and Mels, G (1995) A causal model to evaluate the relationships among supervision, role stress, organisational commitment and internal service quality. *European Journal of Marketing*, 29(2): 2–19.

Bramble, T, Littler, CR & O'Brien, E (1996) Employer labour-use strategies in Australia. *Precarious Employment Conference*. Brisbane.

Brewer, AM (1996) Developing commitment between managers and employers. *Journal of Managerial Psychology*, 11(4): 24–34.

Brown, T (1995) Life without job security. *Business Credit*, 97(9): 15–9.

Burrows, L & Munday, R (1996) Leadership substitutes: their effects on teacher organisational commitment and job satisfaction. *Journal of Instructional Psychology*, 23(1): 3–9.

Caldwell, DF & Chatman, JA (1990) Building organisational commitment: a multi-firm study. *Journal of Occupational and Organisational Psychology*, 63(3): 245–62.

Cohen, A (1991) Career stage as a moderator of the relationships between organizational commitment and its outcomes: a meta-analysis. *Journal of Occupational and Organizational Psychology*, 64(3): 253–69.

Cramer, D (1993) Tenure, commitment, and satisfaction of college graduates in an engineering firm. *Journal of Social Psychology*, 133(6): 791–7.

Davidson, F (1991). *Handbook of executive survival.* Melbourne: Business Library.

DeConinck, JB & Bachmann, DP (1994) Organisational commitment and turnover intentions of marketing managers. *Journal of Applied Business Research*, 10(3): 87–96.

Doherty, N & Horsted, J (1995) Helping survivors to stay on board. *People Management*, 1(1): 26–30.

Elloy, DF & Flynn, WR (1998) Job involvement and organisational commitment among dual-income and single-income families: a multiple-site study. *Journal of Social Psychology*, 138(1): 93–102.

Garcia, J (1997) How's your organisational commitment? *HRFocus*, 74(4): 23–5.

Geiger, SW & Robertson, CJ (1998) The impact of cultural values on escalation of commitment. *International Journal of Organizational Analysis*, 6(2): 165–77.

Glisson, C & Durick, C (1988) Predictors of job satisfaction and organisational commitment in human service organisations. *Administrative Science Quarterly*, 33: 61–81.

Hackman, JR (1977). Work design. In JR Hackman and JL Suttle (eds) *Improving life at work.* Glenview, Illinois: Scott, Foresman.

Hackman, JR & Oldham, GR (1980) *Work re-design.* Reading: Addison-Wesley.

Harrison, JK & Hubbard, R (1998) Antecedents to organizational commitment among Mexican employees of a United States firm in Mexico. *Journal of Social Psychology*, 138(5): 609–24.

Hawk, EJ & Sheridan, GJ (1999) The right staff. *Management Review*, 88(6): 43–6.

Hofstede, G (1980) *Culture's consequences: international differences in work related values.* Beverly Hills: Sage.

Igbaria, M & Parasuraman, S (1994) Work experiences, job involvement, and quality of work life among information systems personnel. *MIS Quarterly*, 18(2): 175–202.

Johns, G, Xie, JL & Fang, Y (1992) Mediating and moderating effects in job design. *Journal of Management*, 18: 657–76.

Jolley, A (1997) *Exporting education to Asia.* Melbourne: Victoria University Press.

Juravich, T (1996). Empirical research on employee involvement: a critical review for labour. *Labour Studies*, 21(2): 60–79.

Kheaomareun, S (1999) Analysing the differences between international students' expectations and the reality they experience. Unpublished report, Department of HRM and ER, Faculty of Business, University of Southern Queensland, Toowoomba.

Knoop, R (1995) Relationships among job involvement, job satisfaction, and organisational commitment for nurses. *Journal of Psychology Interdisciplinary and Applied*, 129(6): 643–70.

Lawson, MB & Angle, HL (1998) Upon reflection: commitment, satisfaction and regret after a corporate relocation. *Group and Organization Management*, 23(3): 289–317.

Leiter, MP & Clark, D (1994) Distinct models of burnout and commitment among men and women in the military. *Journal of Applied Behavioural Science*, 30(1): 63–83.

Littler, CR (1998) Downsizing Australia: the dilemmas of change. *Public lecture series.* Brisbane: QUT School of Management.

Loscocco, KA (1990) Reactions to blue-collar work: a comparison of women and men. *Work and Occupations*, 17(2): 152–78.

Marchant, T (1998) The effects of organisational restructuring on managers' careers in Australia. Doctoral dissertation, Toowoomba: Faculty of Business, University of Southern Queensland.

Marchant, T, Critchley, R & Littler, CR (1997) Managers on the move. *HRMonthly*, October: 6–8.

Marchant, T and Littler, CR (1998) *To avoid redundancy, keep learning and keep moving.* International Conference of Work Psychology, July, Sheffield: Sheffield University.

Maslow, A (1954) *Motivation and personality.* New York: Harper Row.

McClurg, LN (1999) Organisational commitment in the temporary-help service industry. *Journal of Applied Management Studies*, 8(1): 5–27.

Meadows-Taylor, C (1999) War for talented workers hots up. *HRMonthly*, October: 30–1.

Mescon, MH and Mescon, TS (1996) Four ingredients add spice to Orkin pest control operations. *Atlanta Business Chronicle*, 19(26): 4–6.

Mowday, RT, Steers, RM & Porter, LW (1979) The measurement of organizational commitment. *Journal of Vocational behaviour*, 14(2): 224–47.

Naumann, SE, Bennett, N, Bies, RJ & Martin, CL (1998) Laid off, but still loyal: the influence of perceived justice and organisational support. *International Journal of Conflict Management*, 9(4): 356–79.

Norris, R (1998) Equal employment opportunity. In K Parry and D Smith (eds) *Human resource management: contemporary challenges and future directions*, pp. 23–40, Toowoomba: USQ Press.

Ofori-Dankwa, J, Kanthi, MS & Arora, S (1999) A comparison of work attitudes of American R & D automotive engineers employed in a United States corporation and a Japanese subsidiary. *Multinational Business Review*, 7(1): 20–7.

O'Reilly, CA & Chatman, JA (1986) Organisational commitment and psychological attachment: the effect of compliance, identification and internalisation on pro-social behaviour. *Journal of Applied Psychology*, 71: 492–9.

Pasewark, WR & Strawser, JR (1996) The determinants and outcomes associated with job insecurity in a professional accounting environment. *Behavioural Research in Accounting*, 8: 91–114.

Pearson, CAL & Chong, J (1997) Contributions of job content and social information on organizational commitment and job satisfaction: an exploration in a Malaysian nursing context. *Journal of Occupational and Organizational Psychology*, 70(4): 357–71.

Poole, M & Jenkins, G (1997) Responsibilities for human resource management practices in the modern enterprise. *Personnel Review*, 26(5–6): 333–57.

Putterill, MS & Rohrer, TC (1995) A causal model of employee commitment in a manufacturing setting. *International Journal of Manpower*, 16(5): 56–70.

Ramos, M (1999) Gender differences and organisational commitment within a banking and financial institute. Unpublished report, Toowoomba: Department of HRM and ER, University of Southern Queensland.

Robbins, SP, Millett, B, Cacioppe, R & Waters-Marsh, T (1998) *Organisational behaviour: managing and leading in Australia and New Zealand* (2nd ed.) Sydney: Prentice Hall.

Sales and marketing management (1999) A gap in loyalty, 151(4): 84.

Savery, LK & Syme, PD (1996) Organisational commitment and hospital pharmacists. *Journal of Management Development*, 15(1): 14–23.

Schappe, SP (1998) The influence of job satisfaction, organisational commitment, and fairness perceptions on organisational citizenship behaviour. *Journal of Psychology Interdisciplinary and Applied*, 132(3): 277–91.

Stinchcombe, AL (1974) *Creating efficient industrial administrations*. New York: Academic Press.

Stum, D (1999) Workforce commitment: strategies for the new work order. *Strategy and Leadership*, 27(1): 4–8.

Taylor, PJ and Pierce, JL (1999) Effects of introducing a performance management system on employees' subsequent attitudes and effort. *Public Personnel Management*, 28(3): 423–53.

Tan, DSK and Akhtar, S (1998) Organizational commitment and experienced burnout: an exploratory study from a Chinese cultural perspective. *International Journal of Applied Analysis*, 6(4): 310–34.

Webber, T (1997) Strategies for surviving and thriving in organisations. *Career Development International*, 2(2): 90–2.

White, MM and Parks JM (1995) Validity evidence for the organisational commitment questionnaire in the Japanese corporate culture. *Educational and Psychological Measurement*, 55(2): 278–91.

PART 3 Managing groups in organisations

CHAPTER 6

Managing diversity: challenges and future directions

by Robin Kramar

Macquarie Graduate School of Management, Macquarie University, NSW

Robin.Kramar@mq.edu.au

Introduction

During the 1990s, two trends stimulated interest in diversity management. An increasing concern with the predicted changes in the demographic composition of the workforce and customers in the early twenty-first century and a heightened desire to make the most efficient and effective use of people in organisations encouraged interest in the management of differences between individuals and groups in organisations. Despite this increasing interest, the concept of diversity has not been clearly defined.

There are a number of challenges facing the management of diversity in organisations. These include the way the concept of diversity is understood and consequently the way it informs action; the way in which identity is understood in organisations; the implementation of techniques to manage diversity; demonstrating the improvements resulting from diversity management techniques; building a business case; and managing contradictory evidence. Although interest in diversity management in Australian public and private sector organisations will increase during the next 5 years, these challenges are likely to continue.

What is managing diversity?

The concept of diversity has not been clearly defined in organisational contexts (Gilbert, Stead & Ivancevich 1999, p. 61). Definitions range from broad, expansive definitions that refer to differences between individuals to much narrower definitions that focus on differences between particular groups in organisations. When diversity is defined in a broad way, it implies everyone is different and the concept reflects the notion of individualism that underpins much of our understanding of organisations. This broad view allows the identification of a variety of individual characteristics that could influence people's experiences at work, shape their perceptions of their environment and their method and style of communication (Loden & Rosener 1991, p. 21; Jackson, May & Whitney 1995).

These characteristics can be categorised into two dimensions: the primary dimension and the secondary dimension. The primary dimension (which is observable) includes immutable personal characteristics that cannot be changed, such as gender, age, race, physical abilities and sexual orientation. The secondary dimension (which is underlying or non-observable) includes characteristics that can be changed, such as educational background, marital and parental status, geographic location, income, religious beliefs, functional background, organisational tenure and personality (Loden & Rosener 1991, p. 21).

According to Thomas (1991, p. 10), 'Diversity includes everyone, it is not something that is defined by race or gender. It extends to age, personal and corporate background, education, function, and personality. It includes lifestyle, sexual preference, geographic origin, tenure with organisation, exempt or non-exempt status, and management or non-management.' This broad view of diversity has stimulated two main approaches to management actions.

The first approach that this broad view has stimulated is one where actions are taken that acknowledge and value the differences between people in the workplace (Hermon 1996, p. 427; Jamieson & O'Mara 1991). These actions are designed to manage a collective, all-inclusive mixture of differences and similarities along a particular dimension such as parental status or race. They can include sensitivity training, advisory panels and initiatives that manage people with different characteristics along a certain dimension. For instance, the management of the dimension of parental status is not just dealing with the management of those employees with pre-school-age children, school and university-age children or aged parents, but also means dealing with a collective mixture of employees with these responsibilities as well as those employees without these responsibilities. This process involves acknowledging that employees without dependent children could resent the provisions of employment conditions, such as leave without pay, special family leave or child-care facilities for only those employees with dependants.

The broad view has stimulated a second approach involving actions that create a culture that values and appreciates differences between individuals and groups and requires systematic change efforts (Bowens, Merenivitch, Johnson, James & McFadden-Bryant 1993). Managing diversity implies an ongoing, system-wide process that will tap the potential of all employees; it is concerned with developing an environment that works for all employees (Thomas 1991, p. 10). This involves understanding three dimensions of culture: the nature of the existing culture, the dimensions of the desired culture and the way in which the roots of the existing culture hinder the development of the desired culture. The dimensions of the existing culture can be established through cultural audits. To build a culture that values diversity, it is necessary to clarify organisational values so they reflect respect for the needs of individuals.

In contrast, when diversity is defined in a narrow way it refers only to people with particular personal characteristics, such as gender, race or ethnicity. This view of diversity focuses on issues that arise from discrimination based on these personal characteristics. Cross, Kat, Miller and Seashore (1994, p. xxii) indicate diversity focuses on 'issues of racism, sexism, heterosexism, classism, ableism, and other forms of discrimination at the individual, identity group and system levels.' This view of diversity and diversity management is consistent with the view that diversity management is the next generation of affirmative action (Kramar 1996). This narrow view of diversity focuses actions on removing discrimination from the workplace. It encourages the development of policies that provide for equal treatment of members of different groups by making concessions so that employees with certain personal or domestic arrangements can assimilate into the prevailing employment patterns.

Irrespective of which view of diversity is adopted, managing diversity can be regarded as a process of management based on certain values that recognise the differences between people and identities as a strength, but at the same time is directed towards the achievement of organisational outcomes. The processes associated with managing diversity become an integral part of management. When managing diversity is understood from this perspective, it is framed as a broad term that refers to the management practices used to improve the effectiveness of people management in organisations. Failure to value diversity can result in convergent thinking that fosters the belief that there is only one solution to most problems and that it is important to protect existing political and structural arrangements (Gordon 1995, p. 29).

Conceptual models of diversity

Nkomo and Cox (1999, p. 89) argue that, in order to achieve some conceptual clarity in the meaning of diversity, it is necessary to clarify the bases of the diversity. They argue that 'scholars are referring to "diversity in identities" based on membership in social and demographic groups and how differences in these identities affect social relations in organisations' (Nkomo & Cox 1999, p. 89).

Four conceptual models of diversity have been developed to explain the impact of diversity in identities on organisational behaviour and organisational outcomes. Cox (1993), Triandis, Kurowski and Gelfand (1994), Jackson, May and Whitney (1995) and Kossek and Lobel (1996) have each developed models that seek to explain these relationships.

Cox (1993) developed an interactional model of cultural diversity. This model argues that the presence of diversity in organisations will influence effectiveness at the individual and organisational levels. Differences in group identities — both physical and cultural identities — will interact with a complex set of individual, intergroup and organisational factors to influence individual affective outcomes (satisfaction, organisational identification and job involvement) and achievement outcomes (performance, job mobility and compensation). They will also have a direct influence on organisational outcomes such as attendance, work quality and turnover, as well as an indirect impact on outcomes such as profits. According to the model, the organisational context for diversity is critical in determining whether group identities will have a positive or negative effect on individual and organisational outcomes. Because the model is designed around the social psychological phenomena, it has clear applicability across many dimensions of group identity, including members of majority and minority groups, and members of groups with identities based on work function, job tenure, and religion.

The Triandis, Kurowski and Gelfand (1994) model defines and specifies interrelationships among 19 variables. The model is developed around the core concepts of perceived similarity, degree of interaction and rewards. According to the model, under certain circumstances transactions between people of different groups are experienced as rewarding and, as a consequence, positive inter-group attitudes will develop. These circumstances include situations when people perceive themselves as similar, when they have positive contact, when they have a shared sense of goals and when the contact is encouraged by the social setting or authorities.

The model proposed by Jackson, May and Whitney (1995) was developed as a means of understanding the dynamics of diversity in work teams. This is a complex model that includes more than 30 variables, many of which have multiple components. Diversity is defined in terms of two categories specifying dimensions of diversity: a task-related category that includes tenure, education and occupation; and a relationship-oriented category that includes personal characteristics such as race, age, gender and family status. According to the model, one can analyse diversity as a characteristic at three levels: at the level of the individual, at the level of the relationship between the individual and the group and at the level of the group itself. It is argued that outcomes such as personal performance, power balance and team creativity are influenced by personal attributes, interpersonal similarity and team composition. Other factors, such as attention, recall, and stage of socialisation will also influence this relationship.

The framework developed by Kossek and Lobel (1996) seeks to provide a model that identifies diversity management strategies as an integral part of a number of strategies that influence human resource policies and facilitate the achievement of desired individual and organisational outcomes. The framework is designed to increase understanding of the linkages between environmental drivers, managing diversity and other organisational strategic choices, human resource policy areas and individual, group and organisational outcomes (Kossek & Lobel 1996, p. 5). It is based on an open systems framework that indicates that organisations need to take into account external environmental factors, such as labour market composition and global competition, and internal environmental factors, such as business strategy and technology, when making strategic choices about managing diversity. It also indicates organisations need to take into account these strategic choices when developing human resource policies.

These four models indicate that managing diversity in organisations does have an impact on individual, group and organisational performance. They also indicate that diversity-management initiatives need to be developed and implemented in conjunction with other people-management initiatives.

Managing diversity: challenging issues

There are a number of challenges associated with managing diversity. These challenges fall into four categories:
1. the way in which the concept of diversity is understood and informs action
2. implementing techniques to manage diversity
3. demonstrating the improvements arising from diversity management initiatives
4. building a business case for the implementation of diversity management techniques.

Concept of diversity

A major challenge associated with managing diversity is the way the concept of diversity is understood, particularly the concept of identity and the level at which identity is understood in organisations. When diversity is defined in a very narrow way, the prevailing social, economic and political arrangements are taken as given. Consequently, the approach to managing diversity involves providing policies that prevent discrimination and facilitate the integration of these groups into the existing arrangements. When diversity is conceptualised and managed in this narrow way, it fosters the development of policies that provide for equal treatment and compliance with laws and policies, particularly those providing for equal employment opportunity. It distracts attention from the need to integrate employment policies with organisational needs and to take into account the different needs of members of different identity groups. This latter point is illustrated very clearly by Krautil, who makes reference to wild animals in the zoo. She says:

> Imagine your organisation is a giraffe house. Equal opportunity has been very effective widening the door of the giraffe house to let the elephant in, but home won't be best for the elephant unless a number of major modifications are made to the inside of the house. Without these changes the house will remain designed for giraffes and the elephant will not 'feel at home'. (Krautil 1995, p. 22)

The broader concept of diversity allows a redesign of the giraffe house. Dickens (cited in Overell 1996, p. 12) expresses the broader view of diversity in terms of climbing a ladder. She says:

> Rather than helping people from disadvantaged groups to move up the ladder, managing diversity is more about looking at whether the ladder needs changing. It is less about helping different groups to cope within a dominant male, able-bodied culture; more about valuing the differences which people have. (Overell 1996, p. 13)

In Australia, most organisations adopt a narrow view of diversity. Many organisations have widened the door to the giraffe house, but they have not modified the inside of the house, nor have they examined the ladder to see if it needs changing. This is indicated by the tendency for large Australian organisations covered by the *Affirmative Action (Equal Employment Opportunity for Women) Act 1986* ('the Act') to introduce written equal employment opportunity policies concerned with only some of the employment matters specified in the Act, particularly recruitment, selection, promotion and training. However, organisations have not widely addressed other issues such as decreasing satisfaction with the balance between family and work life and issues of sexual harassment (Regulatory review of the Affirmative Action (Equal Employment Opportunity for Women) Act 1986, 1998). Legislation and government policy are critical in establishing expectations about desired standards of behaviour; however, one of the challenges is encouraging organisations to interpret the legislation from more than a very limited perspective.

A further challenge associated with understanding the concept of diversity involves the difficulties of understanding identities in organisations. Individuals have many identities reflecting characteristics such as their gender, ethnicity, function in the organisation, family situation and type of employment. Identities are therefore complex, multifaceted and transient, as characteristics associated with the secondary dimensions of diversity change. The process of managing diversity involves managing individuals with multiple identities. Associated with this challenge is the issue that there are individual differences within groups. Identities are not homogeneous within social groups.

Identity, therefore, needs to be understood at a number of levels of analysis:
- individual
- group/inter-group
- organisational
- societal.

An understanding of diversity at these four levels recognises that initiatives taken to manage diversity involve actions at all four levels, not just one or two levels. For instance, if diversity is understood only at the level of the group, individuals who do not share the norms and values of a group with which they share demographic characteristics will be misunderstood. Although men share the same gender, individual men do not share the same domestic responsibilities. This has been recognised at Esso where all employees, both men and women, have access to 52 weeks' parental leave, a variety of flexible working arrangements such as part-time work, adjustable work hours, working from home and support for dependant care. This dependant care can include care for young children as well as care for elderly dependants.

Implementation of techniques to manage diversity

In the United States, the three most common techniques used to manage diversity are diversity enlargement, diversity sensitivity through training and cultural audits (Kossek & Lobel 1996, pp. 3–5). A fourth technique that is often used is the establishment of advisory panels. The following section examines a number of issues associated with implementing these techniques in organisations.

Diversity enlargement
Diversity enlargement refers to increasing the representation of groups with particular personal characteristics such as ethnic or gender backgrounds. The aim of this technique is to change the organisation's demographic composition, but it usually does not involve changing other human resource practices. Commenting on the situation in the United States, Kossek and Lobel (1996, p. 40) claim:

> Employers seem to assume that increasing diversity and exposure to minority employees will result in improved individual and organisational performance.

They argue that in the United States many employers implementing these changes do not really support them, but feel they are coerced by market demands and the need to appear 'politically correct'. As a result, when a technique of diversity enlargement is viewed as a forced change and is not supported by other policies in the organisation, the effectiveness of the policy is undermined.

In Australia, although the equal employment opportunity and discrimination legislation in the federal and state jurisdictions does not require forced adherence to quotas, it is possible that some employers would feel coerced by expectations in the labour market and by customers to increase the representation of members of particular groups.

Diversity sensitivity through training
Interest in diversity is quite widespread in the United States, with at least half of all major American companies having signed up for diversity workshops (D Sousa 1997, p. 83; D Sousa 1996, p. 43; Gordon 1995, p. 26; Beaver 1995, p. 7). Diversity training usually seeks to promote awareness of and sensitise people to diversity, to promote the understanding, tolerance and workplace harmony that will ultimately produce a more productive workforce (Beaver 1995, p. 7). However, there is evidence (Beaver 1995, pp. 7–9) that these workshops do not achieve their objective of improved cohesion between individuals, but instead heighten tensions, sharpen differences and increase competition and hostility when members of these groups view themselves as competing for jobs.

Research (Kanter 1977; Pfeffer 1983) indicates people feel most comfortable with people who are similar to themselves in terms of socioeconomic status, gender and attitudes. Group differences can foster prejudice very quickly. Although it is not the intention of diversity training, such training can accentuate group differences and fuel prejudice, particularly if it provides information about only the differences between groups.

An instance of this occurred in the Californian-based grocery chain, Lucky Stores. These stores instituted diversity training sessions designed to teach their employees to acknowledge and cope with their racist and sexist assumptions about women and minority groups. Unfortunately, some employees sued the company for discrimination and used the notes taken during the training as evidence. Lucky Stores was found guilty of discrimination and ordered to pay $90 million (D Sousa 1996, p. 42).

Cultural audits

A cultural audit has the potential to assist the process of building a culture that honours diversity. As mentioned earlier, building a culture requires understanding three dimensions of an organisation's culture: the nature of the existing culture; the dimensions of desired culture; and the way in which the roots of the existing culture hinder the development of the desired culture. An organisation's culture can be established through a cultural audit.

Thomas (1991) suggests this audit can be done by either an outside consultant, or, in circumstances where trust is high, by organisational members with the assistance of an outside consultant. This process can involve in-depth interviews, written surveys, reviews of relevant organisational documents, focus groups and direct observation of organisational members' behaviour. The data collected can then be used as a basis for drawing inferences about the attitudes of organisational members toward the issue of diversity. It can identify the major obstacles faced by groups with particular personal characteristics (Morrison, Ruddeman & Hughes-James 1993) and provide an indication of how these obstacles hinder performance (Cox 1993).

Cultural audits are an essential part of managing diversity; however, they are not sufficient in themselves to build a culture that allows all members of the organisation to contribute to their fullest potential (Kossek & Lobel 1996, pp. 4–5). For a cultural audit to be effective, it is essential that the formal procedures such as human resource policies are assessed. This assessment provides the means to examine the extent to which an organisation's policies support or hinder the desired culture values diversity (Kramar 1999, p. 200).

There is also a danger that a cultural audit will leave the impression that the white male culture is the problem and that the white men in the organisation must bear the burden of most of the change (MacDonald 1993). However, if managing diversity is a mutual process then the process must be inclusive to allow all members to contribute to their fullest potential. Cultural audits therefore need to focus on not only the differences between groups, but also on the similarities between groups. It is then possible to acknowledge that these similarities and differences need to be managed through human resource policies and practices.

Advisory panels

Advisory panels can consist of representatives from all groups of employees in the organisation. These panels are responsible for enhancing diversity in the organisation to improve organisational performance. Alternatively, these panels can operate as internal advisory groups, consisting of representatives of particular groups such as women or a particular ethnic group. These groups meet periodically with senior management to have open dialogue about obvious and subtle barriers impacting on various groups. These panels attempt to create a shared understanding of the challenges and opportunities associated with managing diversity (Hermon 1996, pp. 427–8).

A number of organisations in the United States have formed advisory panels. These include Xerox Corporation, Avon, Digital Equipment and US West (Hermon 1996, p. 431). Much of the success of these advisory panels has come from the common understandings and relationships that were built between senior management and the members of the panels who represented only one specified group (Morrison 1992, p. 1).

A study of advisory panels in a large service company located in America's Midwest found both the positive effects and negative effects of the advisory panels. The positive effects included increased sensitivity to diversity issues, improved career advancements and improved relationships within the organisation. More than two-thirds of those interviewed in the study believed the panels raised the sensitivity of senior managers to diversity issues, although only 40 per cent believed the sensitivity of middle managers had been raised. The panels fostered career advancements by encouraging managers to create opportunities by increasing the number of people in these identity groups and by promotion. Relationships in the organisation were improved by the panels facilitating improved communication on racial and gender issues. This communication contributed to culture change; however, the study indicated that it takes time to create the change. It found members of panels that had been in operation for a greater length of time felt more positive about the results of the panels (Hermon 1996, pp. 435–7). The panels also produced negative effects such as increased resentment, a limited effect on middle managers and the development of adversarial relationships between members of groups because of a fear of increased competition. As one woman who served on a panel said:

'There's some resentment. It is somewhat quiet. Midlevel managers feel that being involved in panels gives women and minorities a power that's not readily available to them.' (Hermon 1996, p. 436)

Demonstrating improvements

A further challenge associated with managing diversity is demonstrating organisational improvements. There is evidence that there are many benefits to the employer of managing diversity, such as:
- improved employee performance (Cox 1993)
- enhanced workgroup problem solving, creativity and cohesion (McLeod & Lobel 1992, pp. 227–31; Watson, Kumar & Michaelsen 1993, pp. 590–602)
- a more thorough examination of the assumptions and implications of scenarios (Nemeth & Wachter 1983; Cox & Smolinski 1994)
- a higher level of critical analysis
- a lower probability of group think (Cox & Smolinski 1994, p. 34)
- improved flexibility, innovation and meeting of customer needs (Cox 1993; Wright, Ferris, Hiller & Kroll 1995, p. 272).

However, it is difficult to demonstrate that improvements in individual, group and organisational performance are a consequence of strategies designed to manage diversity. The indirect benefits of managing diversity, such as increased morale, greater job satisfaction, higher productivity and an improved competitive edge are difficult 'if not impossible, to prove' (Stevens 1995, p. 61). Kossek and Lobel (1996, p. 3) report in the United States:

> Despite these reported benefits, their realisation has remained elusive for most firms. This is because traditional HR strategies to manage diversity have largely been introduced piecemeal, lacking integration with other systems. Consequently, they do not change the culture to support the management of heterogeneity; and they end up failing.

It is nevertheless possible to demonstrate the costs of not valuing and managing diversity in organisations. Some of these costs include absenteeism, high turnover, an inability to attract necessary staff, poor morale, increased stress and reduced return on training expenditure. A number of Australian organisations, such as NRMA, Commonwealth Bank, ICI Australia and Pacific Dunlop, have calculated the costs associated with the turnover and absenteeism of staff and realised the importance of limiting these by identifying the cause of the behaviours that contribute to the costs (Kramar 1996).

Building a business case

Another challenge involved in managing diversity is the difficulty associated with building a business case that demonstrates that managing diversity adds value to the organisation. Other organisational initiatives 'that present more compelling, factual evidence of payback on investment win out over diversity initiatives, which seem to offer less predictable and tangible benefits' (Robinson & Dechant 1997, p. 21). The most successful business case for managing diversity is one that focuses on attaining a organisation's long-term specific objectives such as reducing turnover or absenteeism.

For instance, NRMA developed a work and family program as an integral part of its broader strategy, 'improving the way we work'. The major issues associated with building the business case were putting the issue on management's agenda, building the options through exploration, analysis and development, getting started through policy decisions, handling opposition and competing perceptions, keeping the process of development and implementation going through clear identification of responsibilities and monitoring the implementation against a completion date. Factors that were critical for the successful management of these issues were the involvement of employees in all stages and a strong General Manager Human Resources. She was able to convince the executive of the value of a work and family program using financial information describing the costs and benefits of introducing the program (Kramar 1997).

Managing contradictory evidence

In addition, there is evidence that the greater the diversity of observable or primary attributes within a work group or an organisational unit, the less integrated the group is likely to be (O'Reilly, Caldwell & Barnett 1989) and the higher the level of dissatisfaction and turnover (Jackson, Brett, Sessa, Cooper, Julin and Peyronnin 1991, pp. 675-89; Wagner, Pfeffer & O'Reilly 1984, pp. 74-92; Milliken & Martins 1996, p. 415). Negative effects have been found to be greater for the characteristics of race and gender rather than age (Tsui, Egan & O'Reilly 1992, pp. 549-79), thus indicating the possibility that deep-seated prejudices against people with different racial and gender characteristics could be adversely influencing managing diversity efforts.

There is also evidence that there are greater coordination costs associated with managing groups with a wide skill-base, rather than those composed of individuals with more homogeneous skills and backgrounds (Milliken & Martins 1996, p. 415; Tsui & O'Reilly 1989, pp. 402-23). Even similarity on time of entry into an organisation can be important in influencing the interaction frequency and attraction between people (O'Reilly, Caldwell & Barnett 1989, pp. 21-37).

Therefore one of the challenges of managing diversity is to increase problem solving and creativity within the group but at the same time prevent or manage the dissatisfaction and failure to identify with the group associated with group heterogeneity.

Future directions in diversity management

Managing diversity has not become a high priority management initiative in Australian organisations. An understanding of the concept has been framed in terms of a narrow view of diversity that has been shaped by our anti-discrimination and equal employment opportunity legislation. Consequently, initiatives in Australia have primarily focused on the two aspects of the primary dimension of diversity (sex and culture) and one aspect of the secondary dimension (family status).

Initiatives in Australia have included attempts to attract and retain women, develop women for senior management positions and assist them balance their family and employment commitments (Affirmative Action Agency 1996). The initiatives designed to facilitate work-life balance include more flexible working arrangements, vacation care programs and some paid parental leave. In the area of cultural diversity, the two most common activities have involved training managers to manage culturally diverse workforces and promoting English literacy and language training in the workplace (Migliorino, Miltenyi & Robertson 1994).

Diversity management in the future will continue to be influenced by legislation. However, it will also be influenced by the changing nature of the workforce and the nature of the relationships people doing the work have with the organisation. Just as human resource initiatives are increasingly being required to demonstrate the benefits to the organisation, it will become increasingly important for managers to demonstrate the value of diversity initiatives in terms of outcomes that benefit the organisation as well as the individual.

Legislation

The two proposed bills, the *Equal Employment Opportunity for Women in the Workplace Bill* and the *Workplace Relations (More Jobs Better Pay) Amendment Bill*, strengthen the opportunities for organisations to link diversity management initiatives with organisational objectives. This requirement has also been developed in the federal public sector where the *Public Service Act 1999* requires agencies to develop workplace diversity programs and to adopt a strategic approach to employment equity and workplace flexibility.

Although there is no requirement and no apparent intention to require private sector organisations to develop broad diversity initiatives, in the public sector this is now a requirement. Using workplace diversity programs, agencies will be required to develop strategies to attract and retain teams of staff with a diverse range of backgrounds and perspectives. The main objectives of these programs are to build a creative and productive work environment, to improve service delivery and provide a better working environment for employees. Agencies will also be required to make progress in eliminating any employment-related disadvantage attributable to Aboriginality, gender, ethnicity, race, or physical or mental disability (Public Service Merit Protection Commission 1997).

These workplace diversity programs will go beyond the previous requirement to eliminate employment disadvantage and legal compliance by requiring agencies to recognise, value and nurture the different skills and competencies of all people. It is anticipated this will result in the introduction of flexible working practices, agency workforces that reflect the composition of the Australian community and improved agency performance. The programs provide the potential for the adoption of a broad approach to diversity by explicitly stressing the importance of agencies making the best use of the diversity available to them through human resource management processes and stressing that the workplace diversity programs include equal employment opportunity (EEO) legislative requirements, but go beyond this EEO framework (Public Service Merit Protection Commission 1997).

Changing nature of the workforce

Since World War II, the composition of the workforce in Australia has become more diverse. The representation of members of a variety of non-Anglo-Saxon cultures, married women, women with children, including pre-school-age children and two-income-earning families has increased. Labourforce projections indicate that in 2011 the workforce will consist of more people aged over 45 years than under. The Australian Bureau of Statistics (1994) predicts 'major gains will occur in the 45–54 year age group with a projected increase of 36% for men and 75% for women; growth rates for 55–64 year olds will result in a 79% increase, with that group becoming 10.8% of the workforce in 2011' (Hartmann 1998, p. 23). Consequently, as increasing numbers of the workforce belong to these older age groups we could expect the primary dimension of age could become an important basis for the development of diversity management initiatives.

Employment relationships

Not only will the composition of the workforce change in the future, but the nature of the relationships people have with organisations will also continue to change. The 1990s have been characterised by 'an upward trend in all kinds of non-standard forms of employment which undermine people's job security' (ACIRRT 1999, p. 138). There has been increasing use of casualisation of work, temporary work, outsourcing and the use of agencies and other labour market intermediaries (ACIRRT 1999, pp. 138–46; Kramar 1999). Given the predicted changes in the *Workplace Relations Act* and the continuing need for organisations to respond quickly in the marketplace, we could expect these forms of flexible employment to increase.

It therefore seems to be inevitable that the employment relationship will become an increasingly important secondary dimension of diversity that will need to be managed. Saul

(1996, pp. 19–36) argues that different management styles and expectations are required for different individuals, depending on their relationship with the organisation, and that there will be movement of individuals between different relationships. For instance, an older worker might choose to move from full-time employment to the role of consultant to the organisation.

Adding value

Management functions are increasingly under pressure to demonstrate the extent to which they add value to the 'business'. This has been reflected in the widespread retrenchments of managers in Australia (ACIRRT 1999, p. 154) and the intense debate about the value of managers in areas such as human resource management (Ulrich, Losey & Lake 1997). The adding of value to the organisation can be demonstrated in a number of ways. It can be demonstrated by first indicating the impact of the policies on employee behaviour and human resource costs and then by outlining the impact of policies in a diversity program on organisational performance indicators such as stock market prices.

In the United States, it was found that there was a relationship between announcements regarding the management of a diverse workforce and stock market evaluations. Announcements of quality affirmative action programs are associated with positive results on the stock market, while announcements of discrimination settlements against organisations were associated with negative stock price changes (Wright, Ferris, Hiller & Kroll 1995, pp. 281–3).

Similarly, the adding of value to the organisation can be demonstrated by the impact of particular policies that are costly to the organisation on employee behaviour and by changing this behaviour. It has been demonstrated that improved maternity leave benefits increase the retention of employees in Australian (Kramar 1996; Gillespie 1999, p. 214), British (Equal Opportunities Review 1996, pp. 5–6) and American organisations (Cox & Smolinski 1994, pp. 24, 39). Similarly, it has been demonstrated that the provision of child-care facilities and other benefits that seek to manage an individual's work and family lives can improve employee productivity and change employee behaviour (Youngblood & Chambers-Cook 1984; Bruegel & Perrons 1995, pp. 160–1).

Conclusion

Although the concept of diversity management has not been widely used in Australian organisations, it is likely that increasing attention will be paid to managing employees with different identities based on personal characteristics and on different employment relationships. This will be done in the context of using techniques to ultimately improve the organisational outcomes. Managers who are intent on introducing initiatives to manage diversity will need to be able to clarify their notion of diversity and the implications of this notion for the policies used to manage the similarities and differences in their organisation. They will also need to demonstrate the value of the initiatives to the organisation and be able to market a case for the introduction of the initiatives.

References

ACIRRT (1999) *Australia at work: just managing?* Sydney: Prentice Hall.

Affirmative Action Agency (1996) *Best practice in affirmative action: case studies.* Canberra: Australian Government Publishing Service.

Australian Bureau of Statistics. (1994) 1995–2011 *Labour force projections: Australia, catalogue no. 6260.* Canberra: Australian Government Publishing Service.

Beaver, W (1995) Let's stop diversity training and start managing for diversity. *Industrial management*, 37(4): 7–9.

Bowens, H, Merenivitch, J, Johnson, PL, James, AR & McFadden-Bryant, DJ (1993) Managing cultural diversity toward true multiculturalism: some knowledge from the black perspective. In RR Sims and RE Dennehy (eds) *Diversity and differences in organizations.* Connecticut: Quorum Books.

Bruegel, I & Perrons, D (1995) Where do the costs of unequal treatment fall? An analysis of the incidence of the costs of unequal pay and sex discrimination in the UK. In J Humphries and J Rubery (eds) *The economics of equal opportunity.* Manchester: Equal Opportunities Commission.

Cox, T (1993) *Cultural diversity in organizations: theory, research and practise.* San Francisco: Berrett-Koehler.

Cox, T & Smolinski, C (1994) Managing diversity and glass ceiling initiatives as national. economic imperatives. Research Report prepared for the Glass Ceiling Commission, US Department of Labor.

Cross, E, Kat, JH, Miller, FA & Seashore, E (1994) *The promise of diversity.* Burr Ridge, IL: Irwin Professional Publishing.

D Sousa, D (1996) Beyond affirmative action: the perils of managing diversity. *Chief Executive*, 119, pp. 42–8.

D Sousa, D (1997) The diversity trap. *Forbes*, 159(2), p. 83, January 27.

Equal Opportunities Review (EOR) (1996) Proportion of women directors doubles. *EOR*, No 65, January/February: pp. 5–6.

Gilbert, JA, Stead, BA & Ivancevich, JM (1999) Diversity management: a new organisational paradigm. *Journal of Business Ethics*, August, pp. 61–76.

Gillespie, J (1999) Profiting from diversity: the Westpac experience. In G O'Neill and R Kramar (eds) *Australian human resources management.* Sydney: Woodslane, pp. 207–16.

Gordon, J (1995) Different from what: diversity as a performance issue. *Training*, 32(5), pp. 25–34.

Hartmann, LC (1998) The impact of trends in labour-force participation in Australia. In M Patrickson and L Hartmann (eds) *Managing an ageing workforce.* Warriewood: Business and Professional Publishing, pp. 3–25.

Hermon, MV (1996) Building a shared understanding and commitment to managing diversity. *Journal of Business Communication*, 33(4), pp. 427–42.

Jackson, SE, Brett, JF, Sessa, VI, Cooper, DM, Julin, JA & Peyronnin, K (1991) Some differences make a difference: individual dissimilarity and group heterogeneity as correlates of recruitment, promotions and turnover. *Journal of Applied Psychology*, 76, pp. 675–89.

Jackson, SE, May, K & Whitney, K (1995) Diversity in decision making teams. In RA Guo and E Salas (eds) *Team decision making effectiveness in organizations.* San Francisco: Jossey-Bass, pp. 204–61.

Jamieson, D & O'Mara, J (1991) *Managing workforce 2000.* San Francisco: Jossey-Bass.

Kanter, RM (1977) *Men and women of the corporation.* New York: Harper.

Kossek, EE and Lobel, SA (1996) Introduction: transforming human resource systems to manage diversity – an introduction and orienting framework. In EE Kossek and SA Lobel (eds) *Managing diversity: human resource strategies for transforming the workplace.* Cambridge: Blackwell.

Kramar, R (1996) *The business case for a family friendly workplace.* Sydney: NSW Department of Industrial Relations.

Kramar, R (1997) Developing and implementing work and family policies: implications for human resource policies. *Asia–Pacific Journal of Human Resources*, 35(3), pp. 1–19.

Kramar, R (1999) Managing diversity. In G O'Neill and R Kramar (eds) *Australian Human Resources Management.* Sydney: Woodslane.

Krautil, F (1995) Managing diversity in Esso Australia. In EM Davis and C Harris (eds) *Making the link*, no 6, Affirmative Action Agency and the Labour Management Studies Foundation, Sydney: pp. 22–8.

Loden, M & Rosener, J (1991) *Workforce America.* Homewood, IL: Business One.

MacDonald, H (1993) The diversity industry. *The New Republic*, July 5, pp. 22–5.

McLeod, PL & Lobel, SA (1992) The effects of ethnic diversity on idea generation in small groups. *Academy of management best paper proceedings*, pp. 227–31.

Migliorino, P, Miltenyi, G & Robertson, H (1994) *Best practice in managing a culturally diverse workplace — a manager's manual.* Canberra: Australian Government Publishing Service.

Milliken, FJ & Martins, LL (1996) Searching for common threads: understanding the multiple effects of diversity in organisational groups. *Academy of Management Review*, 21(2), pp. 402–33.

Morrison, A (1992) *The new leader's guidelines on leadership diversity in America.* San Francisco: Jossey-Bass.

Morrison, A, Ruddeman, M & Hughes-James, M (1993) *Making diversity happen: controversies and solutions.* Greensborough, NC: Center for Creative Leadership.

Nemeth, CJ & Wachter, J (1983) Creative problemsolving as a result of majority versus minority influence. *European Journal of Social Psychology*, 13, pp. 45–55.

Nkomo, S & Cox, T (1999) Divers identities in organisations. In S Clegg, C Hardy & WR Nord, *Managing organisations: current issues.* London: Sage, pp. 88–106.

O'Reilly, CA, Caldwell, DF & Barnett, WP (1989) Work group demography, social integration, and turnover. *Administrative Science Quarterly*, 34, pp. 21–37.

Overell, S (1996) IPD says diversity is next step for equality. *People management*, 2(24), pp. 12–13.

Pfeffer, J (1983) Organisational demography. In LL Cummings and BM Shaw (eds) *Research in Organisational Behaviour*, Greenwich: JAI Press.

Public Service Merit Protection Commission (1997) *Towards a more diverse workforce in APS.* The public service commissioner's annual report 1996–7 on equal employment opportunity. Canberra: Australian Government Publishing Service.

Regulatory review of the Affirmative Action (Equal Employment Opportunity for Women) 1986 (1998) *Unfinished business: equity for women in Australian workplaces.* Commonwealth of Australia, Canberra.

Robinson, G & Dechant, K (1997) Building a business case for diversity. *Academy of Management Executive,* 11(3), pp. 21–31.

Saul, P (1996) Managing the organization as a community of contributors. *Asia–Pacific Journal of Human Resources,* 34(3), pp. 19–36.

Stevens, J (1995) Weighing up the evidence on managing diversity. *Personnel Management,* 1(13), p. 61.

Thomas, RR Jr (1991) *Beyond race and gender: unleashing the power of your total workforce.* New York: Amacon.

Triandis, HC, Kurowski, LL & Gelfand, MJ (1994) Workplace diversity. In HC Triandis, MD Dunnette & LM Hough (eds) *Handbook of industrial and organizational psychology.* Palo Alto: Consulting Psychologists Press.

Tsui, AS, Egan, TD & O'Reilly, CA (1992) Being different: relational demography and organisational attachment. *Administrative Science Quarterly,* 37, pp. 549–79.

Tsui, AS & O'Reilly, CA (1989) Beyond simple demographic effects: the importance of relational demography and superior-subordinate dyads. *Academy of Management Journal,* 32, pp. 402–23.

Ulrich, D, Losey, MR & Lake, G (eds) (1997) *Tomorrow's HR management.* New York: John Wiley & Sons.

Wagner, GW, Pfeffer, J & O'Reilly, CA (1984) Organisational demography and turnover in top management groups. *Administrative Science Quarterly,* 29, pp. 74–92.

Watson, WE, Kumar, K & Michaelson, LK (1993) Cultural diversity's impact on interaction process and performance: comparing homogeneous and diverse task groups. *Academy of Management Journal,* 36, pp. 590–602.

Wright, P, Ferris, S, Hiller, J & Kroll, M (1995) Competitiveness through management diversity: effects on stock price valuation. *Academy of Management Journal,* 38(1), pp. 272–87.

Youngblood, S & Chambers-Cook, K (1984) Childcare assistance can improve employee attitudes and behaviour. *Personnel Administrator,* February, pp. 93–5.

CHAPTER 7

Using individual and team reward–recognition strategies to achieve organisational success

by Ron Cacioppe

Graduate School of Business, Curtin University of Technology, WA

rc@gsb.curtin.edu.au

Introduction

There is an increasing shift to the use of teams in developed nations. This is occurring for several reasons. First, organisations are downsizing and use teams as a way to make better use of the skills of their workforce. Secondly, there is a marked shift away from directive, hierarchical leadership structures to a more participative equality among group members as a result of changes in social values. Thirdly, technology, competition and customer expectations require that organisations are highly responsive and adaptive to customer requirements. If one organisation does not respond, another will.

Empowered front-line staff and teams are the best way to provide rapid responses to changes in customer needs as they occur. In a 1995 survey of 230 companies on team-based pay, the reasons for adopting teams were customer satisfaction, service/product quality and productivity for over 70 per cent of the organisations (Gross 1995).

Managers know that reward and recognition are important tools for motivating individual employees and teams. 'Employee of the month' schemes, profit sharing and money for higher productivity or commission on sales revenue are widely used and well-known approaches.

There appears to be little understanding, however, of why particular incentives are used in different situations or at specific times. The use of team-based rewards has interested managers, but many hesitate to implement a team-based system since team rewards appear more complex and may have adverse affects on individual performance.

The main focus of this chapter is individual reward strategies that can be used to motivate individuals and teams to achieve organisational success. The types of teams and characteristics of effective teams are discussed first to provide the context for understanding that team rewards are important motivators in accomplishing organisational objectives. Challenging issues associated with individual and team rewards, such as aligning team rewards and business goals, and designing and implementing team rewards, are then discussed. Four factors that need to be considered when establishing team-based rewards are the methods of reward and recognition, the level of individual-team development, the type of team, and the culture of the team and organisation. The research that Motorola conducted with over 150 teams in five sites around the world and Trigon Blue Cross Blue Shield's 4 years' experience with team-based incentives are used as the basis for several of the ideas that are in this paper. Motorola has conducted a worldwide research program examining team reward and has adopted an approach that is relevant to many other organisations based on the findings (Coli 1997). Trigon Blue Cross Blue Shield, a US health insurance company, introduced team-based incentives in 1993 and has found significant positive results since then. As a result of team-based pay, Trigon has increased its service levels, reduced administrative expenses, and improved its employees' understanding of the business.

Forty-four specific reward tools which can be used for individual or team incentives are listed. A comprehensive matrix is put forward that could be used to determine what tools should be used at various stages in a team's development, and with what type of team. Practical implications for managers and organisations are outlined and, finally, a thorough rethinking and restructuring of reward and recognition practices, aligning them with new organisational goals and culture, is suggested.

Types of teams

A team can be defined as a group of people working together towards a common goal. A team can be considered either as a *full-time department*, a *project team*, or a *part-time special team*. A *full-time department team* is the main type of team in most organisations and does not have a targeted or closure date. It continues on permanently and therefore never experiences the adjourning stage. The work or service this team provides is ongoing so it is not planned for elimination or obsolescence.

A *project team* requires its members to be involved full time but disbands at a set date or when the project is completed. It is similar to a full-time department team except that it is often made up of people from various departments and experiences the adjourning process at the end of its life. The *part-time special team* is different from the other teams in that the participation on this team is for only limited times. The members of the team often have other jobs, which usually make more demands on their time. Safety teams, quality teams, selection committees and other types of part-time special teams are common in most organisations.

Rewarding individuals and teams: challenging issues

Aligning team rewards and business goals

Before implementing any team-based incentive program it is important to recognise that pay incentives and rewards are communication and motivation devices. Rewards are one of the loudest and clearest ways leaders of an organisation can send a message about what they consider important. The way in which people behave is influenced to a great extent by the way they are measured and rewarded. If managers want people to work together in teams, they need to set performance goals and reward people as team members. Incentive pay, reward and recognition become an integral part of teamwork. Rewards can be given based on individual behaviours and performance or given to the whole team based on the total team's performance. Giving a reward to the whole team or dividing the reward equally between team members based on the total team performance is referred to as a 'team-based reward'.

Results show that workers currently see little relation between their performance and the rewards they receive and that this link has been decreasing over the last 8 years. In a study of over 500 companies, Hay Management Consultants found less than 50 per cent of middle level managers, 30 per cent of professional/technical workers and 20 per cent of hourly workers felt that their pay is linked to their performance. These percentages have decreased about 5 per cent or more since 1994 for middle management and hourly workers. As many as 20 per cent of people indicated that the team approach has failed, because of lack of team pay (Gross 1995).

Extensive research on teams has shown that five characteristics lead to high team performance (Johnson & Johnson 1997). These are:
1 *'We instead of me'* — *positive interdependence*. This occurs when each team member perceives that he or she is linked with other members in such a way that the individual's

own success is dependent on the internal coordination of efforts in the team. Studies show that when goal, task, resource and role interdependence are clearly understood and when group members see their own contribution as vital to the team success, individuals and teams perform better (Hoskins & Petty 1982; Kerr 1983).

2. *Personal responsibility/accountability.* Each member has to have a sense of personal responsibility to accomplish the group's goals.

3. *Interpersonal and group skills.* The level of interpersonal and small group skills of members greatly influences the level of team achievement and productivity. Good interpersonal skills provide more feedback to team members and build more positive relationships between team members.

4. *Promotive personal interaction.* In high-performing teams, individuals go beyond just having good interpersonal and team skills. They also promote, encourage and facilitate each other's efforts and wellbeing in order to achieve team success. Promotive personal interaction occurs when team members:
   - provide others with efficient and effective assistance
   - exchange resources and information effectively
   - provide each other with useful feedback
   - challenge each other's conclusions and reasoning in order to provide deeper insight into the problem and higher quality decision making
   - encourage each other to make more effort to achieve mutual goals
   - act in trusting and trustworthy ways
   - feel less anxiety and stress with each other.
   - Johnson and Johnson (1997) argue that these positive effects occur often as a result of personal face-to-face teamwork.

5. *Review of team process.* A team makes times to reflect on what member actions were helpful and unhelpful in achieving the team's goals and maintaining working relations and to make decisions about what actions to continue or change.

The challenge to managers is to take a wider, more encompassing approach to teams and aligning team goals to company objectives (see figure 7.1).

Figure 7.1 illustrates that recognition and rewards act as a compass that indicates in which direction the team should be going in order to reach its objectives and goals. Rewards and recognition also provide the incentives and motivation before actions are undertaken and reinforcement once results have been achieved. They therefore are the drivers toward and reinforcement of activities which lead to organisational success.

It is also important to understand the key elements necessary for team effectiveness before the introduction of individual and team-based rewards. The company's business strategy and goals need to be supported by the team vision, goals and values. The team roles, key competencies, and leadership align activities to the achievement of that vision and goals. The systems, structures and procedures, including reward systems, provide the energy

Figure 7.1: Alignment of team rewards to business goals

and control mechanisms so that actions are consistently directed toward the intended aims. The relationships between individuals and managing of differences provide the personal cohesion that keeps a team working as a unit toward a common vision. Finally, in order for a team to provide a useful function to the organisation and its customers, it has to continually learn and develop to avoid mistakes and continually improve. Figure 7.1 also summarises the internal elements that are needed for team effectiveness.

Reward systems and procedures provide the 'glue' that keeps the entire team whole. They:
- help motivate the team members to achieve the vision and goals
- reinforce the key roles and behaviours that are needed for a successful team
- enhance relationships by encouraging co-operation and working toward common goals
- encourage development and learning by stimulating risk-taking and the trying of new initiatives.

Designing and implementing reward systems

While it is easy to accept that rewards and recognition are important when striving to make a high-performing team, the implementation of a reward system in a specific organisation can be very difficult. Two organisations, Motorola and Trigon, have had considerable experience over many years and have provided guidelines for the successful introduction of team-based rewards (Coli 1997; Gross, Amos & Leffler 1997). The major findings in the Motorola study of over 150 teams in five sites around the world and Trigon's 4 years' experience in using team-based pay as an incentive could be summarised under six key areas, which will now be discussed.

Have a clear, strategic purpose for teams and rewards

- Discuss the purpose of the team during the initial stages of team formation. Make sure employees at all levels of the organisation know the reason for teams as well as the role and limits of their team.
- Do not just do teambuilding for the sake of teambuilding — tie teambuilding to organisational objectives and improvement of team functioning.
- Involve team members in setting goals and measures.
- Be careful to recognise and reward employees who are doing the right things, as opposed to rewarding those who fight fires or just blindly follow the team leader's orders.
- Allow teams to mature before implementing team pay.

Communicate about the rewards and the team results

- It is important to ensure the rewards being offered are understood. Team members are often confused about the range of incentives and rewards and who is getting what reward and why. Confusion and misunderstanding about the rewards lead to unfilled expectations, jealousy and cynicism, which could have a negative effect on individuals and the entire team.
- Agree on a process for regular team communication, both within the team and between the team and senior management.

Plan the type, criteria and use of rewards and recognition

- Use non-monetary rewards most of the time. Employers at Motorola were clear in expressing their view that rewarding teams with money was not high on their list of motivators. Non-cash rewards were greater motivators for many people. Spend more time letting employees know you appreciate all they are doing by sincerely saying 'thank you'.
- Encourage the team to develop acceptable risks and returns for their pay. Individuals can take some reduction in pay in order to take the risk of higher team pay. This is usually in a one to three ratio. A 5 per cent reduction in individual pay can lead to a 15 per cent increase in team-based pay.
- Make sure there are clear criteria and measures for team incentives. Agree in advance on these criteria and measures for evaluating the performance of the team.
- Use a variety of recognition and reward programs. Do not use the same program with each team. Teams will need different

approaches and different incentive plans based on their particular situation.
- Focus rewards to fit with the type of team, the culture and the stage of the team's development.

Have financial measures and stretch objectives

- Ensure the goals include at least one financial measure based on benefit versus cost in team performance.
- Make sure the objectives stretch the team; they should be challenging but not impossible, not too easy or too hard to achieve.
- Integrate team contribution as part of an employee's performance appraisal criteria. Include a peer-review process as part of this appraisal.

Include training in interpersonal and teamwork skills

- Ensure everyone, especially specialist/technical groups, agrees to and receives skill training in team processes, interpersonal behaviour and team participation.
- Team leaders should focus on ensuring team processes are maintained. If they maintain effective team processes, hitting specific targets and goals will follow.
- Consider whether the title 'Team leader' is representative of the role as opposed to titles such as 'Supervisor' or 'Manager'. Some teams have used more unusual titles such as 'Builder', 'Conductor', 'Architect' or 'Project leader'.

Evaluate and review the reward system

Monitor the reward, incentive and accountability systems carefully and be prepared to act when necessary. Calculate how much the reward system costs the organisation and how much benefit is coming from it.

Determining suitable rewards for individuals and teams

In determining the rewards that are suitable for individuals within teams and for teams as a whole, four factors need to be considered, according to Coli (1997).

These are:
1 forty-four different ways to reward and recognise individuals and teams
2 levels of team and individual development
3 types of teams (this factor has been discussed earlier in this chapter)
4 the culture of the team and the organisation.

These factors help to establish the best combination of rewards at the most appropriate time.

Forty-four different ways to reward and recognise individuals and teams

The names of various rewards are listed in Figure 7.2 under three different categories: (1) money/prizes/gifts; (2) recognition and praise awards; and (3) development/empowering work. These rewards range from an intrinsic focus of rewards to a very intrinsic focus. This table reflects the rewards listed in Coli's Motorola study and organises them into monetary (M), recognition (R) and development (D) categories.

Levels of team and individual development

Whether a reward should be given to a whole team or to individuals can be a difficult decision for managers. This decision can become further confused if it gets mixed up with salaries and individual bonuses that have already been set through an employee's performance management system. It is necessary to separate reward/recognition schemes from a person's salary level and any specific performance agreements that have already been set. Reward and recognition schemes are intended to motivate people beyond the existing mechanisms of salary and payment and to help individuals and teams achieve goals they might not achieve if only the existing pay and bonus mechanisms are used.

The dilemma of team versus individual rewards involves many different factors and there may be no definite rule of thumb for managers to follow. Two dimensions that need to be considered in allocation of individual or team rewards are the *level of the development of*

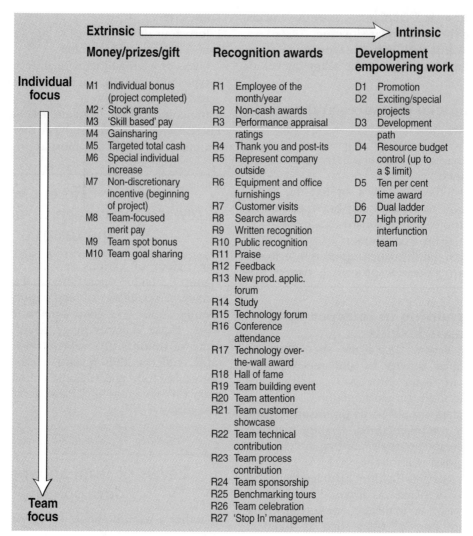

Fig 7.2: Ways of rewarding and recognising individuals and teams

each individual in the team and the *level of team development*. Different teams and different people are motivated by different rewards at different times. A payment of money to a top performer who is struggling to pay his or her mortgage might be much greater incentive than an elaborate free dinner and night out for the team. On the other hand, giving a senior manager a substantial payment when support staff and other professionals in the team have contributed a great deal to the achievement of section goals may be seen as unfair and can diminish the motivation of the team.

Individual development and needs

The theories and research covering individual motivation and development are very extensive and beyond the scope of this discussion. With regard to reward and motivation strategies, it has been established that individuals seek to fulfil a hierarchy of survival, safety and security, belonging, self-esteem and self-actualisation needs. Research has also shown that a person will become less motivated if he or she believes rewards are given to other people on an inequitable basis. Other research has shown that individuals will do those actions that should logically result in the achievement of goals they most value for the least effort (Robbins et al. 1998). It also has been shown that there is a strong relationship between the type of need a person is seeking to fulfil and his or her level of self-development (Wilber 1995). For example, a person who feels lonely and depressed will need a lot of care and attention. Overall, this suggests that some people have a strong desire to fulfil their personal needs or deal with their own problems and are unable to be a fully effective member of a team. The needs and level of development of every individual will vary and therefore the reward or recognition used for every person may have to vary accordingly. A manager has to consider each person's individual needs and level of self-development when considering giving individual or team rewards.

Team development

Team behaviour is a dynamic process that continually changes over time. Most discussions of teams have described general patterns of behaviours as stages of teamwork that evolve over time. The most well-known theory is the stages of teamwork described by Tuckman (1965). The stages Tuckman describes are forming, storming, norming, performing and adjourning. Others have called these stages starting, establishing itself, performing and ending (Coli 1997). More than a dozen field and laboratory task force groups have shown, however, that groups do not develop in the universal sequence of stages that Tuckman and others have described (Gersick 1988). Teams do not move in a neat progression from one stage to the next but they do have a consistent timing regarding when groups form and change the way they work. Specifically, it has been found that the direction-setting of the group, inertia and major changes occur at similar times during the formation and operation of groups.

These two theories of teamwork are sometimes called 'stages of team development'. These frameworks do not adequately describe the development of a team but rather describe the processes that occur within a team as it works toward completion of a team objective. They describe the stages a team goes through in terms of how it performs while completing a project or task but do not provide a description of development. Performing, for example, is not a stage of development; it is a description of people completing a task well. It does not describe the level of sophistication of the intellectual, emotional or interpersonal processes of the team. A team can perform very well on a certain task but may have a low level of development in terms of its internal processes and systems.

The work of Ken Wilber provides an excellent description of development. Wilber (1995) defines development as a process of increasing complexity and increasing integration. Each level of development is described by a particular self-identity, moral framework, type of need and cognitive ability. The following discussion briefly summarises the levels of team development based on Wilber's concepts and incorporates relevant characteristics from Tuckman's and other descriptions of the stages of teamwork.

Initiating

The initiating level is not often described in the literature on teams since it occurs before all of the group members actually contact each other. This first level in the development of a team begins with the recognition that a group of people is needed to fulfil a special purpose or goal. At this level of development, individuals feel only a sense of the team's potential and only some members have a clear idea of the team purpose or task.

Forming

The forming level occurs when individual members come into contact with each other and realise that they are part of the same group. This level starts with the first impressions, information, perceptions and judgments about other members of the team and the team's task. These views begin to form as early as the first few seconds of the group's life and can last for a long time. This level is characterised by low task accomplishment and lack of clarity of individual assignments, goals and measures, procedures and methods of getting information and relationships working between members: 'Members are not using the same book yet.' With complex assignments, this level can take up to 30 per cent of the team's life span or longer.

Near the end of this stage, leadership emerges (to a greater or lesser degree) to keep the group focused on its emerging identity, its purpose and the processes it needs to operate. This level of development is completed when members have begun to think of themselves as part of the team. At this time part of their personal self-identity becomes linked to the whole team.

Solidifying

At the solidifying level, the team begins to form routine operations and procedures for the formal and informal system. The level often involves conflict between team members as the team seeks to establish what it is and how it will operate. The members accept the importance of the team, but there can be resistance to the control the group imposes on individuality. At this level, the team begins to establish its own identity and purpose: 'Members are using the same book but are not on the same page.' As the reality of the task, obstacles and pressures set in, members adjust and align their expectations and behaviours. A hierarchical structure and formal procedures become set. The norms also become established and the team begins to identify itself as an entity. Sometimes, a team at this level takes its purpose for granted and it operates through regular automatic routines.

This level is one in which close relationships develop and the team demonstrates cohesiveness. When this level is complete, there will be a relatively clear hierarchy of leadership within the team and a clear sense of team identity, as well as a sense of 'mateship' between a number of the team members.

Transforming

Once the solidifying level is achieved, the group's direction becomes 'written in stone' and is unlikely to be re-examined throughout the first half of the group's life. This is a period of inertia — the group tends to stand still or becomes locked into a fixed course. New insights that might challenge initial patterns and assumptions might occur to individual members but the group is often incapable of acting on these new insights.

The transforming stage involves going beyond ordinary ways of working and breaks through to a new way of being. At this level, the members of the team recognise that the overall team and its purpose are important and should not stagnate because of complacency. Often conflict, challenge and renewal occur at this level. The team reviews what it is doing and moves to a higher level of team development.

Studies show that each group experiences this transformation at similar points in its life span — precisely halfway between its first meeting and its official deadline — despite the fact that some teams spent as little as an hour on their project, while others spent six months. It is as if the groups universally experience a midlife crisis at this point. The midpoint appears to work like an alarm clock, heightening members' awareness that their time is limited and that they need to come together to 'get on with the job'.

Unified performing

At the unified performing level, each team member is acting as a part of the whole. All members are performing what is required of them to fulfil the purpose of the team. This level includes all of the processes that were set up in the lower levels, but is not limited to them. The team's relationships and structures are set and accepted but the team members can go beyond them if necessary. The team's energy has moved beyond operating as separate individuals to a team focusing on the best ways to achieve the team goals: 'Team members are not only on the same page, they are reading the same words.' When a team is performing at this level the things needed for effective teamwork require no effort, but occur as a natural extension of this level of team development.

Ending: withdrawing collective energy

The ending of a team is not specifically a level of development but a stage in which the unified focus and sense of the collective team identity are dissolved. This occurs when a work team, committee or task force has completed its tasks and no longer has a reason to exist together as a team. Tuckman refers to this as the *adjourning* or *ending* stage. Members in this stage have 'finished the book'.

This stage is a time to end, celebrate, acknowledge and reflect. The responses of team members vary in this stage. Some feel pride in what the team has accomplished; others may be negative and critical of the way the organisation has treated individuals or the team. Some team members may be sad over the loss of friendship gained during the life of the work team. Sometimes team members and managers stay 'attached' to the team and it is hard for them to accept that the team will no longer exist. Sometimes there is an embarrassment that the team has failed or died or ended even when this has occurred through no fault of the team.

Do teams become more effective when they move from the forming to the solidifying stage? The answer to this question is 'no'. Under some conditions, high levels of conflict may help or hinder the development of a team. Teams even occasionally regress to previous levels as a result of failure to achieve their goals or conflict between members or with external managers or other groups.

Anyone thinking about using reward and recognition strategies will need to consider these levels of team development, as well as individual differences. The use of rewards and recognition is an important way to manage and focus the group and to give it energy to achieve its behaviours and outcomes in each of the four levels. Rewards and recognitions can also be helpful in helping individuals deal with and see their experiences in the team positively when it ends. In short, rewards and recognition strategies and knowledge of the stages of team development can help achieve organisational objectives and can contribute to individual fulfilment.

Matching reward/recognition methods with team development stages

There are four broad categories which describe the way rewards and recognition can be used. Using these methods could encourage different behaviours and motivation during the team life cycle. Table 7.1 shows which reward and recognition methods from figure 7.2 should be used at each level of the team development, including the 'ending stage'. The categories are:

- *Direction* — rewards and recognition that help the team members accept and become focused on the goals they have been given and the challenges that go with them. This also encourages actions that will help group members become better acquainted with one another and grasp the different skills required to support team performance.

Table 7.1: Levels of team development reward matrix

Levels of team development	Direction	Support	Recognition	Celebration
Level 1 Initiating	M6, M7, M10, R11, D1, D3, D7			
Level 2 Forming	M6, M7, M10, R10,, D1, D3, D7	M6, R8, R9, R11, R12, R17, R14, R19, R20, D3, D4		
Level 3 Solidifying			M5, R7, R9, R10, R11, R12, R14, R20, R27, D2, D4, D5	
Level 4 Transforming		R9, R11, R12	M8, M9, M10, R4, R9, R10, R11, R12, R23, R24	R19, R26, D7
Level 5 Unified performing			M1, M2, M5, M6, R1, R2, R3, R4, R5, R6, R7, R8, R9, R10, R11, R12, R13, R14	M4, M6, M8, M9, M10, R2, R3, R4, R9, R11, R12, R13, R16, R17, R18, R22
Ending Withdrawing			R15, R17, R20, R21, R25, R26, R27, D1, D2, D4, D5, D7	R23, R24, R26, M1, M9, R4, R11, R18, R26, D2, D3, D7

Note: The letter and number in the matrix refer to the various 'tools' in figure 7.2

- *Support* — rewards and recognition that help a team fully understand and deal with its assignment, agreement to procedures and clarification of expectations members have of each other. These rewards should encourage all team members to support each other and to develop into a team that has its own unique identity.
- *Reinforcement* — recognition that acknowledges the process (or lack of it) of the team as it accomplishes its mission. Informal and formal rewards that provide feedback and encouragement are most effective at the corresponding stages in table 7.1. Pointing out poor performance and the consequences if it continues is very important at this time. This needs to be done in a fair and considerate manner. Ignoring poor performance leads to a lowering of the morale of the team and those who are actively involved in having the team do its best. It is important not to reward poor performance as this would devalue the recognition of those who genuinely performed well.
- *Celebration* — rewards and recognition that acknowledge the achievement of outstanding individuals and the team as a whole. The rewards and recognition should send clear messages that the team is appreciated and the results are important.

How do team and organisational cultures impact on the types of rewards?

When a reward and recognition program is developed, it may be advisable to consider how the culture of the team and organisation may impact on the types of reward employees would prefer. It is important that the reward and recognition systems fit with the organisational mission, vision, values, goals and competitive atmosphere. There are many models that can be used for describing the culture of the team and organisation. Some of the key variables to consider when establishing a reward system are summarised in figure 7.3.

For example, if an organisation has a very formal, materialistic, quantitative, competitive and materialistic culture (e.g., a large steel mill or a chemical manufacturing organisation), the reward system may need to be calculated based on production, conducted in a competitive and formal way, and emphasise monetary rewards. On the other hand, a small health unit that is very informal, focused on personal relationships and works toward cooperative goals may have a more team-based, informal and spontaneous reward system that provides letters of recognition or personal 'thank-you's'. However,

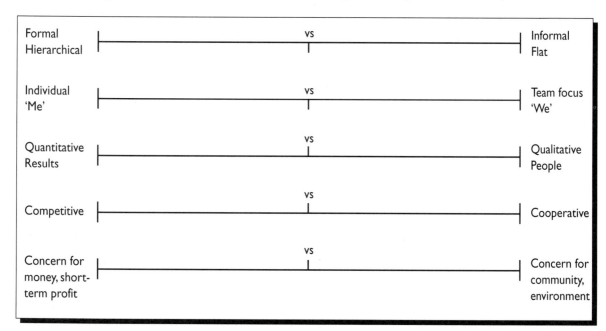

Figure 7.3: Some key variables to consider when establishing a reward system

various combinations of cultural values may occur — an organisation may be informal but fairly materialistic and quantitative (e.g., a small team of scientific researchers) and the reward system needs to suit that culture.

Practical implications for organisations and managers — begin with the end in mind

Steven Covey (1994) in his highly successful book coined a term 'Begin with the end in mind', which is very relevant to the process of establishing team- and individual-based rewards. It is important for any manager who is reviewing an organisation's current reward system to first consider the key results and behaviours that the organisation needs to be successful. It is also important for the leader and the team to determine for the team a meaningful vision and goals which are worthwhile and would make a valid contribution to the organisation.

By working through the following questions when designing individual and team rewards and matching reward categories with stages of team development, an effective team and individual program could be developed:
- What key results and behaviours need to be achieved that are not currently being achieved?
- What team rewards will best motivate people to achieve these results and behave in these ways? The 44 rewards described in table 7.1 could be used.
- What are the indicators of team and individual success? How and when could progress and final results be measured and reported?
- What is the best way to celebrate success?
- What is the estimated cost of each of the reward schemes and what is the total cost of the reward program? How will this be paid for?
- Are there aspects of fairness, group norms and cultural differences that need to be considered?
- How are individuals, teams or the organisation dealt with when targets are not met and there is no reward?

The development and implementation of a program is where the real work occurs and there are several issues organisations need to consider. The way an organisation plans and implements a team-based reward program is as important as the program itself (Gross, Amos & Leffler 1997). One of the key factors that relates to the success of a reward program is the involvement of many of the major stakeholders such as top management, team members, union representatives, other teams, human resource professionals and customers. A study by Hay Research of pay plans showed that employees in companies with successful pay plans rated performance measurement 34 per cent higher, trust 30 per cent higher, encouragement of initiative 28 per cent higher and pressure for performance 18 per cent higher than did employees in companies with troubled programs (Gross 1995).

The introduction of the team-based reward plan involves three phases:
1 feasibility
2 design
3 implementation.

By the end of the first phase, *feasibility*, it is important to have defined the broad objectives of the reward program and to have established a 'charter' which covers which areas the reward program will and will not deal with (e.g., it will not affect base pay but may alter overtime). The planning team should consist mostly of managers whose teams will be affected by the new reward program as well as human resource personnel. It is important to involve the unions since these programs deal with workplace conditions. It is also important that the project has a set time limit and does not take more than 6 to 12 months since the team will lose interest if it does.

The second phase, *design*, involves drafting a system that links reward to organisational objectives and culture. Important considerations of the design include the amount of compensation dollars that will be allocated between fixed and variable pay for different levels of performance. Also, the possible amount any individual person or team will get over other people or other teams needs to be considered. Finally, clear criteria for giving cash or non-cash rewards need to be determined. Based on the type of culture and senior management, these will be either conservative or risk-taking. Testing the reward program by calculating a wide range of scenarios is important so that there are no major surprises. It may even be possible to test and refine the reward program with one or two teams during this stage.

The last stage, *implementation*, involves a strategy for roll out of the program, including an education/communication program for employees and managers. The reward program needs to be integrated with other human resource and management practices (e.g. performance appraisals, promotion systems) or it will send contradictory and confusing messages to staff. The program will need to be monitored and reviewed and feedback from staff will need to be regularly sought to ensure that the program is worthwhile and meeting its objectives. It is also important that financial results be considered in evaluating a program since that will be an important component in management's evaluation of the reward program.

This chapter has not dealt in depth with the theory of pay structures nor how they should be implemented in organisations. Steven Gross' book (1995), *Compensation for teams*, is an excellent and detailed guide on how to implement both a pay- and a team-based reward program. 'People, performance and pay' (Flannery, Hofrichter & Platten 1996) is another useful source that provides a comprehensive approach to how to relate pay and performance in organisations.

Conclusion

This chapter dealt with several challenging issues associated with rewarding individual and team performance and aligning team rewards to business goals. The types of teams, characteristics that lead to high team performance and issues relating to the design and implementation of reward systems were discussed. It was shown how rewards and recognition could be matched with the different stages of team development and the practical implications for managers and organisations were outlined.

Many organisations are transforming into new cultures, flattening their hierarchies, empowering their workers and basing their processes on teams rather than on individual performance. Reward and recognition systems are an important part of the change that is necessary to transform organisations.

Managers and employees can fool themselves if they think that well-meaning directives to 'cooperate and work together' and 'better teamwork' will be enough to create productive, cooperative efforts among individuals. The basic elements of teamwork must be structured into all aspects of the group and its meetings. This especially includes positive interdependence, personal accountability, promotive interaction, the appropriate use of social skills and effective team processes. Reward and recognition systems are one of the most important ways to foster positive interdependence and personal accountability and to help bring together all of the elements of effective teamwork.

A thorough rethinking and restructuring of reward and recognition practices that are aligned with new organisational goals and culture will give companies the focused energy they will need to succeed in challenging times. Those companies that use relevant compensation and rewards as strategic resource tools will be able to tap the tremendous potential of their employees.

This requires leaders of organisations to take the daring step of creating incentive programs that encourage new employee behaviours aimed at achieving team and organisational goals. First, leaders will need to identify the types of teams operating, the level of team development they are at and which incentives should be used to achieve worthwhile team and organisational goals. These reward and recognition programs must also fit in with the culture and values that the organisation wishes to develop. Leaders must be willing to experiment, keep what works, fix what does not and put effort and resources into the reward program so that it works optimally throughout the organisation. Getting this right will not only be rewarding for individuals and teams, but for the organisation's success as well.

References

Coli, M (1997) Strategic team reward and recognition strategies at Motorola. The Best of Team Conference Proceedings, San Francisco: Linkage, pp. 519–605.

Covey, S (1994) *First things first*. New York: Simon & Schuster.

Flannery, T, Hofrichter, D & Platten, P (1996) *People, performance & pay*. New York: The Free Press.

Gersick, C (1988) Time and transition in work teams: toward a new model of group development. *Academy of Management Journal*, March: pp. 419–27.

Gross, S, Amos, S & Leffler, S (1997) Four years of team-based pay at Trigon Blue Cross Shield: what have we learned? From Compensation & Benefits Special Report 'Team Ray Case Studies' *American Management Report*, May 1997.

Gross, SE (1995) *Compensation for teams, how to design and implement team-based reward programs*. New York: American Management Association.

Hoskins, S & Petty, R (1982) The effects of task difficulty and task uniqueness on social loafing. *Journal of Personality and Social Psychology*, 43: 1214–29.

Johnson, D & Johnson, F (1997) *Joining together, group theory and group skills* (6th ed.). Boston: Allyn and Bacon.

Kerr, N (1983) The dispensability of member effort and group motivation losses: free rider effects. *Journal of Personality and Social Psychology*, 44: 78–94.

Robbins, S, Waters-Marsh, T, Cacioppe, R & Millet, B (1998) *Organisational behaviour in Australia and New Zealand*. Sydney: Prentice Hall.

Tuckman, B (1965) Development sequence in small groups. *Psychological bulletin*, 63: 384–99.

Wilber, K (1995) *Sex, ecology, spirituality: the spirit of evolution*. Boston: Shambala.

New communication technologies in organisations: issues and impacts

CHAPTER 8

by Abraham Ninan and Greg Hearn

Purdue University, USA
Queensland University of Technology, Brisbane

aninan@purdue.edu *and* g.hearn@qut.edu.au

Introduction

With the increasing development and application of technology to communicate locally and globally, it has become essential to investigate and analyse the role it plays in communication within and between organisations. Electronic mail, known as e-mail, is a form of computer-mediated communication characterised by the possibility of asynchronous communication in which users have mailboxes and folders, allowing messages to be composed, sent, received, and stored (Donovan 1995).

This form of communication, as well as other forms such as videoconferencing and computer conferencing, have steadily extended to allow and accommodate the crucial need to communicate globally as well as locally. New technologies have been advocated by proponents as being faster and more efficient, permitting communication among geographically dispersed participants, and providing greater flexibility; and allowing asynchronous communication and communication to a wide (even unknown) group of people (Miller 1999).

As technology and computer-mediated communication (CMC) such as electronic mail have become commonplace in society, the significance of research increases (Allen 1995). In an organisational context, a common focus today is whether or not to implement certain technology (Miller 1999). Several models have been developed to explain and predict the adoption of technology. For example, the media richness and social information processing (SIP) models both describe criteria for adopting media choices such as electronic mail (Miller 1999; Walther 1997). Both models are important in an organisational context because they attempt to explain which media choices will be implemented in the organisation. As a result, certain types of CMC are used based on these models of adoption in an organisational context.

The purpose of this chapter is to move beyond the adoption of CMC to consider how organisational culture affects adoption of technology and how this adoption affects organisational culture, specifically the adoption of electronic mail as part of an organisational culture.

First, CMC is defined and discussed. Second, a description of electronic mail, a specific form of CMC and the main focus of this chapter, will be provided. A description of adoption models will explain and predict why certain organisations utilise electronic mail. Finally, the chapter will conclude by focusing on how organisational culture can affect adoption models and the use of technologies such as electronic mail.

Defining computer-mediated communication

CMC-related research is increasing in popularity. Although the focus of CMC research is diverse, a common understanding still exists. In other words, despite diverse focuses, research offers a common definition of CMC. Past research has defined CMC as employing technological systems to communicate to other people or to small groups of people (Barnes & Greller 1994; Bishop & Levine 1999; Donovan 1995; Postmes, Spears and Martin 1998; Witmer 1998). Although this is not the only definition, the fact that studies define CMC is recognised. Witmer (1998) suggests that the first goal for students of CMC education is to develop a conceptual and linguistic understanding of CMC. Researchers have reflected this notion by developing a conceptual understanding of CMC. For clarity, most researchers also emphasise a specific technology when classifying CMC.

Towards a conceptual understanding of CMC

Rice (1996) and Witmer (1998) have emphasised that a computer-based technology such as electronic mail is not an all-inclusive type of CMC. Automated teller machines (ATMs) and touch-screen kiosks are often overlooked as CMC (Rice 1996; Witmer 1998). However, researchers analysing CMC in an organisational context often do not consider ATMs or touch-screen kiosks because, often, they are not applicable to the research. In an organisational context, CMC is characterised by technologies that range from electronic mail to the World Wide Web (Bishop & Levine 1999; Donovan 1995; Miller 1999; Postmes, Spear & Martin 1998). Miller (1999) offered an extensive list of technology that includes electronic mail, voice mail, facsimile (fax), audio and videoconferencing, computer conferencing, management information systems (MIS), group decision support systems (GDSS), local and wide area networks (LANs and WANs),
and the Internet and World Wide Web (WWW). Consideration of specific technologies and what CMC implies offers insight to a conceptual understanding (Bishop and Levine 1999; Donovan 1995; Postmes, Spear & Martin 1998).

CMC is not defined by physical equipment, but by the fact that, through a machine (computer), forms of communication are mediated (Postmes, Spear & Martin 1998). Machines such as television and radio mediate communication but CMC differs from these in how it changes communication. Characteristics include conferencing capabilities (the connection of individuals), information (storage and retrieval), and the ability and ease of broadcasting in organisations (Bishop & Levine 1998; Donovan 1995). Therefore, in an organisational context, CMC does not mean a specific technology such as electronic mail, but any form of communication mediated through technology between individuals or groups (Postmes, Spears & Martin 1998; Witmer 1998). Electronic mail is commonly mentioned because it offers a concrete example of CMC. Beyond this, researchers have classified CMC into dimensions based on how issues such as time, space, and/or feedback mediated through a machine affect communication (Bishop & Levine 1998; Donovan 1995; Postmes, Spears & Martin 1998; Witmer 1998). For example, Miller (1999) indicates that technology allows asynchronous communication and reduces cues, such as verbal and nonverbal, available in other forms of communication. It is clear that many CMC types exist, and characteristically differ, but all mediate communication through a technological system.

Electronic mail

For this chapter, electronic mail as a specific form of CMC is treated as a machine-mediating communication between individuals or groups of people. This connection is important; otherwise, there is a risk of classifying electronic mail other than under a CMC framework. Electronic mail is the most common form of CMC and using it as an example will help attain the goals of this chapter. As Miller (1999) described, a LAN is a common form of CMC. LANs (local area networks) are simply means by which companies send electronic mail. LANs are important because they serve as central locations to store messages and data and route them to their receiver. The advantages of electronic mail include asynchronous communication, storage and crossing geographically dispersed areas (Miller 1999). Organisations often make critical choices whether or not to adopt technology and what form of technology to adopt. The reasons for adopting particular technology will now be discussed.

Why do organisations adopt technology?

The chapter now focuses on models that help explain why an organisation would adopt a technology such as electronic mail.

The first model is the *media richness model* proposed by Daft and Lengel as a framework for understanding choices organisational members make about communication media use (Miller 1999). This model attempts to explain and predict the type of media that organisational members choose to utilise, based on the congruency of the message and media. Advocates of this model predict that people will choose the media, be it face-to-face, telephone, memo, fax, e-mail and so on, based on the extent to which it matches the ambiguity of the message to be communicated. According to this model, all organisational communication tasks can be characterised in terms of their level of ambiguity.

Daft and Lengel argue that communication media differ in their capacity to convey information (Miller 1999). They developed four criteria to differentiate the information-carrying capacity of media:
- the availability of instant feedback
- the use of multiple cues
- the use of natural language
- the personal focus of the medium.

Based on these criteria, a medium is labelled a 'lean' medium (meeting few of the criteria) or a 'rich' medium (meeting all or most of the criteria). Analysing a specific form of communication, based on the media-rich model, face-to-face communication is ultimately the richest medium due to its ability to meet all four criteria. More important to this analysis, electronic mail is considered a lean medium owing to the fact that this form of computer-mediated communication meets only a few of the criteria necessary for a rich medium. Electronic mail fails to provide instant feedback or allow natural language, does not include multiple cues such as nonverbal and verbal cues and provides a less personal focus than face-to-face communication. Since electronic mail is considered a lean medium, it is best for communicating unambiguous messages. For example, a manager may need to communicate the time and place for an upcoming meeting to his employees, a relatively unambiguous message where multiple interpretations are highly unlikely. Using the criterion of media richness, the manager would choose a lean medium, such as electronic mail that matches the ambiguity of the message, to be most efficient (Miller 1999). This model provides a starting point and an insight into what medium is chosen by organisational members to communicate certain messages.

Despite the insight provided by this model, debate concerning its usefulness to predict media selection exists. Consider the previous example: the manager may choose to communicate face-to-face to employees about the upcoming meeting because of the organisation's and manager's value of interpersonal contact. The manager may not even consider the richness of the medium. Studies claim there is more to medium selection than merely matching the medium and the message (Miller 1999). Research has not found support for the model and many question 'the extent to which managers are rational in media choice behaviour and the degree to which the characteristics of media are objective and stable' (Miller 1999). As a result, other theories that attempt to explain more fully the selection of media to communicate messages have developed.

The *social information processing model* as well as considering the richness of the message, ascertains that the decision to use certain media is influenced by social interactions with others in the organisation (Miller 1999). For example, Fulk, Schmitz and Steinfield (1990) found that electronic mail usage by supervisors related to the use of the medium by subordinates. They also found that the decision to use e-mail was strongly influenced by the opinions of peers.

Another finding is that an individual's perception of the social presence of electronic mail was predicted by the individual's impression of how coworkers and supervisors perceived the social presence of electronic mail (Fulk, Schmitz and Steinfield 1990). From these findings, it is clear a model based on media richness may not be complete. Social factors such as interactions, perceptions of the medium and perceptions of the message by the sender and receiver in the organisation play a role in the adoption of technology.

Organisational social factors and their impact on adoption have led to consideration of organisational culture and its impact on adoption. Thus, up to this point, this chapter has described the background of models as well as defined key terms. Specifically, this chapter will emphasise the implications of cultural effects on technology such as electronic mail.

Organisational culture and technology adoption: challenging issues

Organisational culture has been considered to have an impact on technology adoption. Fulk, Schmitz and Steinfield (1990) state that researchers must move beyond adoption models to consider the broader and pervasive influences of the organisational culture. They also state that some firms employ a dominant face-to-face mode as normative for doing business, while others rely more on written media and focus on documentation. Such cultural norms are likely to affect both the media choices and the perceptions of the richness of these media. Using this assumption as a base, this chapter will consider the impact organisational culture has not only on adoption of media, but also the implications culture has on technological characteristics.

To frame cultural impacts, three perspectives of culture were developed by Martin (1992): including:
1 integration
2 differentiation
3 fragmentation.

The first perspective, *integration*, has three defining characteristics. Here, the culture manifests itself consistently in and across an organisation, there is organisation-wide agreement on what is acceptable culture, and culture thus is an area that is considered very clear by all, with little room for ambiguity (Martin 1992). In *differentiation*, the second perspective, culture manifests itself across an organisation inconsistently; what is accepted culture in one department may not be acceptable in another. Also, these varying pockets of culture within an organisation may conflict with one another. Finally, there is some tolerance for this lack of clarity of what exactly is acceptable culture across the organisation; this is also referred to as tolerance for ambiguity (Martin 1992). *Fragmentation*, the third perspective, focuses on ambiguity and has three defining characteristics. The first feature is that the decision as to whether there is agreement or no agreement on a culture is issue-specific in an organisation. Secondly, it may be difficult to define distinct boundaries that separate organisation-wide consensus on an acceptable culture from suborganisational or subcultural schisms. Finally, clear consistencies are rare (Martin 1992). These points of view not only show the limitations of viewing boundaries within and without organisational cultures as explicit, but also set up a way to examine how culture impacts on technology. Before expanding on the linkage between culture and technology, a discussion of interpretive schemes, norms and resources will clarify how humans can affect a technology and likewise be affected by it. As such, tensions are identified as technology mediating human choice and this is central to the thesis of this chapter.

Interpretive schemes

Human interaction involves the constitution and communication of meaning, which is accomplished through interpretive schemes (Orlikowski & Robey 1991, p. 149; Orlikowski 1992: 404). Interpretive schemes are the 'core of the mutual knowledge whereby an accountable universe of meaning is sustained through and in processes of interaction' (Giddens 1979, p. 83). In other words, humans mediate communication and understanding by producing and reproducing interpretive schemes in interaction with one another. In the reverse, interpretive schemes also operate as a means to limit some of the structural factors that guide an organisation's choice of such a scheme (Orlikowski & Robey 1991). Interpretive schemes produce *structures of signification*, which imply the social rules that enable, inform and inhibit the communication process (Orlikowski & Robey 1991; Orlikowski 1992). Interpretive schemes are strengthened or transformed through social interaction, as the institutional rules are reaffirmed or questioned by those who utilise the schemes (Orlikowski 1992). Consider this example: a firm (say, IBM) decides to establish a new security code for entry into its headquarters. The security guard now adamantly sticks to a new rule that says every employee must carry and show a pre-issued identity card to gain entry into the main building. Unfortunately, the CEO himself is refused entry one morning because he does not have his card with him. One then wonders if the institutional rule was reaffirmed properly by the security guard, or does it remain questionable? Either way, the issue is that the interpretive scheme (the way the security guard understood the set of established rules) might strengthen or transform as a result of this social interaction. Either the rule would remain the way the guard interpreted and executed it or IBM would bring about a modification.

Resources

Power comes into interaction also, by providing institutional capabilities for humans to achieve outcomes (Orlikowski & Robey 1991). Power is referred to in terms of a *transformative capacity* over the social and material world (Orlikowski 1992, p. 405). Power in a social system operates through resources that members use in interactions with one another. These resources serve as the media and/or source of power in social interactions (Sewell 1992) and are structural components that constitute *structures of control* (Orlikowski 1992). In other words, power establishes a control structure. For example again, in the IBM security guard case, the situation could pan out two ways. The guard could decide to just stick to the rule and refuse the CEO entry. He or she is doing the right job, really sticking to the rule.

However, the CEO could intervene and use his authority, despite the lack of an identity card, and ask the guard to let him through. Either way, the security guard and the CEO could potentially exercise the legal authority invested in each to transform a social interaction's outcome. Power is a clear resource here.

Norms

Norms are 'conventions or rules governing legitimate or "appropriate conduct" ... expressed through the cultural norms' and are prevalent in social systems (Orlikowski 1992, p. 405). Norms or codes for legitimate conduct are continually produced and confirmed as employees interact with one another to co-create the codes (Orlikowski & Robey 1991). These norms likewise actively shape an organisation's idea of what constitutes legitimate behaviour (Orlikowski & Robey 1991). The normative order of established structures of legitimisation is reinforced through the rituals, traditions and practices of socialisation (Orlikowski 1992). If the IBM guard refused entry to the CEO and this was accepted by the CEO, then the authority vested in the security guard to execute the rule of entry upon showing a pre-issued identity card becomes an acceptable practice or legitimate conduct, also called a norm. Likewise, the adoption of electronic mail in an organisation could have the potential to become a valued resource of power. This is only possible if electronic mail is accepted as a norm or becomes part of the normative order. As a result, the organisational culture and how employees reinforce it through social activities, such as everyday interactions, legitimise electronic mail.

Analysing social and organisational processes through the structuration model of technology

The structuration approach to technology, like e-mail, has been examined by a number of social and organisational researchers in their analysis of social and organisational processes (Poole, Seibold & McPhee 1985; Barley 1986; Poole & DeSanctis 1989, 1990, 1992; Contractor &

Eisenberg 1990; Orlikowski & Robey 1991; Orlikowski 1992, 1993; Yates & Orlikowski 1992; Contractor & Seibold 1993; Kinsella 1993; DeSanctis & Poole 1994; Orlikowski & Gash 1994; Orlikowski & Yates 1994; Tyre & Orlikowski 1994; Orlikowski, Yates, Okamura & Fujimoto 1995; Barley & Tolbert 1997; Brooks 1997; Montealegre 1997).

The structuration model of technology is an attempt to examine the complex interplay of social/cultural/organisational systems, technologies and users. The researchers have adopted aspects of the structuration framework advanced by prior theorists and have modified and refined the concepts of structuration theory for the realm of communication and information technologies. Most importantly, the model has made Giddens' structurational theory methodologically approachable, which, as Willmott (1997) argues, otherwise renders impossible any methodological examination of the conditions for stability or change in organisations. The integrative perspective suggests that e-mail has structures of its own but argues that social practices, like everyday communication between organisational members, affect behaviour relating to the use of e-mail (DeSanctis & Poole 1994) and vice versa.

Thus, the structuration perspective of technology provides a useful framework for exploring issues like electronic mail utilisation, especially with respect to the tension identified between the enabling and disabling properties of electronic mail within an organisational cultural context. A connection between organisational culture and electronic mail can be exemplified through Martin's (1992) three perspectives of culture, as well.

Linking organisational culture and e-mail through Martin's perspectives

Many of the ensuing analyses are intended to form the basis for future research questions for those interested in pursuing them. As outlined before, Martin (1992) establishes three social scientific perspectives of organisational culture. These are: *integration*, *differentiation* and *fragmentation*. It was established that there is a definite, continuous and mutually impacting tie between technology like e-mail and social practices thus far. Martin's (1992) 'integration' perspective says that all organisational members would consistently reinforce the same themes and share an organisation-wide consensus on what an acceptable culture is. With such low tolerance for ambiguity, it is highly possible that the social practices would either quickly appropriate a technology like e-mail on initial introduction or, equally quickly, reject its adoption. This quick turn-around on decision making is made possible by an organisation-wide consistency in attitudes on what is acceptable and what is not, in terms of its culture, as decided by its members. Also, it may be possible, in keeping with the discussion above, that cultures with such low tolerance for ambiguity tend to reify a technology like e-mail, once it has been adopted. These cultures are prone to grow into bureaucracies that establish rigid norms for getting things done and, if e-mail were to be accepted by such a bureaucratic culture, its use would further ossify the already existent, rigid cultural practices. In many senses, then, e-mail would be a bane rather than a boon, a disabler rather than an enabler, in such cultures.

However, with the introduction of a cultural tolerance for some ambiguity, in part or whole, a completely different perspective develops. E-mail, say in the 'differentiation' perspective of organisational culture, may not be adopted with equal speed and ease throughout the organisation. This is because, in this scenario, one faces an organisation that houses pockets of subcultures, which, though consistent within their own boundaries, may conflict with each other. Ambiguity is channelled outside such subcultures. Although the subcultures remain unaffected per se, a holistic picture might reveal that certain cultural manifestations may be inconsistent, such as managers who say one thing and do another. Decision making regarding the adoption of a technology like e-mail would not be as unified as it is in the 'integration' perspective of organisational cultures. Smaller public sector, quasi-government and mid-size private corporations may replicate the differentiation perspective of organisational cultures. If and when e-mail is finally adopted, its use may reflect the mixed culture of such firms. They are caught somewhere between the reification of e-mail, once adopted, and an appreciation for more variety, equity and change in organisational structure and culture terms.

In the final scenario, one looks at the 'fragmentation' perspective. This is a culture with very high tolerance for ambiguity. Ideally, this would be a suitable model for contemporary firms ensconced in turbulent organisational environments. Decision making about the use and adoption of a technology like e-mail would be very decentralised and a final group consensus may be time-consuming, if not almost impossible. Clear consistencies and inconsistencies are rare in such a set-up. Such a culture never risks becoming a bureaucracy or stultifying because of its high tolerance for ambiguity and thus change, variety and equity. It is highly improbable that e-mail will be adopted across the organisation at a single point in time. It may happen that the pockets themselves are prone to change. The greatest thing going for such an organisational culture is its openness to innovation, which is critical to managing rapid change.

Future research implications

A convergence is happening, whereby new systems increasingly mix sources and modes of communication (such as videoconferencing and e-mail), store repositories of communication (Internet and intranet) and mix genres on one screen (TV and e-mail). Questions that arise are:
- Is there a shift from functional mediation to cultural mediation?
- Would the new problem then be not just rates of data flow, but rather the construction of meanings in short time periods?

One speculation is that, currently, e-mail is a tool for disseminating information, which is helpful for efficiently maintaining a social network in its stable phases of organisational evolution (Stacey 1996), but, with increasing rapid change in organisational environments, e-mail may also take on the self-organising properties of complex systems and thus manifest the new patterns of organisational functioning that are required by such turbulent environments (Hearn & Ninan, 1997). E-mail might have a potential to be shaped in the form of networks by human actors and thereby influence and, in turn, be influenced by organisations' cultures. Another question in this context would be: in the above perspective, would it be the functional properties, or the social construction via cultures, that affect e-mail to facilitate variety, diffusion, sense making and networks in the future?

Either way, the key ingredient is to facilitate the ongoing process of communication that will encourage the required variations and new patterns in organisation. Conversations and narratives — the informal side of organisation once thought superfluous — become the seedbed of the future, to be encouraged as a learning exercise. As such this would have strong implications for the study of linkages between technology and cultures.

Related future research issues include investigations of the following:
- Communication technology like e-mail may take on the role of an enabling medium in this learning exercise.
- Communication technology like e-mail could aim to be, in itself, an increasingly efficient system for facilitating rapid information dissemination about continual environmental changes and demands among members of a firm. This is a functional role that could help a firm to learn the limitations of an extant tool and the latest needs of its environment.
- E-mail may be selected and amplified by a set of users or an organisation for more complex use on a larger scale or just reduced to a functional tool level in certain pockets within a firm. All this would be made possible by members, through various types and degrees of consensual decision making.

Implications for managers

Questions organisational development and human resource managers may consider answering may include these:
- Is there a shift from a functional mediation of technology to a cultural mediation in contemporary organisations, especially in view of globalisation facilitated by networks of communication technology, as in e-mail?
- What are the implications for issues of motivation, job satisfaction, training, organisational communication and development,

team management and the future roles of managers in creating a facilitative organisational culture?

Future research should aim to provide a stronger relationship between technology and culture.

Conclusion

Electronic mail has been indicated as the most popular form of CMC (Allen 1995). Characteristics of electronic mail include speed, efficiency and the ability to overcome geographic boundaries. Although adoption models have speculated why organisations utilise specific types of media, organisational cultural influence has not been considered. This chapter not only indicates three perspectives to use as a framework, but also analyses and speculates on the effects organisational culture has on technology adoption. Specifically, a structuration model addresses how organisational culture and e-mail interplay and create a duality. The intent of this chapter is to raise critical issues associated with organisational culture, issues which have implications for organisational behaviour and human resource managers.

References

Allen, BJ (1995) Gender and computer-mediated communication. *Sex Roles*, 32: 557–63.

Barley, SR (1986) Technology as an occasion for structuring: evidence from observations of CT scanners and the social order of radiology departments. *Administrative Science Quarterly*, 31: 78–108.

Barley, SR & Tolbert, PS (1997) Institutionalization and structuration: studying the links between action and institution. *Organization Studies*, 18(1): 93–117.

Barnes, S & Greller, LM (1994) Computer-mediated communication in the organisation. *Communication Education*, 43.

Bishop, L & Levine, DI (1999) Computer-mediated communication as employee voice: a case study. *Industrial & Labor Relations Review*, 52, 213–34.

Brooks, L (1997) Structuration theory and new technology: analyzing organizationally situated computer-aided design (CAD). *Information Systems Journal*, 7(2): 133–51.

Contractor, NS & Eisenberg, EM (1990) In J Fulk and C Steinfield (eds) *Organizations and communication technology*. Newbury Park, CA: Sage.

Contractor, NS & Seibold, DR (1993) Theoretical frameworks for the study of structuring processes in group decision support systems, adaptive structuration theory and self-organising systems theory. *Human Communication Research*, 19(4): 528–63.

DeSanctis, G & Poole, MS (1994) Capturing the complexity in advanced technology use: adaptive structuration theory. *Organisation Science*, 5(2): 121–47.

Donovan, DC (1995) Computer mediated communication and the basic speech course. *Interpersonal computing and technology: an electronic journal for the 21st century*, 3: 32–53.

Fulk, J, Schmitz, J & Steinfield, CW (1990) A social influence model of technology use. In J Fulk & C Steinfield (eds) *Organizations and Communication Technology*. Newbury Park, CA: Sage, pp. 171–41.

Giddens, A (1979) *Central problems in social theory*. London: Macmillan.

Kinsella, WJ (1993) Communication and information technologies: a dialectical model of technology and human agency. *The New Jersey Journal of Communication*, 1(1): 2–18.

Martin, J (1992) *Cultures in organizations: three perspectives*. New York: Oxford University Press.

Miller, KI (1999) *Organizational communication: approaches and processes* (2nd ed.). Belmont, CA: Wadsworth.

Montealegre, R (1997) The interplay of information technology and the social milieu. *Information Technology and People*, 10(2): 106–131.

Orlikowski, WJ (1992) The duality of technology: rethinking the concept of technology in organisations. *Organisation Science*, 3(3): 398–427.

Orlikowski, WJ (1993) CASE tools as organisational change: investigating incremental and radical changes in systems development. *MIS quarterly*, 309–40.

Orlikowski, WJ & Gash, DC (1994) Technological frames: making sense of information technology in organisations. *ACM Transactions on Information Systems*, 12(2): 174–207.

Orlikowski, WJ & Robey, D (1991) Information technology and the structuring of organisations. *Information Systems Research*, 2(2): 143–69.

Orlikowski, WJ & Yates, J (1994) Genre repertoire: the structuring of communicative practices in organisations. *Administrative Science Quarterly*, 39(4): 541–74.

Orlikowski, WJ, Yates, J, Okamura, K & Fujimoto, M (1995) Shaping electronic communication: the metastructuring of technology in the context of use. *Organisation Science*, 6(4): 423–44.

Poole, MS & DeSanctis, G (1989). Use of group decision support systems as an appropriation process. Proceedings of the 22nd Annual Hawaii International Conference on System Sciences, IV, pp. 149–57.

Poole, MS & DeSanctis, G (1990) Understanding the use of group decision support systems: the theory of adaptive structuration. In J Fulk and C Steinfield (eds) *Organizations and communication technology*. Newbury Park, CA: Sage.

Poole, MS & DeSanctis, G (1992) Microlevel structuration in computer-supported group decision making. *Human communication research*, 19(1): 5–49.

Poole, MS, Seibold, DR & McPhee, RD (1985) Group decision-making as a structurational process. *Quarterly Journal of Speech*, 71: 74–102.

Postmes, T, Spears, R & Martin, L (1998) Breaching or building social boundaries? Side-effects of computer-mediated communication. *Communication Research*, 25: 689–715.

Rice, RE (1996) New media and organisational structuring of meanings and relations. In F Jablin and L Putnam (eds) *The new handbook of organizational communication*. Thousand Oaks, CA: Sage.

Sewell, WH (1992) A theory of structure: duality, agency, and transformation. *American Journal of Sociology*, 98(1): 1–29.

Stacey, RD (1996) *Strategic management and organisational dynamics*. London: Pitman Publishing.

Tyre, MJ & Orlikowski, WJ (1994) Windows of opportunity: temporal patterns of technological adaptation in organisations. *Organisation science*, 5(1): 98–118.

Walther, JB (1997) Group and interpersonal effects in international computer-mediated collaboration. *Human Communication Research*, 23, 342–69.

Willmott, R (1997) Structure, culture and agency: rejecting the current orthodoxy of organization theory. *Journal for the Theory of Social Behavior*, 27(1): 93–123.

Witmer, DF (1998) Introduction to computer-mediated communication: a master syllabus for teaching communication technology. *Communication Education*, 47: 162–73.

Yates, J and Orlikowski, WJ (1992) Genres of organisational communication: a structurational approach to studying communication and media. *Academy of Management Reviews*, 17(2): 299–326.

Cooperation and conflict: two sides of the same coin

CHAPTER 9

by Susan Long

Swinburne University of Technology, Victoria

slong@groupwise.swin.edu.au

 Introduction

This chapter examines the nature of conflict in those sociotechnical systems that we refer to as 'work organisations'. The approach is from a psychodynamic and systems perspective. It examines how conflicting interests, values and aspirations at one systemic level (say, between departments or groupings) might be understood as symptomatic of conflict at another systemic level. This implies that workplace conflicts are inevitably the products of displacement. Quite practically, this means that whatever the conflict *seems* to be on the surface, it is also operating at another level. If it seems to be between two people and becomes irresolvable, then you can be sure that it is systemically present somewhere else. Perhaps the conflict is between another two people, or two groups (whom the two people represent), or between the organisation and elements of its environment.

The chapter also examines how conflict might be contained, managed and worked through. What is helpful in examining and working with conflict from the perspective presented here is the idea that what appears overtly to be present and perhaps intractable in one system may well be causally linked to the dynamics of another system where a solution is possible. This is the very essence of a systems approach. It enables one to work, in the face of seemingly irresolvable conflicts, with the possibility that the conflict can be examined and worked through in a different context. The expression of conflict is usually via a suitable vehicle, undercover as it were, in places far from its source. In understanding this, such a vehicle can be freed from having to 'carry' the conflict indefinitely. This concept of 'displacement' (of conflict from one part or systemic level of the organisation to another) is central to a dynamic analysis of conflict in organisations and, indeed, to an understanding of how conflicts might be resolved.

Understanding conflict requires that we also understand the social dynamics of cooperation in the work setting, because they are two sides of the same coin. Or, more correctly, they are both part of a complex web of dynamics that occur when people are organised to work together. The idea of cooperation will be raised towards the end of the chapter.

The term 'sociotechnical' will be used broadly. It depicts those systems of organisation that bring together the social and technical aspects of work. The 'social' refers to systems within, between and among people, taking the stance that individuals internalise and then enact the social relations in the culture where they live, play and work. In short, they take up roles, formal or informal, and act from these roles. The 'technical' refers to specific ways that work is approached. It reflects the term 'technique' and often includes technical equipment such as machinery or electronic equipment. It may, however, simply be a system of technical expertise, as in, say, teaching or counselling.

The human–technical system interface is a major source of conflict in the workplace, not least because both systems have complex communication requirements. The social system includes thoughts and emotions, whereas feeling humans design technical systems. But the sociotechnical interface is encompassed within particular work tasks. Much of what is said later focuses on the ways in which conflicts arise when we engage in work tasks. This includes how we deal with the fears and anxieties aroused when tasks are engaged.

The costs of workplace conflicts

Increasingly, we are aware of the price we pay for workplace conflict. This price is not simply a matter of economics, but also an emotional price to the individual, to families and to the wider community. For example, the effects of chronic and unresolved workplace conflicts are felt in terms of:
- personal stress and ill-health
- interpersonal relationship breakdown
- low morale
- suboptimal teamwork
- decreased productivity
- family stress
- decreased organisational purpose and cohesion
- maladaptive social defence systems (Paine 1982; Menzies 1988a; Hirschhorn 1988).

What's more, chronic, systemic conflicts become an enacted part of an organisation's culture (Stapley 1996). They become part of the way things *are* in that culture and are taken for granted. For example, many senior managers expect to have conflicts when it comes to the division of resources amongst departments. The assumption 'taken for granted' is that resources are limited, must be fought over and are experienced as commodities that are divided into discrete portions. The annual fight for resources thus becomes a chronic part of the culture. This in itself may curb the kinds of collaborative discussions leading to more creative ways of sharing resources or even creating new resources.

Challenging issues associated with the dynamics of conflict

The idea of displacement

Whatever the locus or the source of the conflict, it is often experienced as painful and anxiety-provoking. The organisational response is most often aimed at avoiding conflict because of its disruptive potential. Argyris (1990), for example, argues that organisation members enact various defensive routines as they collectively avoid conflict. Social defence theory puts forward the evidence of organisational cultures based more around reducing anxieties than fulfilling their purported tasks (Menzies-Lyth 1988a; Hirschhorn 1988; Krantz 1998). Chapman (1999) describes how tasks and roles can become corrupted through the systematic avoidance of conflict.

Conflicts do not simply dissolve when they are avoided; they become displaced. The dynamics of displacement imply that we consider two possibilities:
1 Overt directly experienced and observable conflicts may be symptomatic of hidden problems. This raises the issue of conscious/ unconscious or of overt/covert processes. Sometimes conflicts may be what they seem and can be dealt with directly. At other times, conflicts may appear as an overt presenting problem, but mask an issue 'somewhere else' in the system. Yet again, conflicts may be suppressed or repressed and appear as problems in another guise — workplace accidents or poor performance, for example.
2 The differing systemic levels present in the organisation may represent and 'hold' different aspects of a conflict. This implies the operation of such dynamics as splitting, scapegoating, blaming and rendering complex situations in black and white terms. Only when the differing parts can be brought back together, perhaps through dialogue between

conflicting roles, can the conflicts be resolved or at least held in creative tension.

Importantly, the processes that these ideas represent also interact with one another. What may be obvious and overtly experienced by the individual (one systemic level) may be hidden at the organisational level. There are many examples of individuals having to live up to certain informal workplace norms, the challenge of which becomes 'unspeakable' or 'undiscussable' (Archer 1999) (for example, putting in more and more time at the office, with little time left for family, despite the lip service that families are important).

What may be a conflict at a broad social level may be experienced as an interpersonal conflict. Many cross-cultural differences are played out in this way. Yet, again, the individual (or several individuals) may no longer feel what was originally an internal conflict, because it becomes externalised and writ large in the organisation. An example of this, taken from a rehabilitation service, will be noted more fully later in the chapter. These are all examples of displacement.

The displacement is done through processes of 'internalising' (introjection) and 'externalising' (projection) the ideas and feelings at stake. An individual takes thoughts and feelings from outside herself or himself, and makes them her or his own. Sometimes, because a thought or feeling is unwanted, because it causes pain or conflict, she or he may put it out of mind, denying the thought or feeling. This can occur as a projection, where another person is believed to have the thought or feeling. These are normal psychological processes, but can become problematic when the people concerned make assumptions based on their introjections and projections that are not tested in reality. In organisations, these individual processes may occur at a group level, where the members collectively internalise or externalise thoughts and feelings (Menzies-Lyth 1988b). This dynamic may mean that the source of conflict is avoided temporarily. But, despite the movement of conflicts and anxieties, if they are deeply embedded in the structure or culture of the organisation, they can be resolved only through examination and deliberate working through.

Different systemic levels at which conflict may occur

Conflicts may occur at the following levels:
- between individuals
- within individuals
- within or between groups or subgroups
- at the level of the organisation-as-a-whole
- at an institutional level between different groups representing different sets of values and norms.

The following discussion will consider the challenging issues at these levels.

Between individuals

Conflicts occur between individuals, openly or covertly. At this level, although a solution may seem to reside in attempting to improve interpersonal relations between the parties concerned ('the ways people get along with one another'), such a perspective may prove to be oversimplistic. Generations of 'human relations facilitators' have had less overall success than may at first seem apparent. The management literature has described a plethora of ways to solve workplace conflicts through team-building exercises that directly attempt to improve interpersonal trust and communication. They range from massage to outdoor exercises; from simulations and games to group therapy-type exercises. The problem with many workshop 'retreats' that employ such methods is that, while people might get to know and understand each other more fully outside the work situation, this has little effect on actual workplace relations when the pressures of the task and one's specific role are once again in the forefront of interactions.

In contrast to these solutions, it will be suggested here that improved interpersonal relations (including issues such as trust, communication and teamwork — all heralded by modern management gurus as the mainstays of excellent work) are the *by-products* of good role relations. Basically, most conflicts at work are not so much a result of people disliking each other or not, as they are a result of differences between the ways people approach and take up their work. Positive affiliation is a result of factors such as proximity, perceived similarity and (central to our argument) perceived common destiny or working successfully on a task together. The important person-to-person or, phrased more correctly, role-to-role relations become issues of careful negotiation. Trust, for example, becomes an issue of trusting that others are reliable in their approach to a mutual task. This requires that specific role holders have clear understandings about who does what, when and how. These understandings include issues of drawing limits on behaviour and deciding boundaries between tasks and roles. They cannot be taken for granted but must be subject to ongoing negotiation in the work.

Thinking of conflict as a *symptom* (hiding something else), rather than as something that must be directly tackled by showing people how to get on together, allows for new ways of resolving conflicts. Consider the possibility that having people work cooperatively together is achieved primarily as a by-product of successful work. All this is not to devalue the appropriate use of interpersonal skills education. Communication skills, for instance, are crucial for the management of self in the work role. However, such education is not sufficient in itself for reducing workplace conflict.

Within individuals

Another form that conflict takes is that experienced within the individual. Such conflict may be acutely felt and suffered, whether or not it is openly expressed. Conflict may occur at an unconscious level and may be expressed in a variety of ways. These include individuals suffering depression, anxiety or physical symptoms, all of which may lead to a lessening of joy in work, as well as the obvious issues for the organisation of lowered productivity, increase in sickness, high staff turnover and absenteeism. What is not often realised is that conflict felt *by* the individual may be not *of* the individual (Armstrong 1997). This means that the individual may experience conflicts *on behalf of*, or *in the place of*, others, a group or the organisation as a whole. A simple way of putting it is that sometimes organisation members act unwittingly as scapegoats for an issue or conflict not wholly belonging to them. The conflict may be systemically part of the sociotechnical system, yet expressed within the work life of only a few individuals. Just think about the fact that most equal opportunity officers are women. Does this mean women tend to carry or represent the issue of gender inequity and its associated conflicts for the whole?

If internally experienced, conflicts may be the result of a clash of values between the person and what is required of the role. A classic example is the Jehovah's Witness who is trained as a doctor and has to face the issue of blood transfusions. Where staff members do not have the appropriate skills, say, to clearly state the behaviours of others are affecting them, or how to articulate and work through their internal conflicts, then the conflict may go unresolved, or may be displaced into other aspects of work. Personal counselling or interpersonal skills education may be helpful for the resolution and non-escalation of such conflicts. But, more often than not, what gets termed a 'personality clash', or what seems to be only a particular individual's personal problem, is a *symptom* of tensions at other levels (Obholtzer & Zagier Roberts 1994). Workplace conflicts are rarely simply a reflection of a personal problem or an interpersonal clash, even when this is one component of the conflict. Often, such conflicts reflect tensions between the way in which tasks and roles are designed and enacted (Hirschhorn 1988).

Within and between groups

Conflicts within groups (between subgroups) and between groups are sometimes the most openly expressed in organisational life. Very often it is easier to point to a 'them' who are different to 'us'. The dynamic involves seeing negative traits in the 'other' group and seeing mainly positive traits in one's own. To do this appears to preserve one's own integrity and identity and operates even when many group members recognise that this 'splitting' of groupings is a simplification of a more complex reality. The division into 'good' and 'bad' is a comforting fiction that sometimes gets out of hand, say, in the rivalries between different sections of an organisation or, more seriously, in times of war (Sievers, forthcoming). A meglomaniac dictator can bring a population along with him, by appealing to the dynamic of *splitting* exhibited in nationalism. Some misguided organisational leaders (at any level in the organisation) attempt to do the same in their policies of 'divide and conquer'.

In analysing subgroup or intergroup conflicts, the dynamic of splitting should be examined. The question then becomes: 'what is the unconscious or hidden gain in separating (splitting) a complex situation into two simplistic parts?' Just as two conflicting individuals may represent a broader conflict, so may subgroups represent an issue beyond themselves.

An answer may be found partially in the avoidance of change. A comforting status quo may be threatened. The intergroup conflict may be a kind of diversion, taking attention away from another issue, which, if faced, would require the organisation to change. An example follows.

A conflict between an internal information technology unit and a business department of an enterprise reflected a more general issue within the organisation. The presenting problem (that is, the problem that appeared on first consideration of the situation) was an issue of the IT teams getting the software to the business on time. This was often not achieved and disputes, with associated blaming and guilt, would arise. The IT function and its 'inability to meet agreed timelines' could be regarded as the problem. Yet a broader issue in the organisation was the absence of team leaders from their teams. Teams functioned less well because team leaders were constantly taken away to do special projects. This aspect of the culture went unexamined while the conflict was seen to be lodged between the IT function and the business. The respective leaders of the teams were maintaining good relations with each other in a higher-level project while their teams experienced the strains, blames and anxieties associated with not meeting timelines. The negotiations required between leaders were not occurring, perhaps in the interests of keeping relations conflict-free on the special projects. The team members meanwhile felt abandoned, with no real authority to negotiate new work relations between their different functions.

Within the organisation-as-a-whole

Conflict at the level of the organisation-as-a-whole may be expressed in intergroup, subgroup or individual conflicts. Because it is the individuals who think, feel and generally experience the effects of organisational dynamics, it is hard to understand the concept of the organisation-as-a-whole. In everyday language, perhaps the idea of organisational culture is more readily understood. But the organisation-as-a-whole is more than culture. It is a term descriptive of a system such that a change in any one of its parts will have an effect on its other parts. No single person is ever able to see the whole. Organisation members can only consciously experience things from their own role perspective, or perhaps from a team perspective that is part of the whole. Hence, conflicts originating, say, in the way that the organisation-as-a-whole is relating to its environment cannot be viewed clearly from any one position.

Conflicts may occur in the system so that organisation players are quite unaware of the dynamics of their operation but experience their effects, either personally or as a group. Take, for example, the case of a rehabilitation organisation. Because of government policy decisions, this organisation had to change its task. Since World War II it had provided secondary and tertiary rehabilitation services to disabled people. Initially, these services were provided to servicemen and servicewomen, but later the focus was on those who had become disabled in the workplace. This overall task included the rehabilitation of people back into the workforce, but also included providing the chronically disabled with life skills to aid them in their daily lives. The policy change meant that the outcomes by which the organisation would be judged and funded became measured in terms of getting clients into sustainable employment.

As part of an action research project, most staff members, when interviewed, described their own internal conflicts about this change. For the professional psychologists and social workers, the change meant quite a different use of their skills and a conflict with the professional values of aiding people to improve their lives in broader ways. This was particularly important for clients in rural areas where the chances of sustainable employment were minimal. Were these professionals no longer able to help disabled clients develop life skills that might eventually lead them into some form of minimal self-employment, say, on a farm? If the sustainable employment were not quick in coming, then there would be no funding. How would these professionals employ their skills under these conditions? Yet, many saw the inevitability of change because of the government's drive toward reducing unemployment. The managers also felt conflict. As well as challenging personal values, the change in task came with a change in the monopoly that the organisation had in this area. A provider/funder distinction was being made under the government's privatisation policy, and private rehabilitation organisations were entering the field at a rapid rate. In private interviews, many explored their own conflicted thoughts and feelings about the change.

The interviews demonstrated that many staff members were having (or initially had) an internal conflict about the change in task. However, when the organisation was studied beyond the personal and interpersonal levels (at the organisational level) the research team found that the internal conflict had become externalised in quite a rigid manner. We found that, despite individuals recognising an internal conflict when questioned, the organisation, through its public communications and in its formal meetings and strategic discussions, was acting as if the conflict was *between* groups of people. Reference was made to the 'change leaders' and to the 'resisters'. Managers believed that the organisation had to 'cut out its dead wood' because some staff members were holding back the change process. In meetings that planned the change process, and in more general meetings, it was politically incorrect to express doubts about the new way of working. Moreover, some time into the change process, many people who had initially felt internal conflict were now unconflicted and sure of the position that they were taking.

What was happening here? It seems that an internal conflict of values had become an external conflict. Rather than having to endure painful ongoing internal tensions, people took sides. There was a 'good' side and a 'bad' side. The interviews reflected this. Even while seeing the internal tension, staff talked of those who were 'for the change' and those who were not. The interesting thing was that, while most *named* this division between groups, not one person saw themselves in the 'resisters' group. Some named a few doubts, but the real 'resisters' were always elsewhere.

It is clear that organisation members experience the effects of their internal conflicts, say, about change or about the nature of the task they are asked to perform. This becomes ameliorated because the conflict becomes externalised. It is easier to see another person or group as holding on to one side of the picture — one can then stand firmly for the other side. Freed from internal tensions, one can then readily condemn the opposing group. This can be done in a politically correct way that will support an illusion for the organisation. The illusion is as follows: 'Collectively we feel no doubt about the task we must do, or the changes we must make. We can thus get stuck into the work, and perhaps get rid of those "dinosaurs" who won't comply.'

In this way, the conflict is played out at an organisational level, perhaps with leaders even finding a better 'bad' group outside the organisation. The dynamic has been transformed from an internal conflict about values to an external fight with an identified enemy. Perhaps this seems a good resolution. One is less plagued with doubts about the job and is able to get on with it. But I suggest the loss is in the multiple scapegoating of many employees, forcing them into redundancies on the basis of their 'resistance' and assumed inability to change. With their loss, the organisation as a whole loses much of its accumulated knowledge. Moreover, as we know, when the 'dead wood' has been expunged, the problem does not really go away. Internal doubts no longer have a place to be projected. There is no one to take on the bad internal feelings, even if this were only in fantasy. Usually, a new out-group or scapegoat appears. I suggest the organisation must face the internal conflicts of staff around the nature of task, and the nature of organisational change. Processes for working through and discussing these conflicts are required. It is likely that the very category of 'resistance to organisational change' is an epiphenomenon emergent from a collective defence against internal conflict. Understanding the dynamic whereby internal tensions collectively become externalised might be more appropriate for working with resistance than those methods which seek out the resisters in an organisational witch hunt.

The rehabilitation organisation faced the possibility of losing members who held values that may yet be important to the future work if they can be integrated with the new task and new values. In this example, it becomes clear that conflict can move from being experienced internally to being experienced as between groups and at an organisational level.

At an institutional level

Conflict may occur within an organisation because work practices, organisational values, strategic choices and managerial decisions necessarily reflect inherent conflicts within the broader social context. We are speaking here of an institutional level where some very fundamental assumptions about the nature of work get enacted (Sievers 1993).

The social, economic, political and even climatic context of organisations has an impact on the way people work together. Different organisational stakeholders mediate this context. For example, shareholders, suppliers, customers, board members, employees, policy makers and families are each recognisable stakeholder groups. Each group has its own perspective, which brings with it particular tensions. Consider how a conflict might occur *between* shareholders and the management group within an enterprise; or *within* an employee who is asked to work longer hours, yet has several young children, a spouse who works and tensions occurring in the family.

Each stakeholder group is also part of a broader culture surrounding the enterprise. Many social scientists and thinkers have found it useful to see organisations (including their contexts) as having a culture (or more correctly, a subculture) of their own (Smircich 1983; Ouchi 1985; Schien 1990). This may be understood by reference to a few dominant metaphors (Morgan 1986). At a tacit level, such metaphors shape and guide the ways people work. 'This organisation is like a big family,' it might be said. Or, 'this workplace is like a sweatshop' might be muttered constantly in the corridors. Such metaphors provide a container or *psychological space* where thinking and feeling can emerge, be developed and changed.

Western societies in particular have emotionally invested heavily in the producer–consumer partnership (Long 1999). This partnership or pairing, one might say, has become the central metaphor or paradigm for human social relatedness outside the family. It is increasingly dominating the social context of the workplace and is understood in terms of the dual emphasis on (a) the dominant presence of a market economy and (b) the practice of economic rationalism within that economy.

The mass-production of goods and the development of wider communication networks have led to a smaller number of workers employed in direct production and increasing numbers of people employed in industries serving the newly developed consumer market. As a result, service industries have taken up a major role in so far as they now employ more people than production industries in western society.

This development is paradoxical in that, whereas the service industry sector has grown, it has increasingly taken on the rhetoric of production. For example, in the 1990s banks and universities were more likely to describe themselves as providing financial or educational 'products' than services. Universities may well have product managers rather than course directors. Moreover, the services previously provided by governments (in the spirit of public service) are now more likely to be provided through private companies so that medical, rehabilitative, educational and even corrective services are 'delivered' within a business context. All this has brought with it a new focus on the 'customer', now seen primarily as a consumer of goods and services.

Many roles that were once complex — roles such as 'patient', 'student' or 'citizen' — are now rendered in a simplified manner. They are all 'customers'. This becomes their primary appellation. The patient who suffers, the student who learns and the citizen who takes up a place in democratic decision making are now primarily present in the social system as consumers. In such a context, the doctors, teachers and politicians become primarily producers. The more complex aspects of these roles, although necessarily present in the day-to-day work of the relevant professions, become eclipsed in the broader social picture. The business market metaphor dominates where social policy is concerned.

How is this context important to the issue of conflict in the workplace? The dominant producer-consumer metaphor provides the social-emotional context of work. We are forced to assume that work is mainly about *producing something*, goods or services, *for a customer or consumer*. Whatever perfunctory focus is given to wider social issues, the business context is deeply based on the financial success of the producer in pairing with, and keeping, customers (a market). Such an assumption provides the framework or container within which we can think about work. For many, the provider-consumer pair or duality that lies at the basis of the market metaphor is rightly the focus for work and is invested with hope for business growth. Bigger and better markets are hoped for. Diverse and greater production is desired as an indicator of growth and national affluence.

Such basic social assumptions, as the pairing one outlined, provide a conceptual framework or container for thinking. Wilfred Bion (1961) pioneered the work of understanding group dynamics in terms of basic assumptions. He described how group members collectively act on deeply unconscious assumptions about the nature of the group and its leadership. He described three main group assumptions. One was termed flight/fight, where group members acted as if the reason they were together is to fight an enemy either within or, more usually, without. A second basic assumption was called 'dependency', where group members acted as if they were together simply to obey a leader who did all their thinking for them. The third basic assumption identified was termed 'pairing', where group members acted as if the pair would produce a messiah or messianic idea that would save them from their current difficulties. Other basic assumptions have been identified at the group and organisational levels (Turquet 1974; Lawrence, Bain & Gould 1996; Schneider & Shrivastava 1988) and the pairing assumption or metaphor suggested here is postulated to act at a broad societal level.

The reader is encouraged to visit the intriguing and highly practical literature on group dynamics in the Bion tradition. Here I wish to draw attention to one major aspect of group basic assumption behaviour. This is the fact that, while acting upon a basic assumption, group members avoid their agreed work task. Also, the assumption works in such a way that its validity is not tested. It is a taken for granted. It is hard currently to think of organisations in ways other than in terms of the producer-consumer pair. It is a taken for granted that all organisations are basically businesses whether they are schools, hospitals, prisons or genuine businesses. Nowadays, even a small department within a larger corporation is encouraged to see customers in every other department within the same corporation.

A basic social assumption provides a framework for the development and expression of values and the enactment of emotions. For instance, if the provider-consumer pair dominates thinking in the workplace then leadership, for example, will be judged in terms of market expansion rather than the promotion of quality.

We should bear in mind that professional services, community services or even those services that are classed as not-for-profit undertakings are now primarily framed within the producer-consumer pair metaphor with their essential values framed in terms of the values of business. This has caused major conflicts for, say, the Catholic health-care system, where the values of the religious order must constantly be reconciled with business values. Another example can be found in the Victorian school system. Increasingly taking on 'business values', school principals and councils have more independent authority for a variety of issues. Competition for improved educational outcomes may well (unconsciously?) promote finding ways of removing students who are seen as unlikely prospects. The task of 'educating' generational cohorts runs the danger of being corrupted.

Because the market (the producer-customer pair) frames the current thinking in the workplace, the tensions naturally held within that social frame will be played out in our organisations. Overtly, this might indicate that conflicts will necessarily occur between the major producer and customer groups. This would be a case of structural determination. Evidence is found in the increasing growth of consumer advocacy in all industry sectors in the latter part of the twentieth century. A recent example is the need to include consumer groups in policy development in such areas as mental health and corrective services (Wadsworth & Epstein 1998). Conflicts between consumer groups and producers have increased.

More covertly or subtly, this pairing framework may mean that conflicts within organisations become increasingly structured around the producer–consumer issue in specific ways according to how it is experienced at the time. For example, in the 1950s and 1960s there was an increase in functional segregation within organisations. The renewed focus on the customer had begun (Du Gray & Salaman 1992) and large sales departments grew up alongside production departments and separate personnel or other 'staff' departments served these. Intergroup conflicts tended to arise between different organisational functions. They were expressed through issues of job demarcation, problems with logistics and differing perceptions of the primary task of the organisation (different functions understand the 'business' of the enterprise from their own unique perspectives). In an attempt to reduce these conflicts, the management of functional structures was high on the agendas of senior managers and organisational consultants and researchers.

The 1980s and 1990s saw a move toward matrix or project-based organisational structures, in an attempt to break down what were increasingly seen as functional 'silos' that failed to interact appropriately with one another and, most importantly, seemed to be failing to reach the customer. Functional 'silos' were regarded as serving their own institutionalised interests rather than the interests of the market. There was a move toward cross-functional teams that were regarded as more flexible and responsive to consumer needs. Conflict in this context arises, for example, between those who want to work in these new structures and those who are seen as unable to change or as 'lodged in the past'. Other conflicts arise between different multidisciplinary or multifunctional teams. Willshire (1999) describes the conflicts between different teams within a mental health service. Each team was to focus on a different aspect of the task, but some teams increasingly competed with each other and took up a similar task.

In concluding this section, it can be said that the social context for work organisations is important for understanding the nature of conflicts that might arise. This social context is mediated through a dominant symbolic metaphor. Here I have argued that the current dominant metaphor is that of the producer–customer pair. I have argued that this metaphor shapes the ways in which we think and feel at work. It provides a context for our values at work. Various structural configurations within work organisations emerge to fit within the dominant metaphor, and each of these provides an internal organisational context that gives shape to the kind of conflicts that might be experienced. Most importantly, though, the dominant metaphor permeates the way that tasks are understood, structured and engaged by staff and other stakeholders.

Social defence theory: towards explaining the dynamics of conflict

Now we have seen that conflicts expressed at one systemic level in a work organisation may be the result of a covert conflict at another level, it is time to examine a theory that attempts to explain these dynamics. Over the last 30 years, a body of literature has grown around a theory of the social defences against anxiety. Just as an individual may build internal psychological defences against anxiety, so an organisation may build into its very structure and culture defences against the anxieties inherent in the tasks they engage. This is where the sociotechnical notion is important. If we consider the social system alone, then we tend to think of personalities and their interactions. If we include the task and its technical challenges, then we see that we are considering a system of roles. I will give an example in some detail before drawing some conclusions from this theory.

Menzies-Lyth (1988a) considered the nursing task within a major London teaching hospital. The task of nursing brings nurses into close physical and psychological contact with sick and sometimes dying patients. This is stressful enough in itself. However, the organisational context that brings nurse and patient together finds the patient helplessly dependent on the nurse, much as an infant is dependent on its mother. The nurse must provide very personal and intimate care. The Potter television musical 'The Singing Detective' depicts a patient in such a dependent condition. One scene shows how, despite his best efforts, he is unable to control his sexual response to the intimate body wash that he receives. Menzies-Lyth shows this is not all one-sided. Primitive emotional and sexual feelings are unconsciously aroused in both patients and nurses. Moreover, the nursing task is often involved with life-and-death procedures. This gives rise to anxieties around responsibilities when making immediate decisions about treatment after difficulties arise. The nurse must draw heavily on her or his own personal defences to deal with all these feelings and the anxiety that accompanies them.

The additional insight that Menzies-Lyth brings to this picture is her discernment that the hospital system itself provides an additional defence for the nurse. The way the nursing task becomes organised provides such a 'social' defence. The organisation's structure and culture provide a distancing between nurse and patient. Patients become known as their illnesses ('the liver in bed six') rather than as whole people. Nurses become responsible for particular functions rather than for whole persons. This places a curb on intimacy. It also gives rise, however, to secondary problems where patients feel alienated and staff feel guilty because they have little time to spend on providing psychological comfort. Because of the social defences against the fear of making mistakes in a life-and-death situation, the nature of discretion for task becomes rigid so that only the most senior people have the authority to make even the simplest of decisions. Junior nurses are treated as if they cannot be responsible for serious decisions. They become infantilised in their work. Consequently, they are in even greater need of the defensive structure provided by the organisation — hence, the rigid hierarchy found in the hospital studied by Menzies-Lyth.

Others have considered organisational defences in other types of organisations (Hirschhorn 1988; Wastell 1996; Krantz 1998). What becomes clear is the following.

First, it is clear that each particular sociotechnical task has its own anxieties. These may be obvious. One need only think of examples: medical services, working in prisons, teaching adolescents, finding and retaining markets. But all tasks have associated anxieties. These might simply include the anxiety involved in facing a manager with your mistakes, or in admitting to fellow workers that you do not know how to do a part of your job. Such are the everyday anxieties to be found when people need to challenge each other, in role, yet this leads to fears and anxieties about retribution. Perhaps the fear sometimes is simply a fear of not being liked.

Second, defensive structures and cultures develop within the organisation. These aid members in defending themselves against these anxieties. Some structures, for example, help members to avoid each other, thus avoiding the anxiety of open conflict between role holders. Some help members avoid meeting with customers. Needless to say, such social defences are not conducive to improved communications and secondary problems may arise that cause as much, if not more, anxiety than the original causes.

Third, the defensive structures in an organisation may fit with the defensive modes preferred by an individual, or they may not. The nurse who solves her or his own anxieties about intimacy and death by challenging rather than obeying authority would not fit well into the organisational culture described by Menzies-Lyth. Were she to stay, conflict between her way of approaching problems and the ways of others would be sure to occur. Normally, organisations tend to attract those who fit the culture. Hence they tend to reproduce their cultures. The result may seem positive because there may be a reduction of conflict. This, of course, may also mean a reduction of those creative differences that are required for the organisation to prosper.

Fourth, and most germane to our argument here, the defensive structures involve the splitting of complex situations into simpler ones, and the displacement of conflicts from one subsystem or system into another.

Implications for working with workplace conflicts

Conflict in the workplace arises when differing interests (desires), anxieties and fears cannot be managed. While such differences may be partially due to the personal characteristics of those involved, conflict is largely located at the social-system–technical-system boundary. That is, conflict arises from differing interests and anxieties surrounding the way tasks are structured and engaged. One might even go so far as to say that the 'individual' is a kind of temporary container for social dynamics anyway, but I develop that argument elsewhere (see Long 1992).

When conflict does emerge, people normally attempt to avoid or dispel it individually and collectively. At least, that is the norm in the workplace. Conflict is seen as disruptive to organisational life and work, except as a last resort under strained circumstances. One powerful method of avoidance that has been described in this chapter is through the social defences, unconsciously provided within the organisation at both structural and cultural levels. These defences operate through the sociodynamic processes of splitting, projection, introjection and displacement. The effect of such dynamics is that conflicts may be expressed in sociotechnical systems *somewhere other* than they originated. (It should be remembered here that a sociotechnical system may be as small as one person, in role, engaging a task or as large as an enterprise as a whole.)

An associated way of unconsciously managing conflict is that it may become institutionalised as part of the organisational culture. In this way, conflicts become *taken for granted* as ways of working. Let us be clear here. The conflict and the stress involved are experienced consciously by the people involved. It is the collective organisational response to the conflict that occurs unconsciously.

Of course, people may be disguising their interests and anxieties or dissimulating. Perhaps this is part of a political manoeuvre to deliberately gain power (Morgan 1986). Organisation members often believe that holding organisational secrets will be useful to them. The hope may be that, by keeping their own interests and desires as 'hidden agendas', opposing positions will be unprepared when crucial decisions have to be made. Conflicts may thus be implicit and submerged, resulting in reduced cooperation between conflicting parties. This may be an appropriate strategy when dealing with a competing enterprise but may well be destructive within a company.

In a less Machiavellian manner, groups may hide their problems and conflicts from their managers because they are afraid of the embarrassment that might be experienced should they be seen to fail or have problems (Argyris 1990). Such ways of dealing with conflict become an entrenched part of the organisation's culture. They result in defensive manoeuvres where players attempt to avoid their conflicts and anxieties through not communicating them. This can lead to poor communication between those parts of the organisation that need to communicate in order to achieve their tasks.

The creative management of conflict does not involve such automatic or entrenched defences as those described above. It involves working with the conflicts that emerge before they become destructive, and it involves providing an environment where conflicting interests and anxieties are examined rather than avoided.

Given that this argument is valid, what are the implications for working with workplace conflicts? I suggest at least the following.

Overt conflict should not be taken at face value

Individuals or subsystems should be considered in terms of what it is they might represent for other systems or the organisation-as-a-whole. Such an exploration requires quite some maturity on the part of those involved. In the midst of conflict, emotions usually run high and blame is frequently attributed. Managers and teams need to have ways of thinking about conflict so that it is understood as a possible displacement.

Each sociotechnical system requires careful consideration

Each sociotechnical system, from individual roles through to the broader enterprise and its environment, requires careful consideration in terms of the conflicts of interest and anxieties to which they give rise. This requires more than an understanding of the technical or task system by itself. Whatever the 'rational' division of labour seems to be, conflicts will be found in the social–technical interface. Many an organisation discovers this only after, say, an IT systems re-engineering process has occurred and, for example, the best technical solutions give rise to many problems at the sociotechnical interface. An organisational diagnosis (Bain 1976) considering structure, culture and work practice is a useful way of approaching an understanding of the ways conflict might emerge at the sociotechnical boundary. Another associated method of working through the implications of this interface may be found in organisational role analysis and its extension into role dialogue (Long, Newton & Chapman 1999). Sadly, organisations normally turn to such diagnoses and ways of working only after they have experienced crippling problems. Then they often choose to work with consultants whose main task is to excise those parts of the organisation considered problematic. In contrast to this, it may be that the healthy enterprise of the twenty-first century should go in for a regular diagnostic check-up and ongoing preventative work in the form of role dialogue between key areas.

The interests and anxieties of each subsystem or system within the organisation should have available a legitimate forum for expression

If this is not available, then certainly the conflicts become either avoided and displaced or expressed in a destructive manner (Jaques 1989). The forum might simply be the chance to work through issues with one's manager or fellow workers in an appropriate way. Working at the boundary of one's role in relation to other roles requires a constant process of negotiation, settling of differences and finding points of cooperation. This is where interpersonal skills are useful. They are part of a broader picture, though. A role is not static. New tasks, or new ways in which old tasks present themselves, mean that communication, negotiation and cooperation with others tackling linked tasks are ongoing. Moreover, senior managers in organisations that are basically accountability hierarchies need to be in touch with the ways in which people engage their tasks. This means being in touch with the dynamics discussed in this chapter. Less and less is management a process of control. It involves more an awareness of a complex network of sociotechnical systems, and a capacity to intervene at the right times in the right places (Senge 1990; Long & Newton 1997).

A collaborative organisational culture, paradoxically, is not the opposite of a conflicted culture

In fact, if conflicts are to be surfaced and worked through to positive solutions, the organisation members must cooperate (Zagier Roberts 1994; Stokes 1996). It is a misconception that a collaborative culture involves no conflict. Perhaps this is a particularly Australian misconception because a false egalitarianism is often invoked. Sometimes a pseudodemocracy is a disguised flight from the recognition of the differences that are present, including differences of interest, ability and authority. The culture then becomes one where conflicts cannot be surfaced or resolved.

A collaborative organisational culture depends on the development of mature working relations (Long, Newton & Dalgleish 2000, forthcoming). These relations are defined in terms of the following:

- *Clearly negotiated tasks and roles.* Clarity of boundaries, limits, agreements and modes of operation are crucial to a collaborative culture. Basically, such clarity and care with communication and negotiation show respect for the other. Conflicts can then be better understood, examined and resolved.
- *The capacity to learn through experience and action.* This means that one is able to

learn on the job from the experiences that the job presents.

- *The capacity to create and develop a facilitating and emotionally containing environment for the work.* This refers to an environment where it is possible to raise one's concerns about tasks and roles, and others will listen.

Such mature working relations provide the context within which conflict can be explored and examined. But they are conditions hard won, requiring an investment in 'reflective space' where together people can examine their responses to tasks, roles and group dynamics. Without these conditions, defensive avoidance or institutionalised conflict becomes entrenched. Moreover, an approach that avoids rather than examines conflict cannot be truly collaborative. The workplace contains emotions such as envy, shame, rivalry and anger as well as the more positive emotions. Many of these emotions are engendered by the nature of the task (Flynn 2000). They may be worked through in the workplace social system, or they may be destructively denied or enflamed. A collaborative workplace cannot ignore the sources and expression of conflict and its associated emotions.

Conclusion

This chapter examined the nature of conflict in organisations, the costs of conflict and the challenging issues associated with the dynamics of conflict. The social defence theory was then explored to enhance our understanding of the dynamics of conflict. Finally, suggestions of managing and working through conflict were outlined.

Each of the suggestions points to a way of working with conflict that is beyond the treatment of surface symptoms with 'quick fix' solutions. They imply that organisations must value their conflicts, take them seriously and be prepared to trace them beyond their present expression. An examination of organisational conflicts can lead to a richer understanding of the sociotechnical interface. Thus, it leads us to the very heart of the work of the enterprise. And it is here that attention must be paid if the organisation is to achieve its purposes as creatively and effectively as possible. To understand the cost of chronic workplace conflicts, we must first recognise their *symptoms*.

References

Archer, MA (1999) Authentic teaming: undiscussables, leadership and the role of the consultant. Unpublished doctoral thesis, Ontario Institute for Studies in Education, University of Toronto.

Argyris, C (1990) *Overcoming organizational defences.* Needham Heights: Allyn and Bacon.

Armstrong, D (1997) The recovery of meaning. Paper delivered at the Symposium of the International Society for the Psychoanalytic Study of Organisations. New York.

Bain, A (1976) Presenting problems in social consultancy: three case histories concerning the selection of managers. *Human Relations*, 29(7): 643–57.

Bion, WR (1961) *Experiences in groups.* London: Tavistock Publications.

Chapman, J (1999) Hatred and corruption of task. *Socio-analysis* 1(2).

du Gay, P & Salaman, G (1992) The cult[ure] of the customer. *Journal of management studies*, 29(5): 615–33.

Flynn, R (2000) A socio-analytic study of case management in a rehabilitation organisation with specific reference to the dynamic of shame. Unpublished Master's thesis, Graduate School of Management, Swinburne University, Melbourne.

Hirschhorn, L (1988) *The workplace within: psychodynamics of organizational life.* Massachusetts: MIT Press.

Jaques, E (1989) *Requisite organization: the CEO's guide to creative structure and leadership.* USA: Cason Hall.

Krantz, J (1998) Anxiety and the new order. In E Klein, F Gablenick and P Herr (eds) *The psychodynamics of leadership.* USA: Psychosocial Press.

Lawrence, WG, Bain, A & Gould, L (1996) The fifth basic assumption. *Free Associations*, 3(37): 28–55.

Long, SD (1992) *A structural analysis of small groups.* London: Routledge.

Long, SD (1999) The tyranny of the customer and the cost of consumerism: an analysis using systems and psychoanalytic approaches to groups and organisations. *Human Relations*, 52(6): 723–43.

Long, SD & Newton, J (1997) Educating the gut: socio-emotional aspects of the learning organisation. *The Journal of Management Development*, 16(4): 284–301.

Long, SD, Newton, J & Chapman, J (1999) Bridging the tensions: organizational role analysis with members from the same organization. Paper given at the Symposium of the International Society for the Psychoanalytic Study of Organizations, Toronto.

Long, SD, Newton, J & Dalgleish, J (forthcoming, 2000) In the presence of the other: developing working relations for organisational learning. In E Klein (ed) *Dynamic consultation in a changing workplace.*

Menzies-Lyth, I (1988a) *Containing anxiety in institutions.* London: Free Association Books.

Menzies-Lyth, I (1988b) A psychoanalytic perspective on social institutions. In E Bott Spillius (ed.) *Melanie Klein today: developments in theory and practice.* London: Routledge, pp. 284–99.

Morgan, G (1986) *Images of organization.* California: Sage Publications.

Obholtzer, A & Zagier Roberts, V (1994) The troublesome individual and the troubled institution. In A Obholtzer and V Zagier Roberts (eds) *The unconscious at work: individual and organizational stress in the human services.* London: Routledge.

Ouchi, WG (1985) Organizational culture. *Annual Review of Sociology* 11: 457–83.

Paine, WS (1982) *Job stress and burnout.* Newbury Park: Sage Publications.

Schien, EH (1990) Organizational culture. *American Psychologist*, 45(2): 109–19.

Schneider, S & Shrivastava, P (1988) Basic assumption themes in organizations. *Human Relations*, 41(7): 493–515.

Senge, P (1990) *The fifth discipline: the art and practice of the learning organization.* USA: Doubleday.

Sievers, B (1993) *Work, death and life itself: essays on management and organization.* Berlin: De Gruyter.

Sievers, B (forthcoming) *Competition as war: towards a socio-analysis of war in and among corporations.*

Smircich, L (1983) Concepts of culture and organizational analysis. *Administrative Science Quarterly*, 28: 339–58.

Stapley, L (1996) *The personality of the organisation: a psycho-dynamic explanation of culture and change.* London: Free Association Books.

Stokes, J (1996) The unconscious at work in groups and teams: contributions from the work of Wilfred Bion. In A Obholtzer and V Zagier Roberts (eds) *The unconscious at work: individual and organizational stress in the human services.* London: Routledge.

Turquet, PM (1974) Leadership: the individual and the group. In JJ Gibbard, J Hartmann & RD Mann (eds) *Analysis of groups: contributions to theory, research and practice.* London: Jossey-Bass.

Wadsworth, Y & Epstein, M (1998) Building in dialogue between consumers and staff in acute mental health services. *Systemic Practice and Action Research*, 11(4): 353–79.

Wastell, D (1996) The fetish of technique: methodology as a social defence. *Info Systems*, 6: 25–40.

Willshire, L (1999) Psychiatric services: organizing impossibility. *Human Relations*, 52(6): 775–804.

Zagier Roberts, V (1994) Conflict and collaboration: managing inter-group relationships. In A Obholtzer and V Zagier Roberts (eds) *The unconscious at work: individual and organizational stress in the human services.* London: Routledge.

PART 4 | Managing organisations

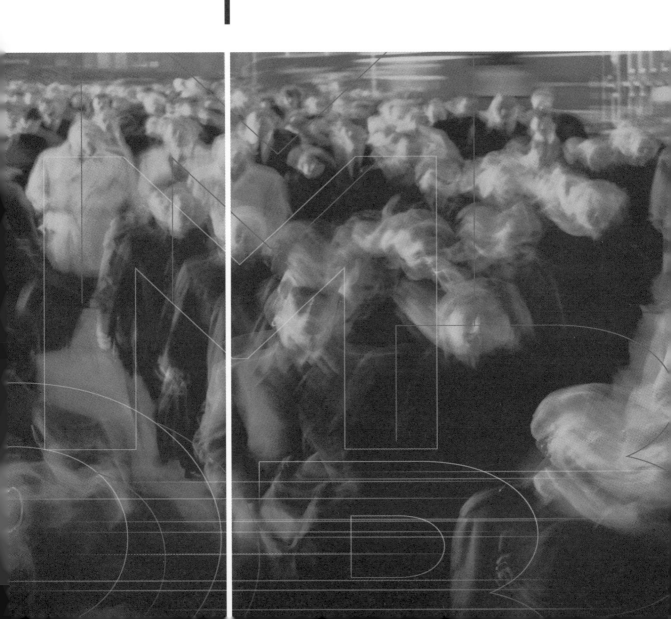

CHAPTER 10

Understanding organisations: the basis of managerial action

by Bruce Millett

Department of Human Resource Management and Employment Relations, Faculty of Business, University of Southern Queensland, Toowoomba

millett@usq.edu.au

 Introduction

This chapter reinforces the need for managers in general, and students of organisational behaviour in particular, to continually seek explanations of organisational behaviour as part of their professional development. The rationale for this is that people of influence need to identify and understand the dominant thinking in managerial practice. They must be able to surface and challenge their own assumptions about managerial behaviour. They need to seek alternative explanations about managerial practice in order to reflect on their own approach. This would assist them in influencing constructive change and continuity in their organisations, and it provides the basis for professional development in an organisation that is committed to the principles of open and continuous strategic learning.

If managers are to respond effectively to the challenges they confront, they need to continually clarify the underlying assumptions they hold about the organisations they manage. This is not only what learning is about, but a basic component of managerial and organisational learning: that is, the way organisations are able to adapt to the challenges and changes in their environments. Intuitively, managers act on sets of assumptions that are deeply woven into their personal psyches and into the cultures that they influence and are influenced by. Managers behave in terms of their theories-in-use or ways of acting (Argyris & Schon 1978) and, in many cases, without hesitation and without thinking about the underlying reasons for their actions. Morgan (1997, p. 4) believes that '...all theories of organisation and management are based on implicit images or metaphors that lead us to see, understand and manage organisations in distinctive yet partial ways.'

For example, Frank Blount took up the position of Chief Executive officer at Telstra in 1992. At the time, Telstra was starting to lag behind other telecommunication companies in terms of the capabilities needed to compete in a deregulated Australian marketplace. In particular, Blount was shocked at the company's deficiencies in technology (Blount & Joss 1999). Using his 38 years of experience in telecommunications in the United States, he set about restructuring one of Australia's biggest businesses.

Blount points out that, while he had some change principles in mind, he relied on his experience rather than the models of change espoused in textbooks. He argues that '...it is important for the leader of change not to articulate or put forward a model of change to the organisation but rather just to manage the change with a considered model or approach in mind' (Blount & Joss 1999, p. 62). An important point about his approach to changing the systems, structures and behaviour within Telstra was the fact that he had a set of guiding assumptions and principles that developed from valuable and diverse experiences.

A manager's ability to act is linked to the assumptions, principles and perspectives that are held about organisations. Particular views can lead to particular actions. While Blount and other change leaders refer to their own unique experiences and assumptions, there tends to be some common threads to many of their assumptions, beliefs and approaches.

For example, Stacey (1991) explains that there are two comprehensive explanations that dominate managerial thinking in the western world. The first is the rational approach. This is based on clear, well-defined policies, procedures and organisational structures. Managerial decision making relies heavily on sound analytical techniques, and control systems are based on the orderly motivation of people. The second is the entrepreneurial approach. Decision making is more intuitive and managerial control is much looser. Organisational structures, policies and procedures are less clear-cut. The leadership style is based on more inspirational characteristics than on position and authority.

The need to explore the nature of organisations as a prerequisite to understanding organisational change should be obvious and is emphasised by Burke and Litwin: 'To build a most likely model describing the causes of organisational performance and change ... we must understand more thoroughly how organisations function' (1992, p. 523).

In the following sections, a range of contemporary theories of organisations is identified and discussed in terms of their contributions to explaining organisational behaviour. Managers' perceptions about organisations are then discussed and their limitations exposed. Finally, some emerging trends in systems theory are highlighted as new ways of explaining organisational behaviour and practical implications for managers and students of organisational behaviour are outlined.

Making sense of the management theory jungle

There is a need for managers to seek out different explanations of organisational behaviour. In the research literature in this area, there is a range of competing theories, assumptions and perspectives about how organisations function. Koontz (1980) refers to this predicament as the management theory jungle. The field of organisation theory has been described in terms of a growing theoretical pluralism (Astley & Van de Ven 1983), as anything but monolithic (Ribbins 1985), as in a state of considerable confusion (Griffith 1982), and as a zoo (Perrow 1974) where different theoretical explanations are on display.

Various authors have attempted to classify theories about organisations. To some authors, organisations are either influenced and dominated by environmental forces or are autonomous units in control of their own destiny (Van de Ven & Astley 1981). Morgan (1986, 1997) provides another classification schema. He uses a range of metaphors to differentiate different types of theories and explanations. Organisations are described in terms of machines, organisms, psychic prisons, brains, cultures and political systems. These metaphors are identified by the consistent themes apparent in different theories and models about the nature of organisations.

Alternatively, Pfeffer (1982) maintains that a critical dimension in terms of distinguishing among theories of organisations is the perspective on action that has been adopted, either implicitly or explicitly, by the various authors. He identified three perspectives based on action. First, action is seen as purposeful, intentional, rational, prospective and goal-directed. Second, action is seen as externally constrained or situationally determined. Third, action is seen as being somewhat more random and dependent on emergent, unfolding processes. According to Pfeffer, the first set of theories classifies action as rational dominates and underpins much of the current prescriptions for managerial behaviour.

Scott (1998) provides a very credible classification of organisation theories in terms of the language of systems. He classifies the major theories and models as either rational, natural or open system perspectives. These three classifications provide a basis for identifying different assumptions that various researchers have about the nature of organisations. The pervasiveness of contingency principles is evident in this work and Scott (1998) makes this apparent by his conclusions about the concept of organisational effectiveness:

> We should not seek explanations for organisational effectiveness in general, since such general criteria are not available, and we must be cautious in celebrating the truism that organisations that are better adapted to their environments are more effective. Adaptation can be achieved in numerous ways, many of which contribute to the survival of the organisation but fail to serve the interests of external constituencies. (Scott 1998, p. 363)

Hall (1991) identifies five contemporary perspectives which he regards as having '... the greatest explanatory power' (p. 274) in terms of theories at the organisational level of analysis. As Hall (1999) points out, each permits those interested in organisations to see and understand the different facets of organisational behaviour and dynamics. The following summaries are intended to illustrate to managers and students the diversity of explanations available. But Hall (1999) also points out that '... each school yields insights; none has been empirically verified as *the* explanation of organisational phenomena' (p. 274).

The first perspective is the *population ecology model* (see Aldrich & Pfeffer 1976; Hannan & Freeman 1977), which has primarily focused on the processes of start-ups and failures of organisations (Kelly & Amburgey 1991). It is concerned with forms and populations of organisations, rather than with individual organisations (Aldrich & Pfeffer 1976), and focuses on the numbers and variations in organisations in society. It suggests that large established firms can become dinosaurs because of their inability to adapt (Daft 1998). Organisations fail or survive according to changing conditions in their environments. This perspective draws from theories of natural selection in biology.

The second perspective is the *rational-contingency model* (see Lawrence & Lorsch 1967). Rationality, in this view, relates to a logical managerial process of setting goals and selecting the means to achieve those goals effectively and efficiently. Managers attempt to design structures and systems that match the contingencies of their situation. Contingency theory is overly concerned with structure as the dependent variable and size, environment, strategy and technology as the independent variables. As such, contingency theory generally ignores the internal organisational processes involved in the dynamics of change, particularly the political aspects of these processes (Katz & Kahn 1978). It relies on linear, rather than mutual and multiple cause-effect, models to determine the appropriateness of particular organisational designs. For example, the Burns and Stalker (1966) model of mechanistic-organic structures is strongly based on a linear and unidirectional cause-effect representation of the environment-design linkage. However, there is no doubt about the influence that this perspective has over many aspects of organisational behaviour. Students often feel some discomfort every time a lecturer explains '... but it all depends'.

The third perspective is the *institutional model* (see Meyer & Rowan 1977). While an organisation's adaptation to its environment is a feature, the focus of organisational change is on responding to broader social norms of legitimacy and resource support, rather than managerial imperatives of efficiency (Thompson & McHugh 1995). Organisations survive by meeting the expectations of a broader community of stakeholders. Organisations are noted for the way they observe other competitors in their field and mimic their structures and processes. The isomorphic or crystallising nature of organisational populations (DiMaggio & Powell 1988) in the institutional perspective directs more attention towards the way organisations conform, rather than the way they change. This is reinforced by Clegg's (1990) reference to isomorphic pressures which, he states, '... are increasingly seen as being regulatorily shaped by organisational bodies of the state and of the professions, as privileged sites of production of what become constituted as rational myths. The iron cage is seen to be composed of rules which enmesh organisations' (p. 84).

The fourth perspective is the *resource-dependence model* (see Pfeffer & Salancik 1978), which is concerned with adaptation rather than selection as espoused by population ecologists. In line with Child's (1972) strategic contingency perspective, the resource-dependence perspective views change as the continuous attempts by decision makers to adapt the organisation to the demands of the environment and, in some cases, to change or enact those environments (Weick 1979). This perspective provides political and economic insights into organisational functioning through the exchange and dependency relationships between various stakeholders. Decision making is a key process as it is central to the distribution of resources. This approach tends not to account for some of the more fundamental attributes expected to be involved in organisational functioning, such as the impact of goals (Hall 1991), or how resources are socially constructed (Pondy 1977, cited in Pfeffer 1982). However, this perspective provides one of the better explanations of the internal dynamics of organisations by considering the political and technical aspects of making decisions, the autonomy of the decision maker, the enactment of the environment, and the impact of multiple stakeholders (Hall 1991).

The fifth perspective is the *transaction-cost model* (see Williamson 1975), which has developed from the field of economics. It focuses on transaction costs in the marketplace, rather than production costs in the organisation. Individuals are seen to act in terms of their self-interest and in a free and open marketplace. This provides the foundation for the efficient exchange of goods and services. However, the costs of each transaction or exchange become more expensive and prohibitive as environments become more complex and uncertain (Daft 1998). When this occurs, transactions, contracts and exchanges are brought within the hierarchical control of an organisation so that behaviour can be monitored and supervised. This model explains the emergence of hierarchical forms of governance in organisations as opposed to alternative forms of governance, such as the influence of price mechanisms in the marketplace. It provides arguments for explaining the status quo (Pfeffer 1982).

These five contemporary perspectives identified by Hall (1991, 1999) contribute significantly to organisation theory by improving our understanding about certain aspects of organisational structure and behaviour. The diversity of explanations adds to the richness of material that managers and students could use to continually reflect on their own views about these matters. The next section focuses on how real managers view their organisations, thereby exploring the gap between theory and practice.

What are managers' perceptions of organisations?

This section summarises the outcomes of a study that investigated the nature of organisational change experienced by four universities. Managers were asked to describe the concept of an organisation and how it functions (Millett 1995). They were asked to:
- define what an organisation is
- draw a picture of an organisation on a sheet of paper
- describe an organisation in terms of a metaphor; that is, they were asked to complete the statement '*an organisation is like a ... because ...*'.

An example of the sort of response received in relation to describing an organisation in terms of a metaphor was 'an organisation is like a dog, because it can be quite vicious and can bite people.' Therefore, metaphors can enable creative thought through the use of associations.

Thirty-eight definitions and graphical representations (which were diagrams rather than pictures) were collected, along with various statements that associated the nature of an organisation with animals, machines and other concepts, which the participants conveniently used to depict the particular attributes and characteristics of their organisations. This method utilises 'imaginization' (Morgan 1993), where the metaphor can be used as a way of thinking creatively and a way of seeing that pervades how managers understand their world generally (Morgan 1986). This is similar to the approaches adopted by other authors (for example, Zbar 1995; Palmer & Dunford 1996). Zbar (1995) used a similar approach to enhance the learning capabilities within management groups by reflecting on different ways that workshop participants described their organisations.

From the analysis of the data, there were no startling discoveries. The majority of participants provided a very basic definition in the form of organisations as 'structured groups of people who seek to achieve goals.' The definitions provided very limited insights into the nature of organisations and how they function. The very fact that they have goals, people and structure, and that people are involved in achieving those goals, does nothing to indicate the extent and types of processes that give organisations their distinctive and dynamic character.

The definitions were similar to the one that Scott (1998) uses to define organisations as rational systems: 'organisations are collectivities oriented to the pursuit of relatively specific goals and exhibiting relatively highly formalised social structures' (p. 26). This definition of a rational system was ingrained in the responses that the majority of participants gave. Therefore, if managers persist with these definitions, then do they in reality believe organisations to be rational and goal-directed entities? Alternatively, definitions may be used as convenient starting points for discussion. Business schools, through the use of popular texts on management and organisational behaviour, seem to have done a sound job of instilling such a rational orientation in students' minds.

In terms of the pictorial representations, participants were generally evenly divided as to what they depicted. Half of the participants described organisations in basic systems terminology. They used diagrams, which reflected a flow of inputs to outputs, or they used overlapping circles to identify subsystems, components and variables and to define the relationship between them and their contexts. The remaining 50 per cent of participants represented an organisation as an organisational chart. However, this pictorial representation of an organisation raises some interesting issues, because the author asked participants to draw a *picture*, and they responded with *diagrams*.

It is of some concern that half of the respondents thought in terms of an organisational chart. This may indicate that participants are strongly influenced by a structural view of organisations, although this is unclear. Waterman, Peters and Phillips (1980) make the point very strongly that organisations are not just structures. They involve much more. The representation of an organisation's structure is acceptable, but to associate such an image with an organisation per se could be problematic. This emphasis on organisations as hierarchies may indicate a deficiency in the graphical imagery that is used to describe organisations conceptually.

The other dominant images that strongly influenced participants were the graphical representations that are associated with general systems theory. The language and symbols of systems theory pervade many discussions on organisations in general. This is understandable given its adoption in most areas of business, science and technology. The input-process-output-feedback linkage, as illustrated in figure 10.1, aligns with the conception of organisations as cybernetic systems where the interactions between operations, control and policy centres are important (Swinth 1974).

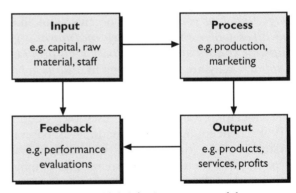

Figure 10.1: A basic systems model

The outcomes of the pictorial representations by participants in the study, like the definitions, were also very limited in terms of highlighting some of the complexities involved in organisational activity. Both the definitions and the diagrams presented a very basic outline of the concept of organisations as used by the participants. This could possibly mean two things.

1 Participants were unable or reluctant to provide a sophisticated or a more complex representation of the concept of an organisation under the circumstances.
2 The definition and the use of diagrams as tools did not provide adequate opportunity for them to do so.

Some participants complained that they were not artists and that they felt uncomfortable about having to think laterally. Also, definitions and diagrams are generally ingrained from the models that are presented in courses on management and these models represent the dominant orthodoxy in organisation theory.

The use of metaphors presents another means of relating to the concept of an organisation. The analysis of the responses produced a whole range of different attributes, which provided new insights into what organisations are. Participants immediately changed from providing a rather clinical and straightforward outline of what the major components are, or what the normative management literature prescribes, to a situation where they had to associate another concept or image with the concept of an organisation. They used animals, machines and the like to assist them in identifying the attributes of an organisation. At this point, it was obvious that this technique forced them to identify some of the realities that go on in organisations. Why are organisations like *dogs that bite you*? Why are organisations like *beehives where the queen bee maintains significant control* and like *mothers who provide support*? Why are organisations like *lions who are predators and kill in order to preserve their family*? The descriptions resulting from the metaphorical analysis resemble Scott's (1998) conception of organisations as natural systems where the informal and behavioural aspects of structure and systems are emphasised, rather than the normative and prescriptive aspects of organisational structure and systems.

One disadvantage of using metaphors as a technique for organisational analysis is the difficulty that managers have in constructing a complex and holistic model of organisations, because they tend to focus on the specific features of an organisation. However, as Morgan (1986) suggests, the metaphorical analysis does provide rich insights into the theory of organisations. Analogies and metaphors provide a means of gathering data about organisations. These data thus provide the basis for constructing a more realistic and descriptive model of what an organisation is, rather than what it should be. What the analogies do is make the participants think of particular situations, particularly attributes and realities that they are concerned with, in terms of this 'thing' called an organisation. If managers are to improve their understanding of organisations, they need to rely on multiple perspectives and a whole range of different reflective techniques in order to challenge their current perspectives and experiences.

Even if managers are unable to develop or articulate sophisticated explanations about the organisations they manage, there is no doubt that they are guided in their actions by some basic and dominant assumptions and imagery regarding what happens at work. As stated previously, the rational approach and the entrepreneurial approach strongly influence their decisions. However, the current definitions and models are not necessarily incorrect, although they tend to be prescriptive and simplistic. More importantly, managers are generally not exposed to the multiple and diverse range of explanations available to them. Their exposure to the concepts, models and language about organisations is limited because organisational behaviour texts tend to emphasise prescriptive and rational definitions and orientations that provide little clues to the realities and vagaries of organisational behaviour.

Emerging themes in systems theory

It is evident from the previous section that systems theory has served us well and will continue to provide managers and students of organisations with metaphors, terminology and explanations about how organisations function. Systems theory has, in fact, dominated as a framework for managerial behaviour and organisational analysis in the last 40 years. For example, Harvey and Brown (1996), Nadler and Tushman (1980) and Burke and Litwin (1992) use systems terminology to describe their own dynamic model of organisational change.

Systems theory is an abstract model for better understanding the nature of the world (Bechtold 1997) and organisations are regularly described by systems terminology. Such descriptions have become an important aspect of explaining the nature of organisations and how they function. As well, these descriptions provide a common language for discussing issues in terms of how to manage them more effectively. Robbins and Barnwell (1998) point out that describing organisations as systems provides insights into their make-up.

In terms of the contemporary use of general systems theory, there are various features that are used to describe the nature of organisations. Three of those features are:
1. the view that organisations constitute a complete system made up of interdependent parts
2. the view that organisations are open systems distinguishable from and interactive with their environment
3. the view that organisations are transforming systems that produce goods and services based on conditions of relative equilibrium and are managed on the basis of cybernetic control loops.

Two other perspectives have emerged in recent years and have started to shed new light on the way organisations are managed. The science of dynamic *nonlinear systems*, or *chaos theory*, is a recent development in mathematics where quite simple equations can model complex and chaotic behaviour. The 'butterfly effect' describes one of its central features through the example of how a butterfly flapping its wings in Mexico can cause a storm in China. This reflects a sensitive dependence on initial conditions; in other words, small changes can have large consequences.

The second perspective is *complexity science*. This refers to the study of the dynamics of 'complex networks of adaptive agents' (Shaw 1997, p. 235). In the case of social organisations, this involves a diverse and wide range of agents as stakeholders. A complex adaptive systems perspective stimulates a different way of looking at organisational change because it '... shifts consultants' attention away from planned change to the "messy" processes of self-organisation that produce unpredictable emergent change' (Shaw 1997, p. 235).

These two perspectives extend the boundaries of normal systems theory that has been described earlier and has dominated the description and analysis of managerial behaviour for much of the latter part of the twentieth century. The two perspectives offer different insights and emerge as exciting new evolutionary system explanations for the nature and development of organisations. The discussion below identifies two central and differentiating features of these perspectives.

Linear versus nonlinear systems

Chaos theory is '... the proposition that systems are neither simply open nor closed, but so complex that minute changes to the system can cause complex and unpredictable change' (Smither, Houston & McIntire 1996, p. 471). Chaos theory recognises that organisations are nonlinear systems. This is also reinforced by complexity science. In western society, the dominant way of thinking about cause and effect relationships is linear and unidirectional (Stacey 1993). Organisational analysts look for a direct causality between dependent and independent variables. However, viewing organisations as nonlinear systems presents a problem for predictability, because multiple forces are engaged in a dynamic way where they have mutual and reciprocal influences on each other.

According to these evolutionary system perspectives, organisations do not achieve success because of their ability to predict and create planned strategies. They achieve success because of their ability to constantly realign with the environment (Burnes 1996). Under these conditions, strategies emerge as behavioural patterns over time. Chaos theory suggests that one cannot predict what will occur in an organisation's environment because small errors in our predictions can have a snowball effect, thereby having a great impact on the accuracy of our predictions (Smolowitz 1996). Put simply, if one of the predictions is incorrect then the strategy that is adopted based on the prediction may not be suitable.

This is contrary to mainstream organisational analysis. Under the dominant logic of Newtonian calculus, small errors of calculation result in small errors in prediction (Stacey 1996a). Here, little importance is attached to nonlinearity where there is the '... possibility that one event may lead to a more-than-proportional response in terms of the next event' (Stacey 1993, p. 128). Mainstream organisational analysis is still focused on linear cause-and-effect relationships, with organisational performance and job satisfaction being key dependent variables.

The practical implication for managers and organisational behaviour students is the need to reappraise their approaches to strategic planning and planned organisational change. Such approaches adopt what Collins (1998) refers to as 'N-step' guides for change. Hence, '... we should not assume, therefore, that the various problems associated with "defining" and "diagnosing" change can be overcome by mechanistic methods which show no sympathy for the diverse drives, orientations, ambitions and yes, the fears of people' (Collins 1998, p. 98).

Dynamic equilibrium versus far-from-equilibrium

If an organisation is not changing, it is not because it is in a state of equilibrium, but because it is not responding to changes in the environment (Smither, Houston & McIntire 1996). This view emphasises the constancy of change. However, the dynamic equilibrium model is fundamental to general systems theory. Dynamic equilibrium is a state of balance between various forces in opposition to each other. While the emphasis is on reaching a state of equilibrium, there is an ongoing dynamic between the forces for change and the forces opposing change.

In change management theory, Kurt Lewin's (1951) model of *unfreezing*, *changing* and *refreezing* an organisation is based on a dynamic equilibrium perspective. Change is about moving the system from one state of equilibrium to another. When equilibrium is disturbed, the forces for and against change move the system to another point of balance. However, under a complex adaptive systems perspective, it no longer makes sense to attempt to refreeze an organisation to a new state of equilibrium, stability and rigidity (Dawson 1994).

Indeed, vision statements, long-term plans and strategies may stifle organisational success if they are not flexible enough to allow an organisation to continually adapt (Crossan, White, Lane & Klus 1996). Change management is about facilitating changeability, rather than change (Michaels 1994).

Therefore, the concept of organisations constantly seeking a state of dynamic equilibrium is coming under increasing scrutiny and an alternative view of a far-from-equilibrium paradigm is being put forward by Stacey (1993) who refers to the studies of Miller (1990) and Pascale (1990) which '... point to the conclusions that: continuing movement towards equilibrium is failure; success requires the maintenance of a position away from equilibrium; contradictions between stability and instability, between tight and flexible controls, between centralised and decentralised structures, are all essential to success' (p. 106). Success, in these terms, is operating in a position of far-from-equilibrium and at the edge of chaos so that the competence of dynamic organisational systems develops from tensions and contradictions rather than from harmony and stability. The implication for organisations is the need for them, to develop their skills relevant to a far-from-equilibrium state.

In conditions that are far from equilibrium, self-organisation becomes a significant alternative to the control-oriented behaviour of management. The failures that have accumulated from attempts at organisational change are related to the fundamental but misplaced belief in the organisation as machine (Wheatley & Kellner 1996). The interventions and control systems used by change agents are straining under the dynamic conditions imposed by the global marketplace. On the other hand, the implication for managers is that '... self-organising systems have what all leaders crave: the capacity to respond continuously to change. In these systems, change is the organising force, not a problematic intrusion. Structures and solutions are temporary' (Wheatley & Kellner 1996, p. 19).

Managers and organisational behaviour students should be aware that self-organisation is the spontaneous development of networks of people around specific issues and these networks generally operate on the shadow or informal side of the organisation, somewhat in tension with the legitimate management system (Stacey 1996b). The need for self-organising is evident in unstable conditions and this raises the issue of the sort of leadership skills necessary to stimulate and facilitate such processes.

Conclusion

The concept of the learning organisation has become a powerful metaphor for contemporary management. Like the other metaphors that Morgan (1986) uses in his ground-breaking book, this metaphor, in particular, emphasises the importance of developing core competencies within the organisation to sustain a successful journey, rather than reach a particular destination. Destinations come and go and the challenges remain. Learning, at the individual, group and organisational levels, is one of the major core competencies we can develop to have a successful journey. The answer resides in the development of managers who see themselves as key participants in the context of a learning organisation. The development of a language about organisations based on novel and diverse theories, models, concepts and emerging themes can only support their learning.

Organisational behaviour texts generally define organisations in simplistic terms and provide limited models that indicate what the basic attributes of organisations are and how they function. While this may be appropriate for such texts, managers and students of management alike need to actively and continuously seek out alternative explanations about the nature of the organisations they are involved with. It is important for managers and potential managers to challenge and expand their understanding of their arenas of influence and accountability.

In this chapter, a range of contemporary theories that could lead to a better understanding of organisations was identified. Some of the issues involved in the initial definitions and representations of an organisation and espoused by a group of managers were outlined, in order to bridge the gap between theory and practice. Finally, some exciting new explanations in systems theory were identified. In conclusion, it would be fitting to ask the reader the question: 'do you realise that you are now in an era of post modernism?'; if you do not, refer to Daft (1998, p. 22).

References

Aldrich, H & Pfeffer, J (1976) Environments of organisations. *Annual Review of Sociology* 2.

Argyris, C & Schon, D (1978) *Organizational learning: a theory of action perspective*. Reading: Addison-Wesley.

Astley, W & Van de Ven, A (1983) Central perspectives and debates in organisation theory. *Administrative Science Quarterly*, 28: 245–73.

Bechtold B (1997) Chaos theory as a model for strategy development. *Empowerment in Organisations*, 5(4): 193–201.

Blount, F, Joss, B and Mair D (1999) *Managing in Australia*, Sydney: Landsdowne.

Burke, W & Litwin, G (1992) A causal model of organizational performance and change. *Journal of Management*, 18(3): 523–45.

Burnes, B (1996) *Managing change: a strategic approach to organisational dynamics*. London: Pitman Publishing.

Burns, T & Stalker, GM (1966) *The management of innovation*. London: Tavistock Publications.

Child, J (1972) Organisational structure, environment, and performance: the role of strategic choice. *Sociology*, 6(1): 1–22.

Clegg, S (1990) *Modern organizations: organization studies in the postmodern world*. London: Sage.

Collins, D (1998) *Organisational change: sociological perspectives*. London: Routledge.

Crossan, M, White, R, Lane, H & Klus, L (1996) The improvising organization: where planning meets opportunity. *Organizational Dynamics*, 24(4): 20–35.

Daft R (1998) *Organization theory and design*. Cincinnati, Ohio: South-Western College Publishing.

Dawson, P (1994) *Organisational change: a processual approach*. London: Paul Chapman Publishing.

DiMaggio, P & Powell, W (1988) The iron cage revisited: institutional isomorphism and collective rationality in organization fields. *American Sociological Review*, 48: 147–60.

Griffith, D (1982) Theories: past, present and future. Paper presented at the 5th IIP of the CCEA, Nigeria.

Hall, RH (1991) *Organizations: structures, processes, and outcomes* (5th ed.). Englewood Cliffs: Prentice Hall.

Hall, RH (1999) *Organizations: structures, processes, and outcomes* (7th ed.). Englewood Cliffs: Prentice Hall.

Hannan, MT & Freeman, J (1977) The population ecology of organizations. *American Journal of Sociology*, 83: 929–64.

Harvey, DF & Brown DR (1996) *An experiential approach to organization development.* Englewood Cliffs, NJ: Prentice Hall.

Katz, D & Kahn, R (1978) *The social psychology of organisations* (rev. ed.) New York: John Wiley.

Kelly, D & Amburgey, T (1991) Organizational inertia and momentum: a dynamic model of strategic change. *Academy of Management Journal*, 34(3): 591–612.

Koontz, H (1980) The management theory jungle revisited. *Academy of Management Review*, 5(2): 175–87.

Lawrence, PR & Lorsch, JW (1967) *Organization and environment.* Cambridge: Harvard University Press.

Lewin, K (1951) *Field theory in social science.* New York: Harper & Bros.

Meyer, JW & Rowan, B (1977) Institutionalised organizations: formal structure as myth and ceremony. *American Journal of Sociology*, 83(2): 340–63.

Michaels, M (1994) Chaos theory and the process of change. In D Cole, J Preston and J Finlay (eds) *What is new in organization development.* Chesterland, OH: The Organization Development Institute.

Miller, D (1990) *The Icarus paradox: how excellent organizations can bring about their own downfall.* New York: Harper Business.

Millett, B (1995) *Identifying a model of institutional change: the transition from college of advanced education to university.* Unpublished PhD Thesis, Griffith University.

Morgan, G (1986) *Images of organization.* Beverly Hills: Sage Publications.

Morgan, G (1993) *Imaginization: the art of creative management.* Beverly Hills: Sage Publications.

Morgan, G (1997) *Images of organization.* Thousand Oaks: Sage Publications.

Nadler, D & Tushman, M (1980) A model of diagnosing organizational behaviour. *Organizational Dynamics*, Autumn: 35–51.

Palmer I & Dunford R (1996) Understanding organisations through metaphor. In C Oswick and D Grant (ed.) *Organisation development: metaphorical explanations.* London: Pitman Publishing, 7–19.

Pascale, R (1990) *Managing on the edge: how successful companies use conflict to stay ahead.* London: Viking Penguin.

Perrow, C (1974) Is business really changing? *Organizational Dynamics*, Summer: 31–44.

Pfeffer, J (1982) *Organizations and organization theory.* Boston: Pitman.

Pfeffer, J & Salancik, GR (1978) *The external control of organizations: a resource dependence perspective.* New York: Harper & Row.

Pondy, L (1977) The other hand clapping: an information-processing approach to organizational power. In T Hammer and S Bacharach (eds) *Reward systems and power distribution.* School of Industrial and Labor Relations, Cornell University, Ithaca, pp. 56–91.

Ribbins, P (1985) Organisational theory and the study of educational institutions. In M Hughes, E Ribbins and H Thomas (eds) *Managing education: the system and the institution.* East Sussex: Holt, Reinhart & Winston.

Robbins, S & Barnwell, N (1998) Organisation theory: concepts and cases. Sydney: Prentice Hall.

Scott, WR (1998) *Organizations: rational, natural and open systems* (4th ed.) Englewood Cliffs: Prentice Hall.

Shaw, P (1997) Intervening in the shadow systems of organisations: consulting from a complexity perspective. *Journal of Organisational Change Management*, 10(3): 235–50.

Smither, RD, Houston, JM & McIntire, SD (1996) *Organization development: strategies for changing environments.* New York: HarperCollins College Publishers.

Smolowitz, I (1996) The disturbing truth about long-term planning. *Production and Inventory Management Journal*, 37(1): 86–7.

Stacey, R (1991) *The chaos frontier.* Oxford: Butterworth Heinemann.

Stacey, R (1993) *Strategic management and organisational dynamics.* London: Pitman Publishing.

Stacey, R (1996a) Management and the science of complexity: if organisational life is nonlinear, can business strategies prevail? *Research Technology Management*, 39(3): 8–10.

Stacey, R (1996b) *Complexity and creativity in organizations.* San Francisco, CA: Berrett-Koehler.

Swinth R (1974) *Organizational systems for management: designing, planning and implementation.* Columbus, Ohio: Grid.

Thompson P & McHugh D (1995) *Work organisations: a critical introduction.* London: Macmillan Business.

Van de Ven, A & Astley, W (1981) Mapping the field to create a dynamic perspective on organizational design and behavior. In A Van de Ven and W Joyce (eds) *Perspectives on organizational design and behaviour.* New York: Wiley-Interscience, pp. 427–68.

Waterman, RH, Peters, TJ & Phillips, JR (1980) Structure is not organisation. *Business horizons*, June: pp. 14–26.

Weick, KE (1979) *The social psychology of organising* (2nd ed.) Reading: Addison-Wesley.

Wheatley, M & Kellner, R (1996) Self-organisation: the irresistible future of organising. *Strategy and Leadership*, 24 (4): 18–24.

Williamson, O (1975) *Markets and hierarchies: analysis and antitrust implications.* New York: Free Press.

Zbar, V (1995) Imaginize: a new way of working. *HR Monthly*, May: pp. 8–9.

Organisational culture — theory, fad or managerial control?

CHAPTER 11

by Dianne Lewis

School of Management, Queensland University of Technology, Brisbane

d.lewis@qut.edu.au

Introduction

Proponents of organisational culture generally consider it to be one of the macro approaches to management, claiming it as the 'one best way' to manage. The early proponents of culture theory, such as Peters and Waterman (1982), expounded it as a means of achieving *excellence* in organisations; but a number of researchers since then have started to look at it as a means of *managerial control*. Both these points of view have some justification, but I will present culture from as unbiased a viewpoint as I can and then critique it as a theory. This may help managers understand their organisations and the people who work in them more effectively. It may also help organisational members in their various roles in those organisations.

The culture approach is simply another way of looking at organisations — another *metaphor* or *image*. There are many ways of looking at organisations, the rational approach being popular during the time of classical management and scientific management theory and the various behavioural approaches being popular when human relations theory was in vogue. Gareth Morgan (1997) says that how you view an organisation determines how you will *manage* it. The classicists saw organisations as machines, so they designed systems that functioned like machines; the human relations theorists saw organisations as living organisms, comprised of people with needs and feelings, so they tried to take account of that. People who see organisations as political arenas are interested in the power relationships between different players in the scene.

Each of these schools of thought views the workplace as a collection of individuals — interdependent in different relationships — but nevertheless as individuals. By contrast, the *culture school* sees the organisation as a collectivity, a social entity, to which employees belong, just as they also belong to the wider collectivity of the society in which they live. We all belong to many collectivities — our family, our university, our class, and our social, community and sporting groups.

Culture theorists would also say that most other organisational theories, such as scientific management, human relations, systems theory and even the political model to a certain extent, have an inherent weakness in that they all consider organisations are run *rationally*:
- People work solely for money
- or they will produce more if treated properly
- or they will respond to changes in the environment and work as a team in a series of interrelated groups;
- or they are politically motivated and will work towards predetermined ends of their own.

Culture theorists say that managers have concentrated on the structures and strategies that *ought* to work and that *ought* to facilitate the management task; and they have forgotten that people are *not* rational; that people do not behave in a certain manner just because they are put into a defined structure, or given a specific task to do. Culture theorists say, sure, you can design structures and implement strategies that will make, for example, communication easier if people *want* to communicate, but no amount of logical organising will make people *want* to communicate. Even the human relations school, whose adherents recognise that people are not motivated solely by rational economics, believed that if you treated people right and were nice to them they would respond and would be motivated to work harder. And this is a rational decision! What culture theorists say is that there are far more indefinable things that motivate people and cause them to act as they do. So, culture theorists search for the *meanings* behind people's actions.

The study of organisational culture has followed many paths and has changed in content and emphasis since Peters and Waterman turned it into a commercial commodity in 1982. Early researchers concentrated on explaining the concept, while later articles have had a more practical purpose, asking the question, 'What use may be made of the gained information?' (Hofstede 1986). In this chapter I will try to cover the main trends in the literature and look at the nature of culture and those aspects of it that researchers have been interested in studying and managers have been interested in finding out about, some of the challenging questions and controversies that surround it, where culture theory appears to be headed and, finally, some implications of culture for both managers and employees alike.

The nature of culture

Culture has traditionally been viewed as one facet of anthropology (Robbins 1983), but an anthropological classification is too narrow. Culture has arisen out of psychology and sociology as well as out of anthropology and, according to Meek (1988), problems of definition always arise when a term is borrowed from another discipline. While some of the elements of organisational culture are obviously similar to those in anthropological culture (hence the use of the term), there are sufficient dissimilar elements to make the use of the word 'culture' inappropriate.

The concept of culture in organisations is not a new one. We tend to think of it as originating with Peters and Waterman's book (Peters & Waterman 1982). But that was only when it took the interest of managers, because Peters and Waterman told managers that the key to corporate success lay in having a strong culture. Managers immediately paid attention, especially as they had listed eight qualities that 'excellent' companies had in common:

1 a bias for action
2 close to the customer
3 autonomy and entrepreneurship
4 productivity through people
5 hands-on, value-driven
6 stick to the knitting
7 simple form, lean staff
8 simultaneous loose-tight properties.

There are many definitions of organisational culture, and part of the criticism that has been made of culture as a theory is that nobody really seems to have worked out exactly what it *is*. One CEO described culture very simply as 'the way we do things around here', so, in looking at an organisation from that viewpoint, people want to know whether it is directly observable behaviour (concrete *forms*) or whether it is underlying shared meanings. That is, can you *see* it, or do you have to *infer* it? Is it fixed or can it be changed? How is it created and transmitted? And how might it be studied?

Forms or meanings

One group of researchers, called 'cultural adaptationists' by Sathe (1983), views culture as the shared assumptions, beliefs, values and feelings that exist, often at an unconscious level, in members' minds, while the other group, called 'ideationists' by Sathe (1983), believes that culture exists in the structure, strategies and observable behaviour of members. Both groups study stories, myths, language, rites, rituals, ceremonies, artefacts and legends, but to the first group these things are merely manifestations of the underlying culture, while to the other they are a part of the culture itself. Most researchers define culture as a combination of forms *and* meanings, but this could be because Peters and Waterman view it this way and their book has had such an important influence on the popular concept of organisational culture. Figure 11.1 illustrates the relationship.

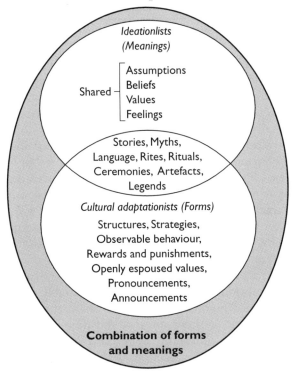

Figure 11.1: Theories of organisational culture

A variation of the ideationist view, which I hold, is that culture is a three-layered thing and can be defined as:

> basic assumptions that people in an organisation hold and share about that organisation. Those assumptions are implied in their shared feelings, beliefs and values and embodied in symbols, processes, forms and some aspects of patterned group behaviour. (Lewis 1992, p. 48)

Symbols, processes, forms and behaviour can all be observed; feelings, beliefs and values have to be inferred from the observable components; and basic assumptions (meanings) are the core of the culture. This view is illustrated in figure 11.2.

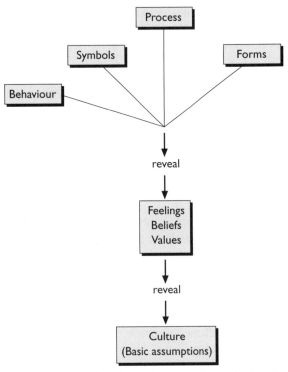

Figure 11.2: The three-layered nature of organisational culture (Lewis 1992, p. 48)

Symbols are things like logos, slogans, rituals, ceremonies, stories that people in the organisation tell, who the power-holders are, ceremonies and day-to-day work practices. *Processes* are the methods an organisation uses to carry out its tasks, such as the line of command, the official communication channels, the strategies used by management, the socialisation procedures for new staff and the rules and regulations about meetings. *Forms* are the directly observable things, like the architecture of the place, the layout of the offices, the furniture, official documents, speeches, newsletters and memos. *Behaviour* is the specific day-to-day actions performed by organisational members as they go about their work. Behaviour belongs in a separate category of embodiment, as not *all* behaviour is cultural. Sometimes people are forced to behave in ways that are contrary to the way they think and feel and their behaviour is a contingency measure and not a reflection of their cultural values at all.

All these things should tell the observant onlooker much about the organisation; but, according to this view, they are *not* the culture of the organisation. They are merely the embodiments of deeper feelings, beliefs and values that members hold about the world in general and the organisation in particular. The culture itself is a deeper thing again. It is the basic assumptions or meanings that people hold about things. Part of the trouble with this definition, and with *any* definition, is that each of the components is in itself an imprecise concept (Lewis 1998, p. 254). Many of the definitions of *feelings, beliefs, values, attitudes* and *behaviour* were taken from the language of psychology, which has still been unable to clearly define them.

Culture is often confused with *climate*. But climate is a measure of people's job satisfaction and whether the realities of life in that job measure up to their expectations. Generally, if employees' views are consistent with the organisation's culture, the climate will be positive. Thus, climate is a much more short-term thing, whereas culture is much deeper and much more long term.

Fixed or changeable?

Apart from whether culture is forms or meanings, researchers are interested in whether it is a variable or a fixed quality; that is, whether it is something an organisation *has* or something an organisation *is*. Most people seem to view culture as a variable. Certainly, those people who believe culture has an impact on the effectiveness of an organisation prefer to see culture as a variable. After all, if it is a variable, it can be changed; whereas, if it is a fixed quality, it is something there is little control over. Culture may be a variable, but in some organisations it has become so deeply and unconsciously entrenched that it is more a fixed quality. It is also a bit simplistic to see culture as a single entity as there are often many subcultures in an organisation.

Creation and transmittal of culture

The third thing culture researchers have been interested in, particularly those interested in culture change, is how culture is created, communicated and transmitted in an organisation. Most researchers seem to believe that certain behaviours lead to shared feelings and only a few believe that shared feelings lead to shared behaviour. The process is probably cyclical, but it seems logical to believe that certain behavioural norms would *initially* create the shared feelings. This proposition is discussed later when looking at Sathe's proposal for changing culture and Schein's 10 means of culture embodiment and transmittal.

Studying and diagnosing culture

People who belong to Sathe's cultural adaptationist school of cultural thought believe that culture can be studied by looking at concrete things. To them, diagnosing culture would be a relatively easy job; all one would have to do is to study the structure, strategies and observable behaviour and say, 'This is the culture.' But if we believe, as most researchers do, that culture is deeper than that — so deep, in fact, that it is largely *unconscious* — then we are faced with the task of trying to unearth the basic assumptions that lie beneath all these physical manifestations of culture.

That type of research is difficult, because assumptions are usually non-debatable and taken for granted. People who share them are not aware of them most of the time, and certainly rarely question them. For example, why do Australian men shake hands when they meet or part rather than embrace and kiss? It is a cultural thing, not followed in all countries. The same is true in organisations — sometimes behaviour is formal, the boss is referred to as 'sir', time books are kept and staff must report when they will be out of the office; sometimes it is very informal, everybody is on first-name terms, times are flexible and staff are free to pursue their own pursuits within certain limits. These different behaviours are examples of different organisational cultures and people who work in those organisations know the rules and, provided they are a part of the culture, usually do not question them.

Techniques for studying culture vary greatly and it is not the purpose of this chapter to describe them in detail. Most of them rely to a certain extent on the study of behaviour but, if culture is not the *only* determinant of behaviour (as is argued) then interpretations of behaviour in purely cultural terms can lead to spurious conclusions. Sathe (1983) and Schein (1983, 1984, 1985), however, assume that culture includes more than just observable behaviour and that one has to infer unconscious assumptions from observable manifestations. Sathe uses shared sayings, things, doings and feelings as his manifestations (1983, p. 7; 1985, p. 17), and Schein suggests categories for studying assumptions (1983, p. 16; 1984, p. 6), as well as 10 mechanisms that founders and managers use to embed and transmit values and assumptions (1983, p. 22). Other researchers whose work shows theoretical underpinnings and who have comprehensively described their methods are Quinn (1988) and Quinn and Rohrbaugh (1983), who devised the competing values model (CVM) for describing culture in terms of what seem to be mutually exclusive value dimensions: structural control versus flexibility, focus on internal versus external stakeholders, and means versus ends; Martin (1992), who investigated three different perspectives of culture — integration, differentiation and fragmentation; and Harris and Ogbonna (1997), who built on Martin's framework and analysed three in-depth case studies.

In my own study of culture (Lewis 1995), I used a combination of methods suggested in the literature and a few I had developed myself. I used qualitative methods (such as ethnographic interviews and focus group interviews, a daily log of observations and a study of formal documents) and quantitative methods to verify the validity of my qualitative findings. Yet uncovering a culture also requires an element of creativity and intuitive skill that may or may not be present in the researcher, and no amount of data or resources can buy creativity. The task remains problematic.

Studying culture: challenging issues

There are more challenging issues in culture research than there are accepted facts. Probably the most challenging issues facing culture researchers at the moment are trying to find answers to the following questions:

- What effects does culture have on an organisation?
- Can culture be changed?
- How can culture and culture change be measured?

Effects of culture on the organisation

Most researchers seem to think that culture has a significant effect on the organisation. After all, if it *hasn't*, then why would anybody in business bother studying it? But, of course, Peters and Waterman made claims of far-reaching effects of culture on performance and claimed a direct link, giving very convincing examples from successful companies. All these companies had strong cultures. I am not really in a position to dispute their claims of excellence in the companies they studied — at the time they studied them! What *is* disputable, though, is the direct link between culture and performance. Peters and Waterman did not take into account any other variables that may affect performance, so it is possible that their high correlation between culture and performance is a spurious one.

There really is no *direct* link between culture and performance. Only behaviour can affect performance, and culture is *not* the only determinant of behaviour. Nevertheless, all the empirical evidence seems to point to some relationship between culture and performance. Perhaps that is why managers are so keen to make use of culture and also why it has tended to last as a theory rather than to be listed among the passing fads.

Can culture be changed?

If culture *does* have an effect on an organisation, it is almost certain that managers of organisations that are not performing as well as they would like are going to look to culture change as the answer to all their problems. If this is the case, it raises the question: *can culture be changed?*

Optimism about changing culture varies greatly between academics (most of whom view it very sceptically) and consultants (who are often prepared to give 'canned' solutions in the form of five-or six-point plans.) There are dozens of these ready-to-use plans, but a word of warning from Allen Kennedy: 'It costs a fortune and takes forever' (Deal and Kennedy 1982). He says it may, in fact, be easier to change the people *in* the organisation than to change the culture *of* the organisation. And, of course, this is one method of changing culture anyway — hiring only people who 'fit in' with the desired new culture. It is a slow method if done purely by attrition, and a dangerous method if done by sacking everyone who does not fit the new mould. Most organisations try it by a compromise between the two methods. I am going to discuss only two researchers who have suggested methods of changing a culture. Vijay Sathe (1983) and Edgar Schein (1983) are two whose work influenced me considerably, though they are very unitarist in their bias.

Sathe provides a guide for managers who wish to intervene to change their organisation's culture. It is prescriptive, but has sound theoretical bases. He says there are five basic processes that cause culture to perpetuate itself, and managers who want to change culture must intervene in each of these five processes:

1 Start by changing people's behaviour.
2 Remove external justifications for the new behaviour.
3 Intervene in the cultural communications; (those things that communicate culture), and try to get people to adopt the new beliefs and values.
4 Intervene in the hiring and socialisation of members. Hire people who would 'fit in' with the desired culture and teach them the rules, norms and expectations of the organisation.
5 Remove any 'deviants' from the organisation. While Sathe does not say exactly how this should be done, I suppose managers with the inclination would use any means they had at their disposal. Some companies use 'golden handshakes', early retirement schemes, mass sackings and psychological warfare that makes someone's life so miserable they leave voluntarily. The culture of the organisation — and the value system of the individual managers — would help determine which methods would be used.

Schein (1983) is not as prescriptive as Sathe, but lists 10 means by which a culture becomes embodied in an organisation and is transmitted to new organisational members. Serious scholars of culture will find these means worth perusing; they range from explicit to implicit mechanisms such as:

- formal statements of organisational philosophy
- design of physical spaces
- deliberate role modelling by leaders
- reward and promotion criteria
- stories, legends, myths and parables about key people and events
- what leaders pay attention to, measure and control
- leader reactions to critical incidents
- how the organisation is designed and structured
- organisational systems and procedures
- criteria used for recruitment, selection, promotion and 'excommunication'.

Measuring culture and culture change

With no consensus of opinion on what culture is or whether it can be changed, one might well ask how it is possible to measure it. The first attempts to measure culture quantitatively came in the mid-1980s, when researchers and practitioners began to ask how culture could be used as a managerial tool. The idea seemed to be that 'you can't manage organisational culture unless you can measure it' (Reynierse & Harker 1986 p. 1). Most quantitative measurements involve surveys, questionnaires and structured interviews, the main weakness of which is that they cannot uncover assumptions that are often non-debatable and unconscious. Attempts to measure culture continue and, while we have not come as far as we need to, research is still being done.

Controversies of culture theory

Culture as a control mechanism

Earlier on, I looked at the question of whether it is *possible* to change a culture. Now I want to look at the far more difficult question of whether one *should* try to change culture. Is culture the prerogative of management and does management have the right to control it?

Until fairly recently, not too many people seemed to worry about such simple questions as culture's effects on the people who were part of it, or the moral and ethical implications of meddling with such things as feelings, beliefs, values and attitudes. Very rarely was culture written about as a *control* mechanism. It was seen as just another tool for managers to use in order to achieve organisational effectiveness and 'excellence'. Your opinion of culture as control will depend on your own view of the world and of management in general.

Strengths and weaknesses of culture theory

In giving an overall evaluation of culture theory, it is obvious that there are a number of both strengths *and* weaknesses. One strength is that the culture metaphor highlights the symbolic significance of every aspect of organisational life, and so focuses attention on a human side of organisation that other approaches ignore or gloss over. The human relations approach would claim to be concerned with 'the human side of enterprise' (Burns 1978), but it was only very superficial, concentrating on being nice to people in order to get them to work harder. Culture theory goes much, much deeper than that, concerned as it is with people's actual feelings, beliefs, values, attitudes and assumptions. People are seen as more complex beings than the early human relationists saw them.

Another strength is that it focuses on other than *design* aspects of organising, and takes things like language, norms and ceremonies into consideration. The rational approach totally ignored these more 'intangible' things. It also gives new meaning to the term 'leadership' and the role of the leader, because it is assumed that it takes a *leader* to change a culture

Finally, the culture metaphor has added to the questions about organisational change, which is now seen as more than changing structures and processes and technologies. For better or for worse, change now includes changes in the beliefs and values that guide actions.

But, of course, there are many weaknesses in culture theory, some of which I have already looked at. One of the most obvious weaknesses, discussed earlier, is the problem of definition and the imprecise understanding of its components. A good theory should precisely define each of its terms so that any study can be replicated by different researchers and yield reliable and valid results. However, each of culture's components remains an imprecise concept. As all management theories are *prescriptive* as opposed to scientific theories, which are largely *descriptive*, for a management theory to be a *good* theory it needs to be a good *prescriptive* theory that will help managers manage (Fulop, Frith & Hayward, 1992). Culture theory, because researchers cannot agree on what culture is or what its components really are, does not do this adequately.

This lack of a clearly defined and universally accepted language and the imprecise nature of the terms used to define culture also make culture difficult to study and reduce its usefulness in measuring inputs and outputs in an economic-rationalist society. It is very difficult to know how to go about changing these things — and even harder to know when you *have* changed them, and *how much* you have changed them. How can you change something you do not fully understand, anyway? This is not very encouraging for those of us trying to research in the field; and my contention is that we have not come any closer to solving these problems in 2000 than the early culture theorists had in the early 1980s. The so-called components of culture are still being defined with reference to the anthropologist Kluckholn (1951) or the psychologist Rokeach (1968) or not defined at all, researchers presumably assuming they have already been adequately defined. In addition, the fact that the concept of culture is an unfamiliar description of an organisation requires people to make a large leap in their thinking.

A second weakness in the culture metaphor is that it makes the assumption of unitarism. Generally, the culture-excellence approach to change is unitary — that is, it assumes that culture is a single entity, that there is 'a culture' that is common to the whole organisation, that culture is the prerogative of management and that managers have the right to change it. Culture *change* also assumes unitarism, because we are assuming that management has the *right* to change people's feelings, beliefs and values — even their basic assumptions about the meaning of work. Most of the culture literature assumes that management has the right to try to change people's values if it deems it necessary. This is extremely unitary, but it is often well disguised in symbolism and fancy words about the 'greatness' of transformational leaders who attempt to change their organisations' cultures (Lewis 1996a).

As far as culture being a single entity, there is really no consensus on that. In fact, many researchers believe there are *many* cultures within the one organisation. This makes 'changing the culture' an academic question. If there *is* no one culture, how can one change it? Unitarist theories do not give full recognition to the existence of differing goals in organisations, but consider that all conflict will be able to be overcome by the presence of a transformational leader, who will be able to unite people with common goals and objectives. All organisation members will work as a team towards these goals and objectives. Thus, the transformational leader will be able to unite the members of the organisation, shape their feelings, beliefs and values, and lead them on to greater heights of self-awareness and achievement (Lewis 1996a).

A third weakness in culture theory is one I mentioned earlier — the very tenuous link between culture and performance. This rather nebulous link makes measurement of culture change a near impossibility. Just because people's behaviours have been changed in some measurable way (which *is* possible to do), it does not mean the culture has changed. Of course, it might not matter; behaviour change is probably all most managers are interested in, anyway. However, as behaviour change does not necessarily indicate culture change, it may be a false claim to say you have changed the culture of an organisation just because you have people behaving the way you want them to. Sathe is very much aware of that when he says you have to remove the external justifications for the behaviour before you can tell whether people have internalised the changes and will continue with their new behaviour patterns regardless of the external rewards or punishments.

A fourth weakness in culture theory is that, with the big hype about the culture-excellence approach in the 1980s and the meteoric rise in the number of consultants advising managers about culture change, people have tried to adopt 'quick fix' methods for achieving organisational success. Many attempts at culture change in the 1980s failed dismally, and there are numerous case studies to give testimony to that.

A fifth weakness of the culture approach is that, if we try to see culture in too concrete a way, then we are in danger of adopting just as mechanistic an approach as did the human relations theorists and the adherents of the rational approach. Culture, whether we like it or not, is not concrete; and trying to measure it and pin it down to specifics is *not* likely to work.

Finally, I question what the culture-excellence approach has done to the quality of life for people in organisations. It may be well and good to be committed to one's organisation and one's product, but it can also be very stressful. Organisations, in times of economic rationalism like the present, are making more and more demands on their employees. They are demanding 150 per cent effort and making people feel guilty if they do not give that effort. People are being encouraged to *devote* themselves to the values and products of the organisation, and then to assess their own worth in these terms.

Organisations are also going for 'lean staffs', which puts extra burdens on those who are left and who are expected to fully internalise the culture of the organisation. It is one thing to 'love the customer' and be 'hands-on, value-driven' (Peters & Waterman 1982), but at what cost to individuality? This is, for me, the greatest drawback to culture theory.

Future directions for the study and use of organisational culture

Predicting the future directions for the study and use of organisational culture is rather like gazing into a crystal ball. The best we can do is survey the current literature and look at where it *seems* to be leading.

Total quality management (TQM)

Around 1989 the concept of *quality* was introduced into the culture literature. The criteria for the Baldrige National Quality Program describe a quality organisation as one operating with certain underlying core values and concepts, including:
- customer-driven quality
- involved and active leadership
- continuous improvement and learning
- employee participation and development
- fast response
- design quality and prevention
- a long-range view
- management by fact
- partnership development
- corporate responsibility and citizenship
- a results orientation (Gore, 1999, pp. 164–5).

Terms like 'participation', 'teamwork', 'empowerment', 'learning organisations' and 'total quality management' have all become buzzwords; though the literature has never seemed to reach agreement on a definition for any of them. In spite of this, most researchers agree that total quality is somehow linked to culture and use the terms 'quality culture' and 'total quality culture'. They disagree, however, on whether TQM involves changing a culture to achieve total quality or whether it means using the existing culture and working with it. In 1990, the Conference Board indicated that TQM probably would involve a cultural change; but whether culture change is needed or not, managers and employees are urged to work together as a team, using training and education, communication, teamwork, customer satisfaction programs, quality processes and tools, sponsoring feedback activities and providing a supportive environment (Conference Board 1994).

Culture change is to be achieved through the media of *empowerment* and *participation*. Unfortunately, the meaning of 'empowerment' is like the meaning of culture itself — confusing and often contradictory — but revolving around the idea of the sharing of responsibility throughout an organisation so that employees at all levels can act as leaders and help the organisation's productivity and 'quality'. The meaning of 'participation' does not seem to be spelled out anywhere in the literature. The kind of organisation in which empowerment, teamwork and participation would occur would be a *learning organisation* (Lewis 1996b).

Not all researchers take this very unitarist and prescriptive approach. Boje and Winsor (1993) see TQM simply as a resurrection of Taylorism by arguing:

> ... whereas total quality management programmes are ostensibly methods of improving product quality, they typically accomplish this goal through the creation of a corporate culture which facilitates the use of psychological and social control and coercion. (Boje & Winsor, 1993, p. 67)

They argue that, rather than engendering employee 'empowerment', these programs 'seek to perfect control systems which produce and enforce uniformity...' (Boje & Winsor, 1993, p. 68). Many employees themselves have since echoed similar sentiments and this raises again the issue of culture as a control mechanism. Perhaps we shall soon see more discussion of culture in terms of control.

Business process re-engineering (BPR)

While interest in TQM remains and the link between it and culture will probably continue, the literature appears to be veering away from an emphasis on TQM and business process re-engineering (BPR) seems to be emerging as a preferred management initiative. While there are a number of similarities between TQM and BPR, TQM focuses far more on people. BPR involves a redesign of business processes to improve measures of performance such as cost, quality service and speed.

Both systems concentrate on *process* and start with the customer. However, TQM seems to work more — though not always — within the existing framework (the culture), while BPR seeks to break from existing practices. TQM is based on continuous incremental improvement, while BPR seeks a breakthrough. Gore (1999) believes that TQM provides a way to build a culture that supports improvement and that BPR is a result of frustration with the time it takes to carry through on a TQM initiative. A focus in BPR on 'tools' and specific improvement rather than on people, the use of outsiders and specialised personnel, all work against employee confidence and involvement.

Organisational learning

Organisational learning has recently been defined as 'the capacity of organisations to change themselves in response to experience' (Mahler 1997, p. 519), and learning organisations are defined by Senge as 'those that continually expand their abilities to shape their own future' (Senge 1992). Culture has recently become associated with the concept of organisational learning, with the idea that culture guides learning, and Mahler argues that 'specific elements of an organisation's culture may affect the capacity of the organisation to learn and may influence what it learns and how it learns' (Mahler 1997, p. 520).

Of course, there is nothing new in all this. Argyris and Schon had introduced the term 'learning organisations' as far back as 1978 and reiterated it in 1996 (Argyris & Schon, 1978; 1996). And culture theorists have *always* believed that culture has an effect on an organisation. Surely, then, it is only commonsense to believe that an organisation's culture will affect how that organisation reacts to new situations and whether the organisation is likely to learn from them or ignore them. Culture has always been a storehouse for past history and lessons, an interpreter for events and actions, and a designer of strategy. As such, the culture would determine whether an organisation learned from its mistakes or ignored them, saw events as opportunities or threats, and was pro-active or reactive in its strategies.

The newness of the learning organisation concept is that researchers and managers are beginning to realise the potential that culture has to influence the long-term learning of an organisation. The latest culture literature is verbalising and formalising the force that was always there in the background.

Competence-based management (CBM) and sustainable organisations

The most recent directions for culture have been links with the theory of competence-based management, which argues that an organisation can increase its productivity and create a sustainable organisation by developing competences that span business activities and by engaging in competence leveraging (Sanchez, Heene & Thomas, 1996). The creation of *sustainable organisations* will probably be the next direction for organisational culture, as organisations seek to change their culture to create a learning organisation that will enable organisations to create long-term sustained performance. Competence-based management is concerned mainly with increasing productivity, but those who are concerned about long-term sustainability say that managers of future organisations must do much more than this if they are going to survive in the long term. They must change their present economic-rationalist mindset, which is often exploitative of people and ecological resources, and take into consideration the interests of broader stakeholders than shareholders — the interests of the community in general, the biosphere and future generations. They must stop contributing to or subtracting from the ultimate viability of life on this planet, stop reducing topsoil, polluting oceans and rivers, and pouring toxic gases into the atmosphere (Hart 1997). According to Hart, the challenge for the organisations of the future is to develop a 'sustainable global economy: an economy that the planet is capable of supporting indefinitely', and that presently, 'in meeting our needs, we are destroying the ability of future generations to meet theirs' (Hart 1997, p. 67). This will require a major shift in terms of reference — a radical change in culture, which will transform organisations from being part of the problem to being part of the solution.

Strategic alliances

Business mergers have long been a fact of business life and many have failed because they did not take account of the differing cultures of the organisations concerned. Almost inevitably, mergers have become takeovers, with one business dominating the other in 'the way things are done around here' (Deal & Kennedy 1982). While mergers are continuing, many organisations are increasingly seeking to leverage their resources and maximise member benefits through setting up *strategic alliances* — not total mergers, but more cooperative efforts on specific ventures and the undertaking of joint projects. Such alliances are not likely to cause as much cultural trauma as mergers do, but lack of understanding of one another's culture and the effects it has on business activities can cause problems for an alliance as well as for a merger. The culture literature is only now beginning to show awareness of the problem, as alliances become more common.

Knowledge management

The latest buzzwords in the culture and related literature are 'knowledge management' and 'knowledge transfer', which are claimed to be successful ways of implementing culture change. The questions that remain to be answered about the concept of knowledge management are whether it really is something new and different or just a repackaging of old ideas that have always been part of management activity. Schein described knowledge transfer in the fifth of his 10 mechanisms that founders and managers use to embed and transmit values and assumptions: 'stories, legends, myths and parables about key people and critical events' (Schein 1983, p. 22). And Sathe implied it in his shared sayings, things, doing and feelings (1983, p. 7; 1985, p. 17). In fact, the study of human knowledge is as old as human history itself, having been a central subject matter of philosophy and epistemology since Greek times.

Even if knowledge management and transfer is not a new idea, it may turn out to be an effective way to transmit culture, as it reinforces the value of people and their contribution to organisations and makes use of the new technology of sophisticated information systems. Schein and Sathe did not have the benefit of the information systems now available to enable 'a policy of knowledge exploitation' (Gumbley 1998, p. 175). Perhaps it will wake managers up to the need to take more notice of it now as *one* method of culture change. An organisation in which knowledge transfer occurs is surely going to be a learning organisation and an organisation open to change.

Implications for organisations, managers and employees

Many of the implications of culture and its various offshoots have been discussed within this chapter. What *is* culture? Can you see it or do you have to infer it? Is it fixed or can it be changed? How can you study it? What effects does it have on an organisation? Can you measure it? Can it be used by management as a control mechanism? These are all questions the answers to which will affect organisations, managers and employees alike. Yet there are many other implications that still remain to be investigated. Many of the issues relate to culture change, which, in spite of the huge volume of articles and books written on the subject, is not satisfactorily dealt with in the literature.

What implementation process should be used?

The culture literature has traditionally stated that culture change is difficult and time-consuming and cannot be rushed into directly. Early researchers used the organisation development (OD) model of slow, planned change that concentrates on organisational effectiveness and employee well-being without disrupting the organisation's natural life cycles. OD emphasises participation, teamwork and problem solving. It was not until Dunphy and Stace (1988) suggested that sometimes change needs to be made fast if the organisation is to survive in a rapidly changing environment that the idea grew of rapid change (an action stage) followed by longer periods of consolidation. As yet, there are very few empirical studies that have been done on the success of transformations whose 'action stage' consists almost solely of power-coercive strategies by management. However, with the new interest in transformational leadership and the push to achieve quality, reengneering and knowledge management, a few authors are beginning to advocate coercion as a legitimate primary strategy for change under some circumstances. Dunphy and Stace, for example, consider coercion as a strategy for use when time is short, support for change is low, but radical change is necessary for the organisation's survival (Dunphy & Stace 1988, 1990; Stace & Dunphy 1994). In my own research I have attempted to investigate their theories, though much more research is needed (Lewis & Cunnington 1993).

What facets of organisational behaviour should be targeted?

If symbols, processes and forms are the embodiment of culture, then transformation should involve attention to all three areas. However, as I have tried to show in this chapter, not all suggestions for culture change consider all three. TQM, BPR and CBM concentrate on the *processes*; knowledge management concentrates on the *information*. Very few recently suggested methods of culture change follow the OD method of a focus on the whole organisation. Perhaps this is why so many attempts at culture change have been unsuccessful — managers wanting a 'quick fix' rather than being prepared to spend the time and money on a long-term, all-inclusive program.

What problems are likely to be encountered?

The pitfalls associated with attempting to change a culture are well chronicled in the literature and include such topics as management communication style, resistance to change, differentiation in the organisation and the incompatibility between different styles of strategies used to effect change. Overcoming resistance to change seems to be the problem that receives the most attention. However, of more use to managers and employees alike would be information on the *value* of resistance. Most books and articles on change assume that the changes that management wants to implement are all necessary and worthwhile and that resistance is something to be overcome. Yet they have forgotten that resistance may carry benefits, such as feedback on the changes. If nothing else, negative feedback may cause management to make more careful decisions and avoid rushing into some ill-considered action (Lewis 1996b). Resistance may also provide management with a gauge of the strength of employee feelings; it may uncover dominant power coalitions; and it may encourage management to rethink its communications with employees (Davis 1981).

Conclusion

This chapter has covered a number of themes. It has investigated the main trends in the culture literature, showing how interest changed from defining the concept to asking how it may be *used*. It discussed those aspects of culture that have been researched: whether it is observable forms or underlying shared meanings, whether it is fixed or can be changed, how it is created and transmitted, and how it might be studied and diagnosed. Challenging issues associated with studying culture were presented: exactly what effects it has on an organisation, how it might be changed to achieve better organisational performance, and how one might measure culture and culture change. Controversies that remain are debates on whether it is the prerogative of management to attempt to change culture and to try to control people's feelings, beliefs and values; and arguments on the strengths and weaknesses of culture as a *useful* management tool.

Where the study of culture goes from here is difficult to predict, but so far it has been tied to TQM, BPR, organisational learning, CMB and sustainable organisations, strategic alliances and knowledge management. Yet there still remain many questions to be answered, particularly for managers wishing to attempt culture change. What implementation process should be used? What facets of organisational behaviour should be targeted? And what problems are likely to be encountered?

The final question we need to ask ourselves is, 'Is culture a genuine theory or just a passing fad?' It is my belief that the idea of organisational culture has been around for long enough not to be considered as just another fad. Whatever its shortcomings, culture has added a whole new human dimension to organisational life. Perhaps we will never understand it, and it is unlikely we are going to be able to rely on it for precise measurements of relationships between inputs and outputs in the foreseeable future. But analyse the theory for yourselves. Do not accept *any* theory at face value. Most management theories are value-laden, unitarist and prescriptive. They tell people what to do and they usually take a particular point of view (or bias). They are therefore open to interpretation and analysis.

References

Argyris, C & Schon, DA (1978) *Organizational learning: a theory of action perspective*. Reading, MA: Addison-Wesley.

Argyris, C & Schon, DA (1996) *Organizational learning 11: theory, method and practice*. Reading, MA: Addison-Wesley.

Boje, DM & Winsor, RD (1993) The resurrection of Taylorism: total quality management's hidden agenda. *Journal of Organizational Change Management*, 6(4): 57–70.

Burns, J (1978) *Leadership*. New York: Harper & Row.

Conference Board (1994) *Global perspectives on total quality*. New York: The Conference Board.

Davis, K (1981) *Human behavior at work: organizational behavior* (6th ed.). New York: McGraw-Hill.

Deal, TE & Kennedy, AA (1982) *Corporate cultures: the rites and rituals of corporate life*. Reading, MA: Addison-Wesley.

Dunphy, D & Stace, D (1988) Transformational and coercive strategies for planned organizational change. *Organization Studies*, 9(3): 317–34.

Dunphy, D & Stace, D (1990) *Under new management*. Sydney, NSW: McGraw-Hill.

Fulop, L, Frith, F & Hayward, H (1992) *Management for Australian business: a critical text*. South Melbourne: Macmillan.

Gore, EW Jr (1999) Organizational culture, TQM, and business process reengineering: an empirical comparison. *Team Performance Management: An International Journal*, 5 (5): 164–70.

Gumbley, H (1998) Knowledge management. *Work study*. 47(5): 175–7.

Harris, LC & Ogbonna, E (1997) A three-perspective approach to understanding culture in retail organizations. *Personnel Review*, 26(2): 104–23.

Hart, SL (1997) Beyond greening: strategies for a sustainable world. *Harvard Business Review*, January–February: 67–76.

Hofstede, G (1986) The usefulness of the 'organizational culture' concept. *Journal of Management Studies*, 23: 253–7.

Kluckhorn, C (1951) The study of cultures. In D Lerner and HD Lasswell (eds) *The policy sciences*. Stanford, California: Stanford University.

Lewis, D (1992) Communicating organisational culture. *Australian Journal of Communication*, 19(2): 47–57.

Lewis, D (1995) Researching strategic change – methodologies, methods and techniques. In DE Hussey (ed.) *Rethinking strategic management*. Chichester: John Wiley and Sons.

Lewis, D (1996a) New perspectives on transformational leadership. In K Parry (ed.) *Leadership research and practice: emerging themes and new challenges*. Melbourne, Australia: Pitman.

Lewis, D (1996b) The organizational culture saga – from OD to TQM: Part 11, applications. *Leadership and Organizational Development Journal*, 17(2): 9–16.

Lewis, D (1998) How useful a concept is organizational culture? *Strategic Change*, 7(5), 251–60.

Lewis, D & Cunnington, H (1993) Power-based organizational change in an Australian tertiary college. *Journal of Strategic Change*, 2(6), 341–50.

Mahler, J (1997) Influences of organizational culture on learning in public agencies. *Journal of Public Administration Research and Theory*, 7(4), 519–40.

Martin, J (1992) *Cultures organizations: three perspectives*. London: Oxford University Press.

Meek, VL (1988). Organizational culture: origins and weaknesses. *Organization Studies*, 9(4), 453–73.

Morgan, G (1997) *Images of organization*. San Francisco: Sage Publications.

Peters, T & Waterman, R Jr (1982) *In search of excellence*. Sydney: Harper and Rowe.

Quinn, RE (1988) *Beyond rational management: managing the paradoxes and competing demands of high performance*. San Francisco: Jossey-Bass.

Quinn, RE & Rohrbaugh, J (1983) A spatial model of effectiveness criteria: towards a competing values approach to organizational analysis. *Management Science*, 29: 363–77.

Reynierse, JH & Harker, JB (1986) Measuring and managing organizational culture. *Human Resource Planning*, 9(1): 1–8.

Robbins, S (1983) *Organizational behavior* (2nd ed.). Englewood Cliffs, New Jersey: Prentice Hall.

Rokeach, M (1968) *Beliefs, attitudes and values: a theory of organization and change*. San Francisco: Jossey-Bass.

Sanchez, R, Heene, A & Thomas, H (1996) Introduction: towards the theory and practice of competence-based competition. In R Sanchez, A Heene and H Thomas (eds) *Dynamics of competence-based management*. Oxford, UK, pp. 1–35.

Sathe, V (1983) Implications of corporate culture: a manager's guide to action. *Organizational Dynamics*, 2: 5–23.

Schein, EH (1983) The role of the founder in creating organizational culture. *Organizational Dynamics*, Summer: pp. 13–28.

Schein, EH (1984) Coming to a new awareness of organizational culture. *Sloan Management Review*, Winter: pp. 3–16.

Schein, EH (1985) *Organizational culture and leadership*. San Francisco: Jossey-Bass.

Senge, P (1992) *The fifth discipline: the art and practice of the learning organisation*. Milsons Point, NSW: Random House Australia.

Stace, D & Dunphy, D (1994) *Beyond the boundaries: leading and re-creating the successful enterprise*. Sydney, NSW: McGraw-Hill.

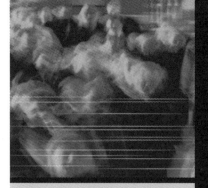

CHAPTER 12

The professionalising of management? Functional imperatives and moral order in societal context

by David E. Morgan and Ian Hampson

School of Industrial Relations and Organisational Behaviour, Faculty of Commerce and Economics, University of New South Wales, Sydney

D.Morgan@unsw.edu.au *and* i.hampson@unsw.edu.au

Introduction

What we know as modern management is a relatively recent phenomenon, confined largely to the twentieth century. We here define management as the control, coordination and development of economic activities, encompassing operational (internal) and external (strategic) domains. Management as currently conceived is *business* management, oriented to profit making, which originated with *industrial* management that emerged from the production demands of large organisations in the United States after 1860 (Chandler 1962, 1990). Through the twentieth century, business management recast the conduct of management across all sectors and institutions beyond the corporation, in a project known as 'managerialism'. The more recently coined term 'neo-managerialism', however, captures the novelty of its claims for societal influence since the early 1980s. The broad scope of these claims has given rise to intense questioning about the nature of management, in particular its moral stature and societal role.

The assertion of management professionalisation has long been contentious. The conception of 'profession' connotes technical competency, ethical probity, and selfless service — attributes often lacking in modern management. Public administration, management's antecedent, had little effect in shaping business management, despite the American adoption of the term 'business administration' for university-based management education. Indeed, this term partitioned the notion of 'public' or 'civil service' and *mere* 'administration' from what went on in business. Managerialist claims were altogether more grandiose, even encompassing notions of Platonic 'guardianship' and civic leadership. But it was always doubtful that profit making could provide a sufficient ethical basis for the putative profession of management, given the evident tensions between market and social processes (see Polanyi 1964). Even so, neo-managerialism has intensified in the past decade, the process prompting examination of its moral role. The latter comprises, first, behaviour that complies with moral principles; and, second, the contribution of management to the welfare, progress and leadership of society, entailing a social compact of institutionalised trust (see Preston et al. 1995, pp. 508–9). Evident tensions exist between this ideal moral role and actual management practice, which professionalisation may help resolve.

The issue of 'professional management' remains a vexed one at the beginning of the twenty-first century. Some argue that the trajectory of change is inexorably towards professionalisation (Andrews 1969; Schein 1988 [1968]), based on the technical demands of the work and skills set required, although some limit this to senior executive management (Raelin 1997).

While stopping short of advocating professional organisation in the traditional sense, recent writers have called for an occupational professionalism based on a critical education (Reed & Anthony 1992). Others advocate a professional attitude by management, which eschews management 'fads' in deference to the 'scientific' basis of management knowledge (Hilmer & Donaldson 1996). Still others argue that the nature of the management function precludes professionalisation (Whitley 1989) or may impair its societal role (Raelin 1990). This range of views points to an instability or incongruity at the core of the managerial function and its societal role, an instability that differentiates it from the recognised professions.

This chapter discusses the broad literature on professionalism, drawing out the key features of the prevailing conceptions of professionalism. Against these, assertions of management 'professionalisation' can be tested. It also explicates managerialist and neo-managerialist conceptions of the nature and role of management. We argue that the professionalisation of management suffers from tensions between the profit-making and 'ethical' roles of management. These tensions can corrupt the conceptions of managerial activity propagated in management schools, undermining the 'scientific' pretensions of its knowledge base. Further, while we have considerable sympathy with the ambition of professionalising management, particularly the injection of ethical considerations into management decision making (in contrast to their frequent absence), the mechanisms to ensure civic accountability are only weakly developed, and clash with prevailing notions of capitalist control. Finally, we sketch what we see as the path towards the professionalisation of management.

Understanding professionalisation

Interest in the professions and their role appeared before 1900 (Durkheim 1957; Flexner 1915; Carr-Saunders 1933; Parsons 1954), but only fully emerged as a research area in the 1940s and 1950s. Collins (1990, pp. 11–5) identifies four periods in the study of the professions that may be labelled the pre-conceptual period, 1930s–1950; the attribute or classic period, 1940s to mid-1960s; the control or revisionist theory, late 1960s to 1980s; and an emergent post-revisionist period in the 1990s. Each period is characterised by different assumptions about the nature of the professions and these shape the questions addressed, the research undertaken and the theory that emerges.

In Collins' so-called *pre-conceptual period*, the striking feature is that concern over professional status long predates the systematic theoretical consideration. In this period, the professions were largely considered as a particular category of occupation in broader studies of modern industrial occupations. In the second period, the *attribute model* emerged where a profession was defined by a number of attributes centred on the three core components of knowledge, discretionary judgement and positive societal role (see Collins 1990; Goode 1957; Moore 1970; Parsons 1954, 1968; Greenwood 1957; Merton 1960; Elliot 1972). Generally, they possessed a body of abstract knowledge deployed via the use of specialist skills and competencies that depended on a high level of discretionary judgement. In particular, the growth of science and specialisation has provided the abstract knowledge for more occupations to seek the prestige and status of the older professions. Moreover, the acquisition of this knowledge is associated with formal education from accredited universities or other specialist institutions.

While the traditional professions — medicine, law, the clergy — may be traced back to medieval universities, it is the modern state that has delegated to professional bodies the right to govern standards of qualifications and practice through systems of registration and licensing. In part, the reciprocal feature of the social compact this entailed was the ethic of altruistic service, characteristic of the professions. Disinterested expertise and altruism legitimated their functions, facilitating the acceptance of their expertise as authoritative and objective in institutions such as courts of law, from which flowed high esteem and prestige. Thus,

> the professions are marked by 'disinterestedness'. The professional man is not thought of as engaged in the pursuit of his personal profit, but in *performing services* to his patients or clients, or to *impersonal values* like the advancement of science (Parsons 1954 [1939] p. 35, emphasis added)

and knowledge and competence is

> put to *socially responsible uses* ... such as the application of medical science to the cure of disease. (Parsons 1968, p. 536, emphasis added)

By the late 1960s, writers came to question the usefulness of this approach and even labelled it little more than misguided special pleading for sectional interests (e.g. Roth 1974, p. 17). Accordingly, the analytical focus shifted to why and how the professions came to hold their privileged societal position — the essence of what Collins calls the *power/control*, or *revisionist* perspective. This approach focused on the manner in which the professions achieved privilege by actively shaping professionalising processes (Friedson 1970a, 1970b). The key lay in state protection and the support of political, economic or social elites (Friedson 1970b, p. 188), which could secure ongoing dominance over cognate occupations. However, over time the professions came to act independently of the initial sponsoring elites, via their potential to define social reality in their area of interest.

In an apparent paradox, the structure of the modern professions was grounded in the formation of the market for expert services, while at the same time the professions pursued exclusive and anti-market control — or exclusive jurisdiction — over their area of expert practice (Larson 1977; Abbott 1988). With a solid base in the social division of labour, the 'system of professions' (Abbott 1988) was seen to play a key role in the constitution of new markets in intangible and exceptional products. With the state's regulatory support, the autonomy of corporate professional groups allowed them to define their products, set standards and control occupational practice. In return for this monopoly, the professions allegedly demonstrated commitment to the values of probity and ethical conduct (Larson 1977, pp. 56–63).

Recent work on the professions has taken a different tack, characterised by what Collins calls a *post-revisionist perspective*. Recent market-based rationalisation has precipitated fundamental changes in the role and even challenges to the existence of the professions (Casey 1995; Crompton 1990). Deepening commercialisation is associated with issues such as:
- demands to lift restrictions on competition and advertising
- attacks on registration as monopoly
- the increasing redundancy of specialist knowledge.

Ironically, the response of professionals has accelerated the effects of the commercialisation process by blurring of differences between their work and that of non-professionals. Work fragmentation and specialisation, organisational rationalisation and market orientation have repositioned many professionals as a 'commercialised' service class (Hanlon 1994, 1996; Sommerlad 1995). New research has indicated a shift in the very meaning of professionalism away from technical competence to the mode of self-conduct and presentation, and the construction of knowledge fields (Grey 1998; Fournier forthcoming). 'Professionalism' can act as a discursive resource of control — as a disciplinary mechanism applied to other employee groups, to ensure that appropriate work identities and modes of self-conduct are adopted in the workplace (Fournier 1999).

This brief sweep through the literature on professionalism reveals two broad approaches. The attribute model emphasises:
- the acquisition of specialist scientific knowledge and skills
- the high social esteem and privilege consequent on the deployment of the skills and knowledge governed by an ethic of altruistic public service enforced by institutions of civic accountability, including peer review and state licensing.

The power, or 'revisionist', perspective and, following on, the post-revisionist perspective stress the role of power in the gaining of recognition by the state, and the social construction of relevant knowledge. There are profound issues here that cannot be addressed in this chapter, in particular the epistemological status of the knowledge underpinnings of professionalism. Nevertheless, it is clear that the claims to professional status of management are of the first 'attribute' kind, while analysis based on the second kind may be more useful to understand these claims.

Professional management and managerialism

Modern management emerged in the United States in the decades following the 1860s. The stratum of full-time non-owner salaried managers who controlled the functioning of organisations was seemingly ripe for professionalisation. This section explicates some key managerialist claims, and locates their emergence within a certain industrial milieu — the new mass-production industries in the United States.

The size and complexity of organisations created the demand for new functions in firms — initially in American railway companies (Chandler 1962). Here the production process required the standardisation of equipment and procedures to transport passengers and freight across wide geographical areas. A new group of employees — managers — provided the essential supervision and coordination functions for production. More generally, management integrated the multitude of pre-existing crafts required to supply mass-production markets, which involved the development of new activities and skills. The latter included large-scale design and redesign of jobs; the design of efficient machinery; and the coordination of more numerous and complex organisational functions — that is, 'recoupling' organisational parts to the whole (Litterer 1963). Thus the systematic management movement emerged (Litterer 1961) and spread to industries like armaments, agricultural machinery, machine tools, chemicals, petroleum, and many others.

A key factor in these processes was the significant expansion in the scope of managerial activities. An early advocate of such an expansion was the American Frederick Taylor, the founder of scientific management. In addition to work on developing extensive methods for organising operations in industrial management, he also insisted that the techniques of scientific management had general application to all organisations (Taylor 1964). Moreover, if his ideas were adopted, society as a whole would benefit, a view underpinned by a sense of moral obligation. For Taylor, scientific management was a *universal* organisational *theory*, rather than just a method of work design (see Braverman 1974, pp. 85–8), and applicable to whole organisations, whether government, churches, farms and even the home. It required no less than a complete 'mental revolution', as it entailed a new conception of management and its role in generating wealth for employees, customers and society.

Ideas promoting specialist functions and expertise found a responsive environment in the last decades of nineteenth-century America. Managers, engineers, economists, and a long list of others in middle-class America searched for status and authority. The culture of professionalism provided an ideal vehicle for occupational and social progress — it promised individual autonomy, technical mastery, and social status to all who could qualify:

> The culture of professionalism incarnated the radical idea of the independent democrat, a liberated person seeking to free the power of nature within every worldly sphere, a self-governing individual exercising his trained judgement in an open society. The professional person grasped the concept behind a functional activity, allowing him both to perceive and to predict those inconspicuous or unseen variables which determined an entire system of developments ... The professional did not vend a commodity, or exclusively pursue self-interest. (Bledstein 1976, pp. 87, 88, 89)

A primary source of qualification came via the American university. It provided the external source of legitimation based on 'non-partisan expertise and technical know-how' for the professional image of American business and management (Bledstein 1976, p. 289). The first students' 'business school' was planned in 1869, although the first established was the Wharton School of Finance and Commerce in 1881 at the University of Pennsylvania (Urwick 1952, p. 14). The central professional qualification, a Master of Business Administration degree, appeared in 1908. By 1950, some 160 business schools were established in the United States, with over 600 other tertiary schools offering business and management degrees — far in excess of any advanced capitalist country.

By 1910, American management was established as a separate occupational group that specialised in the administration of large business organisations. The emergence of the multi-divisional organisational form increased the complexity of large corporations, creating further demand for administrative functions for organisational recoupling via integration and coordination. The new stratum of managers who performed this work were professional in the sense that its members were employees and not owners, derived their income from salaries and not profits, pursued a career in one firm (and were not independent agents), and claimed special *expertise* and authority. They came to control all the everyday activities of corporations.

The emergence of a hierarchy of management up to the board level saw the authority of the capitalist owner diminish to the extent that professional managers' control rose. Indeed, this separation of ownership and control was identified in the early 1930s by Berle and Means (1932) as a central feature of the changing nature of capitalism. They asserted that as a corporation grew its share-ownership became more dispersed, delivering effective control to professional managers. By the 1920s senior executives in large corporations emerged as prominent figures in public debates in the United States. Part of their aspiration to economic leadership was the claim of *social responsibility* of professional management who held the reins of power in corporate America.

The wide-ranging claims of managerialism centred on moral authority and guardianship, now spanning private and public management. Echoing Plato's ideal conception of rulership by Guardians, management elites, it was claimed, possess specialised knowledge, apply rational techniques and exhibit personal qualities of integrity, personality and wisdom that combine to build societal prosperity and good governance (see Scott 1992, pp. 1–13). These features legitimated societal leadership, and legitimation was crucial to any profession. Chester Barnard, a leading American executive who spanned the corporate and academic worlds, viewed management as a calling that required 'a self-less commitment to a profession of transcendent social importance' (Scott 1992, p. 148).

Twenty years later, the doyen of management writers, Peter Drucker, echoed these views. His seminal book, *The practice of management* (1955), begins:

> The manager is the *dynamic*, *life-giving* element in every business. Without his leadership 'the resources of production' remain resources and never become production. Management is also a *distinct and a leading group* in industrial society. We no longer talk of 'capital' and 'labour'; we talk of 'management' and 'labour'. The 'responsibilities of capital' have disappeared from our vocabulary together with the 'rights of capital'; instead we hear of the '*responsibilities of management*' and ... the '*prerogatives* of management.' (Drucker 1955, p. 1)

Drucker concludes by arguing that the business enterprise is not an island, but 'an organ of society and serves a social function.' While the primary role of management is profit-making, its leadership role springs from its capacities to recast its own interests as part of the general interest (Drucker 1955, pp. 337, 345–6).

Later writers have also pointed to the importance of management in the latter part of the twentieth century and echoed Drucker's sentiments. For example, in a comprehensive survey of research on management behaviour and effectiveness, four eminent American management academics began:

> The *key* occupational group in an industrial society is management. Effective direction of human efforts — whether in the public or private sectors of the economy — is central to the *wise* and *efficient* utilisation of human and material. (Campbell et al. 1970, p. 1, emphasis added)

In an account of an American history of management thought, George concluded:

> Management is the determiner of our economic *progress*, the employer of our educated, the amasser of our resources, the *strength* of our *national defence*, and the *moulder* of our society. It is the *core of all* our *public* as well as *personal* activities ... As we know it today, it is in some respects, a twentieth century concept. (George 1967, quoted in Mant 1977, p. 10)

In a recent large inquiry into management leadership and skills in Australia, the authors wrote:

> Improving management skills is a *key* area of leverage for sustaining higher rates of growth in the Australian economy. ... management skills are the *foundation* for workplace *reform*, international *competitiveness* and improved *standards of living*. (Karpin Report 1995, p. 54, emphasis added)

Such claims span over a century of writing on management and display remarkably similar components. First, management is a *key, leading* or even *foundational* group in society, the very *moulder* of it. Second, the functional roles and technical skills of management are broad in scope and comprehensive in depth respectively. Management is the *active, life-giving* element in society that must and will deliver *progress*, ensure *efficiency*, drive *reform* and achieve *competitiveness* for organisational and national performance, at all levels and in all sectors. Third, the basis of the decisions must be technically competent, reflectively *wise*, and balance its *prerogatives* with *responsibilities*, as our very *standard of living* and even *national defence* is dependent upon it.

Management professionalisation: challenging issues

As we have seen, the essence of the 'attribute' model of the professions comprises:
- practice based in scientific knowledge
- an ethic of service and altruism
- state licensing and discipline by professional bodies which control practice
- occupational identity.

While in practice these features of professionalism may be rarely met in their entirety, they still provide a checklist against which professions can be assessed. The 'power' model points to the role of an active agency in securing professional status. This section argues that viewing management as a profession in the traditional sense is implausible. First, there have always been disagreements over the nature of management work, and there are strong tensions between earlier and recent conceptions, the latter laying greater emphasis on the fragmentation in management work. Second, the relation between the putative content of management knowledge — what corresponds to a 'science' of management — and management practice is profoundly unclear. In this discussion, we attempt to impose some conceptual clarity on this issue. And third, the nature of institutional regulation of professional management activity is similarly unclear, not least because it clashes with the nature of enterprise control in a capitalist society. This power dimension is unique among professions. This third issue will be discussed in the next section.

Management work

Specifying the nature of professional work should be a reasonably clear process — yet this is not the case for management. Early conceptions of the nature of management — associated with the 'classical' theory of management — saw it as primarily an objective, detached and mechanistic process. A much-used acronym summed up the nature of management work — PODSCORB (planning, organising, directing, staffing, coordinating, reporting and budgeting) (Gulick 1937, p. 13). It was essentially a prescriptive classification of management work, or for Max Weber an ideal type. He stressed that it is only 'from a *technical point of view* [that bureaucracy is] capable of attaining the highest degree of efficiency' (Weber 1964, p. 327, emphasis added). In general, the prescriptions of the classical theorists were rarely based on systematic research, but more on speculation cloaked in scientistic language.

Management is more than the exercise of technical skill, as a leading managerialist, Chester Barnard, noted as early as 1938. His classic book, *The functions of the executive*, discounts the view that organisations 'can apparently be reduced to organisational charts, specifications of duties, and descriptions of divisions of labour, etc.' (Barnard 1968 [1938], p. 267). Against this, Barnard (1968, p. 217) stressed the informal aspect of organisation, defining the executive function as 'first, to provide the system of communication; second, to promote the securing of essential efforts; and third, to formulate and define purpose.' Mere management utilised technical skills and competencies, whereas senior leadership required a wide range of 'general abilities' which are 'relatively difficult to appraise because it [the general abilities] depends upon innate characteristics developed through general experience. It is not greatly susceptible to immediate inculcation' (Barnard 1968, pp. 268-9). Barnard here points to the difficulties in specifying the nature of management work in terms of formal processes, of categorising underlying knowledge and abilities (now labelled 'competencies') required to perform the work, and the difficulty of inculcating these skills (apart from their mere technical foundations) through formal education and development. These are powerful obstacles to management professionalisation, which can be overcome only with difficulty.

Systematic research after the late 1940s has confirmed the multiplicity of capacities and skills required in management work. Reviews by Hales (1986) and Whitley (1989) stress the fragmented nature of management work and its multiple and conflicting demands and time pressures. Tasks are relatively unstandardised, and subject to inadequate provision for reflective planning and consideration. Yet, although fluid and difficult to predict, tasks are highly interdependent, and subject to an overarching concern with system maintenance and change, the consequences of competitive pressures and seemingly continual organisational restructuring (Hales 1986, 1993: pp. 9-14, 221-37; Whitley 1989). Recent bouts of organisational restructuring and downsizing, over the past decade and a half, have intensified these features. If the classical model of 'stable' organisations was ever applicable, it certainly is not today.

The characteristics just outlined have several consequences for management's knowledge base, and managers' attitudes to the latter. First, managers prefer verbal communication, and are reluctant to commit too much to writing. Managers prefer methods and knowledge that deliver an immediate payoff; they eschew concern over past events and 'academic' speculation, or explorations of the subtleties of 'mere' theoretical knowledge. These attitudes are a rational response to the nature of managerial work (Mintzberg 1980, pp. 29-53). Second, the rationality of 'theory aversion' is reinforced by the 'organisation-specific' nature of many problems, where standardised procedures are often ineffective. Third, distilling universal principles from the maelstrom of management activity or developing a research-derived broad knowledge base is a complex and difficult process. Management inherently involves the *discretionary application* of knowledge and ideas. Accordingly, no clear relation has been established between the acquisition of research-derived knowledge as such and organisational performance — for managers are often faced with the constraints of 'unstructured' problems, and the bounded rationality of action this involves (Simon 1957). Finally, access to the labour market, control over task allocation, performance assessment and rewards are all controlled by employers — not by any 'professional' standards, developed by a relevant professional body. Managerial work is even subject to a high degree of interpretation and manipulation, involving the 'management of meaning' (Gowler & Legge 1983) that creates a close normative alignment between management and its employers (Raelin 1990). This would make professionalisation difficult, a point to which this chapter later returns.

Tension between knowledge and practice

The above characteristics of management work precipitate problems in the relation between knowledge and practice, since the discretionary application of knowledge lies at the heart of professionalism. Two critical issues emerge here: first, the content of management knowledge and, second, the latter's relation to actual practice. First, in traditional professions, knowledge is essentially 'certified' and legitimated by 'scientific' procedures, whereas management has a highly porous knowledge base. This has given rise to the phenomenon of management 'fads', in which 'knowledge' that lacks intellectual credibility can still gain considerable appeal, and acquire purchase on management thinking and practice. Indeed, the lack of intellectualism itself is often a source of appeal. In response, fads have spawned a generation of 'fad spotting' (or revisionist) writing among management academics. One type seeks to repackage 'fads', by separating the useful aspects from the excesses (Micklethwait & Wooldridge 1997; Shapiro 1995). Another seeks to liberate management from their influence. In this view, good knowledge breeds good practice, bad knowledge (fads) the opposite. Therefore, fads must be weeded out, the scientific knowledge base of management asserted, and professionalism of management thereby advanced (e.g. Hilmer & Donaldson 1996).

Second, the relation of knowledge to practice is highly complex for management. In our view it is not at all clear that bad ideas lead to ineffective practice. Nor is the converse the case — that accurate analysis will improve management effectiveness. The question of ethics may be seen in the same light. Indeed 'bad' (incomplete) knowledge often has the effect of masking tensions between ethical standards and the consequences of corporate practices. Thus, increasing awareness is often the first step in a political strategy seeking redress arising from poor practice. These tensions are endemic to capitalist business, where the imperatives of market competition may mean that following ethical considerations leads to loss of market share ('if we don't sell it to them, someone else will'), or otherwise diminish competitiveness in some manner. In these circumstances, an education incorporating and inculcating ethical considerations — and nurturing virtuous conduct — or an education enhancing awareness of the unsavoury consequences of corporate endeavour may diminish managerial effectiveness measured in terms of the bottom line. Here ethics can constrain ruthlessness where the latter is seen as necessary for performance.

While this analysis may be controversial, the following applies it to the 'professional dilemma' of management. We seek to classify types of management knowledge, and types of orientation to that knowledge, to achieve conceptual clarity with respect to the professionalisation of management. Despite the attendant difficulties in professionalising management, we contend that it presents a fruitful path for an improved practice of management.

Orientation to knowledge and moral order

Identifying a core of positive scientific management knowledge is epistemologically complex, in part as a result of the operation of the ideas market. On the supply side, Huczynski's (1993) review of management 'best sellers' shows that writing about business is itself big business. It is naive to believe that the motivation for this endeavour is simply a desire to spread 'the truth' about management. For what 'sells' is what counts. On the demand side, and as we have argued in the previous section, management work predisposes managers towards ideas they believe will be useful and practical — so much so, that the quest for 'useful' ideas swamps intellectual or analytical quality. Sensing this, even serious management 'theorists' have developed an eye for 'customer' demand and have simplified complex ideas and skirted analysis of the political role and nature of management. We take these latter two points in turn.

The pragmatism engendered by much management writing has tended to corrode the intellectual integrity of management ideas. As Lee puts it, ideas need to be presented to management students in an 'appropriate' manner, one that does not confuse them by 'overemphasising the complexity of life' (Lee, in Huczynski 1993, p. 9). Even academic researchers have advocated that theories offensive to managers be abandoned, since such theories may lead to the breakdown of cooperation between managers and academic researchers, resulting in loss of management support and research access (Donaldson 1995, pp. 184–6). Not surprisingly, educational and research practice based on this view has led to considerable oversimplification of many key ideas. But further, for Lee, the point of a management idea is not primarily its explanatory power, but rather its widespread *acceptance* by practitioners because of its perceived high 'usefulness' to them. The 'aim of an appropriate theory was not to be right, but to be useful' (Huczynski 1993, pp. 9-10) — to help managers' 'effectiveness'.

However, as we have suggested above, effectiveness might actually be *improved* by the application of ideas that obfuscate, disguise or mask the clash between the imperatives of capitalist competition and ethical considerations. Put another way, ideas may be useful because of their ideological nature. Such ideas may disguise the *political* nature of management. Thus, according to Huczynski, much organisation theory fails as an analytical endeavour, precisely because of its 'conscious or formulated refusal to ask any *fundamental* questions about the nature of organisation' (Huczynski 1993, p. 5, emphasis added). Such fundamental questions might probe too deeply into the relations between the managers and the managed, and unearth the 'capitalist imperative' — the way profit maximisation overrides other perhaps more worthy considerations. As Huczynski has observed:

> ... the capitalist system rejected any questioning of either the basic terms on which the management of the organisation was conducted, or of the political disposition in which it existed. These potentially troublesome questions were simply bracketed, acknowledged in asides, or obliquely referred to in externally determined matters such as the contracts of employment and their regulation by law. The political nature of organisation is rarely referred to directly in any of the popular management literature. (Huczynski 1993, p. 7)

Management theory, therefore, is built on a profound tension between prescription and understanding. Many analytically incisive and intellectually meritorious ideas lack recognition, while some truly suspect notions attain wide currency, enormous popularity and large sales. There is, therefore, no direct connection between an idea's intellectual significance and its popularity (Huczynski 1993, p. 3). If anything, management ideas grow in popularity if they can blend simplicity and practicality and in doing so challenge neither the intellect nor the sense of ethics. Accordingly, Huczynski argues, writers like Peters and Waterman convey simplified ideas through alliteration and memory hooks at the expense of intellectual depth and precision. The genre of 'Heathrow organisation theory' is defined by its simple, easy-to-read style and its 'absent centre' (Morgan 1989). It is popular *because* it shuns any consideration of philosophical and moral issues or deeper understanding of organisations. For the publisher and the writer, 'the use of a book ... [is] seen to be how many copies it sells and not what it tells us about the world of organisations' (Morgan 1989, p. 308).

However, the concepts of 'good' versus 'bad' knowledge can take us only so far. The market for management ideas is more diverse, and we attempt to impose some order on this diversity. Whitley (1988, pp. 48–55) identifies four types of knowledge about management, which we will call 'practitioner', 'consultant', 'prescriptive' and research-based. Each primarily addresses a particular audience — organisational colleagues, clients, managerial public and other researchers respectively — with a different goal. Consultants' goals are market-based — expansion, profit and repeat business. Similarly, the purveyors of popular prescriptions, whether consultants, writers or publishers, also seek to sell books, videos and similar commodities. Their audiences are driven predominantly by a pragmatic concern with what works and accordingly purchase 'idea' commodities with a reasonable expectation of measurable gain. In contrast, research knowledge is aimed at intellectual influence on which the reputations of researchers are built. This orientation rests primarily on theoretical coherence, explanatory power, validity and similar measures of research excellence, rather than on the immediate concerns of management or publishers. Thus, knowledge ranges along a continuum from the practitioners' useful knowledge through to the researchers' abstract knowledge, and there is clearly tension between them.

The tension may be seen as a function of two dimensions that permeate management ideas. First, the *theoretic* dimension, which, although primarily concerned with understanding, must also contend with some users' preference for practical guidance. The second dimension concerns the manner in which the knowledge gained is actually used — what we shall term the *normative* dimension. Here we may distinguish between the instrumental orientation and ethical orientation associated with the traditional philosophical dualism between what 'is' happening and what 'ought' to happen in the practice of management. From this distinction flows a focus on ethics as constitutive of behaviour, rather than just formal reasoning. So in proposing a normative dimension we are concerned with the analytical delimitation of the foundations of behavioural decisions *irrespective* of the basis on which knowledge is derived. Thus, ethical action is intrinsically concerned with considerations of moral right, whereas instrumental action aims to achieve given ends whatever the moral consequences. These dimensions yield four ideal types, as set out in figure 12.1.

The four types may be summarised as follows. A practical orientation presents knowledge as essentially derived from experience but underpinned by a concern with 'doing the right thing' — a kind of moral intuitiveness. The professional orientation relies more heavily on generalised abstract knowledge and is applied with a similar concern for 'right conduct', although embedded in a framework of (constructed) professional ethics. This orientation is concerned with the constitutive role of ethical judgement in professional practice. The 'culture of mastery' and understanding of a specialism found in German management demonstrates a model based on the accumulation of expertise based on technical knowledge (*Fachwissen*) (Stewart et al. 1994, pp. 61–2, 112–3, 120–7, 160–4).

		Theoretic dimension	
		Guidance	Understanding
Normative dimension	Moral	Practical	Professional
	Instrumental	Realist	Strategic

Figure 12.1: Types of orientation to managerial knowledge

The strategic orientation is also based on the use of abstract knowledge, but is more concerned with securing net advantage from its application. It is oriented more to instrumental success than understanding and the maintenance of mutual relations (cf. Habermas 1984, pp. 327–35). In this sense, the strategic orientation may — and invariably does — consider the ethical aspects of a specific scenario only to the extent they contribute to, or detract from, net advantage. This orientation may be seen as employing a thoughtful consequentialist or utilitarian ethic. The realist orientation presents knowledge as essentially experiential and is often disparaging to the value of abstract knowledge. It is generally unconcerned with, even dismissive of, normative considerations, unless they have a material effect on behaviour or the capacity to secure advantage.

We have shown that the uncertainty and variation in the practice of management generates demand for knowledge and information, with a bias towards useful guides for action. Many managers see themselves as pragmatic, assuming (or not caring about) a moral basis for their actions. As we have seen, the prescriptive literature has responded, albeit with little concern over the moral implications of its ideas. The consultancy market has supplied similar guidance and neglect of moral implications, particularly where 'hard edge' advice is provided. Moreover, the little time for reflection that managers have tends to preclude issues seen to be outside everyday and direct business problems. Even influential and detailed outlines of the occupational standards of general managers fail to list ethical considerations (e.g. Management Charter Institute 1989). Thus managers remain concerned with what 'works', writers and consultants with what sells.

In summary, the unreflective concern with practical, hard-edged management can spell disaster. The absence of a broad, rigorous and critical education can result in an incapacity to evaluate the impact of management ideas on performance. In addition, low ethical and political awareness can result in a community backlash against corporate excesses, for which corporate leaders may be held personally accountable.

Professionalising opportunities and constraints: future directions

The rise of management has been accompanied by calls for ever greater societal power and influence. Indeed, the emergence of neo-managerialism centres on the claimed capacity of market-based managerial methods and techniques to deliver organisational efficiency and societal progress (Considine & Painter 1997; Terry 1998; Enteman 1993). It is in this context that the professionalisation of management must be viewed.

The ideal model of the professions (examined earlier) has three key characteristics:
1. a scientific knowledge base
2. adherence to ethical standards of pracice
3. regulation by professional bodies and the state to ensure civic accountability.

The previous section pointed to major problems for the assumption of any simple linkage between knowledge and practice, and to the tensions between ethical behaviour and the pursuit of private advantage. These tensions, to be sure, are present for any professional activity, but are surely more intense for management, driven as it is by the pressures of capitalist competition. However, these tensions on their own do not prevent professional orientation to knowledge and practice. It is argued in this section that appropriate forms of regulation ensuring civic accountability could greatly assist the professionalisation of management.

As noted earlier, the American culture of professionalism entailed a high degree of autonomy, a characteristic of most Anglophone countries. The professional operates as an individual, subject only to client assessment of service, authoritative licensing and enforcement of competence by the relevant peer professional body and the state. The attractions of this model must be balanced against the position of managers. Three components are central, which we will term 'ideal', 'technical' and 'behavioural' professionalism.

Ideal professionalism stresses professional practice oriented to an ideal. For medicine, there is the Hippocratic oath devoted to health, for law there is 'justice', for the clergy, spiritual salvation — each with a purpose beyond the corporeal world and self-interest. For management, the 'lofty ideal' of adding value is proposed by some (Hilmer & Donaldson 1996), echoing Peter Drucker's call of 40 years earlier. Grounded in this ideal, Drucker thought professionalisation appropriate for management, since it was 'the organ of society specifically charged with making resources productive, that is, with the responsibility for organised economic advance' (Drucker 1955, p. 4) and so deserved high status and reward. However, several flaws exist in this view. First, the nature of the service provided by managers is not unambiguously linked to any single or independent user, client or (in current argot) 'customer'. While shareholders and society may derive benefit or otherwise from the activities of managers, there is no direct link from the latter to the former. Second, performance is not easily measured, as it lacks a natural referent. Safe construction is an outcome of engineering, but what is the corresponding outcome of management? Value creation, wealth and/or profits (see Hilmer & Donaldson 1996). Yet each of these is subject to definition, shifts in accounting procedures, distribution and other factors. Moreover, high (short-term) profits can disguise maladies to be reaped in the longer term. Third, much management work, despite its outer individualist coating, is profoundly collective in nature, offering ample space for the misallocation of credit or blame.

Arguments for *technical* professionalism appear to be on stronger ground. These assert that a body of management knowledge exists, incorporating core disciplines (data analysis, economics, organisational behaviour and others), applied subjects (corporate strategy, change management, human resource strategy and so forth) and key skills (such as communication, negotiation and so on). These can be found in MBA curricula or in-house courses in Japanese or European firms. Yet the links between this academic curriculum and organisational performance are weak and complex, as we have pointed out.

Behavioural professionalism rests on ethical standards of behaviour. But it is worrying that two leading management academics in Australia admit having 'no ready answer' to the question of how ethics should be taught in business schools, despite ethics being central to the professionalisation project, as they themselves conceive it (Hilmer & Donaldson 1996, pp. 186, 190). Arguably management's greatest weakness is its *lack* of behavioural professionalism, deriving in part from tensions between the imperatives of competition and moral right. A constant stream of research, from Barnard's (1938) appeal for management freedom to exercise 'moral creativeness', to Dalton's (1959) approval of 'protective coloration' of compromise in the context of complexity and ambiguity, and Jackall's (1988) description of 'morality in use', all testify to the subordination of moral virtue to organisational expediency and positional power. Indeed some (Feldman 1996; Jackall 1988) have argued that the *very core* of management culture and practice obscures the *basis* of ethical choice, since management is rooted in instrumental rationality that denies legitimacy to alternative normative orientations. The introduction of ethical considerations in these circumstances is likely to present major difficulties.

If management is to adopt a professional orientation to knowledge and action, a system of enforcement of professional responsibility, in line with those of the established professions, must be adopted. This would oversee the implementation of managerial codes of conduct, and offer redress to victims of managerial moral transgressions. In our view, if management is to acquire the legitimacy of the established professions, civic accountability is the necessary and vital concomitant. Civic accountability may be defined as responsibility for professional performance encompassing technical competence and, ethical probity, whereas public accountability refers to compliance with established regulatory and procedural rules. Incompetence, incapacity and ethical transgressions are all grounds for exclusion from the right to practise — one is struck off, debarred as the case may be — in the professions. At present, no equivalent sanction may be brought to bear on management, although association with failed companies can bring temporary exclusion. The project of management professionalisation, as conceived by Hilmer and Donaldson for example, is a plea for management to be accorded the 'status' of professionalism, with few of the regulatory procedures that ensure civic accountability (Morgan & Hampson 1998).

The responsibility and high rewards claimed by management can be expected to attract increasing calls for civic accountability. The practice of management has been made subject to the provisions of legislation on human rights, antidiscrimination, environmental protection and a range of other issues over recent years (see Fisher 1996). This, we contend, is not purely the result of growing public distrust, suspicion or even anger towards management (although we agree this plays a part), but a predictable and systemic corollary of the claim to a key societal role. Moreover, since the provision of specialist services (inherent in the professions) is a central feature of the social compact between providers and the wider society, the responsibilities of this compact have been increasingly registered by the judicial system. Thus, the traditional individual and subjective assessment of standards of the skill of company directors in law has been recently raised to a higher objective standard with respect to duty of care and negligence. No longer is culpability limited by lack of personal knowledge and experience, but directors *must* possess *relevant* skills to exercise reasonable judgement (Lipton & Herzberg 1999, pp. 314-6). Appropriate education, experience, judgement and integrity must all play a part in such a legal assessment. The principle of accountability for the duty to exercise care and skill has been extended to senior management officers. As one judge commented: 'as the chief executive officer and managing director ..., he [Clark] was obliged to bring to bear an *appropriate level of skill having regard to the responsibilities* which the office entailed ... he must *unquestionably be regarded as responsible* for the overall control of operations ... both in a day to day sense and in giving effect to the broader policies [of the bank]' (Perry J, *South Australia v. Clark*, 1996 cited in Lipton & Herzberg 1999, p. 317, emphasis added).

The imposition of greater civic accountability in this manner has implications for management education and the formation of the knowledge base of management. The bifurcation between instrumental (non-ethical) and professional approaches would tend to disappear. For, as ethical standards became imposed on management actions with more serious consequences, playing down the political and ethical dimensions of management activity, in deference to discomforted 'customer' — students, would no longer be tacitly acceptable educational practice. Moreover, the imposition of greater accountability on management educators would necessitate the latter making due efforts to ensure their students are aware of the political aspects of the role of management, its ethical correlates, and the consequences of non-compliance.

Conclusion

This chapter examined the issues and justification surrounding the professionalisation of management. It drew out the key features of the prevailing conceptions of professionalism. It also examined managerialist and neo-managerialist conceptions of the nature and role of management. We argued that the professionalisation of management suffers from tensions between the profit-making and 'ethical' roles of management. We made it clear that while we have considerable sympathy with the ambition of professionalising management, particularly the injection of ethical considerations into management decision making, the mechanisms to ensure civic accountability are only weakly developed. Finally, we sketched what we see as the path towards the professionalisation of management.

Management is a central occupational group in modern society. It holds considerable sway over the everyday work experience of millions of employees; over the life chances of these employees and their families; over the formulation of government policy and the type and scope of government services; and over public debate, in the formation of agendas, problems and questions, as well as putative solutions and answers. The importance of management to modern society is unquestionable. What is questionable is the basis on which management exercises its considerable influence. Clearly, institutions that enforce civic accountability on other professions exist, if at all, only in a very rudimentary manner in the case of the putative management profession. As Anthony (1986, pp. 168, 182–3, 198–9) emphasises, the authority of management rests on the latter's consistency with wider social values embedded in the moral order of society. It is not sufficient, as Anthony (1986, p. 173) stresses, for management to take a purely instrumental attitude to ethics, under fear of legislative and political control. Management must take active responsibility for its actions. Advocating a practical and comprehensive *behavioural* professionalism, that incorporates technical mastery, critical reflection *and* ethical reasoning, and is policed by appropriate professional bodies and the state when necessary, is one way forward.

References

Abbott, A (1988) *The system of professions: an essay on the division of expert labor*. Chicago: University of Chicago Press.

Andrews, KR (1969) Towards professionalism in business management. *Harvard Business Review*, 47 (Mar-Apr): 49–60.

Anthony, PD (1986) *The foundation of management*. London: Tavistock.

Barnard, C (1968) [1938] *The functions of the executive*. Cambridge, MA: Harvard University Press.

Berle, AA & Means, GC (1932) *The modern corporation and private property*. New York: Macmillan.

Bledstein, BL (1976) *The culture of professionalism: the middle class and the development of higher education in America*. New York: Norton and Co.

Braverman, H (1974) *Labor and monopoly capital: the deregradation of work in the twentieth century*. New York: Monthly Review.

Campbell, JP, Dunnette, MD, Lawler, EE & Weick, KE (1970) *Managerial behavior, performance and effectiveness*. New York: McGraw-Hill

Carr-Saunders, AM (1933) *Professions: their organization and place in society*. Oxford: Clarendon Press.

Casey, C (1995) *Work, self and society after industrialism*. London: Routledge.

Chandler, A (1962) *Strategy and structure: chapters in the history of the industrial enterprise*. Cambridge, MA: MIT Press

Chandler, AD (1990) *Scale and scope: the dynamics of industrial capitalism*. Cambridge, MA: Belknap Press.

Collins, R (1990) Changing conceptions in the sociology of professions. In R Torstendall & M Burrage (eds) *The formation of professions*. London: Sage, pp. 11–23.

Crompton, R (1990) Professions in the current context. *Work, employment and society*. Special Issue, 4: 147–66.

Considine, M & Painter, M (1997) *Managerialism: the great debate*. Melbourne: Melbourne University Press.

Dalton, R (1959) *Men who manage*. New York: Wiley.

Donaldson, L (1995) *American anti-management theories of organisation: a critique of paradigm proliferation*. Cambridge: Cambridge University Press.

Drucker, P (1955) *The practice of management*. London: Heinemann.

Durkheim, E (1957) *Professional ethics and civic morals*. Translated by C Brookfield. London: Routledge and Kegan Paul.

Elliot, P (1972) *The sociology of the professions*. London: Macmillan.

Enteman, W (1993) *Managerialism: the emergence of a new ideology*. Madison: University of Wisconsin Press.

Feldman, SP (1996) The ethics of shifting ties: management theory and the breakdown of culture in modernity. *Journal of Management Studies*, 33(3): 283–99.

Fisher, S (ed.) (1996) *The law of commercial and professional relationships*. Melbourne: FT Law and Tax.

Flexner, A (1915) *Is social work a profession?* New York: New York School of Philanthropy, Studies in Social Work, no. 4.

Fournier, V (1999) The appeal to 'professionalism' as a disciplinary mechanism. *Sociological Review*, 47(2): 280–307.

Fournier, V (forthcoming) Boundary work and the (un-)making of the professions. In N Malin (ed.) Professionalism, boundaries and the workplace.

Friedson, E (1970a) *Profession of medicine: the structure of medical care*. New York: Dodd, Mead and Co.

Friedson, E (1970b) *Professional dominance: the structure of medical care*. Chicago: Aldine-Atherton.

Goode, WJ (1957) Community within a community: the professions. *American sociological review*, 22: 194–200.

Gowler, D & Legge, K (1983) The meaning of management and the management of meaning: a view from social anthropology. In MD Earl (ed.). *Perspectives on Management*. Oxford: Oxford University Press.

Greenwood, E (1957) Attributes of a profession. *Social Work*, 2 (July): 44–55.

Grey, C (1998) On being a professional in a 'big six' firm. *Accounting, organizations and society*, 23(5/6): 569–87.

Gulick, LH (1937) Notes on the theory of organization. In LH Gulick and LF Urwick (eds) *Papers on the science of administration*. New York: Columbia University Press.

Habermas, J (1984) *The theory of communicative action*. Boston: Beacon.

Hales, C (1986) What do managers do? A critical review of the evidence. *Journal of Management Studies*, 33(6): 731–56.

Hanlon, G (1994) *The commercialisation of accountancy: flexible accumulation and the transformation of the service class*. Basingstoke: Macmillan.

Hanlon, G (1996) Casino capitalism and the rise of the "commercialised" service class — an examination of the accountant. *Critical Perspectives on Accounting*, 7: 339–63.

Hilmer, F & Donaldson, L (1996) *Management redeemed: debunking the fads that undermine corporate performance*. Sydney: Free Press.

Huczynski, AA (1993) *Management gurus: what makes them and how to become one*. London: Routledge.

Jackall, R (1988) *Moral mazes*. New York: Oxford University Press.

Karpin Report (1995), Industry Task Force on Leadership and Management Skills. *Enterprising Nation, Renewing Australia's Management*. Chairman, D. Karpin. Canberra: AGPS.

Larson, MS (1977) *The rise of professionalism: a sociological analysis*. Berkeley: University of California Press.

Lipton, P & Herzberg, A (1999) *Understanding company law*, (8th ed.). Sydney: LBC Information Services.

Litterer, JA (1961) Systematic management: the search for order and integration. *Business History Review*, 35: 461–76.

Litterer, JA (1963) Systematic management: design for organizational recoupling in American manufacturing firms. *Business History Review*, 37: 369–91.

Management Charter Institute (1989) *Occupational standards for managers: key roles and their associated units of competence*. MCI: London.

Mant, A (1977) *The rise and fall of the British manager*. London: Macmillan.

Merton, R (1960) Some thoughts on the professions in American society, Graduate Convocation Speech, Brown University paper No. 37, 6 June.

Micklethwait, J & Wooldridge, A (1997) *The witch doctors*. London: Mandarin.

Mintzberg, H (1980) *The nature of managerial work*. Englewood Cliffs, NJ: Prentice Hall.

Moore, WE (1970) *The professions: roles and rules*. New York: Sage.

Morgan, DE & Hampson, I (1998) The management of organisational structure and strategy: The new professionalism and managerial redemption. *Asia-Pacific Journal of Human Resources*, 36(1): 1–24.

Morgan, G (1989) The absent centre: the neglect of philosophy in Anglo-American management theory. *Human Systems Management*, 8: 307–12.

Parsons, T (1954) The professions and social structure. In Parsons, T. *Essays in sociological theory* (revised edition), New York: Free Press

Parsons, T (1968) Professions. In D Sills (ed.). *International encyclopaedia of the social sciences*, Vol. 12, Macmillan.

Polanyi, K (1964) *The great transformation: the political and economic origins of our time*. Boston: Beacon.

Preston, AM, Cooper, DJ, Scarborough, DP & Chilton, RC (1995) Changes in the code of ethics of the US accounting profession, 1917 and 1988: The continual quest for legitimation. *Accounting, Organizations and Society*, 20(16): 507–46.

Raelin, JA (1990) Let's not teach management as if it were a profession. *Business Horizons*, 32(2): 23–8.

Raelin, JA (1997) Executive professionalization and executive selection. *Human Resource Planning*, 20(2): 16–27.

Reed, M & Anthony, P (1992) Professionalizing management and managing professionalization: British management in the 1980s. *Journal of Management Studies*, 29(5): 591–613.

Roth, J (1974) Professionalism: the sociologist's decoy. *Sociology of Work and Occupations*, 1(1): 6–23.

Schein, EH (1988) Organizational socialization and the profession of management. *Sloan Management Review*. Fall, 53–65 [first published 1968].

Scott, WG (1992) *Chester I Barnard and the guardians of the managerialist state*. Lawrence, KA: University of Kansas Press.

Shapiro, EC (1995) *Fad surfing in the boardroom: reclaiming the courage to manage in the age of instant answers*. New York: Addison-Wesley.

Simon, HA (1957) *Administrative behavior* (2nd edition). New York: Macmillan.

Sommerlad, H (1995) Managerialism and the legal profession: a new professional paradigm. *International Journal of the Legal Profession*, 2(2): 159–85.

Stewart, R, Barsoux, J, Ganter, H, Kieser, A & Walgenbach, P (1994) *Managing in Britain and Germany*. Basingstoke: Macmillan.

Taylor, FW (1964) *Scientific management*. New York: Harper & Row.

Terry, LD (1998) Administrative leadership, neo-managerialism, and the public management movement. *Public Administration Review*, 58(3): 194–201.

Urwick, L (1952) *Management education in American business*. New York: AMA.

Weber, M (1964) *The theory of social and economic organization*. Trans. T. Parsons. New York: Free Press.

Whitley, R (1988) Management sciences and management skills. *Organization Studies*, 9(1): 47–68.

Whitley, R (1989) On the nature of management tasks and skills: their distinguishing characteristics and organization. *Journal of Management Studies*, 26(3): 209–24.

PART 5
Managing the processes of organisational behaviour

CHAPTER 13

Exploiting differences: the exercise of power and politics in organisations

by Terry F. Waters-Marsh

Central Queensland University, Rockhampton
t.waters-marsh@cqu.edu.au

 ## Introduction

One of the most salient aspects of organisations is the exercise of power, yet few if any textbooks give managers and students of organisational behaviour any substantive understanding of this phenomenon. Two major reasons are cited for this failing. The first is the antipathy experienced by most whenever the topic is raised — we all need power and engage in political behaviours to create, maintain and strengthen our power, but at the same time we are very loath to admit it. Worse still, the creation and maintenance of power through political behaviour is often treated as a taboo topic of discussion. No one succeeds in organisations without power and its exercise through political behaviours; however, few are willing to admit they possess and use it. The second reason for the lack of understanding of the concepts of power and political behaviours is the lack of clear definitions of just what they actually are. In the new millennium, we can no longer permit such ignorance to permeate the management and organisational behaviour literature. Therefore, an alternative definition of power is proposed, one which focuses on the notion of differences.

The aim of this chapter is to make a preliminary attempt to engage the reader in a journey of discovery and reflection on power and political behaviour, by offering some divergent views on the topic. Some emerging themes in the study of power and political behaviours are also presented. In doing so, it is intended or hoped that readers will question their own conceptualisations of power and political behaviour and that they will seek to find new approaches and understandings, appropriate for the emerging organisational forms. However, the intention of this chapter is not to provide an omnibus treatment of the topic, nor is it intended to reach a definitive conclusion. Rather, if this chapter stimulates reflective thought and reflection on power, what it may involve and the resultant political behaviours that attend power, then it will have achieved its stated aims.

 ## Alternative definitions of power

When the plethora of textbooks on organisational behaviour is perused, it is noticeable that a significant portion of these texts is devoted to the topic of power and politics. Indeed, most textbooks provide a whole chapter dedicated to the topic. Similar definitions of power emerge from these texts. For instance, Robbins, Millett, Cacioppe and Waters-Marsh (1998, p. 437) define power as 'a capacity that A has to influence the behaviour of B so that B does things s/he would not otherwise do.' This is very similar to Gordon's (1993, p. 392) definition of power as 'the potential or actual ability to influence others in a desired direction.' Hellriegel, Slocum and Woodman (1992, p. 534) come up with an almost identical definition, that 'power is the capacity to influence the behaviour of others.' What these representative definitions have in common is probably their genesis in the seminal work *Power in organizations* by Jeffrey Pfeffer, published in 1981. Pfeffer analysed power from a sociological perspective in which power was seen as deriving from the division of labour that forms the predominant feature of organisations and hierarchical structures. He noted that, 'power becomes defined as force...sufficient to change the probability of B's behaviour from what it would have been in the absence of the application of the force' (1981, p. 3). He went on to note that power is relationship- or context-specific; that is, it is dependent upon the social relationship of the actors involved in the power process. As such, power in organisational settings is contextualised to the structural relationship between the actors created by the division of labour inherent in the organisational arrangement. Thus an actor will have power in one context but be powerless in another — the manager may have significant power in the office but be powerless in a community activity centre to which he or she belongs.

If so many writers of textbooks dealing with organisational behaviour adopt this general definition of power, does that not in and of itself lend credence to the definition? After all, if everyone believes the same illusion, does that illusion not become a reality? If the definitions could stand closer scrutiny, then we would probably agree that the rather normative definitions of power presented in textbooks were valid enough to rely upon them. However, there are many aspects of these definitions, which suggests that new definitions and/or conceptualisations bear further investigation and study. Dunford (1992) was very critical of these normative, rational definitions of power. He criticises these definitions as follows (Dunford 1992, p. 194).

> Power is a topic that has traditionally been off centre-stage as far as the study of organisational behaviour is concerned. Associated with the dominance of machine models of organisations ... has been the idea that organisations are neutral machines for achieving objectives and, if not performing in this way, that they 'damn well should be'. That is, any hint of power or politics has immediately been associated with the undesirable, with insufficiency. *Power* [original italics] has been treated as a pejorative term with its manifestation seen as indicative of the intrusion of vested interests and/or irrationality into what should be a rational objective exercise.

Another perspective on power was put forward by Kanter (1979, p. 65) who commented: 'Power is [the] last dirty word. It is easier to talk about money — and much easier to talk about sex — than it is to talk about power.'

Dunford correctly identifies the superficial nature of the definitions of power used at this stage in most organisational behaviour textbooks. Part of the problem lies in the assumption of a rational-logical arena in which the exercise of power occurs. Along with Kanter and the post-modern Foucault-inspired organisational theorists, this rational-logical assumption of organisations is challenged (Barnett & Finnemore 1999; Kanter 1979; Collins 1998). Central to the assumption of power being an influence attempt is that members of organisations share common perceptions and goals. As such, power would then be simply a means whereby these objectives are achieved and in ways which are collectively viewed as fair and legitimate. Clearly, this assumption does not stand close scrutiny. If all members of the organisation shared the same goals and objectives, then why would power need to be applied to persons to behave in a way contrary to the way they would have originally behaved? One would have to infer that the members of the organisation do not all share the same outcome expectations, necessitating some process to coerce desired behaviour. Hence, there is a need to exert power over the organisation's members. Further, it implies that organisations are rational entities where decisions and actions should all support the rationally determined goals and objectives. Therefore, any acts by members contrary to achieving the goals and objectives are viewed as deviancy and power must be exerted to effect the necessary remedial actions.

This criticism of rational views of power in organisations appears to be gaining increased attention over the last decade. In 1990, Drory and Romm argued that political behaviour as a result of the exercise of power could be divided into three broad elements — outcomes, means and situational characteristics. The first two elements will be referred to later in the chapter. They distinguished the third element, situational characteristics, by:
- conflict and uncertainty over the correct choices in resource allocation
- leadership approaches and styles
- goals and objectives
- the optimal input of ideas and information into the decision-making process.

These uncertainties precluded any assurance that the courses of action chosen by managers were the best of the possible choices and that political behaviour was certain to both shape and be shaped by the conflict inherent in such uncertainty (Drory & Romm 1990). Another facet to the exercise of power that Drory and Romm (1990) introduced to the rational organisation debate was the confounding impact of individual self-interest. Thus, the likelihood of the rational choices being the only ones selected was further tested by the notion that some decision makers would choose alternatives which satisfied self-interest needs, rather than rational organisational needs. In turn, power would need to be exercised by these individuals to 'coerce' other organisation members to accept and comply with these objectives chosen to satisfy self-interest needs.

Post-modern views of power give us an alternative to this rationalist view of power. In an article that attacks the rationalisation of organisational life, Feldman (1999) provides a clear exposition of critical post-modern theory with respect to power in organisations. Feldman's argument, founded on the work of Foucault (1977), is that power '… is a kind of social production process through which collective meaning is created and maintained. It is created and maintained in knowledge. Knowledge, then, becomes an instrument of power that people use in making sense of the world without fully grasping its implications' (p. 229). Thus, rationality is a construct created by persons attempting to make sense of their world, not that rationality is, in and of itself, real. Definitions of power, which imply rational decision making about goals and objectives, must therefore be suspect, to say the least. In Foucault's view, it is power itself that creates the reality and the illusion of any rationality is a construct developed to support the power creating the reality (Foucault 1977).

Feldman (1999) also provides a clue to a possible new view of defining power. He states that a key to modern power/knowledge regimes is the 'ethos of individualism' (Calas & Smircich 1992, p. 233). This can be seen clearly in the discipline of organisation theory that focuses on concepts such as competition, motivation, and leadership, all of which assume 'an autonomous, acultural, and ahistorical self' (Calas & Smircich 1992, p. 233). By focusing on the autonomous self, they tend to de-emphasise the relational aspect of organisational behaviour, such as conflict, class, and power (Steffy & Grimes, p. 1992). This decontextualisation results in the limiting of the self in the workplace because it leaves the effects of power/knowledge discourses unanalysed (p. 230).

But what if that power comes from some intangible inner aspect of self? This inner aspect does not need to be defined, only recognised that it exists and is somehow different from the situation, context or reality around it. Further, this inner aspect or difference is of sufficient nature to create a force which leads to altered outcomes in those around the individual possessing the difference. Whereas post-modern writers would argue that power is a social construct created to give shared meaning to the environment, this view of power argues that it needs only be an aspect of the inner self which, when given expression, creates a difference from which force is an outcome. Such a view of power opens new vistas to examine both past definitions of power and also opportunities to redefine the role of power in new types and forms of organisations. It also presents opportunities to reconceptualise power and political behaviour in organisations in such a manner as to liberate discussion and to remove the pejorative stigma often attached to political behaviour. In the same way that the interactionist view of conflict liberated the discourse and study of conflict, so too does the definition of power as a force created by difference have the potential to carry forward debate about power and political behaviour in organisations.

Power and politics: challenging issues

Sources of power

Most organisational behaviour textbooks present a framework or schema on the sources of power, after attempting to define what power is. The most common of these is that proposed by French and Bell (1958). They proposed that there were five bases of power: referent, coercive, expert, reward, and legitimate power. A closer examination of each of these five broad categories reveals that each represents something possessed by the holder of the power that creates its force. Thus, coercive power is predicated on the ability of the power holder to create fear within or possible retribution against the object of the power exercise. The difference between the power holder and the object over which the power is exercised is the perception of the difference shared by both the possessor of the difference and the object of the influence. In other words, it is not the fear, per se, that the powerholder imbues the recipient with which creates the power but the difference in power possessed by the power holder. Similarly, for example, expert power is reliant upon the difference in knowledge between the power holder and the object of the power exercise. Thus, if each party held equal knowledge, no difference would exist and, therefore, power would be absent. It could be argued from this perspective, then, that French and Bell's (1958) classification of power sources is really a list of the possible sources of differences from which power may emanate. French and Bell's (1958) five sources of power can be collapsed back to their main constituent, difference.

Foucault (1977, p. 194) argued that power was the source of reality and that it produced '... domains of objects and rituals of truth.' Thus, the distinguishing element between those with power and those without power was in the construction of realities or shared meanings — a sort of collective construction of reality. If this constructed reality included some form of recognition that one party held something that the other party did not, and that the first party had power over the second, then the real source of power was the perception, not of power in its own right, but of the difference that formed the foundation of the power force. In other words, power according to post modernism could be reduced to being a result of differences between the actors in the construction of the reality. It builds on Foucault's view that power is relational (Townley, 1994) and that it defines social identities by prescribing how the individual is in the world (Alvesson & Deetz 1996).

In the case of legitimate power, it is construed as the power conferred upon people as a feature of their role within the structure of the organisation. As Barnett and Finnemore (1999, p. 698) argued about Weberian arguments on the subject of bureaucracies and in relation to the sociological institutionalist approaches to organisational behaviour, structures '... by definition, make rules, but in so doing they also create social knowledge.' In other words, the structures, through divisions in labour and responsibilities, create differences between and among the social actors. It is these differences that are the genesis of the power, not the structures themselves. Thus, arguments for legitimacy as a source of power are not sustainable when viewed in light of the structures being based on differences, not the rules and authority constructs as the originators of the power. This argument does allow room for the sociologists to expand their institutionalist perspectives on structures in a constructive manner.

Political behaviour

How does the view of power being a force created by differences liberate thinking in regards to organisational behaviour? Most important, it releases the straightjacket of conceptualisation of power from an endless examination of the sources of the power. If we accept that power is a force created by differences, then an understanding of the potential types and nature of differences can yield a richer understanding of the possibilities of different human interactions within social contexts. It also creates the possibility for the social actors to move past the view of behaviours primarily driven by power as being somehow taboo or abhorrent. It may even liberate our view of political behaviour as being potentially healthy and, dare one say, desirable within organisational settings. Bate (1994) argued that organisations were strategies and that strategies and organisational culture were interchangeable concepts. Thus, he argued, organisations were cultures in which all their actors shaped and created and constructed not only their realities but also their shared meanings and understandings. In such a view of organisations, the exercise of power and power attempts to shape and mould the shared meanings and understandings would not only exist but would present both functional and dysfunctional potentialities. In the interactionist view of conflict, functional conflict is argued to be vital to the health of the organisation (Kanter 1979; Pascale 1990). Similarly, political behaviour that arises as part of the ever-shifting construction of shared meanings and understandings can be notionally construed as part of the conflict such activities would naturally give rise to. How could we then argue to support functional conflict while in the same breath decrying political behaviours? Indeed, one could reasonably argue that political behaviours and conflict are so inextricably linked that an attempt to eradicate one could be viewed as an attack on both. Political behaviours have as their foundation interaction between social actors on the basis of realities containing differences that create forces in terms of power as a reality. Conflict also occurs when there are perceptions of differences, particularly when those differences relate negatively to the objects valued by the perceiver of the conflict.

As noted earlier, some very interesting insights into political behaviour are starting to emerge. In 1990, Drory and Romm reviewed the literature on power and politics and found the definitions to be categorised around the purpose of behaviours (outcomes), the behaviour itself (the means) and the relevant context (the situational characteristics). This allowed a wider analysis of political behaviour: an analysis that encompassed conflict and organisational change. This had not been seen much before this time. Similarly, political behaviours and cultural change within organisations had not been widely studied. Part of this gap in the literature was due to a cultural bias that argued that change agents in cultural change activities needed to be apolitical and removed from the political arena. French and Bell (1995, p. 313), for instance, argued that, 'the role of the OD practitioner is that of a facilitator, catalyst, problem solver and educator. The practitioner is not a political activist or power broker.' Yet, as mentioned earlier, organisations are cultures and any change activities are going to change the culture. In changing the culture, the shared meanings that constitute not only the culture but also the construed realities will be altered, thereby stimulating a change in differences held by individuals and groups, and in the power thus created. In turn, political behaviours will be stimulated as losers of differences fight to protect their 'turf', and others who stand to profit in terms of differences being created by the changed shared meanings will attack the established 'turf' (Buchanan & Badham 1999a, 1999b). To argue that change agents should then remain aloof from the political behaviours in the resultant conflict is highly problematic, particularly when many authors present significant warnings on the political and influence tactics that may be observed in the change process (French & Bell 1995; Ackroyd & Thompson 1999).

Incorporating political behaviour into the study of cultural change emphasises the need to also seek some integration with the research into conflict within organisational behaviour analysis (Valle 1999). This point was emphasised by Ackroyd and Thompson (1999, p. 10) when they argued, 'texts or chapters dealing with organisational politics and power do have to come to terms with conflict.' Conflict is not something that can be 'managed away'; it has to be dealt with in ways that get at the underlying genesis of the phenomenon. By looking at political behaviour as an outgrowth of the forces associated with differences, understanding conflict can extend past the rather sterile analysis of organisational behaviour as being primarily about structure, contingency and performance (Donaldson 1985). In other words, conflict is an integral feature of power and political behaviour and should not be seen as having a separate identity or as being merely '... relatively routine "office politics", (Ackroyd & Thompson 1999, p. 20).

Another interesting area of study in the area of power and politics that is emerging is the extent to which the new communication technologies are playing an increasing role in mediating or accentuating political behaviours within organisations. Romm and Pliskin (1997), building on the work of Markus (1994a, 1994b), found in a number of case studies strong support for a model of *virtual politicking*. This model of virtual politicking was built on two dimensions:
1. direction — the direction of the influence attempt in the politicking behaviour being upwards or downwards
2. scope — whether the virtual politicking was confined to small groups or across the whole organisation.

Romm and Pliskin (1997) found that political players increasingly use e-mail at all levels of the organisation and the potency of e-mail's use as political behaviour is presenting organisations with significant new challenges and risks. Indeed, in and of itself, e-mail represents a power because of the 'difference' it confers upon those who possess access to it and/or can use it for political means. Romm and Pliskin (1997) identified four features of e-mail that create this power and its use as a political behaviour:
1. speed — giving its users the ability to act almost instantaneously
2. multiple addressability — giving individuals the ability to reach as many people as possible or as required by the situation
3. processing — the ability to store, retrieve or even alter email messages before resending them to others; and
4. routing — being able to create mailing lists for the routing of some or all of an email, depending on the intended political influence being sought.

In the same way that fax machines prevented the government of the People's Republic of China from silencing the events surrounding the Tiananmen Square, e-mail now threatens the power holders within organisations. Indeed, attempts to silence staff or control their political behaviours by restricting access to e-mail have become virtually impossible (Romm & Pliskin 1997).

Before leaving the focus on political behaviours, it is worth noting that there is a growing awareness that the pejorative view of political behaviour so widely reported in the organisational behaviour textbooks is starting to disappear in the research literature. Two factors account for this. The first is the view enunciated earlier in this paper that power and politics are as much a part of organisational culture as conflict is; indeed they are often closely related. 'Hardy (1996) argues that political forces provide a critical source of dynamic energy for strategic organisational change. To shut down the political action is to turn off this source of creative energy' (Buchanan & Badham 1999a, p. 14). In the same way that Pascale (1990) argued conflict is vital for healthy organisations, others argue for politics as being of beneficial value in organisations. Harrison (1987, as cited in Buchanan & Badham 1999a, p. 14) contends that politics has the following value to management:

- Such tactics can be used to counter the use of otherwise legitimate means to non-legitimate ends, such as the unreasonable assertion of authority by a manager.
- The political system makes visible those members of the organisation with the skills in dealing with power-plays and the intrigue and helps them to develop their political capabilities.
- Political debate helps make explicit all the dimensions of an argument, perhaps including issues that would not be readily recognised or encouraged by the legitimate system.
- Political action may be required to remove (bureaucratic?) blockages raised by the legitimate system.
- Political tactics can be used to facilitate the implementation of decisions reached by legitimate means.

To ignore the functional benefits of power and political behaviours would be to rob the organisation of a 'difference' that creates a power of its own.

The second factor that is leading to a breakdown in the pejorative view of organisational politics is the recognition that dysfunctional behaviour within organisations cannot be adequately addressed until it can be separated from political behaviours. In the past, without some legitimisation of political behaviours, it was difficult to distinguish between political behaviours and non-violent dysfunctional behaviours within organisations (Analoui 1995; Griffin, O'Leary-Kelly & Collins 1998). One set of behaviours has value, the other (the dysfunctional behaviours), necessitates remedial action by the organisation. This is particularly true in terms of performance — the first can actually improve performance (Egan 1993) whereas the second can damage or put the organisation at grave risk (Abraham 1999). Applying the wrong actions and measures to the acts of individuals and/or groups could cost the organisation dearly. Thus, by removing the pejorative view of political behaviour within organisations, increased value and diminished risk can ensue. In this era of increased litigation against organisations for stress-induced injuries, being able to differentiate between political and non-violent dysfunctional (often stress-induced) behaviours can save the organisation from significant legal liabilities (Quinn, O'Neill & St Clair 1999), not to mention the loss of valuable human resources.

Conclusion

The treatment of power and politics in most organisational behaviour textbooks is superficial, out-dated and in urgent need of radical overhaul. The first priority is to develop consensus around new definitions of what power is and what political behaviours are. The view that power is the force created by differences is advanced here as a more feasible definition than those commonly cited in organisational behaviour textbooks. Second, the superficial, rational-logical perspectives of organisations need to be re-examined and discarded where they are not appropriate in the power and political behaviour arenas of organisations. Third, a broader view of power and political behaviour must be incorporated into the analysis of organisational behaviour so that power is seen in the context and situational aspects of conflict, culture and organisational change. Finally, the pejorative view of politics needs to be discarded for a more profitable view that recognises both the functional and dysfunctional benefits/costs of political behaviour. It is hoped that this brief discussion and review will encourage the next generation of management and organisational behaviour students and scientists to at least examine the possibilities enunciated in this paper.

References

Abraham, R (1999) Emotional dissonance in organizations: conceptualizing the roles of self-esteem and job-induced tension. *Leadership & organization*, 20(1): 18–25.

Ackroyd, S & Thompson, P (1999) *Organizational misbehaviour*. London: Sage.

Alvesson, M & Deetz, S (1996) Critical theory and postmodernism: approaches to organizational studies. In S Clegg and C Hardy (eds) *Handbook of organizational studies*. London: Sage.

Analoui, F (1995) Workplace sabotage: its styles, motives and management. *Journal of Management Development*, 14(7): 48–65.

Barnett, MN & Finnemore, M (1999) The politics, power and pathologies of international organizations. *International Organization*, 53(4): 698–723.

Bate, P (1994) *Strategies for cultural change*. London: Butterworth-Heinemann.

Buchanan, D & Badham, R (1999a) *Power, politics and organizational change: winning the turf game*. London: Sage.

Buchanan, D & Badham, R (1999b) Politics and organizational change: the lived experience. *Human Relations*, 52(2): 609–29.

Calas, M & Smircich, L (1992) Voicing seduction to silence leadership. *Organization Studies*, 12: 567–602.

Collins, D (1998) *Organizational change: sociological perspectives*. London: Routledge.

Donaldson, L (1985) *In defence of organizational theory*. Cambridge: Cambridge University Press.

Drory, A & Romm, CT (1990) The definition of organisational politics: a review. *Human relations*, 43(11): 33–54.

Dunford, RW (1992) *Organisational behaviour: an organisational analysis perspective*. Sydney: Addison Wesley.

Egan, G (1993) The shadow side. *Management today*, September 1993: 32–41.

Feldman, SP (1999) The levelling of organizational culture: egalitarianism in critical postmodern organization theory. *The Journal of Applied Behavioral Science*, 35(2): 228–44.

French, WL & Bell, CH (1958) The bases of social power. In D Cartwright (ed.) *Studies in social power*. Ann Arbor, Michigan: Institute for Social Research.

French, WL & Bell, CH (1995) *Organizational development: behavioral science interventions for organization improvement*. Englewood Cliffs, NJ: Prentice Hall.

Foucault, M (1977) *Discipline and punish: the birth of the prison*. Harmondsworth: Penguin Books.

Gordon, J (1993) *A diagnostic approach to organizational behavior* (4th ed.) Boston: Allyn & Bacon.

Griffin, RW, O'Leary-Kelly, A & Collins, JM (eds) (1998) *Dysfunctional behavior in organizations, part A: violent and deviant behaviors, part B: non-violent dysfunctional behavior in organizations*. Stamford, CT: JAI Press.

Hardy, C (1996) Understanding power: bringing about strategic change. *British Journal of Management*, 7: 3–16.

Harrison, EF (1987) *The management decision-making process*. Boston: Houghton Mifflin.

Hellriegel, D, Slocum, JW & Woodman, RW (1992) *Organizational behavior* (6th ed.) St. Paul, Minnesota: West Publishing.

Kanter, RM (1979) Power failure in management circuits. *Harvard Business Review*, 24: 65–75.

Markus, ML (1994a) Finding a happy medium: explaining the negative effects of electronic communication on social life at work. *Association for Computing Machinery*, 12(2): 119–49.

Markus, ML (1994b) Electronic mail as a medium of managerial choice. *Organization Science*, 5(4): 502–27.

Pascale, RT (1990) *Managing on the edge: how the smartest companies use conflict to stay ahead*. New York: Simon & Schuster.

Pfeffer, J (1981) *Power in organizations*. Boston: Pitman.

Quinn, RE, O'Neill, R & St Clair L (eds) (1999) *Pressing problems in modern organizations (that keep us up at night): transforming agendas for research and practice*. AMACOM.

Robbins, S, Millett, B, Cacioppe, R & Waters-Marsh, T (1998) *Organisational behaviour: leading and managing in Australia and New Zealand* (2nd edition) Sydney, Australia: Prentice Hall.

Romm, CT & Pliskin, N (1997) Towards a virtual politicking model. *Association for computing machinery*, 40(11): 95–100.

Steffy, B & Grimes, A (1992) Personnel/organization psychology: a critique of the discipline. In M Townley (1994) *Reframing human resource management*. London: Sage.

Townley, M (1994) *Reframing human resource management*. London: Sage.

Valle, M (1999) Crisis, culture and charisma: the new leader's work in public organizations. *Public Personnel Management*, 28(2): 245–57.

CHAPTER 14

Could leadership theory be generalised?

by Ken W. Parry

Victoria University of Wellington, New Zealand

Ken.Parry@vuw.ac.nz

 Introduction

One challenge for leadership scholars and would-be leaders is the extent to which the findings about successful or effective leadership can be generalised across a range of situations and contexts. Management and leadership textbooks work through trait theory and behavioural theory, and punctuate that progression with the emergence of situational leadership. The latter debunks the generalisability of the preceding theories, but bogs itself down in a multitude of combinations and permutations of situational variables for which there is no successful taxonomy of leadership styles or behaviours. Next, the textbooks move on to the 'new leadership', which claims to have explanatory applicability around the world in most, if not all, countries, societies, and contexts. However, the new leadership is challenged in turn as being a rehash of the behavioural theories, or insufficiently situationally contingent, or neglecting of critical management roles and functions. So the cycle perpetuates itself.

The recurring theme is the extent to which 'leadership' is something that we can learn and apply readily to the leadership challenges we face, vis-à-vis the extent to which leadership is something that each of us has to 'recalculate' each time we are faced with a leadership challenge.

This theme is important for students and practitioners to work through in their own minds. If we think that leadership is a readily applicable general theory, then we would be frustrated by a difficulty in trying to apply the 'new leadership' theories (charisma, transformational leadership, and so on) to all the different situations we face each day. On the other hand, if we have to reassess our own theory and strategies of leadership for every situation we face, we will become frustrated by the mental workload. In reality, we probably have to do a little of both. There are some critical elements of 'general' theories that do hold up in the vast majority of our managerial situations, and there are times when we have to work out our own explanations and strategies. Perhaps if all practitioners can work out their own explanations of phenomena, and therefore their own 'theories' of leadership, the understanding and the application will come much more readily.

An appreciation of this theme raises the important issue of the extent to which 'leadership' has become blurred with the more traditional organisational challenge of 'management'. One way of resolving this issue is to find a new partner for leadership, instead of management.

Therefore, there are three themes covered in this chapter. The first theme is that, because of the lack of evident resolution of the leadership/

management debate, we need to rethink the nature of the relationship between leadership and management. A second theme is an outcome of the first. It is the proposition of a style of management called 'managership'. Managership is a style of management that contrasts with the leadership style. The third theme is rather different from the first two, but it is at least as important, certainly in a practical and applied sense. The third theme revolves around a perceived need to audit the social capital of organisations. These audit outcomes could be used as the basis for developing the capability of managers to improve the social capital of their organisations for the good of the individuals, of society and of the organisational bottom line.

Leadership and managership

Many scholars have examined the distinction between management and leadership explicitly and implicitly. There are various explanations of this distinction. Four options for summarising the relationship between management and leadership are:
1 two very different constructs
2 two overlapping constructs
3 leadership is one part of management
4 management is one part of leadership.
These explanations are now examined.

Leadership and managership are different

John Kotter (1990) has asserted that leadership and management are two very different things. He refers to leadership and management as having two very different sets of roles, functions and activities. Kotter argues that 'leadership' has been left out of 'management', with an overemphasis, reinforced by most MBAs, on planning, budgeting, organising, staffing, controlling and problem solving. He asserts that leadership is a different beast, consisting of establishing direction, aligning people, motivating and inspiring, and that successful organisations are good at both leadership and management. The point is that organisations that do their planning and budgeting without being strong at establishing direction and aligning people to that direction will achieve only limited success. Similarly, those organisations that are good at motivating, inspiring and establishing direction, but not effective at organising and problem solving, will face failure in a short space of time. Kotter insists that leadership and management are very different sets of functions, roles and activities in practical terms as well as conceptual terms.

Leadership and management are different but overlapping

Mintzberg (1973) determined that managerial work consisted of three roles — interpersonal, informational and decisional. 'Leadership' appeared specifically within the interpersonal roles, but many of the dimensions of the other roles also contained what could be called leadership imperatives. Similarly, Luthans (1988) categorised managerial activities into four headings: routine communication, traditional management, networking and human resource management. 'Leadership' never appeared in any of the detail of these categories, but one could interpret aspects of all four of them as being leadership activities. The same can be said of Yukl's (1998) taxonomy of managerial practices. Hence, it would appear that, far from being clear about the relationship between leadership and management, these authors have shown that leadership is part of a range of management roles and activities. Also, by exclusion, they have shown that leadership is part of a range of other roles and activities that do not come under the headings of 'management' or 'managerial work'.

Other authors (Stewart 1982; Kraut, Pedigo, McKenna & Dunnette 1989) have determined similar categorisations of managerial work. Stewart categorised styles, and Kraut et al. categorised activities. Neither mentions 'leadership' per se. This is not necessarily to say that they consider leadership not to be part of managerial work. Rather, it reinforces the suggestion that leadership is partly within the domain of 'managerial work', and partly something else. The extent of the overlap is not clear, however.

Similarly, Wright (1996) discussed 'managerial leadership'. The title of his book suggests that there are various forms of leadership, one of which is managerial. Within his work, Wright discusses 'management', and implicit within this discussion is the implication that there are various forms of management, some of which have a leadership dimension to them. Wright's work further reinforces the notion that leadership and management are different, although overlapping, beasts.

Mumford's concept of utilitarian leadership states that there is more to effective leadership over time than the combination of charisma, transactional management, and transformational leadership. He suggests a utilitarian 'hands on' approach to clarifying the benefits for all stakeholders, which will culminate in ultimate organisational success. Utilitarian leadership emphasises organisational problem solving through day-to-day leadership rather than through exceptional leadership (Mumford & Connolly 1991; Mumford, Zaccaro, Harding, Jacobs & Fleishman, in press). In addition to explaining an overlap between charisma, transactional management and transformational leadership, Mumford is almost suggesting another overlapping circle to explain the managerial 'task' of problem solving.

Leadership is a part of management

On the other hand, most management texts construct their content according to the four main functions of management: planning, organising, leading and controlling (or POLC for short). So conveyed, it is quite explicit that leadership is one of the functions of management. In other words, leadership is one of the things that managers do. This is a widely held viewpoint, and a very persuasive one. In a comprehensive assessment of the management and leadership literature, McKenna (1999) has concluded that our understanding of managing (vis-à-vis management) should embrace leadership theory as well as traditional management theory, and that, while there may be leaders who are not managers, managers must always be leaders.

Management is part of leadership

It is more implicit than explicit that some authors suggest that management is a part of leadership. Bass and Avolio (1994) refer to transformational and transactional leadership, and go on to elaborate that transactional leadership has most in common with the traditional concept of management. In fact, transactional leadership consists of management-by-exception and contingent reward, the latter of which is contractual in nature, and parallels the management-by-objectives function of HRM. The word 'management' occurs frequently in conjunction with the word 'transactional'. The main point is that effective leadership comes when managers enact (transactional) management *and* supplement it with (transformational) leadership. The key is to have a sound basis of transactional management/leadership and augment that with transformational leadership.

Kouzes and Posner (1987) have identified a range of (transformational) leadership factors that they have called challenging the process, inspiring a shared vision, enabling others to act, modelling the way and encouraging the heart. What some researchers have identified is that certain managerial actions are necessary to make this leadership work. Jackson (1999) has called it 'supporting the process', and echoes Mumford's utilitarian leadership.

Whilst explicitly stating that management and leadership are different constructs, it is implicit within Bass, Avolio, Kouzes and Posner's conceptualisations that 'leadership' is 'where it is at', and that management is a necessary component of making the leadership 'big picture' work.

Gary Yukl (1998) has summarised the literature under both headings, and acknowledged correctly that management and leadership can be thought of as two very different things, or two overlapping constructs, or even one subsumed by the other. In effect, Yukl's summation has confirmed that there is confusion about the relationship between management and leadership and therein lies the challenge for scholars and practitioners.

To summarise, leadership and management are different, with varying degrees of overlap or no overlap at all. Alternatively, leadership might be a part of management, or management might be a part of leadership. There is no obvious consensus about the correct answer to this potentially multiple-choice question, as Yukl (1998) has correctly identified.

Management and leadership: challenging issues

What conclusion can we draw from the previous discussion? One conclusion is that attempting to relate management to leadership is folly. Because we can find no answer perhaps we are asking the wrong question. Instead, perhaps we should recognise that we are not comparing apples with apples here. Leadership is an ability, and a style, and a process, which can be translated into a range of roles, activities, skills and behaviours. Management is normally thought of as roles, activities, skills and behaviours. Management is *not normally* written up as an ability or a style or a process.

In attempting to compare and contrast management with leadership, many authors are outlining the following very different conceptualisations of 'management':
- The first conceptualisation is the totality of the challenge that faces anyone who has to manage an organisation.
- The second conceptualisation of management is as the converse of leadership. It is within this conceptualisation that the confusion arises.

The many popular listings of the 'differences' between management and leadership are summarised in Table 14.1. These listings represent management as being the converse of leadership. Almost everyone has trouble with these listings. These problems take two forms. The first problem is that management is about things like initiating, delegating, and risk taking as much as it is about accommodating, controlling, and risk avoidance. Hence, management and leadership are not really mutually exclusive.

TABLE 14.1: Traditional contrasting notions of management and leadership

Management	Leadership
Accommodating	Initiating
Control	Delegation
Risk avoidance	Risk taking
Planning	Envisioning
Reactive	Pro-active
Distant relationship	Face-to-face relationship
Group orientation	Individualised orientation
Formal	Informal
Impersonal	Personal
Coercion	Encouragement
Transaction	Transformation
Avoid change	Thrive on change
Do things correctly	Do the correct things
Follow a plan	Communicate a vision
Stabilisation	Advancement
Position power	Personal power
Organising	Aligning people
Staffing	Motivating and inspiring
Monitoring	Empowerment

Source: Adapted from Kotter 1990; Parry 1996

The second problem with such listings is that when people say that 'leadership' is more effective than 'management', they are implying quite clearly that envisioning is better than planning, or that initiating is better than accommodating, or that risk taking is better than risk avoidance. This is an inappropriate conclusion to draw. The management characteristics listed in table 14.1 are just as important in organisations as the leadership characteristics.

Perhaps management and leadership are non-contrastable entities. Consequently, we may have been incorrect in attempting to reconcile management with leadership. Perhaps the listings above are extremes on a continuum of dimensions of the managerial challenge. On the other hand, perhaps the listings above actually reflect alternative styles or processes by which organisations can be managed — in effect, alternative styles of management. Each style is mutually exclusive according to each dimension, and one style might be superior to the other in certain situations. Certain activities, skills, roles and behaviours are required in order to enact both styles. Those activities, skills, roles and behaviours are 'management', and have been discussed in great detail in the management literature, and summarised very effectively in the opening chapters of management texts and organisational behaviour texts worldwide.

Proposing managership

In other words, we should be contrasting leadership with something other than management. Therefore, if we think of the converse of leadership, we should be thinking of it as ability, style or process. This can be contrasted with the abilities, styles and processes that are covered in the leadership literature.

I will call this contrasting conceptualisation 'manager*ship*', and suggest that managership + leadership = management. In so saying, I would support the stance that management represents the totality of the challenge that faces anyone who has to manage an organisation. In other words, leadership is one style of management and managership is the other style of management.

Let me now posit some characteristics of the 'managership' style that would contrast it with the 'leadership' style. These characteristics are presented in figure 14.1.

Both styles can be reflected in the ways in which management roles and activities are carried out. For example, Mintzberg's informational roles can be carried out in a *managership style* with an emphasis on:

- seeking information in order to determine exceptions and correct them, assign accountability for outputs, determine deviations from contractual obligations, and ensure conformity with planned performance
- passing on information directly to subordinates formally and impersonally in only sufficient quantity to enable them to undertake their immediate task.

Managership style	Leadership style
Transactional	Transformational
Monitor and control	Delegate and empower
Corrective transaction	Constructive transaction
Contingent transaction	Constructive transaction
Formal and impersonal	Informal and personal
Contractual mind-set	Collaborative mind-set
Prefers written contract	Prefers psychological contract
Emphasises accountability	Emphasises responsibility
Emphasises detailed written plans	Emphasises goals, strategies, outcomes
Emphasises conformity	Emphasises development
Rigid	Flexible
Hoards power	Disperses and develops power
Tends to Theory X	Tends to Theory Y
Favoured compliance strategies:	Favoured compliance strategies:
• assertiveness	• inspirational appeal
• appeal to authority	• consultative appeal
• sanction	• reason
• bargaining.	• coalition.

Figure 14.1: Managership vis-à-vis leadership

Alternatively, Mintzberg's informational roles can be carried in a *leadership style* with an emphasis on:
- seeking information in order to construct future goals and objectives, determine responsibility for outcomes, and determine developmental needs in order to achieve goals
- passing on information directly to subordinates informally and personally in sufficient quantity to allow them to see how their immediate tasks lead to goal achievement.

Of course, both styles can and probably should be employed, but an emphasis on managership at the expense of leadership will likely lead to less than optimum levels of job satisfaction, satisfaction with leadership, motivation, and performance.

Managers are responsible for the management of their organisation, even if the organisation consists of only two people. People who concentrate on the leadership style are 'leaders'. People who concentrate on the managership style could be called 'managerialists'. For want of a better term, let us stick with that one. 'Managerialism' is a concept from the public sector management literature, and bears a strong resemblance with the managership style of management.

By representing managership in this way, we can find an explanation that integrates the various existing conceptualisations of the relationship between 'management' and 'leadership'. This is explored in the following section.

Links to the management/leadership debate

John Kotter (1990) has said that management and leadership are very different entities, and that the most successful organisations are good at management and leadership. Perhaps he could have said that manager*ship* and leader*ship* are very different entities, and that the best-managed organisations (which are the most successful) are good at managership *and* leadership. In other words, all the aspects of Table 14.1 are done well and at the appropriate times. Put another way, successful organisations have a managership style that does the planning, budgeting, organising, staffing, controlling and problem solving well. They also have a leadership style which does the direction setting, aligning of people, motivating and inspiring well. In total, they are well managed.

Mintzberg's roles, Luthans' activities, Yukl's practices, Stewart's styles and Kraut et al.'s activities are all about the totality of management. As stated earlier, 'leadership' is implicit and explicit across these roles, activities and practices. They can all be undertaken with a managership style *and* with a leadership style (Mintzberg 1973; Luthans 1988; Yukl 1998; Stewart 1982; Kraut et al. 1989). Other research, particularly Kotter's and the transformational/transactional research, has shown that both styles will contribute to optimum effectiveness, although Mintzberg and Yukl were not concerned with effectiveness outcomes per se. Luthans' work showed that the most effective and successful managers were good at all four sets of activities and, therefore, good at both styles of carrying out those activities.

Distinguishing between managership and leadership is not inconsistent with Wright's notion that leadership can operate independently of management. He discusses 'managerial leadership', so by implication there also exists 'non-managerial leadership'. For instance, there is informal leadership, which we know to be dysfunctional if not managed well. Similarly, Wright (1996), Kotter (1990) and others have noted that management can operate independently of leadership. In effect, they are saying that a managership style can operate independently of a leadership style. Kotter has established that this can greatly reduce management effectiveness.

To the extent that Mumford's utilitarian leadership emphasises problem solving through leadership, he is advocating both managership and leadership (Mumford & Connolly 1991). After all, problem solving is a management challenge, according to Kotter (1990), and, in any case, utilitarian leadership includes traditional management activities which specifically refute 'new leadership' characteristics. Mumford's explanation of utilitarian leadership goes beyond transformational leadership, and in fact he is at pains to distinguish it from transformational and charismatic leadership. Implicitly, utilitarian leadership has a strong component of transactional management. Transactional management is central to the managership style.

Managership parallels the transactional management part of Bass and Avolio's transformational/transactional theory of leadership. Leadership, of course, is reflected in the transformational part of the theory. Bass and Avolio's theory demonstrates that organisational effectiveness is enhanced when transactional and transformational behaviours are present in substantial portions, and that organisational effectiveness is optimum when transactional behaviours do not outweigh transformational behaviours (Bass & Avolio 1997). Some situational contingencies for transformational leadership have been established. However, more specific ratios of managership to leadership are still subject to research confirmation. Because Kouzes and Posner's leadership theory reflects transformational leadership but not transactional management, it would reflect leadership but not managership (Kouzes & Posner 1987).

That leadership is one component of management is central to the POLC formulation of management. What the POLC formulation does not do is to couch the POLC components in terms of a style. Instead, discussion is normally couched in terms of functions and activities for managers to undertake. What managership provides is a synthesis of the POLC components of management, especially in terms of a managerial style that certainly does translate down into an already established range of activities and functions.

Relationship of managership to extant leadership theories

In terms of behavioural leadership theory, I would posit that the managership and leadership are conceptually similar to the long-standing categorisations of leader behaviours shown in figure 14.2. Each categorisation reflects a style of behaviour, and all of us have relative capability at each style.

Leadership approximates:	**Managership approximates:**
• Concern for people	• Concern for production
• Employee-centred	• Production-centred
• Supportive	• Directive
• Consideration	• Initiating structure
• Relationship-oriented	• Task-oriented

Figure 14.2: Traditional behavioural-leadership styles

In terms of an attitudinal style of management, managership also reflects McGregor's Theory X, whereas leadership more closely reflects Theory Y. Behavioural theories like Blake and Mouton's agree that the best leaders are effective at both categorisations of behaviours. However, it could also be suggested that management is most effective when leaders are effective at both styles. For example, Reddin's 3-D theory establishes situational contingencies for the application of Blake and Mouton's two factors. This does not mean that the managership-leadership dichotomy is just another initiation-consideration two-factor model. Rather, it is to suggest that the managership-leadership dichotomy helps to explain the two-factor theories of leadership. The two-factor theories have their limitations, but one should be wary of throwing out 30 years of two-factor behavioural research. Instead, one should acknowledge that they did concentrate on the 'leadership' domain at the expense of the wider implications for 'management' generally (see Robbins, Millett, Cacioppe and Waters-Marsh 1998 for a discussion of these theories).

In terms of situational leadership theory, I would posit that Fiedler's high and low control environments would favour the managership style, whereas the moderate control environment would favour the leadership style. High LPC scores might reflect a leadership orientation; while low LPC scores might reflect a managership orientation. Hersey and Blanchard's matrix of 'leadership' styles probably reflects a progression from a strongly managership style to a strongly leadership style of management. House's path-goal theory adds situational contingency to a similar continuum of managerial styles (see Robbins et al. 1998 for a discussion of these theories).

In summary, the emerging theory of 'managership' involves the following points:
- Management represents the totality of the challenge that faces anyone who has to manage an organisation.
- Management and leadership are not opposites.
- Manage*ment* = manager*ship* + leader*ship*.
- Leadership and managership are alternative styles with which to manage organisations.
- Managership is a managerialist style of enacting the roles, activities, and practices of management.

- The roles, activities, and practices of management are represented in both managership and leadership. However, they are carried out differently for each style.
- Managership is best represented by Bass and Avolio's transactional factor.
- Managership is best reflected in the list called 'management' in figure 14.1.
- Managership is also reflected in a managerialist, contractualist mind-set.
- Managership largely reflects 'management' as proposed by Kotter to be an adjunct to leadership.
- Managership partly reflects the behavioural styles known as directive, task-oriented, initiating structure, and concern for production.
- Managers can and should alternate between both styles, although personality is likely to favour one style over the other.
- Success and effectiveness are maximised when managers can reflect both styles, but with leadership exhibited much more frequently than managership.

Of course, much more work is needed on the concept of managership, but it does help to provide a means of understanding and reconciling the debate about the relationship between management and leadership. It also provides a readily applicable format with which managers can analyse their own styles, practices, systems and processes. Finally, 'managership' provides a means of determining a successful management style and strategy, and of predicting the effectiveness of that management style.

Attempting to resolve the issue of the relationship between leadership and management illuminates some allied challenges for managers of organisations. Those challenges, and the potential future directions that arise from them, are now discussed.

Future challenges and directions

One future challenge for practitioners is to be able to audit their organisations for the presence of leadership and managership. Organisations have sophisticated mechanisms to audit for financial and accounting outputs, but the auditing for social outcomes is quite rudimentary. The National Institute for Governance, in Canberra, is furthering the argument in favour of auditing for social capital in organisations and in society generally. The argument for organisational leadership audits has been put by Parry (1999b), and the case for auditing for social outcomes in organisations by Parry (2000).

Auditing the social capital of organisations

Social capital includes:
- social networks that help a society to function effectively
- voluntary associations that provide linkages between people
- a sense of connectedness between citizens.

These three components enable those citizens to be effective in their business and social activities (Institute of Policy Studies 1997).

Such social capital requires trust, voluntary association between groups and individuals, and opportunities to meet and discuss. As such, social capital is usually considered to be external to an organisation, is considered as a process, and is about 'community' development.

However, the challenge of generating social capital has much in common with the challenge of generating leadership in organisations. For the purposes of the debate, let us consider the *internal* social capital of organisations. The component parts of social capital that are listed above can be reflected within our organisations as well as external to them in the wider society. The internal social capital of organisations is reflected in such phenomena as:
- organisational citizenship — willingly doing more than is normally expected for the good of the organisational 'community'; organisational citizenship correlates strongly with the presence of leadership in organisations (Podsakoff et al. 1990)
- social processes — the linkages, interactions and outputs over time of social interaction; found to be crucial to understanding of effective leadership (Parry 1998b)
- transformational leadership — generating trust, being a role model, transforming motivations to higher and less self-serving levels of endeavour, encouraging performance beyond expectations.

Such concepts are frequently mentioned in the leadership literature, because leadership is largely about investing in the social capital of organisations. Let us now examine the example of leadership further, together with its impact on the social outcome goals of organisations.

Leadership as an example

Leadership outcomes can be identified and measured. Subsequent discussion will elaborate on how leadership outcomes such as motivation, perceptions, commitment, and so on can be identified, if not measured.

Leadership and its impact on the bottom line

Leadership improves the bottom line. In a major meta-analysis of the transformational leadership literature Lowe, Kroeck and Sivasubramaniam (1996) determined that effective leadership consistently has a positive impact on a number of financial and other measures of organisational performance.

Leadership is a source of sustained competitive advantage. Leadership is a long-term investment in the future, not a quick fix for the balance sheet. Because the investment is long-term, the advantages are also long-term.

Figure 14.3 helps to represent the last three items of understanding about leadership. It shows that leadership has a positive impact on the 'bottom line' of organisational output. However, that impact is not a direct impact. Leadership has an immediate effect on the psychology of the workforce. It improves the motivation, perceptions, attributions, commitment, persistence, understanding, organisational citizenship, integrity and satisfaction of the workforce. In turn, any improvements in these psychological outcomes will improve the behaviours and performance of the workforce, which in turn will have a positive impact on the 'bottom line'.

Figure 14.3 emphasises that one must ensure the organisation is meeting the intermediate social outcome goals (the social psychology of followers) as well as meeting the 'bottom line' output goals. This is for three reasons. First, meeting the intermediate goals indicates that effective leadership exists, and we know that leadership works. Second, the intermediate social outcome goals are important in their own right. They are a reflection of the social capital of the organisation. Third, meeting the intermediate goals helps to ensure the achievement of the 'bottom line' goals further down the line.

The problem of just concentrating on bottom-line output goals is that outputs might be achieved *because* of short-term and unsustainable actions, and *in spite* of the more sustainable benefits of leadership. For example, many organisations have pursued restructuring and downsizing strategies that have an immediate and quantifiable impact on the accounting bottom line. However, the loss incurred to the social capital of the organisation has often outweighed any short-term financial gain (Parry 1998a). It is akin to an athlete taking painkillers — the performance is achieved short-term, but the real problems are merely disguised. The athlete knows that sustained long-term advantage will accrue through a longer-term investment in treatment for the injury so that a career might be salvaged and lengthened. A tendency to concentrate on the bottom line outputs at the expense of the intermediate social outcomes is characteristic of the 'managership' style of management.

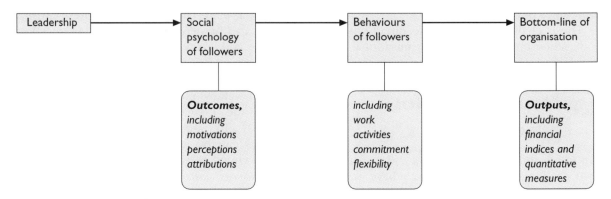

Figure 14.3: Leadership and its impact on the bottom line (adapted from Parry 2000)

Impact of the contemporary climate of work

Trends in restructuring, reform and downsizing have generated a number of outcomes in the perceptions, attitude, motivation, commitment and behaviour of workers. When assessed collectively, these outcomes amount to an increased sense of job insecurity and worker alienation from within large sections of the workforce (Littler et al. 1997). In summary therefore, the climate of work is often characterised by a selfish, cynical, short-term transactional, contractual attitude to social networks and relationships. This climate is representative of an excess of the managership style of management over the leadership style of management. This climate also reflects negative social process outcomes and a potential paucity of social capital. There is less time for the development of social networks. There is less discretionary time at work to engage in 'organisational citizenship' behaviours. There is less 'connectedness'. There is less trust. Therefore, there is less social capital.

On the one hand, leadership has a role to play in reversing these negative attitudes. On the other hand, and simultaneously, these negative attitudes have the impact of negating much genuine leadership throughout organisations. This paradox is a challenge for those in leadership positions. It is also a challenge for organisational systems and processes to maintain positive social outcomes in the face of rising job insecurity and worker alienation.

An HRM challenge to respond to this climate of work is to develop (including train), select, design jobs and manage careers according to leadership criteria. A concomitant challenge is to audit for the presence of the processes and outcomes of leadership.

These challenges and future directions provide some implications for organisational practice. These implications are now examined.

Implications for practice

An implication for practitioners and a concomitant challenge is to identify, and where possible to measure, the outcomes of leadership. As discussed earlier, the value of these outcomes is well known. What is neither so well known, nor built into organisational systems, is the routinised evaluation of the achievement of these outcomes. Some of the measurable leadership outcomes are:

- *Level of follower motivation.* Increased motivation has long been identified as an outcome of effective leadership (Bass 1990) and there exist several instruments with which to measure levels of follower motivation.
- *Types of follower perceptions.* The perceptions of followers and others about the effectiveness of leaders can be assessed with the multifactor leadership questionnaire (MLQ) of Bass and Avolio (1997) and other instruments.
- *Level of follower commitment and persistence.* The level of organisational commitment of followers can be measured with the organisational commitment scale (Mowday, Steers & Porter 1979).
- *Nature of organisational culture.* The organisational description questionnaire (ODQ) developed by Bass and Avolio (1997) is one means of identifying effective and ineffective organisational cultures.
- *Degree of understanding of organisational vision.* A clearly articulated direction for the department is characteristic of the accepted notion of the vision of a leader (Nanus 1992). Open-ended and semi-structured interviews can determine whether or not followers have taken in, absorbed and understood the strategic organisational vision of the manager.
- *Nature of follower attributions.* It is an established phenomenon that followers attribute very successful and very unsuccessful organisational outcomes to leadership, while they attribute moderate organisational success to factors other than leadership (Meindl 1990; Parry 1999a). The presence of these attributions can be determined readily via questionnaires and interviews.
- *Nature of leader values and of follower values.* The presence of a set range of validated values measures can be determined with the Rokeach value survey (Rokeach 1973). In addition, organisation-specific values can be identified via semi-structured open-ended questions.
- *Employees' satisfaction with their leadership.* The satisfaction of followers with the leadership of their managers can be assessed

with the multifactor leadership questionnaire (MLQ) of Bass and Avolio (1997), and with other instruments.
- *Organisational citizenship.* The organisational citizenship questionnaire (OCQ) (Smith, Organ & Near 1983) measures this important aspect of social capital.
- *Perceived leader integrity.* Employees' perceptions about the integrity of their leaders can be measured with the perceived leader integrity scale (PLIS) (Craig & Gustafson 1998).
- *Perceived follower integrity.* Perceptions about the integrity of followers, or subordinates, or colleagues, can be measured with the subordinate integrity rating scale (SIRS) (Parry, Craig & Gustafson 2000).

A further challenge is to *develop* managers (and therefore potential leaders) on the basis of these outcomes. It is a very different challenge to reward managers on the basis of these outcomes, because *reward* and punishment are the soulmates of 'accountability', and 'accountability' is the backbone of managerialism. 'Managerialism' is a style or philosophy normally associated with the public sector, and has a negative tone of being overly contractual, prescriptive, retrospective, corrective and punitive. After all, the social outcome goals of leadership are *means* to the end of improving outputs, not the *end* itself. The ends are the outputs that organisations must provide, and for which managers are accountable. Managers should be rewarded for achieving outputs and they should be accountable for outputs; they should be developed to achieve the outcomes that result in the outputs. Improving internal social outcomes is a responsibility, not an accountability. It is a strategy to achieve desired outputs, not the output itself.

Implications for individual employees

Each individual has certain strengths and weaknesses in their future leadership capability. The weaknesses should be interpreted as areas in which to concentrate future development, rather than as criteria for sanction or punishment. This development should be geared toward improving their managerial style so that leadership is emphasised over managership. This message is just as important for process, clerical and supervisory employees as it is for managers. The Centre for Leadership Studies in New Zealand has had success in improving the manifestation of desirable transformational leadership behaviours by 11 per cent, with only 4 days training, over a 3-month period. It has also been able to improve the satisfaction and extra effort of workers by 11 per cent in that 3-month time frame. Importantly, these improvements are consistent whether the leader is at the lower levels of an organisation, or at the highest levels.

Therefore, five implications for employees can be proposed. First, use the managership style *and* the leadership style of management in your daily work life. To couch this in terms of other conclusions drawn from research into leadership in Australia and New Zealand (Parry 1998c), be both transactional and transformational in your managerial style. This combination has a proven beneficial impact on individual and collective success. Second, develop both styles. Use activities and behaviours that are consistent with both styles of management. These activities and behaviours have been chronicled at length in the mainstream 'management' literature, and, as explained above, can be applied with a leadership style and with a managership style. Third, individual employees could have a leadership audit, or profile, done on themselves. Employers are looking for leadership capability in prospective employees. So, employees could use an existing validated instrument to profile their own leadership capability. This is hard evidence of leadership style, and would be personally beneficial for career enhancement. Fourth, employees should attempt to 'lead upwards'. Leadership relies more on personal power than managership does. All employees have personal power, whereas managers have positional power as well. So, leadership is open to all employees, and all employees can have a leadership impact on their managers. Remember that the transformational/leadership compliance strategies of inspirational appeal, consultative appeal, reason, and coalition do not require formal authority, and can therefore be used by anyone in an organisation. Fifth and finally, employees can expect that leadership from the top will filter down through the organisation. This filtering effect will improve the social capital of the organisation. As a result, the organisation as a whole will benefit, but importantly for the individual, their quality of work life will improve also.

An associated implication for practice is to understand the nature of the social processes of leadership, which in turn lead to the generation of social outcomes in organisations. Parry (1998b) has already identified this challenge. Most leadership research has been about the manifestation of certain behaviours that we know lead to desirable outcomes. However, social process research is about identifying the linkages, interactions and outputs over time of social interaction between and among people, found to be crucial to the understanding of effective leadership. These social processes will probably vary between organisational and industry cultures.

Conclusion

Three themes have been covered in this chapter. First, we need to rethink the nature of the relationship between leadership and management. This need comes from an inability after more than 20 years to resolve the leadership/management debate. Leadership and management are not comparable entities. Consequently, this chapter has proposed that we consider *managership* and *leadership* as two styles of management that together will contribute to organisational success. Therefore, the second theme is the proposition of a style of management called 'managership'. The third theme revolves around a perceived need to audit the social capital of organisations. These audit outcomes could be used as the basis for developing the capability of managers to improve the social capital of their organisations for the good of the individuals, of society and of the organisational bottom line. There exist several social capital criteria that are measured by existing validated instruments. The social capital of organisations can be audited as effectively as can the economic and financial capital of organisations.

References

Bass, BM (1990) *Bass and Stogdill's handbook of leadership: theory, research and managerial applications* (3rd ed.) New York: Free Press.

Bass, BM & Avolio, BJ (1994) *Improving organisational effectiveness through transformational leadership.* Thousand Oaks, CA: Sage.

Bass, BM & Avolio, BJ (1997) *Full range leadership development: manual for the multifactor leadership questionnaire.* Palo Alto, California: Mindgarden.

Craig, SB & Gustafson, SB (1998) Perceived leader integrity scale: an instrument for assessing employee perceptions of leader integrity. *Leadership quarterly*, 9(20): 127–45.

Institute of Policy Studies (1997) *Social capital and policy development.* Wellington, NZ: Victoria University.

Jackson, CRA (1999) *Managing and leading organisational change.* Master's Degree Thesis. Brisbane: University of Queensland.

Kotter, JP (1990) *A force for change: how leadership differs from management.* New York: Free Press.

Kouzes, JM & Posner, BZ (1987) *The leadership challenge: how to get extraordinary things done in organizations.* San Francisco: Jossey Bass.

Kraut, AI, Pedigo, PR, McKenna, DD & Dunnette, MD (1989) The role of the manager: what's really important in different managerial jobs? *Academy of management executive*, 3(4): 286–93.

Littler, CR, Dunford, R, Bramble, T & Hede, A (1997) The dynamics of downsizing in Australia and New Zealand. *Asia-Pacific Journal of Human Resources*, 35(1): 65–79.

Lowe, KB, Kroeck, KD, & Sivasubramaniam, N (1996) Effectiveness correlates of transformational and transactional leadership: a meta-analytic review of the MLQ literature. *Leadership Quarterly*, 7(3): 385–425.

Luthans, F (1988) Successful versus effective real managers. *Academy of Management Executive*, 2(2): 127–32.

McKenna, R (1999) *New management.* Roseville, NSW: McGraw-Hill.

Meindl, JR (1990) On leadership: an alternative to the conventional wisdom. In BM Staw and LL Cummings (eds) *Research in organisational behaviour*, 12, 159–203. Greenwich. Connecticut: JAI Press.

Mintzberg, H (1973) *The nature of managerial work.* New York: Harper and Row.

Mowday, R, Steers, R & Porter, L (1979) The measurement of organisational commitment. *Journal of Vocational Behaviour*, 14: 224–47.

Mumford, MD & Connolly, MS (1991) Leaders as creators: leader performance and problem-solving in ill-defined domains. *Leadership Quarterly*, 2: 289–315.

Mumford, MD, Zaccaro, SJ, Harding, FD, Jacobs, TO & Fleishman, EA (in press) Leadership skills for a changing world: solving complex social problems. *Leadership Quarterly*.

Nanus, B (1992) Visionary leadership: how to revision the future. *The Futurist*, September-October: 20–25.

Parry, KW (1996) *Transformational leadership: developing an enterprising management culture*. Melbourne: Pitman Publishing.

Parry, KW (1998a) Leadership competency: the human resource management challenge of the contemporary organization. *Management Development Forum*, 1(2): 7–27.

Parry, KW (1998b) Grounded theory and social process: a new direction for leadership research. *Leadership Quarterly*, 9(1): 85–105.

Parry, KW (1998c) The new leader: a synthesis of leadership research in Australia and New Zealand. *Journal of Leadership Studies*, 5(4): 82–105.

Parry, KW (1999a) Enhancing adaptability: leadership strategies to accommodate change in local government settings. *Journal of Organisational Change Management*, 12(2): 134–56.

Parry, KW (1999b) The case for organizational leadership audits. *Management Development Forum*, SUNY-Empire State, 2(1): 133–41.

Parry, KW (2000) Auditing for social outcomes: a new direction for management capability. *Canberra Bulletin of Public Administration* (accepted for publication).

Parry, KW, Craig, B & Gustafson, S (2000) Subordinate integrity rating scale (SIRS): an instrument for assessing leader ratings of subordinate integrity. *Leadership Quarterly* (under review).

Podsakoff, PM, MacKenzie, SB, Moorman, RH & Fetter, R (1990) Transformational leader behaviors and their effects on followers' trust in leader, satisfaction, and organizational citizenship behaviours. *Leadership Quarterly*, 1(2): 107–42.

Robbins, SP, Millett, B, Cacioppe, R & Waters-Marsh, T (1998) *Organisational behaviour: leading and managing in Australia and New Zealand* (2nd ed.). Sydney: Prentice Hall.

Rokeach, M (1973) *The nature of values*. New York: The Free Press.

Smith, CA, Organ, DW & Near, JP (1983) Organizational citizenship behavior: its nature and antecedents. *Journal of Applied Psychology*, 68: 653–63.

Stewart, R (1982) *Choices for the manager. A guide to managerial work and behaviour*. Berkshire, England: McGraw-Hill.

Wright, PL (1996) *Managerial leadership*. London: Routledge.

Yukl, G (1998) *Leadership in organisations* (4th ed.). Upper Saddle River, New Jersey: Prentice Hall.

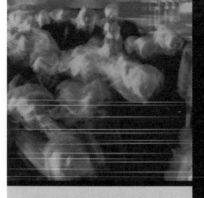

CHAPTER 15

The heroic archetype for leaders: integrating the old with the new

by Greg Latemore

Latemore & Associates Pty Ltd, Queensland

gml@ozemail.com.au

 Introduction

Back in the third century A.D., King Ts'ao sent his son, Prince T'ai, to the temple to study under the great master Pan Ku. Because Prince T'ai was to succeed his father as king, Pan Ku was to teach the boy the basics of being a good leader. When the prince arrived at the temple, the master sent him alone to the Ming-Li forest. After one year, the prince was to return to the temple to describe the sound of the forest.

When Prince T'ai returned one year later, Pan Ku asked the boy to describe all that he could hear. 'Master,' replied the prince, 'I could hear the cuckoos sing, the leaves rustle, the hummingbirds hum, the crickets chirp, the grass blow, the bees buzz and the wind whisper and howl in the trees.' When the prince had finished, the master told him to go back to the forest to listen to what more he could hear. The prince was annoyed and deeply puzzled by the master's request. Had he not discerned every sound already?

For days and nights on end, the young prince sat alone in the forest listening. But he heard no sounds other than those he had already heard. Then one morning, as the prince sat silently beneath the trees, he started to discern faint sounds unlike those he had heard before.

The more acutely he listened, the clearer the sounds became. A feeling of enlightenment enveloped the boy. 'These must be the sounds the master wished me to hear,' he reflected.

When Prince T'ai returned to the temple, the master asked him what more he had heard. 'Master,' responded the prince reverently, 'when I listened most closely, I could hear the unheard — the sound of the flowers opening, the sound of the sun warming the earth and the sound of the grass drinking the morning dew.'

The master nodded approvingly. 'To hear the unheard,' remarked Pan Ku, 'is a necessary discipline to be a good ruler. For only when leaders have learned to listen closely to the people's hearts, hearing their feelings uncommunicated, pains unexpressed and complaints not spoken of, can they hope to inspire confidence in their people, to understand when something is wrong, and meet the true needs of their citizens'.

The demise of state comes when leaders listen only to superficial words and do not penetrate deeply into the souls of the people to hear their true opinions, their true feelings and their true desires.

(Adapted from Kim & Mauborgne 1992.)

This story illustrates that while every leader must to some extent blaze his or her own path, every leader stands upon the shoulders of his or her ancestors. It is recognised that the study of organisational behaviour is indebted to many disciplines, including psychology, sociology, anthropology and political science (Robbins, Waters-Marsh, Cacioppe & Millett 1994, p. 22). Students of management and organisational behaviour are also encouraged to read literature and mythology to enhance their knowledge of leadership.

There is an amazing array of literature on leadership but, as Burns (1978, p. 25) said over 20 years ago, there is still much to learn:

> The fundamental crisis underlying the mediocrity of leadership and leaders is intellectual. If we know all too much about our leaders, we know far too little about leadership. Leadership is one of the most observed and least understood phenomena on earth.

More recently, Gary Yukl (1994) asserted that the sheer volume of publications, disparity of approaches and the proliferation of confusing terms is to blame for the confused state of leadership. Furthermore, the constructs of management and leadership are often misconstrued: each is necessary but not sufficient to produce organisational effectiveness. Bennis and Nanus (1985) were right in saying that many organisations were over-managed and under-led: there is much activity to ensure the planned and wise use of resources (efficiency) but often little commitment to ensure quality outcomes (effectiveness) among managers and staff generally.

The human element of a passionate dedication to higher ideals is also given scant and often cynical attention. What seems to be needed is a renaissance, a transformation of energy among managers and executives to ensure that new pathways are explored while honouring the 'treasures' of the past. Executives and managers must discern wisely, make decisions and mobilise genuine commitment towards goals. They must do this in a changing and turbulent operating environment where the boundaries are more confused than ever and the executive must manage ambiguity and diversity. As the demands made by stakeholders and clients increase, managers must discern and focus scarce resources more acutely than ever. As the need for organisational performance and effectiveness increases, the quality of leadership must be assessed and developed.

This chapter encourages a critical openness to the past by discussing the power and types of archetypes and integrates certain older viewpoints on leadership with more contemporary approaches. It draws upon the 'heroic journey' as an action-metaphor for courageous leadership and then addresses more recent understandings of leadership.

The approach used in this chapter draws upon the best of current thinking and practice in the realms of leadership while acknowledging the lessons of the past. As the ancient Persian princes were taught to 'ride a horse, shoot an arrow and tell the truth', so too modern managers must get the basics right (ride a horse), understand the opposition well (shoot an arrow) and relate well to their people (tell the truth). Closer to our own time, another leader summarises his experience as, 'Leaders stand alone, take the heat, bear the pain, tell the truth' (De Pree 1991, p. 45).

The cult of individualism that appears to pervade much of the American writing on leadership is acknowledged. While the heroic myth is indeed useful to tap the deeper aspects of leadership, this chapter endorses the post-heroic, 'virtual leadership sentiments with emerging Australian models of leadership (see Sarros & Butchatsky 1996). Some wrongly assume that the quality of leadership will be enhanced by focusing on charismatic, almost heroic traits when in fact most real organisational change occurs within and by teams.

Finally, much that has been written and said about leadership is more exhortative than emulative — that is, we are urged to exhibit worthy leadership qualities, but given little guidance about what actually to *do* as a leader. This chapter will attempt to equip the modern leader with a range of strategies which draw upon the wisdom of both the past and the present.

Leadership: an old approach

It seems that leaders in the past were acutely aware of their 'connectedness', not just with the task to be done and with their followers, but also with history and life itself. Analytical psychologists, especially Carl Jung (1875–1961), highlight the importance of recognising a deeper dimension than a purely conscious view of the world. Jung even suggested in the 1930s that 'the mental state of European man shows an alarming lack of balance'. He asserted that people were living undeniably in a period of the greatest restlessness, nervous tension, confusion and disorientation of outlook (1933, p. 231).

Maybe this is still the case nearly 70 years later. We are witnessing the successes as well as the increasing exhaustion and disquiet among managers on a daily basis. Disillusionment and cynicism seem to match many managerial achievements. If Jung is correct, such achievements may even be at 'the cost of a diminution of personality' (1933, p. 104). If leaders are tired, cynical and disillusioned, something else might need to be honoured and nurtured rather than simply developing more knowledge, skills and robustness — even if these are important, too.

What is missing? Could it be the power of myth? In Campbell's (1971, p. xxi) words:

> ... it struck me what it means to live with a myth, and what it means to live without one ... [a person without a myth] is like one uprooted, having no true link either with the past, or with the ancestral life which continues within him, or yet with contemporary society. This plaything of reason never grips the vitals ... Individual consciousness is only the flower and the fruit of a season, sprung from beneath the earth ...

This is not to argue for an uncritical sentimentality or to recommend the denigration of consciousness and reason! If the ancients might have been more susceptible to poetic and spiritual posturing, modern managers are indeed too complex, too educated and too cynical to do so! (See Jung 1933, pp. 125–51). What is suggested here is the evocation and fostering of a critical openness to the past as a way of rekindling the passion for leadership.

Power of archetypes in leadership: challenging issues

Archetypes are patterns of instinctual behaviour that are contained in the collective unconscious. The collective unconscious is that part of the unconscious that is not individual but universal in contents and modes of behaviour that are more or less the same everywhere and in all individuals (Jung 1933; see also Latemore 1989, 1990).

The collective unconscious certainly includes the shared attitudes and assumptions of a group. But it goes much deeper. Jung believed that there was a kind of racial memory, a myth-creating level of mind shared by people across time and cultures. This level of mind, this common psychic substratum, he came to call 'the collective unconscious'.

Archetypes are manifestations of this 'collective unconscious'. In other words, they are prototypes or original models of how people respond to life. 'Archetype' is derived from the Greek *arche* (origin, primordial) and *tupos* (imprint, image) and literally means 'primordial impression or form' (McBride 1979). As Peter O'Connor (1985) clarifies:

> Archetypes are simply the predispositions to act, the moulds, if you like, into which we pour specific images from life's experiences. Archetypes are the tendency, one might even say the necessity, to apprehend and experience life in a manner conditioned by the past history of humankind; in this sense they are pre-existent forms of apprehension.

Archetypes embrace a whole range of basic human experiences from birth to death. The language of archetypes is the language of symbol — and therein lies their power (Jacobi 1962). A word or an image is symbolic when it implies something more than its obvious and immediate meaning. No one can fully define or explain it because it lies beyond the grasp of conscious reason (Jung 1933). For example, a wheel might lead us to the concept of the sun and then to a sense of unity or wholeness.

Recurring archetypal images have been isolated at the personal level in dreams, visions and fantasies. At the collective level, archetypes are glimpsed in tradition, metaphor, liturgy, ceremony, rituals, rites, folklore, fables, legends, religion, the occult, epics and sagas, mystery cults and fairy tales. Echoing Jung's own discovery, June Singer (1972) points out that the study of mythology, fairy tales, literary forms and comparative religion helps in understanding and recognising the power of the archetypes within people. This then puts one's own personal experiences into a larger perspective.

Archetypes are not just passive 'instincts', but dynamic reservoirs of energy. Archetypes, as manifested in moving ceremony, great literature, music and drama, for example, touch a level of humanity that transcends or, better, underlies the conscious ego. The power of the archetypes can be depicted as a kind of 'magnetic field' (Jacobi 1962) where the subjective ego is pulled and pushed by deeper forces.

Jean Houston (1990) has also given eloquent expression of the dynamic nature of archetypes. She speaks of our 'pushing' and 'being pushed' by archetypes: the collective transformation of mind and body when fully alive manifests and even reconstitutes the archetypal images themselves. Human creativity will be harnessed and constellated when we honour our own inner space and relearn our own mythic stories (Houston 1982). This is not to suggest that we lose free will or that we should relinquish the power of choice — simply that there are forces deeper than the ego that are also operative within and between us. It is argued that these are forces that exist, albeit unconsciously, and within which we participate (Jung 1933, p. 141). Further, these archetypal forces possess a motivating character.

Of course, to suggest such a thing is risky. As Jung (1933, p. 45) wryly points out:

> These things seem very remote to our modern 'enlightened' eyes. When I speak of this hinterland of the mind, the unconscious, and compare its reality with that of the visible world, I often meet with an incredulous smile.

If the archetypes express the 'ancestral heritage of possibilities' (Jung 1933, p. 38), and contain the 'spiritual heritage of humankind's evolution' (Jung 1933, p. 45), one archetype seems especially relevant for the modern manager — the heroic archetype.

The heroic archetype

Carol Pearson (1989) and Jean Shinoda Bolen (1984) make it clear that the hero is masculine or feminine — there is no gender monopoly on heroism. Campbell (1971) compares the adventure of the hero with the three phases of religious rites of passage: the call and departure; the initiation and quest; the return and renewal (see also Moore & Gillette 1993, p. 114). Campbell summarises the heroic journey in this way:

> A hero ventures forth from the world of common day into a region of wonder: fabulous forces are there encountered and a decisive victory is won: the hero comes back from this mysterious adventure with the power to bestow boons on his fellows.

It would appear, to some extent at least, that organisational leaders engage in tasks that psychologically echo the universal figure of the hero and the heroine:

> To maintain our integrity and self-awareness is frequently a battle against long odds, involving hard work that seems to require the cleverness, help, luck and perseverance of a figure larger than life. This 'battle' ... often recurs in cycles that parallel the cyclic defeat and renewal depicted in heroic legends (Hopcke 1992, p. 114).

Some of the primary features of the heroic myth (with some examples from art and history) include the following:
- Heroes are often born under extraordinary circumstances (Moses, Jesus, Mother Teresa of Calcutta).
- The trials both prove and prepare the hero (the prophet Jeremiah, Ripley in the *Alien* movie series);
- The hero is and is not one of the people (Superman, Xena, Warrior Princess).

- The tasks are often difficult and dangerous (Jason and the Argonauts, the movie *Dragonslayer*)
- Sometimes the enemies and the monsters are misunderstood (*Beauty and the Beast*, Darth Vader in the *Star Wars* series).
- The hero has difficulty convincing people upon returning home (Ripley in the *Alien* movie series, Odysseus in Homer's *Odyssey*).
- The hero returns home a reluctant leader (Gandhi, Mother Mary MacKillop).
- The hero protects and rescues the helpless (Rambo, Mad Max, Caroline Chisholm).
- The hero will die for his or her people (Florence Nightingale, Joan of Arc, Martin Luther King, Gandhi).
- The hero is not always a warrior but can be a magician or a sage (Merlin, Confucius)

The essential qualities of heroes or heroines seem to be:
- They have a destiny, even a messianic vocation (Buddha, Luke Skywalker in the *Star Wars* series);
- They are choice-makers, not victims.
- They are not loners, but team players.
- They are not just travellers, but pioneers and pathfinders.
- They are resourceful (Sarah Connor in the *Terminator* movie series).
- They may have a lifelong mission or a specific task to perform (the captain of the starship 'Enterprise' in the *Star Trek* television series).
- The hero or heroine has fatal flaws (Macbeth and Lady Macbeth).
- The hero or heroine saves the people (*Neverending Story* and *The Dark Crystal*).

Neumann (1993) claims that the heroic myth is a psychoanalytic fable of the perils of achieving selfhood or autonomy. The timeless appeal of the heroic myth is well stated by Mitroff (1983):

> Since every individual and every generation has to fight this battle — for every person it is a first time — little wonder that the myth or story of the hero is endlessly recurring. It merely changes its form to suit the times. For one age, it is Jesus; for another, it is E.T., it is a character who brings love to life and is brought back to life by love.

A note of caution is important here. Heroic leaders can delude themselves and seduce their devoted followers. This is the danger that haunts the charisma of the hero or heroine. In other words, leaders of today would do well to behold the heroes and heroines of yesterday in so far as they can learn from their courageous example. However, it is just as important to 'beware the heroes and heroines of yesterday' in so far as blind imitation could trap us into dangerous activity. We need only recall the disastrous consequences of a Stalin, a Hitler, a Pol Pot, a Mao — the list goes on.

Of course, what is at issue here is that the heroic archetype is but one archetype that can potentially educate and enrich the leaders of today. There are other powerful archetypes that clearly do apply: the sage, the mother, the father, the trickster, the ruler. Recent books in these areas are rich resources for contemporary leaders.

The Odyssean hero and heroine

It might be instructive to explore, for a moment, one of the heroic myths in more detail. Homer's epic in the Odyssey is painted on a grand scale with subtlety and complexity. The *Odyssey* is a magnificent display of courage, endurance and resourcefulness — and not just by Odysseus, the warrior king of Ithaca, but by his wife, Penelope, his son, Telemachus, the family teacher, Mentor, and the goddess Athene, to name a few of the characters.

In his masterful work on the *Odyssey*, Stanford (1992) distinguishes four dramatic aspects of Odysseus within the Odyssean saga:
- the man of policies (the politician)
- the mournful exile
- the adventurous traveller
- the avenger in disguise/returning husband and king.

Stanford points out that post-Homeric commentators usually selected one or a related group of the heroic roles to suit their own artistic purposes and the mood of the times (1992, p. 211). Homer alone presented the whole person as a reintegrated hero.

> The wise king, the loving husband and father, the brave warrior, the eloquent and resourceful *politique*, the courageous wanderer, the goddess-beloved hero, the yearning exile, the deviser of many ruses and disguises, the triumphant avenger, the grandson of Autolycus and the favourite of the goddess Athene.

As a hero, Odysseus is not a typical 'grunt'. There is nothing simple about Odysseus. He differs from the typical warrior hero, such as Hercules. Plato regarded Odysseus as a *polutropos*, one displaying 'many-sidedness, versatility of mind ... changefulness, complexity, versatility' (Liddell & Scott 1968). Grant (1962, p. 68) also highlights the exceptional feature of Homer's Odysseus as cleverness. Curiously, early Greek artists dismissed him as being overly clever: Pindar apparently said: 'May I never have a character like that, but walk in straight-forward ways' (Grant 1962, p. 69).

Legend had it that Odysseus came unwillingly to the Trojan war (he feigned madness to avoid the draft but was caught out). He came from Ithaca, a western island, somewhat apart from the city-kingdoms of Mycenae, Athens, Thebes or the eastern islands. Chiefly, he was distinguished by his qualities of mind — clever, inventive, crafty, wise. Mythologically, he was descended from Autolycus, the arch-thief and son of Hermes (Zabriskie 1972).

Odysseus possessed a civilised gentleness (especially in his relationships with women) but also an incredible savagery. His reckless ferociousness needs to be curbed even at the very end of his journey. Circe gives him good advice when she says: 'Do you have to have battle in your heart forever? Won't you ever yield to the immortal gods?'

Further, it has been pointed out (Liddell & Scott 1992 p. 1309) that later commentators regarded Odysseus as *paradoxos* — a paradox. The term in Greek means 'contrary to all expectations, incredible' and was also 'a term given to distinguished athletes, musicians, and artists of all kinds, the admirable, the marvellous.' Odysseus certainly displays a wide range of human strengths and foibles: he is frequently tutored to restrain his warrior anger by the goddess Athene just as she tutors his son, Telemachus, to discover his manly courage. Further, Athene gives to Penelope gifts of artistry and wit to survive her own ordeals back at the palace.

Odysseus' relationship with women is also significant. Zabriskie (1972) explores this aspect by saying that 'she is leading Odysseus to a renewed, mature kind of masculinity ... for young men, like Telemachus, Athene's special role seems to be that of making them become heroes ... For men both young and old, Athene's chief role is to support the process of becoming or being a man ...' Athene gives plain fighting courage to both Telemachus and Odysseus.

There are heroines in mythology, legends, folklore and history, but according to Brooks (1988) in his writing of the failed hero, they are not nearly as numerous as their male counterparts. Joan of Arc, Penelope and Antigone were heroines, but 'one does not detect a "failed individual" anywhere among them; heroines seem always to have fulfilled their archetypal pattern' (Brooks 1988).

There is a worldwide renaissance in discovering the benefits of a deep masculinity just as there are encouraging moves to empower women to rediscover deep femininity. These aspects are beyond the scope of this chapter; however, it is important for the modern leader, female or male, at least to understand such endeavours.

In summary, in the light of the Odyssean myth, some implications for the modern leader are:

- Younger leaders need to learn courage and assertiveness.
- Older leaders need to develop patience and compassion.
- The way of the warrior is not the only path for the heroic leader.
- Cleverness and resourcefulness are hallmarks of the mature leader.
- Complexity of character is an asset, not a hindrance, when dealing with ambiguity.
- Male leaders should develop authentic relationships with female peers and subordinates that honour and develop all concerned.
- Female leaders need to discover their own strength and a decisiveness that transcends passive stereotypes.
- The leader needs to know when to attack, when to retreat and when to form alliances.
- The leader needs to know how and whom to mentor.

- The leader must recognise the time to step down and to train successors.
- The leader rarely works alone: heroic leaders are part of teams.

Post-heroic leadership

Curiously, modern interpretations of the heroic leader seem to imply that the leader individually fights the dragon as a warrior, wins the treasure and returns home personally triumphant. The heroic archetype does not presume a lone individual who battles the odds and wins the day. Even Cairnes (1998) in her excellent work, *Approaching the corporate heart*, seems to equate the warrior with the hero. As we have seen above, the 'hero as warrior' is a shallow and stereotypical interpretation of the heroic myth; the authentic hero or heroine is far more nuanced and complex than this.

Notwithstanding this, there is much to commend a post-heroic interpretation of leadership. This viewpoint rightly avoids a purely patriarchal, military and individualistic approach to leadership. In similar vein, Sinclair (1998) argues for new paths for leading men, other than the traditional path of 'heroic' masculinity.

Sarros and Butchatsky (1996, p. 283) elaborate on 'virtual' leadership:

> Virtual leadership is in vogue today. This type of leadership is where the leader works closely with all workers and managers to deliver the organisation's objectives. A virtual or post-heroic leader does not seek the adulation of his or her peers; in fact, this leader feels as comfortable out of the spotlight as on the stage. The post-heroic leader is committed to developing leaders at all levels of the [organisation] by modelling appropriate behaviour and willingly distributing the power to make decisions and be held accountable for the outcomes to all workers.

In the light of their research among Australian leaders, Sarros and Butchatsky (1996, p. 283) itemise the key features of virtual leaders as:

- They lead from within instead of from out in front.
- They promote responsibility among their followers.
- They make leadership a shared activity, not the prerogative of the elite few.
- They guide and nurture, not command.
- They are not concerned with power.
- They earn respect because of what they do, not what they say.
- They communicate often and clearly.
- They monitor the messages they send out.
- They work with people at all stages of implementing new programs and ideas.
- They are committed to instilling a sense of 'belongingness' in workers.
- They achieve credibility through honesty, competence, forward-looking behaviour, and intelligence.
- They delegate often.
- They are visible and accessible.
- They do not interfere, but know what is happening.
- They listen well and with empathy.
- They captain and coach, guide and counsel as well as direct and control.

Parry (1996b) gives us a glimpse of what the Australian leader might look like. He recognises that Australians are very hard on their leaders, they are quick to blame them, they are cynical about authority, and they do not tolerate indiscretions. He has found that, to be considered good leaders by Australians, leaders must possess the following characteristics:

- They must be positive role models.
- They must engage in individually considerate behaviour at all times.
- They must espouse positive visions about the future only when this is accompanied by credible action.
- They must keep monitoring and controlling behaviour to a minimum.
- They must be intellectually stimulating when the occasion arises.

The Karpin report (Karpin 1995) has suggested that Australian leaders are moving from the autocrats of the 1950s, through the communicators of the 1970s, to the 'enablers/leaders' of the new millennium. Parry (1996b) too offers a profile for future leaders, a profile that is based upon an iterative process of interpreting a variety of research findings. He believes that future leaders will:

- be developed rather than trained

- be continuously learning
- develop and train other leaders
- have a desire to be changed as well as to change
- possess ethical and socially responsible values
- be part of a team as much as the 'head' of a team
- possess 'feminised' characteristics
- communicate up, down, and sideways
- be transformational and transactional.

Integrating the best of the past and future

Managers, of course, live and operate in the present to produce positive outcomes for their organisation. This cannot be done without one eye on the future (the vision) and one eye on the past (the values). The construct of the 'servant-leader' might be a way of integrating the best of the past and the present, and so facilitate a more authentic way of embracing the future.

Servant-leadership

The 'servant-leader' is a well-defined idea within the Old Testament of the Bible, especially among the prophets. The prophets were both representatives of and challengers to their own people. The true prophet didn't so much tell the future but proclaimed what the people needed to do: they were more *forth*-tellers than *fore*-tellers. They worked for justice. The prophets were never passive mouthpieces, but active participants in a salvation drama. Like Job, they often disagreed with their commissions!

The prophets were commissioned for a specific purpose, were called to serve the people and were supported in the process. Such service was a vocation, not just a job: 'servant-leadership' engaged the mind, heart and body. These leaders were engaged not just for something to do, but to do something, something of real importance for the community. They rarely were well-received and were persecuted, but produced the desired outcomes, however reluctantly (like the prophet Jeremiah). Such leaders paid attention to the people's true needs and 'heard the unheard' (see the example in the introduction to this chapter). The 'suffering servant' was the highest development of the prophetic voice (see Anderson 1966; Leon-Dufour 1967).

The full development of the servant-leader within the Christian tradition is in the life of Jesus of Nazareth who 'gave his life for many' (Matthew 20:28). The servant is not one who craves power, but one who seeks to serve.

Robert Greenleaf has been one of the clearest and most passionate modern advocates of this ancient viewpoint (Spears 1995, p. 55). For him, a servant-leader is one who is a servant first:

> It begins with the natural feeling that one wants to serve, to serve first. Then conscious choice brings one to aspire to lead. The difference manifests itself in the care taken by the servant — first to make sure that other people's highest-priority needs are being served. The best test is: do those served grow as persons; do they, while being served, become healthier, wiser, freer, more autonomous, more likely themselves to become servants?

He stresses that servant-leadership is not a quick-fix approach. Nor is it something that can be quickly installed within an organisation. At its core, servant-leadership is a long-term, transformational approach to life and work — in essence, a way of being that has the potential to create positive change throughout our society.

Why be a servant-leader? Greenleaf suggests four basic reasons (Spears 1995, pp. 81–3):
- It works.
- It reinforces the nature of one's profession and calls upon its more noble instincts.
- It is action-oriented.
- It is a commitment to the celebration of people and their potential.

The characteristics of the servant-leader include listening, empathy, healing, awareness, persuasion, conceptualisation of a new way, foresight, stewardship, commitment to the growth of people and building community (Spears 1995, pp. 4–7). Contemporary writers on emotional intelligence would agree with Greenleaf; they also argue for leaders who are self-aware and interpersonally 'smart' (Goleman 1999; Cooper & Sawaf 1997).

There is nothing soft or wimpish about servant-leadership. The strategic toughness of this approach requires the congruent living within the organisation of such core values as honesty, integrity, fairness, respect, good citizenship, accountability and protection of the public trust. We see these values increasingly being both espoused and expected of Australian leaders, both in the private and the public sector.

The heroic greatness of Mother Teresa of Calcutta, Fred Hollows and Victor Chang of Australia, and Nelson Mandela of South Africa lies in their being servant-leaders. They did not focus on their own reputation or career, but on the needs of their people. They provided something worthwhile and gave of themselves with true dedication.

Applying the ancient to the modern

Leaders of today must deal with current reality. Problems and opportunities within the marketplace and within the community demand immediate and careful attention. Managers clearly cannot ignore their own social and organisational context. Nonetheless, it is arrogant and naive to act as though the current reality and a modern approach are the only viewpoints worth adopting.

Managers of today do not have a monopoly on truth. It might therefore be useful to pay some attention to older ways of approaching things and not merely for historical interest. If the mythologists are correct, we do indeed 'stand on the shoulders of our ancestors'; we do share a rich psychic tradition that transcends the purely personal and the purely conscious. The trick is to approach this psychic realm with a critical openness, but an openness nonetheless. Heraclitus claimed that there was nothing new under the sun; if this is so, we might well learn from the past and build upon it to co-create a living tradition that actually makes a difference.

Kaye (1996) would agree when he argues that leaders need to be 'myth-makers and story-tellers', who unleash the power of myths to understand the past, envisage the future and create lasting and positive cultural change in organisations.

Some strategies that might foster and provide access to the 'collective unconscious' of leadership include the following:
- Openly trust older viewpoints, not as automatically valid or as precedents, but to learn from them.
- Keep a personal learning journal that expresses our hopes and fears, successes and failures as leaders.
- Honour the 'corporate memory' by contracting in the retired, experienced managers as mentors and sounding boards.
- Establish good mentoring programs that connect new managers with their older (and younger!) colleagues.
- Appoint a corporate archivist to create an attractive 'tribal elders kiosk' through interactive multimedia.
- Encourage and reward managers who travel abroad, work overseas and learn another language.
- Include on the corporate agenda serious discussion of the successes and failures from the corporate history.
- Include elements on the developmental program that tap into good mythology: art galleries, live theatre, concerts, opera, ballet, film.
- Invite managers from diverse ethnic backgrounds to present workshops which draw upon their own tradition.
- Ensure that diversity is honoured within the organisation, perhaps by engaging outsiders as provocateurs, catalysts and teachers.
- Educate younger leaders about the dangers of the 'hero as warrior'.
- Guard against idealising the organisation's heroic leaders of the past by recognising their flaws as well as their strengths.
- Restore a sense of balance by recognising the redeeming features of the organisation's heroic 'villains'.
- Initiate programs that protect against the consequences of negative, collective projection as racism, sexism, fascism and fundamentalism.
- Foster pride in one's organisational culture and heritage without condoning absolutism or arrogance.

- Critique other organisational heritages and incorporate positive aspects of such heritages (where appropriate) into one's own organisational ethos and practices.
- Consider development programs that include aspects of post-heroic leadership.
- Foster a culture that respects and encourages 'servant-leadership'.

Conclusion

Perhaps the ancients were correct in urging self-mastery and patience. The young prince in the introduction to this chapter needed to curb his bias for action and allow his wisdom to emerge through attentiveness and reflection. Credibility and effectiveness as a leader surely begin with valuing the lessons of the past and attuning to the needs of today *all at once*. Sophisticated managers do not stand in a vacuum any more than they stand alone. The challenge is to be critically open to the past. This is possible by acknowledging the power and types of archetypes and their integration with more contemporary approaches.

The 'heroic journey' as an action-metaphor for courageous leadership and more recent understandings of leadership were discussed. The chapter focused on the best of current thinking and practice in the realms of leadership while acknowledging the lessons of the past. As the ancient Persian princes were taught to 'ride a horse, to shoot an arrow and to tell the truth', so too modern managers must get the basics right (ride a horse), understand the opposition well (shoot an arrow) and relate well to their people (tell the truth). Closer to our own time, another leader summarises his experience as 'Leaders stand alone, take the heat, bear the pain, tell the truth' (De Pree 1991, p. 89).

The approach in this chapter showed that, despite the confused state of writings on leadership, much more is known about these skills than is usually recognised. For the manager trying to gain insight, it is difficult to 'see the forest for the trees'. As Hughes, Ginnett and Curphy (1993, p. 18) assert: 'Being able to analyse your experiences from multiple perspectives may be the greatest single contribution a formal course in leadership can give you.'

References

Anderson, W (1966) *The living world of the Old Testament* (3rd ed.) London: Longman.
Bennis, W & Nanus, B (1985) *Leaders: the strategies for taking charge*. New York: Harper and Row.
Bolen, JS (1984) *Goddesses in every woman: a new psychology of women*. New York: Harper & Row.
Brooks, V (1988) *The failed hero: an unfulfilled archetypal pattern*. Unpublished doctoral dissertation, CG Jung Institute, Zurich.
Burns, JM (1978) *Leadership*. New York: Harper and Row.
Cairnes, M (1998) *Approaching the corporate heart: breaking through to new horizons of personal and professional success*. East Roseville: Simon & Schuster.
Campbell, J (ed.) (1971) *The portable Jung*. New York: Penguin Books.
Cooper, R and Sawaf, A (1997) *Executive EQ: emotional intelligence in business*. London: Orion Books.
De Pree, M (1991) *Leadership jazz*. Melbourne: Wilkenson Books.
Goleman, D (1999) What makes a leader? *Harvard Business Review*, November–December: 92–105.
Grant, M (1962) *Myths of the Greeks and Romans*. New York. Mentor.
Hopcke, RH (1992) *A guided tour of the collected works of CG Jung*. Boston: Shambalah.
Houston, J (1982) *The possible human: a course in enhancing your physical, mental and creative abilities*. Los Angeles: JP Tarcher.
Houston, J (1990) The art and science of human transformation. A workshop conducted at the University of Queensland, sponsored by the Institute of Cultural Affairs, April.
Hughes, RL, Ginnett, RC, Murphy, GL (1993) *Leadership: enhancing the lessons of experience*. Boston, MA: Irwin.
Jacobi, J (1962) *The psychology of CG Jung*. London: Yale University Press.
Jung, C (1933) *Modern man in search of a soul*. San Diego: Harcourt Brace.
Karpin, DS (ed.) (1995) *Enterprising nation: renewing Australia's managers to meet the challenges of the Asia-Pacific century*. Canberra: Australian Government Publishing Service.
Kaye, M (1996) *Myth-makers and story-tellers*. Chatswood: Business & Professional Publishing.
Kim, WC & Mauborgne, R (1992) Parables of leadership. *Harvard Business Review*, July–August: 124.
Latemore, G (1989) Celebrating heroes and heroines: a strategy for managing organisational culture. Unpublished paper for the Centre for Strategic Leaders, Brisbane.

Latemore, G (1984) The change agent as partner, prophet and magician. Unpublished paper for the Centre for Strategic Leaders, Brisbane.

Leon-Dufour, X (1967) *Dictionary of biblical theology*. London: Geoffrey Chapman.

Liddell, H & Scott, R (1968) *A Greek-English lexicon*. Oxford: Clarendon Press.

McBride, T (1979) The Dreamtime of the Aborigines and present day Australia with special references to the role of the healer. Unpublished doctoral observation. Zurich: C Jung Institute.

Mitroff, I (1983) *Stakeholders of the organizational mind: towards a new view of organizational policy making*. San Francisco: Jossey Bass.

Moore, R & Gillette, A (1993) *The magician within: accessing the shaman in the male psyche*. New York: William Morrow & Co. Inc.

Neumann, E (1993) *The origins and history of consciousness* (10th ed.) Princeton, NJ: Princeton University Press.

O'Connor, P (1985) *Understanding Jung, understanding yourself*. North Ryde, NSW: Methuen.

Parry, K (1996a) *Transformational leadership — developing an enterprising management culture*. Melbourne: Pitman Publishing.

Parry, K (ed.) (1996b) *Leadership research and practice — emerging themes and new challenges*. Melbourne: Pitman Publishing.

Pearson, C (1991) *Awakening the heroes within: twelve archetypes to help us find ourselves and transform our world*. San Francisco: Harper Collins.

Robbins, SP, Waters-Marsh, T, Cacioppe, R & Millett, B (1994) *Organisational behaviour concepts, controversies and applications in Australia and New Zealand*. Sydney: Prentice Hall.

Sarros, JC & Butchatsky, O (1996) *Leadership — Australia's top CEOs: finding out what makes them the best*. Sydney: Harper Business.

Sinclair, A (1998) *Doing leadership differently: gender, power and sexuality in a changing business culture*. Melbourne: Melbourne University Press.

Singer, J (1972) *Boundaries of the soul: the practice of Jung's psychology*. Garden City, NY: Anchor Books.

Spears, L (1995) *Reflections on leadership*. New York: John Wiley & Sons.

Yukl, G (1994) *Leadership in organisations* (3rd ed.). Sydney: Prentice Hall.

Zabriskie, P (1972) *Odysseus and the Great Goddess: psychological studies from Homer's Odyssey*. Unpublished doctorial dissertation. Zurich. CG Jung Institute.

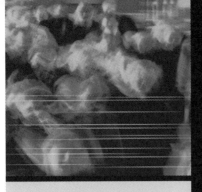

CHAPTER 16

The dynamics of strategic learning in an era of industry restructuring

by Bruce Millett and Chris Marsh

Dept of Human Resource Management and Employment Relations, Faculty of Business, USQ, Toowoomba
Director of Nursing at the Peninsula Private Hospital, Redcliffe, Queensland

millett@usq.edu.au

 Introduction

The Australian manufacturing industry has experienced tremendous challenges and changes in the past two decades. Those responsible for guiding firms through these times could be regarded equally as heroes and villains. The 'hero' title is appropriate for those leading an organisation through a minefield and surviving. The 'villain' title has more appeal to those who were emotionally scarred and drained through the years of hard decisions, realignment and downsizing.

It was therefore refreshing to hear another view from a person who experienced tremendous challenges and changes in his career. This person is the current general manager of the Toowoomba Foundry. Not long after his appointment in 1993, he observed, 'In the last seven years, the foundry has had seven general managers.' He was a local and long-time employee and he had experienced first-hand the turmoil, challenges and changes that the organisation confronted during those years. In response to a question about the impact that the previous general managers had, he recalled that the foundry had learnt something from each of them, even though their period of strategic leadership was relatively brief in terms of the firm's history and tradition, which has developed over 120 years.

The case of the Toowoomba Foundry is significant, because it allows us to gain some further insights into the dynamics of behaviour in organisations and into the tensions of managing continuity and change. It allows us to integrate two important concepts from the field of organisational behaviour — leadership and organisational learning — by relating them to the context, content and processes of organisational experiences. As Pettigrew (1985) stresses, we need to better understand the dynamics of organisational change by taking account of the historical, contextual and processual aspects involved in each case. This also allows us to illustrate the importance of organisational identity as a central concern for managing change and strategic learning.

The purpose of this chapter is to describe the influence that various executive leaders had on the way the Toowoomba Foundry was able to respond to a crisis of identity and to illustrate the importance of an organisation's identity as a strategic focal point for action. The information provided about the case was taken from interviews of staff and from company and other public documents.

The chapter first outlines the background to the organisation and discusses the concepts of organisational learning and organisational identity as a relevant prerequisite for explaining the case. This is followed by a description of the change in the firm's identity over a 10-year period of major restructuring and the phases of identity change that were apparent in this period. Finally, the impact that various general managers had on the changes that occurred is discussed in relation to Lenz's (1994) model of executive leadership.

Background to an organisation that reinvented itself in a time of crisis

The Toowoomba Foundry is a medium-sized manufacturing company that has a long and proud tradition. It began in 1871 as an ironmonger's shop in regional Queensland and in 1876 the business became a foundry with workshops for sawing, casting and machining, as well as facilities for the blacksmith and boilermakers. One of its first products was Australia's first windmill. The company grew in strength and in 1882 was producing a wide variety of products including windmills, railway wagons, pumps, wool presses, tanks, troughs, steam engines and boilers.

While its strategy focused on agricultural products predominantly for Australian farmers, the company sought and gained contracts with various organisations such as the State Railways and firms within the automobile industry. The contracts helped to balance out the fluctuations in agriculture, particularly during recessions and droughts. For 100 years, the Toowoomba Foundry not only survived, but it symbolised the persistence and achievements of a proud pioneering family.

In the 1950s and 1960s, the firm capitalised on the post-World War II boom and sold almost everything it produced. By the 1980s, the company's fortunes had changed and, like many other Australian manufacturers, the Toowoomba Foundry began to feel the impact of increasing globalisation, the devalued Australian dollar and tougher market competition. By global standards, the company was starting to become uncompetitive. The traditional markets of agricultural and resource commodities had declined in recent years and various Australian governments attempted to address the issues of declining economic growth by implementing a range of macro and micro strategies in response to changing world markets. During this period, increasing inflation further eroded economic growth.

In 1973, the Whitlam government examined the extent of tariffs within manufacturing and began to reduce the degree of protectionism within this sector. The 1980s saw further reform with the float of the Australian dollar in 1983 and the deregulation of financial markets. These were significant events which opened the way for reforms in manufacturing where the flow of capital on global financial markets impacts on international as well as domestic trade. The 1980s recession also added to the decline in economic growth and many Australian companies failed.

It was recognised that effective change was required and significant strategic reforms were put in place within the manufacturing sector. The Australian Business Council's report of 1986 recognised that the Australian manufacturing sector needed serious reform and indicated areas of concern: real unit labour costs which had increased dramatically relative to international competitors; relatively high costs of production owing to industrial disputes as well as failure to upgrade technology; reductions in tariffs and protection; and the impact of a relatively high real exchange rate on competitiveness (Business Council of Australia 1985).

The Toowoomba Foundry was one of many manufacturing firms that felt the pressure in the mid-1980s. The firm had experienced the classic conditions for corporate collapse (Shadur & Bamber 1991). The foundry is a special case of an organisation that has learnt to reinvent itself in a time of crisis. The following section outlines the concepts of organisational learning and organisational identity.

The challenge of executive leadership and strategic learning

There are many perspectives on organisations in the organisational behaviour and theory literature. One perspective that is relevant to this case is that organisations are conceived as problem-finding and problem-solving entities where decision-making processes are seen as central leverage mechanisms for managing organisational change (Lenz 1994). While decision making pervades all aspects of an organisation's operations, there is no doubt about the important role that senior executives play in making strategic choices about the future.

This case highlights the influence that various general managers had on the restructuring at the Toowoomba Foundry. Executive leadership is very much concerned with the co-alignment of key factors that impact on an organisation's future (Thompson 1967). Such co-alignment means that executives are continually attempting to influence the intensity and rate of learning that occurs within their organisations. Prahalad and Hamel (1990) introduced the concept of core competencies as the *collective learning* in the firm that, in the long run, has the potential for competitive advantage.

Organisational learning is concerned with the dynamics and processes of collective learning that occur both naturally and in a planned way within and between organisations and their stakeholders. It is the process of continual realignment between the organisation and its environment as both change (Maznevski, Rush & White 1994). These processes and dynamics of learning are seen as more than just the management of change. They are seen as fundamental to the way that organisations develop (Crossan, Lane & Hildebrand 1994). They are seen to be strategic in the way learning affects the fundamental nature of an organisation.

Particular authors identify various types of learning; for example:

- Fiol and Lyles (1985) distinguish between higher and lower levels of learning.
- Senge (1990b) differentiates generative from adaptive learning.
- Argyris and Schon (1978) relate single-loop and double-loop learning to different activities within organisations.
- Dodgson (1991) detects a difference between strategic and operational learning.

These types of learning differentiate between different levels of complexity. However, while these types are prominently identified in the literature on organisational learning, they do not provide a useful framework for analysing leadership and organisational learning.

Lenz (1994) has specifically developed a theoretical framework that is more relevant to explaining the influence that executives have on strategic learning. As illustrated in figure 16.1, he has identified four alternative influence processes for leading organisational change. Each process fosters learning and affects the rate of learning.

Sufficient competence	Orchestrated learning	Execute now
Insufficient competence	Orderly transition	Shock treatment
	Low sense of urgency	High sense of urgency

Figure 16.1: Organisational influence and learning processes (adapted from Lenz (1994))

According to Lenz (1994), two factors account for most of the variation in the decisions of effective executives. These factors are:

1 the extent to which managerial and support personnel are competent in technical and administrative tasks
2 the sense of urgency felt by an executive for initiating change.

Based on these two dimensions, four approaches to leading change are identified.

Orchestrated learning is a leadership influence process where the executive of an organisation focuses most attention on the design aspects of the organisation. If the management and support teams are competent and the sense of urgency is low, the executive can set about developing an organisation that can learn to take care of itself. Such a design would attract and retain talented people, stimulate commitment and creativity, and provide an environment where effective learning and adaptation take place across the entire organisation. In this approach, the executive follows the lead given by Senge (1990a), who suggests that those who lead learning organisations are designers, teachers and stewards. This is in contrast with the traditional view of executives as the centrepiece of the organisation, setting direction, making the key decisions and motivating the troops. The executive stimulates and supports learning across all aspects of the firm's operations.

Execute now is a leadership pattern applicable to a situation with a high sense of urgency and talented people to work with. The senior management determines the strategic agenda and sets out the requirements for action for the rest of the organisation. The executive tends to be personally involved in the implementation of strategy, as well as assertive and directive in style. There is little time for developing broad-based learning strategies across the organisation as is the case with orchestrated learning. The focus is on the senior management team's learning by doing.

Shock treatment is a leadership pattern where the sense of urgency is high and the extent of talented people to work with is limited. Such a situation is generally apparent in turnaround situations where a company is on the brink of collapse, and decisive and immediate measures need to be put in place. Executives move very quickly by getting the bad news out of the way and then undertaking downsizing and/or major restructuring initiatives. There generally needs to be a revolution in the organisation's culture to enable new ways of thinking about and doing business. There is little time to have the management team unlearn old ineffective practices, so members of the management team are the first target of downsizing or replacement. Learning becomes a little more erratic due to the dismissal of some of the existing role model staff, new priorities in budget allocations, new goals and changing job definitions and expectations.

Orderly transition is a leadership pattern where the sense of urgency is low and the extent of talented people to work with is limited. The main challenge for the executive is to manage a change in culture through evolution rather than revolution. Because the sense of urgency is low, the executive feels that a longer time period is available to get key staff to unlearn old, ineffective practices. This is done by replacing key personnel and/or by introducing appropriate training and development programs. The leader is more directive and adopts a counselling approach towards members of the management team.

While these four leadership patterns emphasise the sense of urgency in taking action and the degree of managerial competence in the organisation, there is still a broader question relating to executive leadership — what is the main focus of strategic learning? Organisational learning involves some change in the knowledge base of an organisation as well as behavioural change (Maznevski, Rush & White 1994). But this does not necessarily mean that strategic learning has taken place. Strategic learning basically relates to the way the fundamental nature of the organisation is changed through learning by action.

Shrivastava (1983) described three types of organisational learning that emphasise the strategic nature of learning. *Adaptive learning* focuses on adapting and changing the goals, rules and routines of the organisation. Routines in organisations include the:

- forms
- rules
- procedures
- conventions
- strategies
- technologies
- beliefs
- paradigms
- cultures that organisations operate in (Levitt & March 1988).

Such routines are fundamental to the development of collective memories and shared knowledge (Nelson & Winter 1982).

Fundamental changes in the means and ends specified by organisations are considered to be strategic. *Assumption learning* involves the development and sharing of a set of assumptions and norms across the organisation. Changes to these assumptions and norms are strategic when they relate to the fundamental nature of the organisation. The third type is *developing a knowledge base*. This form of learning is strategic when there is a change to the core knowledge assets of the organisation that give it a competitive advantage.

While these three types of learning help to depict aspects of what is strategic about organisational learning, they emphasise only aspects of what is strategic. From a holistic perspective, when executives are involved with strategic learning and attempt to influence it, they are concerned about the development of a desirable organisational identity.

What is organisational identity?

The concept of an organisation's core identity is a holistic one (Hall 1994). It covers every aspect of a company's activities and is a central feature in times of crisis and change. Because of the pace of technological, economic, political and social change in the current global arena, many organisations are in a constant state of reaction. However, responsiveness is a more appropriate strategy than reaction when it comes to organisational renewal — the ability of a company to remain successful through managing change effectively. True responsiveness demands that organisations understand and manage their own identity, just like the chameleon organisation, which generates cynicism about its outputs and outcomes, confusion about its function as an employer and concern about its contributions to society (Hall 1994).

The concept of organisational identity has gained some attention only in the last decade. While marketing academics have focused on the concept of corporate identity, the organisational behaviourists have emphasised the broader concept of organisational identity (Balmer & Wilson 1998). *Corporate identity* focuses on securing a competitive advantage for an organisation by developing a favourable corporate image and corporate reputation, which leads key stakeholders to be favourably disposed toward it (Balmer & Stotvig 1997). *Organisational identity*, on the other hand, refers to the way that personnel identify with their organisation by what they think and feel (Hatch & Schultz 1997). It also refers to the way that members of a particular organisation perceive their organisation as enduring, central and unique (Albert & Whetten 1985).

Within this framework, organisational identity emerges from the experiences of people directly involved with their organisation on a regular basis, as well as from some degree of consensus about particular attributes that become apparent from those individual and collective experiences. Those attributes can be tangible (like structures, policies, appearance, products and systems) or intangible (like vision, culture, strategy and values) (Hall 1994).

Another perspective on organisational identity is put forward by Kanter, Stein and Jick (1992). The authors maintain that an organisation's identity changes through the relationships between the organisation as an entity and its environment. The relationships can involve the assets it owns and the markets it approaches and the particular segments it occupies. The relationship with the environment is more specifically dependent on its relationship with customers in particular and all stakeholders in general, particularly those that fund it and confer legitimacy on it.

This view of identity is grounded in some basic assumptions about organisations. According to Kanter, Stein and Jick (1992), organisations are based on bundles of activity and they are made up of multiple stakeholders. Hence, organisational identity is apparent in the elements and boundaries that define those activities and in the way the relationships with major stakeholders are defined and redefined. Fundamental change to an organisation's identity means that an organisation has become something entirely different. However, Kanter, Stein and Jick (1992) point out that this is an elusive idea, because there is always a question over whether an organisation ever remains the same. They argue that the answer lies in the nature of the relationships between key stakeholders. It is the value-generating aspect of such relationships that gives an organisation its identity. When the nature of the relationships is altered, then the identity has changed.

Dutton and Penner (1994) provide some support for the claim that organisations have identities. First, it is normal for senior managers to identify and communicate those attributes that are unique, central and enduring. Second, an organisation's identity is created and diffused throughout the various social and cultural systems in the organisation. The beliefs and actions of individuals impact and are impacted by these systems. The unique, central and enduring attributes become embedded in rituals, symbols, ceremonies and stories as part of an enculturation process. Individuals are likely to exhibit some degree of consensus about the attributes when they are institutionalised and preserved in the organisational culture. Members' perceptions and interpretations are influenced more by the culture than by leadership behaviours. Organisational identity is taken to be a subset of the collective beliefs that constitute an organisation's culture (Beyer 1981).

There are six points that need reinforcing, as evident from the foregoing discussion on the nature of organisational identity:

1 Organisations are made up of key stakeholders including staff, customers, and shareholders.
2 While most organisations are recognised as entities through a legal framework, the essence of identity is contained in the nature of the relationships between stakeholders, including the personnel who are recruited to represent the organisation.
3 There is a degree of consensus about the attributes that is enduring, central and unique to the entity.
4 Stakeholder perceptions about these attributes are impacted by the activities of the organisation.
5 Any change to an organisation's identity means a fundamental change to the relationship with stakeholders, as well as a change to the way participants articulate the defining attributes.
6 Organisational identity can be a tool for organisational renewal by focusing attention on what the organisation is now and what it needs to be in the future (Hall 1994).

The following section outlines the nature of the identity change experienced by the Toowoomba Foundry during the period 1986 to 1996.

Phases and nature of the identity change: a practical example

In 1986, the Toowoomba Foundry responded to a major challenge that eventually led to a change of ownership and, during the following 10 years, a different organisational identity emerged. The 10-year period from 1986 to 1996 could be described as a period that was concerned with managing an identity crisis. As shown in figure 16.2, the Toowoomba Foundry was a self-sufficient family company in 1986. By 1996, it became quite clear that a different identity had emerged, one that could be described as the *lean business unit*.

As mentioned previously, an organisation's identity relates to those characteristics of the firm that are seen by its stakeholders as enduring, central and unique. For 110 years, the firm had developed as a responsive and

	1986	'87	'88	'89	'90	'91	'92	'93	'94	'95	1996
The change in organisational identity	The self-sufficient family										The lean business unit
The three phases of the identity change	Crisis		Doubt						Shared vision		
The approaches to leadership	Orderly transition		Shock treatment			Execute now		Orchestrated learning			

Figure 16.2: The Toowoomba Foundry responding to a crisis of identity

entrepreneurial organisation guided by four generations of the founding fathers. There were some distinguishing attributes of the old identity: a private family company owned the firm and the major shareholders were descendants of the original founders. The significance of this type of ownership was that the resources of the family limited the amount of investment capital available. This eventually led to the change of ownership. The other facet of this family company was the paternalistic style of the executive management.

Employees identified with the family. They were local and were seen to contribute to the community. Being local and parochial provided the foundation for a strong sense of community, commitment and loyalty to the firm and the family. The strategy was one of unrelated diversification as described by Galbraith and Nathanson (1979). The foundry was involved in a very broad range of products and contracts, including ferrous and non-ferrous materials. The family company also ran a retail outlet for building supplies, a Ford dealership and a brick factory. Right from the outset, the operation had developed as a self-contained unit with a large sales organisation located around Australia to ensure that the interests of the factory were protected and controlled.

The structure was bureaucratic and had a large 'techno' component which Mintzberg (1983) described as a supporting group of professionals (in this case, predominantly engineers) who provided technical advice to management and operational employees. This group was very influential in terms of work practices. The technology can be described as traditional mass production, characterised by dedicated machines (Jones 1995). These machines can generally perform one operation at a time, take long periods for retooling for a different operation, and cater for narrow product ranges and large production runs to obtain efficiencies of scale. This also meant the creation of large inventories of finished products.

These characteristics described the identity of the firm up until the early 1980s. In 1986, a crisis began to emerge in relation to the production technology and this signified the first phase in the change of the firm's organisational identity. The semiautomatic ferrous moulding line that had served the organisation well for many years was no longer cost-effective for competing in domestic as well as global markets.

The family shareholders decided to borrow $7.5 million to upgrade the outdated technology. In 1987, a modern semiautomatic cast-moulding line was installed in an effort to retain existing contracts within the automotive industry. During this period, an additional $6.5 million was spent on upgrading computer systems, machine tools and the melting furnaces. However, the company had major problems in financing its debt from an overseas source due to high interest rates and fluctuations in the Australian dollar. These were typical in the economy at the time. Non-current liabilities increased from $6 million to $23 million in 1988. The debt to equity ratio changed from 90 per cent in 1987 to 158 per cent in 1989 (Harker 1995).

In 1988, the family responded to the crisis and gave up 49 per cent of its shareholding to an investment company, National Consolidated Ltd, in return for an injection of capital to reduce the debt. In 1990, National Consolidated Ltd acquired the controlling share in the company and immediately took complete control of its management. The crisis was triggered by the financial situation. But it was not just a crisis of outdated technology and systems. In 1986, it became a crisis of identity because the family began to ask some serious questions about their involvement in the business.

With the entry of National Consolidated Ltd in 1988, a period of doubt began in relation to the firm's identity. This phase of the identity change signified uncertainty about the organisation's future, uncertainty about the new owners and their commitment and support, and uncertainty about its own ability to survive. The new owners were instrumental in bringing in consultants to assess the extent of the firm's problems. They were also instrumental in appointing the new general managers who were predominantly from outside the organisation. The first of the outsiders arrived in 1988 and this heralded the start of serious restructuring with a view to cutting the organisation to the bone, so that competitive cost structures could be realised. This cost cutting strategy was prominent for the next 6 years and made it difficult for staff to share a common view about the nature of this changing entity.

The period of doubt continued until July 1993 when the Toowoomba Foundry became an independent unit in National Consolidated Ltd's portfolio of manufacturing companies. From this point, a new phase emerged in relation to the firm's identity with the emergence of a shared vision by the local staff who were left with the responsibility to make it succeed. The emergence of a shared vision represented a collective and determined effort on the part of key people to identify what the Toowoomba Foundry represented, where it was going and how it should get there. This final period of the identity change is the recognition of a new future and new possibilities for a new set of attributes.

By 1996, the Toowoomba Foundry had significantly changed to a lean business unit, and operated relatively autonomously as part of a portfolio of manufacturing companies, owned by a public rather than a private company, National Consolidated Ltd. Being owned by a holding company specialising in manufacturing and residing in Melbourne did not engender the same sense of being a big fish in a small pond. It was the reverse. The new owners were not as flexible as the old when it came to company performance and returns on investment. They wanted results. The impact on employees was also significant. Although they had difficulty in identifying with a distant and remote landlord, they could identify with the opportunity to contribute to an autonomous unit confronting the daily challenges of surviving a dynamic and competitive environment. They had a bigger stake in their own future, whereas previously the family had looked after their future.

As a lean business unit, the foundry now had a *focused strategy*, which means that it had made significant investments in assets dedicated to a particular strategic direction (Kim & McIntosh 1999). The sales organisation had been sold along with the non-ferrous production facilities. The structure was lean, with the main focus being on what Mintzberg (1983) referred to as the *operating core* — the people who were directly involved in the prime activities of production. The support areas were reduced to a bare minimum. The technology had moved from a mass production site to one more characteristic of an advanced manufacturing technology site. Jones (1995) described this as a move that offsets some of the limitations of mass production, including flexibility, costly inventories, narrow-skilling, and limited usage of new computer-enhanced technologies.

This section has mapped out in very general terms the change that had taken place in the firm's identity. The significance of the changes could be seen in the reorientation of some fundamental attributes. The discussion also identified three phases of the change in the identity over the 10-year period: a phase of crisis, a phase of doubt and a phase of emerging shared vision. This is significant, because it provides managers with a context to view their actions as appropriate or otherwise. In this context, we will now discuss the intervention of a number of general managers during this period of identity change and what each one contributed to the way the organisation was able to learn strategically.

From orderly transition to orchestrated learning: a practical example

In the context of the three phases of identity change, we can detect the four different approaches to leadership that were identified by Lenz (1994) and previously described. As illustrated in figure 16.2, the different interventions could be described as 'orderly transition', 'shock treatment', 'execute now' and 'orchestrated learning'. These approaches could be associated with the appointment of various general managers at the organisation during this 10-year period, and their influence on strategic learning.

The *orderly transition* pattern of leadership began with the retirement of the managing director of the family holding company in 1984 and the appointment of his son as successor. The new managing director saw the need for change and proceeded over the next 4 years to restructure the organisation and undertake a program of downsizing. Employee numbers in the factory declined from 700 in 1983 to 570 in 1988 and to 260 in 1998. As a family member, he appreciated the difficulties in changing a culture that was deeply entrenched. His sense of urgency was moderated by the realisation that it would take a medium to longer time frame to achieve the changes he felt were necessary.

In 1986, the long-serving general manager of the foundry retired and a new person was appointed from the ranks. Although there was a very competent group of technical experts and line managers, they tended to be specialised in particular areas of responsibilities and were closely linked to the old identity. In order to restructure the company for a much more competitive future, there was a need to develop a new set of skills in the managerial and technical ranks — a set of skills that were more broadly based and able to exploit the capabilities of the emerging manufacturing technologies. The potential capabilities of some key staff were insufficient for the new environment. It is common for organisations whose ability to change has atrophied to adopt an orderly transition approach to leadership (Lenz 1994).

Strategic learning tended to be concentrated in the top management team. Under the new leadership, the senior executive team had changed because of the retirement of some of the key 'old guard' figures. The new team began to focus their attention on developing a new identity, but in an evolutionary way. A company newsletter was developed to keep staff informed of developments. In the first edition, the new managing director announced that the company was adopting a new image and a new direction that was to be more marketing oriented, rather than production oriented. He said that there was too much complacency with the company's old established image, and too much reliance on the reputation built up over 100 years. He believed that the magazine reflected a new beginning and would give all employees a feeling of belonging and a sense of importance of their roles in the corporate structure. The training department was expanded to support the restructure. A small research and development section was allowed to continue to stimulate new product development.

The *shock treatment* pattern of leadership became noticeable in 1988 with the appointment of a new general manager, who had a brief, particularly from National Consolidated Ltd, to get serious about cutting costs in the organisation. He was a consultant and an outsider. Suddenly, the sense of urgency was greater and it became more apparent that some of the existing staff were not up to the task of running a lean operation or that their skills were no longer required in the new scheme of things. Employees became very unsettled during the next few years as desperate measures were put in place to stop the firm from failing financially.

This was the start of a phase of leadership where the strategic focus was on downsizing and trimming the factory to a point of leanness that was unimaginable a few years previously. The objective was to get production costs to a minimum without detracting from the quality and quantity of the production output. The general manager made it quite clear to his management team that the foundry and machine shops were process operations and competed in a very competitive market which required low overheads and the lowest cost of production possible. He was told by Toyota and Nissan, two major clients, that the foundry's products were too expensive. This was during a period of unprofitability.

During the downsizing, a lot of skills, knowledge and support literally walked out the door. The training section and the research and development group were closed down. This put greater pressure on the people left behind to learn quickly. The process entailed identifying what the basic skills and knowledge were that enabled the plant to still function effectively. A lot of attention was placed on reducing defects and the amount of rework required. An interesting aspect of this period was that there was an expectation that a dictatorial style would persist. To the contrary, the general manager with consulting experience adopted a more consultative style and allowed staff much more freedom in making decisions and solving the problems of cost cutting than they had been used to. While this caused staff some concern and frustration, the seeds were sown for developing independent thinking and more involvement across all levels of staff. This was a small thing that was observed at the time, but a big positive in terms of strategic learning.

The *execute now* pattern of leadership could be associated with the appointment of another general manager in 1991. The new appointee had a wealth of international experience in various manufacturing plants, including the Rolls-Royce factory in the United Kingdom. The sense of urgency was still high in terms of cost cutting and developing the organisation into a competitive unit. In a statement to staff, he made it clear that the phrase 'times are tough' was an understatement. He added that all cost-related activities had been thoroughly worked on and there was an imperative to preserve the skill base to effectively and safely operate the plant. The smaller team of managers and professionals were starting to gain sufficient confidence and competencies in relation to the new requirements. The new man had quite a different style to his predecessors. He liked to get down into the factory where the action was.

In this phase, the focus of strategic learning continued to emphasise a broader involvement of employees throughout the factory to create an organisation that tapped the talents of all staff. His vision was to galvanise the brainpower of all employees, by allowing his managers to make mistakes in order to learn valuable lessons, and to develop a clean and safe environment as part of a program to rebuild self-esteem. His first impressions of the foundry were that it needed some tender loving care and management needed to keep faith with employees during the hard times.

While he was driving change from the top, through his particular vision and strategic agenda, he was promoting a philosophy of self-development and involvement that started in a small way during the shock treatment period. There was intense personal involvement in his style and he encouraged learning by doing. He used the introduction of AS 3901 international quality standard as a vehicle for change at the foundry. The strategy was to develop a culture where quality and customer service were important to every employee. The enterprise bargaining agreement also provided the firm with some new options through flexible work arrangements.

The *orchestrated learning* pattern of leadership that more explicitly promotes a vision of a learning organisation where people '...continually expand their capacity to create the results they truly desire' (Senge 1990b, p. 3) and the organisation becomes '...skilled at creating, acquiring and transferring knowledge, and at modifying its behaviour to reflect new knowledge and insights' (Garvin 1993, p. 78). The current general manager was appointed in 1993 and represented the shift to the new identity of a lean, effective business unit. He built on what had been learnt from the general managers who preceded him. In 1993, the large sales organisation that had been associated with the family company and provided the distribution for the factory was sold, along with the small non-ferrous production facility. This left the foundry entirely to its own devices in terms of sales and distribution and allowed it to concentrate solely on ferrous-based castings and products.

One of the current managers' observations was that the revolution was over and the organisation needed to concentrate on an evolution of continuous improvement. He was an insider, had been with the foundry for many years, and was part of the senior management team during the previous years of revolutionary restructuring. He gained the respect from employees for his commitment to them and to making the firm successful. He was a firm believer in the old adage 'our people are our greatest asset' and this was apparent in his style as coach, teacher and role model.

In 1993, the managing director of the holding company, National Consolidated, was concerned with the profitability of the foundry and indicated the possibility of selling it. This was a galvanising challenge for the new general manager and his team. A strategic planning seminar was held off site. This was unheard of and some people were uncomfortable, because of the 'junket' tag generally attached to such events. While there had been planning seminars back in the 1980s, this one involved the 'grass roots' managers. These were the people directly associated with the shop floor and who understood the issues of the factory. While some senior executive planning sessions tend to be remote from shop-floor activity, this was different because the participants were directly connected to the factory; this helped to bring the vision, decisions and sentiments of the seminar back to where it counted.

This event represented a strategic milestone and illustrated that the organisation had moved to a lean, dedicated business unit where the involvement, energy and talent of everyone were the real strategic asset. Their owners had set a target of $300 000 profit for the coming year. The firm responded with a higher target that took the owners by surprise. The planning seminar was an event that laid the foundation for the team to develop a shared vision and framework for succeeding in the future. The future was in their hands, rather than in the general manager's hands. In the first year under the new leadership, the foundry returned a profit in excess of four times the original target.

In strategic terms, learning was more distributed. The management team consisted of nine people and the layers of management were reduced to four, allowing communication and decision making to flow more effectively. The vision became more formal and visible, with a clear mission to be the preferred manufacturer of machined ferrous castings through exemplary customer service. Relevant performance indicators were developed and used effectively to drive continuous improvement. Astute incentive schemes were developed to link the performance indicators to performance across all sections of the factory.

Conclusion

The case of the Toowoomba Foundry provides valuable insights into leadership and organisational learning during a time of crisis and major restructuring. The chapter described some of the basic characteristics of the old identity and the new. This allowed us to see how the organisation had changed. Three phases of identity change were also identified: crisis, doubt and shared vision. This provided some context in which to view the actions of the various general managers. Finally, the chapter related how the firm had learnt from each of the general managers during this time of restructuring. Particular aspects of strategic learning were discussed in the context of Lenz's four executive leadership approaches.

A number of insights are apparent from an organisational behaviour perspective. First, leadership, change, learning, structure and individual and group development must be viewed in context. The case identifies various stages of development that are important to understanding the actions of key leaders. Second, the case highlights the importance of employee involvement in developing a high-performance culture. Third, it emphasises the importance of identifying the fundamental attributes of an organisation's identity as central to strategic learning. The substance of any learning is the sense that all stakeholders make of their relationship with an organisation. Part of the leader's role is to help the key stakeholder groups clarify their own identity along with that of the organisation, so there is little doubt about the positive aspects of the relationship.

There is no doubt that the future for manufacturing companies will continue to be clouded in uncertainty and turbulence. The challenge for general managers is to develop an organisational identity based on a unique and enduring set of core competencies. Such competencies will be dependent on technology but general managers need to be reminded that it is people who make the difference in terms of flexibility, responsiveness, creativity and customer service. The implication for all managers is that such competencies emerge from the leadership roles and behaviours that are appropriate and special for supporting high-involvement workplaces — environments where everyone can learn to achieve their potential and enjoy their work.

References

Albert, S & Whetten, DA (1985) Organizational identity. In LL Cummings and BM Staw (eds) *Research in organizational behaviour*. Greenwich, CT: JAI Press, 7: 263–95.

Argyris, C & Schon, D (1978) *Organizational learning*. London: Addison-Wesley.

Balmer, J & Stotvig, S (1997) Corporate identity and private banking: a review and case study. *International Journal of Bank Marketing*, 15(4–5): 169–82.

Balmer, J & Wilson, A (1998) Corporate identity: there is more to it than meets the eye. *International Studies of Management and Organisation*, 28(3): 12–31.

Beyer, JM (1981) Ideologies, values and decision making in organizations. In P Nystrom and W Starbuck (eds) *Handbook of organization design*. London: Oxford University Press, 166–202.

Crossan, M, Lane, H & Hildebrand, T (1994) Organisational learning: theory to practice. In J Hendry, G Johnson & J Newton (eds) *Strategic thinking: leadership and the management of change*. Chichester: John Wiley and Sons, pp. 229–65.

Dodgson, M (1991) Technology learning, technology strategy and competitive pressures. *British Journal of Management*, 2(3): 132–49.

Dutton, JE & Penner, WJ (1994) The importance of organizational identity for strategic agenda building. In J Hendy, G Johnson & J Newton (eds) *Strategic thinking: leadership and the management of change*. Chichester: John Wiley, 95–7.

Fiol, C & Lyles, M (1985) Organisational learning. *Academy of Management Review*, 10(4): 803–13.

Galbraith, JR & Nathanson, DA (1979) Role of organizational structure and process. In D Schendel and S Hofer (eds) *Strategic management. A new view of business policy and planning*. Boston: Little and Brown.

Garvin, D (1993) Building a learning organization. *Harvard Business Review*, July–August: 78–91.

Hall, J (1994) WYSIWYG: perception, reality and organizational focus: core identity as a holistic framework for the management of change. In H Thomas, D O'Neal, R White & D Hurst (eds) *Building the strategically-responsive organization*. Chichester: John Wiley & Sons, pp. 29–44.

Harker, M (1995) Company turnarounds: a context, content and process perspective. PhD dissertation, Griffith University, Brisbane.

Hatch, M & Schultz, M (1997) Relations between organisational culture, identity and image. *European Journal of Marketing*, 31(5–6); 340–55.

Jones, G (1995) *Organisational theory: text and cases*. Reading, MA: Addison-Wesley Publishing Company.

Kanter, RM, Stein, BA & Jick, TD (1992) *The challenge of organisational change: how companies experience it and leaders guide it*. New York: The Free Press.

Kim, E & McIntosh, J (1999) Strategic organisational responses to environmental chaos. *Journal of Managerial Issues*, 11(3): 344–57.

Lenz, R (1994) Strategic management and organisational learning: a meta-theory of executive leadership. In J Hendry, G Johnson & J Newton (eds) *Strategic thinking: leadership and the management of change*. Chichester: John Wiley and Sons, pp. 153–79.

Levitt, B & March, J (1988) Organisational learning. *Annual Review of Sociology*, 14: 319–40.

Maznevski, M, Rush, J & White, R (1994) Drawing meaning from vision. In J Hendy, G Johnson & J Newton (eds) *Strategic thinking: leadership and the management of change*. Chichester: John Wiley, Chichester, pp. 13–45.

Mintzberg, H (1983) *Structure in fives: designing effective organizations*. Englewood Cliffs, NJ: Prentice Hall.

Nelson, R & Winter, S (1982) *An evolutionary theory of economic change*. Cambridge: Belknap Press.

Pettigrew, A (1985) *The awakening giant: continuity and change in ICI*. Oxford: Basil Blackwell.

Prahalad, CK & Hamel, G (1990) The core competence of the corporation. *Harvard Business Review*, May/June: 79–91.

Senge, P (1990a) The leader's new work: building learning organizations. *Sloan Management Review*, Fall: 7–23.

Senge, P (1990b) *The fifth discipline: the art and practice of the learning organisation*. New York: Doubleday.

Shadur, M & Bamber, G (1991) Towards total quality and human resource management: changing management strategies and work organisation in an Australian company. Paper presented at ANZAM, Bond University, Gold Coast.

Shrivastarra, P (1983) A typology of organisational learning systems. *Journal of Management Studies*, 20(1): 7–28.

Thompson J (1967) *Organizations in action*. New York: McGraw Hill.

CHAPTER 17

Layers of meaning: understanding organisational communication

by Mara Olekalns

Melbourne Business School, University of Melbourne, Victoria

m.olekalns@mbs.unimelb.edu.au

Introduction

Communication is central to an organisation's activities. From simple functions such as explaining tasks to more complex functions such as giving normative information about an organisation's culture, communication is the tie that binds organisational members. Done well, it creates a positive climate in which individuals feel more committed to their organisation; done poorly, it lowers job satisfaction and increases stress and burnout. Good organisational communication is built on good interpersonal communication. The two are inseparable and without good interpersonal communication skills we cannot establish a positive communication climate. However, because organisations must share information across networks, they face additional challenges to communicating well. In this chapter, I provide an overview of both interpersonal and organisational communication, and identify some of the challenges that organisations face in their efforts to communicate with their members. This chapter starts with a description of two well-established models of communication: a mechanistic model that describes how messages can be transmitted most accurately and a psychological model that focuses on how the individuals sending and receiving messages may inadvertently distort the communication process. I then move on to discuss newer perspectives on communication, especially the idea that it is not just *what* we say but *how* we say it that influences the message received. Finally, I identify the issues that organisations face in communicating with their employees, and how the quality of organisational communication affects both individuals and organisational processes.

Traditional models of communication

The two best-known models of communication are based around Shannon and Weaver's (1948) depiction of communication as information transfer. The first of these, the mechanistic model, concerns itself with how information is transmitted. The second, the psychological model, recognises that transmission is never perfect and focuses on the barriers to communication (Chatman, Putnam & Sondak 1991).

A mechanistic model of communication

The original Shannon and Weaver (1948) model characterised communication as a process of inputs and outputs. An individual (the sender) formulated a message, selected a medium in which to transmit the message, and this message was received and 'decoded' by a listener.

According to these authors, the communication process starts when individuals want to pass information or ideas on to another person. They need to think about their aim in passing this information on, and make several decisions about what will be included in the final message, as well as how that message is to be conveyed. Speakers need to 'encode' their messages. Will the message be written or verbal? If it is verbal, will it be face-to-face or through some other medium? Will it be in a forum that allows for comments and questions, or one that restricts opportunities for feedback? It ends when the receiver — the individual hearing the message — 'decodes' what has been said. As we will see in the next section, both the encoding and decoding processes are open to distortion.

Mechanistic models of communication focus on the accuracy of transmission and argue that, if communication fails, it is because the sender has chosen an inappropriate medium for transmitting the message. What options are available to the individual? As we saw in the previous paragraph, senders must make several decisions. One is whether to allow feedback. Communication that is *one-way* does not encourage feedback. Its main advantage is that it allows us to prepare in advance what we will say and to deliver the message without disruption. Because of this, it provides a mechanism for rapidly delivering large amounts of information. The main disadvantage is that we have no idea about how someone listening to us has interpreted our message, and so have no way of correcting any misinterpretations that arise. In comparison, *two-way* communication encourages and actively seeks feedback. Although this means that our messages cannot be as well planned, and that the communication process takes longer, the big advantage is that we can verify whether our message has been interpreted correctly (Greenberg & Baron 1993).

Not surprisingly, the issue of getting feedback is intimately linked to the choices we make about how we communicate. We can obtain feedback most easily when we engage in face-to-face communication. Face-to-face communication improves communication in several ways. First, it makes it easier to engage in a question-and-answer process that provides an immediate check on how our message has been interpreted. Second, it provides the other person with a set of nonverbal cues that help clarify our intentions. And, third, it gives us access to a range of nonverbal behaviours that provide important cues to how our message has been interpreted. As we move away from face-to-face communication, and use other media such as the telephone or letters, we decrease the opportunities for soliciting feedback. More importantly, we decrease access to the nonverbal cues that help others interpret our intentions. Not only does this reduce our ability to communicate accurately, but it worsens our overall relationships. Research in the field of conflict management and negotiation has long demonstrated that, in comparison to individuals in face-to-face negotiations, individuals who cannot see each other escalate conflicts far more rapidly and adopt a much more contentious approach to negotiation (e.g., Carnevale & Isen 1986).

New directions for mechanistic models

As the use of computers and e-mail increases, we clearly reintroduce the possibility that communication will be misperceived and misinterpreted. Access to e-mail creates the risk of misinterpretation coupled with an unprecedented speed in communicating. Can we anticipate the likely consequences of this style of communicating? Anyone familiar with e-mail will also be familiar with 'flames': the denigration and abuse of another person. Flames start an escalating cycle of conflict and can result from very simple misunderstandings. For example, some one might send a message in upper-case, possibly accidentally, not realising that the 'Caps Lock' key is on. This is interpreted as 'shouting' by the receiver, who writes back: 'I HATE BEING SHOUTED AT BY E-MAIL. HOW DARE YOU SPEAK TO ME LIKE THIS. IF THIS IS HOW YOU ARE GOING TO TREAT ME, I DON'T WANT TO COMMUNICATE WITH YOU'. And so the cycle of conflict starts. Sproull and Kiesler (1991) show that people are more likely to 'flame' when using e-mail than when communicating in person. Already, in order to address this issue, 'emoticons' have entered our electronic communication; these are symbols that denote our intent and help remove ambiguity from our messages (Thompson 1998). It appears that the introduction of e-mail has magnified all of the problems in transmission and introduced some new ones. It has simultaneously eliminated the nonverbal cues that help interpret messages and increased the speed with which we respond (sometimes rather unthinkingly) in a way that serves to escalate tension and conflict. For example, negotiations conducted via e-mail have a much greater likelihood of ending in impasse than those conducted face-to-face (Moore, Kurtzberg, Thompson & Morris 1999). Interestingly, this can be offset if individuals take the time to get to know each other before they commence their negotiations. Of greater concern — for organisations — is recent research showing that the increasing use of e-mail is associated with an overall decrease in communication. Furthermore, much of what is lost turns out to be casual forms of conversation such as greetings (Sarbaugh-Thompson & Feldman 1998) — precisely those forms of communication that build relationships.

A psychological model of communication

If mechanistic models focus on the key components of communication (encoding, transmitting and decoding), then psychological models focus on the links between these components. These models are concerned with analysing the characteristics of senders and receivers that result in faulty transmission. The end point of these models is the identification of specific skills and behaviours that will help us to communicate better.

Senders face several problems in constructing their messages. The likelihood that their message will be 'faulty' is increased if they filter their messages, use in-group language, or fail to adopt their receivers' frame of reference. *Filtering* describes several ways in which we alter messages before passing them on. Anyone who has played 'Chinese whispers' will know that, as we construct and pass messages on to others, so we shape the content of those messages. Filtering reflects problems with message construction. The best-known example of filtering is deletion, in which information is selectively left out of a message. We make decisions about what is or is not important, and what the listener should or should not hear. In either case, especially if we are passing information on through an organisational hierarchy, the original intent of the message may be lost. At the other end of the continuum, we may also see additions: those little pieces of information that we add to an original message to make it more newsworthy! Senders may also use *jargon*. They include in their messages words and phrases that have a common meaning to others who share their background, be it organisational, professional or social. This immediately excludes those from a different background from understanding the message. Lastly, the *frame of reference* that we adopt as senders may differ from that of our listeners. It raises the possibility that our past experiences will shape how we interpret a message. If senders and listeners do not have a common background or a common set of experiences, the intention and interpretation of a message may be substantially different (Ivancevich, Olekalns, & Matteson 1997).

Listeners also have a role in improving the accuracy of communication. Although there are a number of specific issues that listeners need to consider, perhaps their greatest sin is inattention. Because we can process speech more rapidly than we can produce it, listeners have a lot of spare cognitive capacity. Unfortunately, most of us do not use that capacity productively, preferring instead to daydream, plan what we will do tomorrow or prepare our response while waiting for our turn to speak. None of this helps improve communication. Good listeners try to follow and understand the intention of a speaker, and provide feedback to ensure that the message is accurately sent and interpreted. A number of factors, other than inattention, stand in the way of effective listening.

First, listeners may display *selective listening*, hearing only those portions of a message that they want to hear. We are most likely to 'hear' messages that fit with our existing worldview and most likely to block those messages that do not. Second, we frequently make *value judgements* about the worth of a message or the person sending the message. For example, when we judge messages as having no relevance to us, we fail to hear them. Third, only when the sender is *credible* do we listen to her or his message. And finally, since we are limited in our capacity for processing information, our ability to accurately interpret messages decreases when we experience *information overload* (Ivancevich, Olekalns & Matteson 1997; Greenberg & Baron 1993).

All of this points to the need for senders and listeners to work together to increase the clarity of their messages. First and foremost, both senders and listeners should actively seek feedback to ensure that the message as sent is how it is received. Senders need to ensure that they match their verbal message with their non-verbal one, that they take into consideration their listener's frame of reference, and that they build some redundancy into their message by sending it through more than one medium. Listeners must be willing to prompt the other person for more information by asking open-ended questions that encourage speakers to elaborate and clarify their messages. In both cases, individuals must avoid communication 'stoppers': a range of responses that evaluate, judge or criticise the other person. Instead, as communicators, we need to focus on conveying our thoughts and feelings in a clear and non-evaluative manner. We can do this by describing specific actions (when you arrive at work late) rather than our interpretation of those actions (your laziness ...), and by adding our feelings about the situation (Bolton 1987; Johnson & Johnson 1987; Kolb, Rubin & Osland 1991).

New directions for psychological models

Perhaps the underlying message in this section concerns how we treat others in the course of our interactions. Although many of the recommendations for improving interpersonal communication centre on the effective management of blocks, a second theme in these recommendations is that our interactions display respect for the other person. This idea has more recently been captured in a new form of justice. We are already familiar with two types of justice: distributive, which focuses on the fairness of resource distribution, and procedural, which focuses on the fairness of the decision-making process. We can now add to this a third kind of justice: interactional justice, which focuses on the fairness of interpersonal treatment. We perceive interpersonal treatment to be fair when the other party is truthful, shows respect and propriety, and provides adequate justification of his or her decision (Cohen 1991; Greenberg 1990). This idea has recently been applied to managing organisational change. Novelli, Kirkman and Shapiro (1995) argue that the implementation of large-scale change will be judged as more interpersonally fair if employees perceive managers to be sincere and empathic.

New perspectives on communication

Newer models of communication focus neither on how messages are transmitted, nor on how this process may fail. Instead, they focus on communication as a mechanism for building shared meanings. In this approach, communication acts as a symbol; and the interpretation of these symbols provides information about values, beliefs and ongoing relationships (Putnam, Phillips & Chapman 1999). These models recognise the inherent uncertainty in social interactions (Hinde 1979; Snyder & Swann 1978) and the role of communication in reducing uncertainty (McCann & Higgins 1990). The underlying theme in these models is that the context in which we communicate is critical to how messages are interpreted. The interaction goals that we hold and their impact on emergent relationships provide part of this context. In the next sections, we will consider how two interaction goals — maintaining status and fostering relationships — shape our interactions.

Meta-messages in speech styles

A long-standing line of research links *how* we send our messages to the impressions that others form of us. This research focuses on the form rather than the content of our speech. Researchers have linked attributions of dynamism (power) and aesthetic quality to the differential use of linguistic markers. Speakers are perceived as powerful (high in dynamism and low in aesthetic quality) when they use linguistic forms such as the first person singular pronoun, present tense, judgemental adjectives and vocalised pauses. Conversely, they are perceived as powerless (low in dynamism and high in aesthetic quality) when they use tag questions, disclaimers, qualifiers, indirect requests and adverbial sentence beginnings (e.g., Aries 1996; Bradac 1990; Bradac, Mulac & Thompson 1995; Mulac & Bradac 1995). So, how we choose to express our messages influences the judgements others make about our power relative to theirs. Interestingly, as we go on to discuss in subsequent sections, precisely those speech forms that convey powerlessness are also those that foster closer relationships.

At a more general level, messages about social distance may also be sent by patterns of speech. Communication accommodation theory (Burgoon, Stern & Dillman 1995) identifies two distinct patterns of speech: convergence and divergence. *Convergence* describes a speech pattern in which an individual adapts her or his own speech style so that it becomes more similar to that of other person. Convergence results in increasingly greater perceptions of similarity. As perceived similarity increases, so does a person's predictability and perceived supportiveness. Consequently, convergent communication is expected to lead to greater closeness and a reduction in social distance. Conversely, *divergence* describes a speech pattern in which individuals emphasise and amplify their own speech characteristics and thus distance themselves from the other person. The aim of divergence is to increase social distance and to display power. Divergence acts to highlight distinctiveness rather than commonality and reinforces individual rather than group identity. Consequently, it does not lead to trust or the development of a shared perspective, but does lead to negative evaluations and attributions about the other person.

Some organisational consequences of meta-messages

Research has shown that a speaker's status, message content and delivery styles influence the perception of performance feedback. Supervisors who use negative assertive messages when responding to criticism or refusing a request are rated differently to those using positive assertive messages: they are perceived as less likeable, their behaviour is considered inappropriate, they lose respect and the relationship is weakened (Bryan & Gallois 1992). Similarly, in the context of recruitment decisions, speech style influences how recruiters view job candidates — job candidates who use an assertive speech style are rated as more likeable and similar to interviewers than those who use either an aggressive or an unassertive speech style (Gallois, Callan & McKenzie Palmer 1992).

Gender, culture and communication

Recent work by Deborah Tannen (1995) also typifies the social constructionist perspective described earlier. Tannen argues that speech can serve one of two functions — it can be used to establish and maintain relative power and status, or it can be used to foster relationships. She further links these goals to gender differences, arguing that, whereas men are socialised to view interactions from a power perspective, women are socialised to view interactions from a relationship-building perspective.

Importantly, she proposes that the same speech forms (for example, questions) may be interpreted differently, depending on which of the two interaction goals — power or relationship-building — that we hold. Following this line of argument, consider the tag question, 'That was a good movie, wasn't it?' From a power perspective, a tag question puts the communicator in a one-down (or low power) position whereas, from a relationship-building perspective, it fosters relationships by allowing for differences of opinion. Tannen extends this argument to an examination of workplace interactions. She argues that the way in which we give and interpret criticism and praise, and our willingness to engage in arguments, is influenced by gender. Consequently, the kinds of behaviours that women engage in to foster workplace relationships will be interpreted by men as an indicator of low power; and the kinds of behaviours that men engage in will be interpreted as detrimental to workplace relationships by women.

Similar arguments have been made about the relationship between culture and communication. Before turning to these arguments, let us consider how culture might more broadly impact on communication. Due to the work of Hofstede (1980) and others (Trompenaars 1993; Schwartz 1994), we are aware of the many dimensions on which cultures differ. Our concern here is with how these dimensions might influence the communication process. The discussion below draws on the work of Gibson (1997), who identifies two clusters of communication. One cluster is associated with cultures that hold communal values, are collectivist, and are characterised by high power distance and high context communication. The other cluster is represented by agentic (masculine) and individualistic values, and is characterised by low power distance and low context communication. What becomes apparent in Gibson's description is that individuals who are characterised by the first cluster are more likely to value communication as a mechanism for fostering social relationships and decreasing social distance. Individuals characterised by the second cluster are more likely to use communication as a mechanism for establishing status and increasing social distance. Consequently, many of the issues identified by Tannen in the context of cross-gender communication will apply equally to cross-cultural communication.

First, there is the possibility that culture will impact on what we choose to put in our messages. For example, cultures that are high in agentic (masculine) values are more likely to include rational, task-relevant information in their messages, whereas cultures that are high in communal (feminine) values may add a component of emotion to their messages. Similarly, whether cultures emphasise collectivist or individualistic values may impact on how they form their messages. Because relationships are enhanced, collectivists may choose to phrase their messages in a more implicit way by using qualifiers and ambiguous words; individualists, on the other hand, may choose more direct and explicit speech forms that include words such as absolutely, certainly, positively. Cultures also differ in the extent to which meaning derives from the context in which a message is sent. For high context cultures, much of the meaning derives not from the specific message, but from the context in which it is sent, for example who else has heard the message. In low context cultures, messages are treated in a more abstract way. They are interpreted literally for meaning and the surrounding context plays a lesser role in shaping how we interpret those messages. Finally, low power distance cultures are more likely to choose informal over formal channels of communication, whereas high power distance countries are more likely to prefer formal to informal channels of communication (Gibson 1997).

Extending these models to organisations

In the preceding sections, I have described two broad patterns of communication: one has goals of maintaining status and increasing social distance, the other has the goals of building rapport and decreasing social distance. Perhaps not surprisingly, these styles of communication map onto different types of organisational communication climate. *Communication climate* describes an organisation's attitude to communicating with employees. Generally, organisations that are characterised by norms of openness and trust are also thought to have a more positive communication climate, and one that fosters higher levels of organisational commitment and job satisfaction (Lamude, Daniels & Smilowitz 1995; Miles, Patrick & King 1996; Putti, Aryee & Phua 1990). Dysfunctional climates are characterised by communication that emphasises evaluation, control, strategy, emotional neutrality, superiority and certainty. Conversely, functional climates are characterised by communication that emphasises information exchange, a problem-solving orientation, spontaneity, empathy, equality and provisionalism (Gordon 1993).

Interestingly, these different communication climates may be linked to organisational structure. Research shows that not only do mechanistic organisations emphasise one-way communication aimed at gaining control, but also that patterns of communication between managers and employees are much more competitive. In these organisations, both managers and subordinates use communication to gain or regain control of conversations. Conversely, in organic organisations, two-way communication is emphasised and flexibility is a key to organisational interactions. In these organisations, the interaction styles of managers and employees are similar and both place an emphasis on participation and information exchange (Courtright, Fairhurst & Rogers 1989).

These findings suggest that communication climate is shaped by several factors, including the interaction goals of organisational members. If organisations are concerned with fostering a functional communication climate, they would be well advised to attend to the ways in which employees speak to each other, and particularly how they use language to manage relationships. Donnellon (1994), for example, has identified a number of ways that language may be used to foster either collaboration or competition. Donnellon argues that conversational forms can serve the following purposes:
- emphasise interdependence or independence
- increase or decrease social distance
- create or minimise power differences
- emphasise either the individual or the group.

Interestingly, extending this theme, research has shown that when individuals frame conflict in terms of 'we' rather than 'I', they achieve better outcomes (Simons 1993)

Organisational communication

Although the quality of individual communication underpins the quality of organisation communication, managing organisational communication is more complex because the social relationships in organisations are more complex. Essentially, we have moved from one-on-one conversations to conversations with multiple parties; and we often need to communicate through the layers of an organisation rather than directly with the target individual. Consequently, the communication process becomes much more like the processes that we observe in small groups. Before we go on to consider some of these issues in more detail, let us review the 'basics' of organisational communication. In organisations, communication can flow in three directions: *down*, from the top levels to the lower levels in an organisation; *up*, from the lower levels to the top levels in an organisation; and *laterally*, between peers. Although relatively little is known about the last of these patterns of communication, the first two have been extensively investigated.

Downward communication serves five functions:
1 to give job instructions
2 to provide a rationale for specific jobs
3 to communicate organisation procedures, policies and regulations
4 to provide performance feedback
5 to establish an organisational culture (Katz & Kahn 1978).

From a mechanistic perspective, the key issue for downward communication is that it makes feedback difficult — much of the information that flows down organisations comes in a written form. Returning to the psychological model, key issues here include:
- the likelihood that filtering — especially deletion — will occur as information passes down through organisational layers
- that managers will violate rules of interactional justice when they provide performance feedback.

Good downward communication also requires that managers do not see interactions as power struggles; rather, they need to be open and willing to share information. Finally, good downward communication is both timely and relevant (Luthans 1985).

Upward communication also serves several vital functions. First, it provides feedback about the effectiveness of downward communication. It also assists managers to identify potential problems in organisational procedures and provides information about workplace morale (Kreps 1990). If overload is one of the biggest problems for downward communication, then underload is surely one of the biggest problems for upward communication. Again, returning to the psychological model, several factors will affect the flow of upward communication. First, because employees need to communicate what is essentially 'bad' news, for example potential problems with organisational procedures, they may engage in distortion by minimising the negative aspects of their message. Second, and especially if communication is viewed as a means of maintaining power and status, a manager may fail to 'hear' the message. A subordinate may lack credibility in the manager's eyes, or the manager's ability to understand the meaning of the message may be influenced by selective perception and value judgements. There is no easy solution to these problems.

Although there are many prescriptions for improving upward communication (Greenberg & Baron 1993), none of these will work if the organisation's communication climate is dysfunctional. In the absence of openness and trust, it is unlikely that any strategy will encourage subordinates to honestly pass information back up the organisational hierarchy. The issue, for organisations, is how they create the type of communication climate that fosters information flow.

Communication networks

A further issue for organisations is the need to understand how information *flows* around the organisations — that is, the communication network. There are two types of communication networks: centralised and decentralised. In *centralised* networks, one individual holds a key (central) position and all information flows through that individual. Not surprisingly, this individual holds considerable power and frequently emerges as a leader in the network. However, this role can be stressful — the person at the centre of a network must coordinate large amounts of information and make many decisions about what will be passed on to whom. In these networks, it is also possible that some individuals become isolated; that is, they receive no information at all. And being an isolate is even more stressful than being at the centre of the network (Leiter 1988; Roberts & O'Reilly 1979). In *decentralised* networks, there is a free and open flow of communication between all members in the network. Although which of these networks is more effective depends on the nature of the task, decentralised networks always result in greater participant satisfaction (Johnson & Johnson 1987).

Remembering that communication must flow not just around, but also between networks, we can consider two further roles in networks. Both describe the functions of individuals who bridge the gap between two networks. First, individuals may act as *gatekeepers*, determining what information passes into (or out of) a network. Middle managers, because they provide a bridge between senior management and staff, are likely to find themselves in this role. Second, individuals may act as *boundary-spanners*: they may provide a link between two or more organisational units. While boundary-spanning positions can create role conflict and ambiguity for their incumbents, they serve the important function of breaking down organisation barriers and increasing communication flow (Mitchell, Dowling, Kabanoff & Larson 1988).

New directions for organisational communication

Thinking about communication networks raises a number of issues for organisations. First, we need to understand not just the formal networks (those defined by organisational charts) but also the informal networks. Understanding informal networks provides insight into lines of influence that are not recognised by the formal organisational structure. This links to an emerging trend in organisational research, the investigation of social networks or *relational demography*. Relational demography describes the extent to which the characteristics of group (or organisational) members are (dis)similar. This concept captures differences along many demographic dimensions, including age, gender and cultural background. In short, it is a measure of a group's diversity. This becomes important when we realise that perceived similarity leads to higher levels of attraction and increased communication (Tsui & O'Reilly 1989). These kinds of differences can create organisational 'faultlines' — dividing lines that define subgroups within a larger group (Lau & Murnighan 1998). One consequence of such faultlines is to restrict communication, so that it does not cross this invisible division (Lau & Murnighan 1998). For organisations, this implies that informal communication networks will develop around perceived demographic similarities and may affect communication flow within work groups. It further implies that, within work groups, fault lines may restrict communication to minority group members, creating isolates. As organisations become increasingly diverse, the challenge for managers is to develop communication strategies that will facilitate communication across faultlines.

Second, we need to consider the relationship between organisational structure, communication networks and communication climate. As we saw earlier in this chapter, it appears that mechanistic structures, centralised networks and 'dysfunctional' climates group together, as do organic structures, decentralised networks and 'functional' communication climates. A more immediate issue, for organisations, is the fact that organisational forms are undergoing rapid change. As organisations move from traditional structures to new structures for organising work, so the very nature of communication and communication networks will change. A yet to be addressed issue is how we will create positive communication climates and manage organisational communication when new organisational forms, such as matrix and cellular organisations, are introduced.

How communication affects organisations

Communication is the lifeblood of organisations. As we saw in the preceding section, without it we cannot convey information about tasks, roles, policies or procedures. Nor can we determine how well the organisation is working or identify potential problems. More importantly, communication affects individuals day-to-day experiences of their workplace. For example, research shows that communication can reduce the uncertainty encountered by newcomers, lower stress, and influence the quality of group decisions. In the next few paragraphs, I go on to review the relationship between communication and individual experiences in the workplace.

Organisational socialisation

When individuals join an organisation, they experience uncertainty about their tasks and their interactions with others. Communication provides one means of reducing this uncertainty. By providing information about organisational norms and values, organisations can not only reduce this uncertainty but can also shape the values and behaviours of their new employees. Newcomers are not, however, passive and research shows that they seek information about their jobs, their roles and the social norms of their work group. According to Chao, O'Leary-Kelly, Wolf, Klein and Gardner (1994), individuals need to obtain information about their tasks, organisational jargon, organisational politics, goals, values and history. This information may be obtained through observation, limit testing or, importantly from our perspective, through direct and indirect questions (Miller & Jablin 1991). Research shows that individuals learn their jobs more effectively when they receive technical information from supervisors (Morrison 1993). Similarly, performance feedback increases role clarity and a willingness to request normative information increases social integration (Morrison 1993). Importantly, acquiring this kind of knowledge not only improves work performance; it also accelerates career progression (Chao et al. 1994).

Stress and burnout

Uncertainty has long been recognised as a source of workplace stress. Like other forms of communication, organisational communication has the potential to reduce uncertainty and, consequently, stress (Miller, Ellis, Zook & Lyles 1990). Several authors have investigated two forms of organisational communication — social support and participation in decision-making — for their impact on burnout. Burnout is observed in professions that require a high level of interpersonal contact. It is characterised by a group of three symptoms: high emotional exhaustion, or the feeling that you are emotionally drained; depersonalisation, or feeling negative about or alienated from clients; a sense of low personal accomplishment, characterised as a lack of work-related fulfilment or esteem. Social support is able to reduce both the experience of emotional exhaustion and depersonalisation, as well as increasing feelings of personal accomplishment (Lee & Ashforth 1991; Miller et al. 1990, Miller, Zook & Ellis 1989). The mechanisms by which this is accomplished are not well understood, but these researchers provide some evidence to suggest that social support reduces the symptoms of burnout because it decreases work load and role stress (Lee & Ashforth 1991; Miller et al. 1989, 1990). Additionally, it appears that participation in decision making is able to alleviate feelings of depersonalisation and emotional exhaustion, while increasing feelings of personal accomplishment. Again, this appears to be because it reduces role stress (Miller et al. 1989, 1990).

Teams and decision making

Another long-debated issue centres on the relative merits of individual and group decision making. The question that arises is whether groups make 'better' decisions than individuals. Research has yielded mixed results and it is unclear that groups consistently outperform individuals. One of the reasons for this is that the situation faced by groups is considerably more complex. Group members need to manage more perspectives on the issues being discussed and more information. Part of the reason that groups do not always outperform individual decision makers may lie, then, in faulty group process. Salazar (1995), for example, argues that communication may either facilitate or disrupt the quality of group decision making. He argues that as decisions become more complex they create more uncertainty and that this uncertainty creates obstacles to effective decision making. In this context, communication can either disrupt the decision-making process by steering discussion away from the task or it can facilitate decision making by ensuring that alternative viewpoints are considered. Salazar (1995) speculates that high-quality group decisions are reached when facilitative influences dominate communication, and poor quality group decisions are reached when disruptive influences dominate communication.

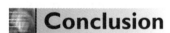

Conclusion

In this chapter, I described several models of communication. For each model, I also identified the challenges that organisations must address in order to ensure high-quality communication. Traditional models, which emphasise the accuracy with which messages are sent, must meet the challenge of electronic communication. As the use of electronic media increases, we reduce the informal social contact between individuals. One consequence of this is that we find out less about the people we are communicating with and any faultlines in the organisation are more likely to be maintained; new ones may be created. These models also emphasise the way we interact with others and highlight the role of interactional justice in maintaining a good communication climate.

Newer perspectives on communication highlight the context within which messages are sent and received. They provide a unifying theme for understanding how diversity influences the communication process. This highlights the challenges posed by increasingly diverse workforces, in particular the need to foster understanding and communication across faultlines. Because such faultlines form natural barriers to successful communication, managers must develop strategies transcending these boundaries. Finally, my discussion of organisational communication turned our attention to the changing nature of work and organisation structure, which is increasing the complexity of organisational communication. We have yet to determine the demands that new organisational forms and work arrangements will place on organisational communication. Underlying all of these challenges, however, is a challenge that is far from new. How to foster a positive communication climate and increase employees' communication satisfaction has been — and continues to be — a challenge for organisations. One of the principal criteria for achieving this is a willingness to view communication as a means for building better relationships, rather than as a tool for gaining power and control. And, as we have seen in this chapter, its attitude to communication is intimately linked to an organisation's structure and culture.

References

Aries, E (1996) *Men and women in interaction: reconsidering the differences.* New York: Oxford University Press.

Bolton, R (1987) *People skills.* Australia: Simon and Schuster.

Bradac, JJ (1990) Language attitudes and impression formation. In H Giles and WP Robinson (eds) *Handbook of language and social psychology.* Baffins Lane, Chichester: John Wiley and Sons.

Bradac, JJ, Mulac, A & Thompson, SA (1995) Men's and women's use of intensifiers and hedges in problem-solving interactions: molar and molecular analyses. *Research on Language and Social Interaction*, 28: 93–116.

Bryan, A & Gallois, C (1992) Rules about assertion in the workplace: effects of status and message type. *Australian Psychologist*, 44: 51–9.

Burgoon, JK, Stern, LA & Dillman, L (1995) *Interpersonal adaptation: dyadic interaction pattern*. Cambridge, New York: Cambridge University Press.

Carnevale, PJ & Isen, AM (1986) The influence of positive affect and visual access on the discovery of integrative solutions in bilateral negotiation. *Organizational Behavior and Human Decision Processes*, 37: 1–13.

Chao, GT, O'Leary-Kelly, M, Wolf, S, Klein, HJ & Gardner, PD (1994) Organizational socialization: its content and consequences. *Journal of Applied Psychology*, 79: 730–43.

Chatman, JA, Putnam, LL & Sondak, H (1991) Integrating communication and negotiation research. *Research on Negotiation in Organizations*, 3: 139–64.

Cohen, RL (1991) Justice and negotiation. *Research on Negotiation in Organizations*, 3: 259–81.

Courtright, JA, Fairhurst, GT & Rogers, LE (1989) Interaction patterns in organic and mechanistic systems. *Academy of Management Journal*, 32: 773–802.

Donnellon, A (1994) Team work. *Research on Negotiation in Organizations*, 4.

Gallois, C, Callan, VJ & McKenzie Palmer, J-A (1992) The influence of applicant communication style and interviewer characteristics on hiring decisions. *Journal of Applied Social Psychology*, 22: 1041–60.

Gibson, CB (1997) Do you hear what I hear? A framework for reconciling intercultural difficulties arising from cognitive styles and cultural values. In PC Earley and M Erez (eds) *New perspectives on international industrial/organizational psychology*. San Francisco: Jossey-Bass.

Gordon, JR (1993) *A diagnostic approach to organizational behavior* (4th ed.) Boston: Allyn and Bacon.

Greenberg, J (1990) Organizational justice: yesterday, today and tomorrow. *Journal of Management*, 16: 399–432.

Greenberg, J & Baron, RA (1993) *Behavior in organizations: understanding and managing the human side of work* (4th ed.) Boston: Allyn and Bacon.

Hinde, RA (1979) *Toward understanding relationships*. New York: Academic Press.

Hofstede, G (1980) *Culture's consequences: international differences in work-related values*. Newbury Park, CA: Sage.

Ivancevich, JM, Olekalns, M & Matteson, M T (1997) *Organizational behavior and management*. (1st Australasian ed.) Sydney: Irwin.

Johnson, DW & Johnson, FP (1987) *Joining together: group theory and group skills* (3rd ed.) Prentice Hall.

Katz, D & Kahn, R (1978) *The social psychology of organizations* (2nd ed.) New York: Wiley.

Kolb, DA, Rubin, IM & Osland, Y (1991) *Organizational behavior: an experiential approach* (5th ed.) Prentice Hall.

Kreps, GL (1990) *Organizational communication*. New York: Longman

Lamude, KG, Daniels, TD & Smilowitz, M (1995) Subordinates' satisfaction with communication and managers' relational messages. *Perceptual and Motor Skills*, 81: 467–71

Lau, D & Murnighan, K (1998) Demographic diversity and faultlines: the compositional dynamics of organizational groups. *Academy of Management Review*, 23: 325–40.

Lee, RT & Ashforth, BE (1991) A further examination of managerial burnout: toward an integrated model. *Journal of Organizational Behavior*, 14: 3–20.

Leiter, MP (1988) Burnout as a function of communication patterns. *Group and Organization Studies*, 14: 15–22.

Luthans, F (1985). *Organizational behavior* (4th ed.) New York: McGraw-Hill.

McCann, CD & Higgins, ET (1990) Social cognition and communication. In H Giles and WP Robinson (eds) *Handbook of language and social psychology*. Baffins Lane, Chichester: John Wiley and Sons.

Miles, EW, Patrick, SL & King, WC Jr (1996) Job level as a systemic variable in predicting the relationship between supervisory communication and job satisfaction. *Journal of Occupational and Organizational Psychology*, 69: 277–92.

Miller, KI, Ellis, BH, Zook, EG & Lyles, JS (1990) An integrated model of communication, stress, and burnout in the workplace. *Communication Research*, 17: 300–326.

Miller, KI, Zook, EG & Ellis, BH (1989) Occupational differences in the influence of communication on stress and burnout in the workplace. *Management communication Quarterly*, 3: 166–90.

Miller, VD & Jablin, FM (1991) Information seeking during organizational entry: influence, tactics, and a model of the process. *Academy of Management Review*, 16: 92–120.

Mitchell, TR, Dowling, PJ, Kabanoff, BV & Larson, JR (1988) *People in organizations: an introduction to organizational behaviour in Australia*. Sydney: McGraw-Hill.

Moore, DA, Kurtzberg, TR, Thompson, LL & Morris, MW (1999) Long and short routes to success in electronically mediated negotiations: group affiliations and good vibrations. *Organizational Behavior and Human Decision Processes*, 77: 22–43.

Morrison, EW (1993) Longitudinal study of the effects of information seeking on newcomer socialization. *Journal of Applied Psychology*, 78: 173–83.

Mulac, A & Bradac, JJ (1995) Women's style in problem-solving interaction: powerless, or simply feminine? In PJ Kalbfleisch and MJ Cody (eds) *Gender, power and communication in human relationships*. Hillsdale, NJ: Lawrence Erlbaum.

Novelli, L, Kirkman, BL & Shapiro, DL (1995) Effective implementation of organizational change: an organizational justice perspective. In CL Cooper and DM Rousseau (eds) *Trends in organizational behavior* (2nd ed.), John Wiley and Sons.

Putnam, L, Phillips, N & Chapman, P (1999) Metaphors of communication and organization. In SR Clegg, C Hardy, and WR Nord (eds) *Managing organisations: current issues*. London: Sage Publications.

Putti, JM, Aryee, S & Phua, J (1990) Communication relation satisfaction and organizational commitment. *Group and Organization Studies*, 15: 44–52.

Roberts, KH & O'Reilly, CA (1979) Some correlates of communication roles in organizations. *Academy of Management Journal*, 22: 42–57.

Salazaer, AJ (1995) Understanding the synergistic effects of communication in small groups: making the most out of group member abilities. *Small Group Research*, 26: 169–99.

Sarbaugh-Thompson, M & Feldman, MS (1998) Electronic mail and organizational communication: does saying "hi" really matter? *Organization Science*, 9: 685–98.

Schwartz, SH (1994) Beyond individualism/collectivism: new cultural dimensions of values. In U Kim, HC Triandis, and G Yoon (eds) *Individualism and collectivism*. London: Sage.

Shannon, C & Weaver, W (1948) *The mathematical theory of communication*. Urbana: University of Illinois.

Simons, T (1993) Speech patterns and the concept of utility in cognitive maps: the case of integrative bargaining. *Academy of Management Journal*, 36: 139–56.

Snyder, M & Swann, WB (1978) Behavioral confirmation in social interaction: from social perception to social reality. *Journal of Experimental Social Psychology*, 14: 148–162.

Sproull, L & Kiesler, SB (1991) *Connections: new ways of working in the networked organization*. Cambridge, MA: The MIT Press.

Tannen, D (1995) The power of talk: who gets heard and why. *Harvard Business Review*, 73: 138–48.

Thompson, L (1998) *The mind and heart of the negotiator*. Prentice Hall.

Trompenaars, F (1993) *Riding the wave of culture*. London: Economist Books.

Tsui, A and O'Reilly, C (1989) Beyond simple demographic effects: the importance of relational demography in superior-subordinate dyads. *Academy of Management Journal*, 32: 402–23.

PART 6 Managing organisational dynamics

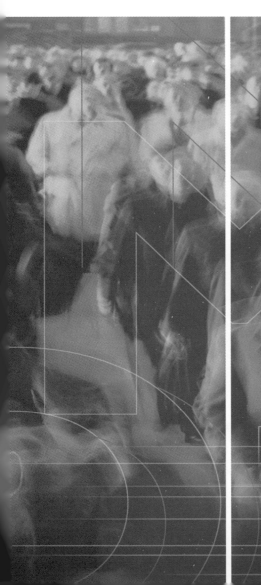

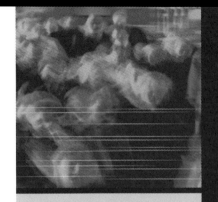

CHAPTER 18
Organisational change

by Patrick Dawson

University of Aberdeen, Scotland

p.dawson@abdn.ac.uk

Introduction

The new century has already witnessed a number of company mergers and transformations, and developments in technology continue to offer new ways of organising work. How we navigate these changes and remake and remodel organisations have important implications not only for employees directly affected by change but also for the society in which we live. In this chapter, we examine some of the conceptual and practical issues which surround discussions on change management. The intention is both to inform and educate the reader, and to present new material which will hopefully promote further discussion and debate. The chapter commences by examining what we mean by the term 'organisational change'. A number of definitional concerns are discussed and some key dimensions are identified. This is followed by an historical overview of change management, which briefly documents the importance of the industrial revolution and the establishment of the factory form of organisation. A number of external and internal triggers to organisational change are outlined and the importance of context in shaping the uptake of change is highlighted. The notion of employee resistance to change is then addressed and a range of reasons is listed as to why people are often unwilling to accept change. Following on from this, attention is directed towards change theories and frameworks.

In evaluating the literature on conventional change models, two approaches are discussed: first, an organisational development approach which stresses the importance of participation and communication; and, second, a situational model which draws on contingency theory and emphasises the importance of varying company change strategies to achieve optimum fit with the business environment. Following a critical evaluation of these two approaches, a processual framework is developed and advocated. This processual perspective is then drawn on in a section which outlines practical guidelines on the management of change. Finally, the chapter concludes by looking forward into the first decade of the new century and suggesting that process is likely to remain a key concept in the study of organisational change.

Defining organisational change: navigating the four dimensions

Organisational change is difficult to conceptualise because it involves rather complex processes that do not lend themselves to simple definition. Attempts to simplify change processes into a series of rational linear events or N-step phase models are at face value attractive but in practice they tend to lose their relevance to the actual process of managing change. This leaves us with the question of how we define organisational change.

At a general level, we could formulate a definition of organisational change which encompasses all aspects of change within any form of organisation. Under such a broad definition, change initiatives could range from corporate restructuring and the replacement of key personnel through to the minor modification of basic operating procedures within a particular branch or plant. One problem, which arises from these commonsense definitions, is that organisational change is not differentiated from the more general study of organisations. In other words, the study of organisational change virtually becomes the study of organisations. For our purposes, a simple definition of organisational change is 'new ways of organising and working'. However, this tells us little about the nature of the change in question. For example, should we differentiate an individual's decision to use an electronic diary, which is networked into the main office, from the decision of some large corporation to de-layer and downsize in all major operations worldwide?

In tackling this conceptual problem and moving beyond lay definitions, academics have sought to identify a number of defining characteristics of organisational change. Although this has resulted in the development of competing conceptual frameworks, two common dimensions which run through a number of these more sophisticated characterisations relate to, first, the movement over time from a present state of organisation to some future state (Beckhard & Harris 1987) and, second, the scale or scope of change (Dunphy & Stace 1990). On this second dimension, the main focus has been on examining the more permanent, influential, large-scale operational and strategic changes that are affecting organisations (Burnes 2000). In examining these forms of organisational change, the question arises as to whether change outcomes have been brought about through a rapid transformation or more incrementally over a longer period of time (Quinn 1980). According to Buchanan and Badham (1999), strategies for extensive participation may be used under apolitical programs of incremental change as change is accepted and occurs at a more relaxed pace. They argue that whether change is generally accepted or challenged is another central dimension and a key determinant of the type of strategy required to successfully manage the process. For example, they claim that radical change programs, which are critical to the survival of the company and yet are highly politicised and contested, will need to be driven by what they term 'power-coercive solutions'. They note that any form of contested change will necessitate political activity in dealing with opponents and building support for the initiative (Buchanan & Badham 1999, pp. 180–1).

Three dimensions can all be used to characterise change. These are:

1. the temporal element of change (the time frame, for example, whether change is to occur quickly or over a longer period of time)
2. the scale of change (whether small incremental change or large-scale radical change)
3. the political dimension of change (whether change is generally accepted as being central and worthwhile or whether is it perceived as a threat and hence challenged).

The fourth and final dimension discussed here is the substantive element of change. This is taken to refer to the essential nature and content of the change in question. For example, are we talking about a cultural change program, the introduction of new technology or the implementation of a quality assurance system?

Within the literature, some combination of the four dimensions outlined above is often used in defining and classifying organisational change. However, the dimensions, which have been stressed and developed by authors, vary considerably and, as a consequence, considerable debate and some conceptual confusion can occur. This is further exacerbated when certain elements of new theories and concepts are taken up by consultants in their drive to meet the growing demand for business solutions. As a result, the last decade has witnessed a mushrooming of consultants and consultant firms who variously modify, refine and repackage change concepts and theories. If they are successful in popularising their change initiative, then the high visibility of these programs (especially if supported by government funding and taken up by large multinational corporations) can stimulate more widespread implementation. In practice, some of the consultant packages may differ considerably from the concepts and theories which formed the basis of initial formulation. Thus, not only is there a greater sense of competitive urgency for change, but the emerging offerings may themselves be transformed from initial conceptualisation, through to popularisation, consultant or change agent modification and eventual adaptation during implementation and uptake. It is no wonder that the area of change management continues to stimulate simple recipes for success, which do not provide accurate reflections of what is a complex and muddied process.

A brief history of organisational change

There is nothing new about organisational change; we could study early forms of organisation in China or the changing face of government and military organisation under the rise and fall of the Roman Empire. However, our interest is with the rise of commerce and the birth of the factory system following the British Industrial Revolution (c. 1730–1850). The mechanisation of the textile industry in the late eighteenth century marked a significant societal transformation from a mainly agricultural society into an industrial economy. The abundance of rich mineral resources, particularly in coal and iron ore, led to the construction of bridges and canals, the building of ships and the development of railways. New industrial towns developed around Glasgow, Newcastle, Manchester and Birmingham, and new forms of industrial organisation were imposed on workers seeking employment in these growing urban centres. In its infancy, the industrial revolution offered wealth to the new industrial owners and hardship for working families who often had to suffer long hours and poor working conditions for little pay.

New methods for organising work followed the principles put forward by Adam Smith in 1776. He used the well-known example of pin making to demonstrate how, through distributing tasks to workers (so that an employee would constantly perform one simple task rather than doing all the tasks required to make a pin), output could be significantly increased. These ideas were taken up by pioneering factory owners such as James Watt, Matthew Boulton and Josiah Wedgwood (Burnes 1992, p. 8). By the twentieth century, early forms of factory organisation were superseded by the new fixed-speed moving assembly lines of Henry Ford (see Hobsbawn 1969, pp. 172–8).

The systematic organisation of mass production and the breaking down of work tasks into ever smaller elements is associated with job fragmentation and the rise in scientific management (Taylor 1911). Taylor argued for the systematic collection of data on work processes, the simplification and minimisation of tasks with a concomitant reduction in workers' discretion and, finally, the establishment of standard procedures and times for carrying out tasks. Although there is considerable debate on the extent and uptake of scientific management, Taylorite forms of work organisation can still be found in various guises throughout the industrialised world and his principles have further influenced the development of change theories. For example, some of the problems associated with Taylorite forms of work organisation have been tackled by human relations theory and the more participative change strategies advocated by the field of organisational development (French & Bell 1985). In other cases, some change initiatives such as business process re-engineering (Hammer & Champy 1993) have been accused of simply reintroducing a type of ICT-mediated form of Taylorism, where 'the silicon chip plays an equivalent role in BPR to that performed by the stop watch in Scientific Management' (Willmott 1995, p. 96). In short, the twentieth century witnessed the emergence of a range of new theories on organisational change and interest in the area has heightened under the current climate of a new century.

Developments in technology, notions of the virtual and the boundary-less organisation, the growth in trade in the Asia-Pacific region, wars, the transition and changes within Europe and issues of globalisation all form part of the broader context in which organisations are a part. It is not surprising, therefore, that an organisation's ability to manage change is perceived to be increasingly central to its competitive position and ultimate survival.

Organisational change: challenging issues

The triggers to organisational change

Within the literature, a range of 'triggers' to organisational change have been identified. These are seen to consist of elements both within and outside an organisation. Some of the main external factors are seen to comprise:

- government laws and regulations (for example, legislation on age discrimination, world agreements and national policies on pollution and the environment, international agreements on tariffs and trade)
- globalisation of markets and the internationalisation of business (the need to accommodate new competitive pressures both on the home market and overseas)
- major political and social events (for example, some of the changing relationships and tensions between America and the Middle East, and Australia and its East Asian neighbours)
- advances in technology (for example, companies who specialise in high-technology products are often prone to the problem of technological obsolescence and the need to introduce new technology)
- organisational growth and expansion (as an organisation increases in size, so may the complexity of the organisation, requiring the development of appropriate coordinating mechanisms)
- fluctuations in business cycles (for example, changes in the level of economic activity both within national economies and within major trading blocs can influence change strategies significantly).

Four internal triggers to change, which are generally characterised in this field of study, are:
1. technology
2. primary task
3. people
4. administrative structures (Leavitt 1964).

The concept of 'technology' can be used broadly to refer to the plant, machinery and tools (the apparatus) and the associated philosophy and system of work organisation which blend together in the production of goods or services. Thus, a change in an organisation's technology may involve the installation of a single piece of equipment or the complete redesign of a production process. The 'primary product' and/or service of an organisation refers to the core business, whether this is providing a health service, refining oil, or developing computer software. 'People', or human resources, refers to the individual members and groups of people who constitute an organisation. 'Administrative structures' refers to elements pertaining to the administrative control of work, such as formalised lines of communication, established working procedures, managerial hierarchies, reward systems and disciplinary procedures.

With the turn of the century and the growing expectation of the need to change, the managerial careers and political aspirations of business leaders can also promote visions and strategies for change. Essentially, there are external influences as well as a range of internal factors which may all interlink and overlap in determining the speed, direction and outcomes of change within an organisation. One important element identified in the literature centres on the unwillingness of employees to accept change (or resistance to change) and this area is discussed briefly in the section which follows.

Resisting organisational change

Organisational change may break the continuity of a working environment and create a climate of uncertainty and ambiguity. Old-established relationships may be redefined, familiar structures redesigned and modified, and traditional methods of work may be called into question. Understandably, some employees may seek to maintain the status quo and resist change. Typically, resistance has been identified as resulting from one, or a combination, of the following factors:

- substantive change in job (skill requirements)
- reduction in economic security or job displacement
- psychological threats (whether perceived or actual)

- disruption of social arrangements (new work arrangements)
- lowering of status (redefines authority relationships).

According to Gray and Starke (1988, pp. 575–80), a substantive change in the nature of work and the skills required to perform certain functions is likely to engender distrust and resistance, particularly in situations where employees are not informed of the change prior to its implementation. Even if these threats reflect an individual's perception of change rather than an actual threat, employee resistance to change is likely to result. Bedeian (1980) agrees that parochial self-interest, misunderstanding and lack of trust are common causes of resistance to organisational change. In addition, he notes that individuals will differ in the way they perceive and evaluate change and that some employees may have a lower tolerance for change.

In examining reasons why employees may resist change, Eccles (1994) identifies 13 possible causes:

1. The employee fails to understand the problem.
2. The solution is disliked because an alternative is preferred.
3. The employee feels that the proposed solution will not work.
4. The change has unacceptable personal costs.
5. The rewards from change are not sufficient.
6. The employee fears being unable to cope with the new situation.
7. The change threatens to destroy existing social arrangements.
8. The employee is afraid that sources of influence and control will be eroded.
9. New values and practices are repellent.
10. The willingness to change is low.
11. Management motives for change are considered suspicious.
12. Other interests are more highly valued than new proposals.
13. The change will reduce power and career opportunities.

According to Collins (1998), there is a tendency for writers on change management to view employee resistance as a negative, individual problem rather than a positive response to changing conditions, and one which might require further consideration. He states:

> Workers who 'resist' change tend to be cast as lacking the psychological make-up to deal with change, and so are said to be weak and fearful of change, whereas those who support or manage change are regarded as 'go-ahead' chaps who have the 'right-stuff' for career success. (Collins 1998, p. 92)

In seeking to overcome resistance to change, a number of strategies have been identified; they centre largely around methods of participation, communication and support at one end of a continuum through to negotiation, manipulation and coercion at the other. As we shall see in the section that follows, those who adopt an organisational-development approach have tended to opt for more participative methods, whereas those following a contingency perspective recognise the need for more coercive strategies under certain contingent circumstances.

The study of organisational change: conventional theories and models

Organisational change is a growing area of study and has its roots in organisation theory. In the conceptual developments of modern management initiatives, such as knowledge management, the learning organisation or best practice management, social science knowledge is used to formulate 'new' approaches to change management. Following the conceptualisation of a change philosophy or strategy, these ideas may become popularised through various forms of publication and media coverage. In some cases, such as the uptake of quality management programs, these processes have been bolstered by the setting up of prestigious quality awards, the development of national and international quality agencies and the support of governments. With the liberalisation of world trade and the entry of new fast-growing economies into a more highly competitive and global market place, many companies are continually in search of change programs which can improve their competitive position. As already noted, this concern with the successful management of change in order to sustain competitive advantage has stimulated demand for simple change recipes to solve complex organisational problems. These managerial prescriptions for change are generally presented in the form of a rational historical development, with each new development representing an improvement on previous ideas. In this way, new recipes for change are often presented as combining the best of earlier movements (for example, quality management can be shown to combine social and cultural ideas from earlier human relations and socio-technical systems theories with technical and administrative prescriptions from scientific management and bureaucratic theories). However, academics who have sought to explain organisational change have been quick to show how there can be significant variation in the adoption of managerial ideas (Hofstede 1991), how any fundamental change is likely to engender at least some employee distrust and resistance, and how different strategies and structures may be appropriate under different circumstances (Donaldson 1987). These and other competing views have resulted in a large body of empirical research and the development of a number of competing perspectives of change (Collins 1998). Two competing models are now presented.

Planned change models

The foundational work of Kurt Lewin has had a significant and long-lasting effect on the way academics have researched and taught the topics of change management. The ghost of Lewin, in the form of an established orthodoxy, has generated considerable resistance to new frameworks for understanding change. This is perhaps ironic, given that Kurt Lewin championed minority claims, questioned conventional assumptions and prejudices and, throughout his life, remained a strong advocate for democracy at the workplace (de Board 1978). For those practitioners and academics within the field of management known as organisational development (OD), his classic work on intergroup dynamics and planned change has proven to be particularly influential (see Kreitner & Kinicki 1992, pp. 723-61). Basically, he argued that in order for change to be successfully managed it is necessary to follow three general steps (Hellriegel, Slocum & Woodman. 1995, pp. 667-9). The three general steps identified by Lewin (1951) are:
1 unfreezing
2 changing
3 refreezing.

Unfreezing is the stage in which there is a recognised need for change and action is taken to unfreeze existing attitudes and behaviour. This preparatory stage is deemed essential to the generation of employee support and the minimisation of employee resistance. For example, in his pioneering research (some of which was published after his death in 1947; see Lewin 1951), Lewin found that, in order to minimise worker resistance, employees should be actively encouraged to participate in the process of planning proposed change programs (see Clutterbuck & Crainer 1990, p. 105).

Managing change through reducing the forces that prevent change, rather than through increasing the forces that are pushing for change, is central to Lewin's approach and his technique of force-field analysis (1947, pp. 5-42). He maintained that within any social system there are driving and restraining forces which serve to maintain the status quo, and that organisations generally exist in a state of quasi-stationary equilibrium. Thus, in order to create conditions conducive to change it is necessary to identify the restraining and driving forces and to change one or other of these in order to create an imbalance.

In the management of organisational change, the focus of OD specialists has been on providing data that would unfreeze the system through reducing the restraining forces rather than through increasing the driving forces (Gray & Starke 1988, pp. 596-629; Weisbord 1988, p. 94). Once an imbalance has been created, the system can be altered and a new set of driving and restraining forces put into place. A planned change program is implemented and only when the desired state has been achieved will the change agent set about 'refreezing' the organisation. The new state of balance is then appraised and, where appropriate, methods of positive reinforcement are used to ensure employees 'internalise' the attitudes and behaviors consistent with new work regimes.

This planned model of change remains an integral part of the conventional orthodoxy taught in business departments and management schools around the world. Although academics have generally been slow to criticise the relevance of this model and continue to spread the Lewinian view of change management among their students, there is now a growing recognition of the need for alternative strategies for change and of the political process involved in the successful management of change.

Situational or contingency approach

Dexter Dunphy, who has a background in the OD area (see Dunphy 1981), has developed a model for identifying key contingencies and which can be used by managers to determine the most appropriate change strategies given the prevailing circumstances (Dunphy & Stace 1990, pp. 81–92). The two dimensions of their model are, first, the scale of change and, second, the style of leadership required to bring about change. With regard to the former, the authors identify four types. 'Fine tuning' and 'incremental adjustment' refer to small-scale changes ranging from the refining and clarification of existing procedures through to the actual adjustment of organisational structures. 'Modular transformation' and 'corporate transformation' refer to large-scale changes from divisional restructuring to revolutionary changes throughout the whole organisation. In the second dimension, the appropriate style of leadership is seen to range along a continuum from participative to autocratic, namely 'collaborative', 'consultative', 'directive' and 'coercive'. By using these dimensions, Dunphy and Stace identify four types of change strategies. 'Participative evolution' and 'forced evolution' refer to incremental change through collaborating and directive change respectively. 'Charismatic transformation' is described as large-scale discontinuous change achieved by collaborating means; and, finally, 'dictatorial transformation' describes major coercive change programs.

The model developed by Dunphy and Stace is clearly influenced by Lewin's work and, while it attempts to tackle some of the problems associated with the universality of OD, as David Wilson (1992, p. 31) notes, 'the addition of an extra variable — whether or not the organisation is out of fit with its environment — merely adds to the list of driving and restraining forces.' Perhaps one of the major failings of this model is the way change is characterised as an apolitical process. There is a surprising lack of reference to notions of power (Pfeffer 1993) and the political nature of workplace change (see, for example, Mangham 1979; Pettigrew 1973). As Dunford (1990) points out, 'managers are portrayed as neutral conduits' who ignore their own self-interests in making rational decisions that seek to promote organisational effectiveness and survival.

On this count, Buchanan and Badham (1999, p. 189) point out that, while there are no simple strategies for effective change management, there is the paradox that change programs should appear to significant others (such as the public) as rational and linear. Increasingly, however, these linear stage models of change are being called into question (Kanter, Stein & Jick 1992, p. 10). It is no longer deemed appropriate to view change as a discrete series of stages but, rather, as an ongoing complex process with various twists, turns and restarts. In accommodating this shift in emphasis, there has been a theoretical and empirical movement towards more fluid, dynamic and *processual accounts* (Hatch 1997).

Organisational change: towards a processual perspective

In the past, the push to identify and define strategies to aid change management under prevailing contextual conditions has led to a tendency to downplay the processual and ongoing nature of organisational change. However, there are a growing number of academics in Europe and, more recently, North America and Australia, who are starting to recognise the importance of processual research for understanding the dynamics of organisational change

(Van de Ven & Huber 1990). For example, the early work of Pettigrew (1985) charted the unfolding and non-linear aspects of change at Imperial Chemical Industries. He has criticised the aprocessual character of a lot of the material on change management in advocating the need for the adoption of particular types of research strategy and methodology (Pettigrew 1990). In contrast to the dominant approach in organisation theory which emphasises the importance of sophisticated quantitative analyses (Ledford, Mohram, Mohram & Lawler 1990, pp. 6–8), the processual approach is concerned with the collection of longitudinal qualitative data which facilitate a more detailed understanding of the complex and dynamic processes of change (see Ropo, Eriksson & Hunt 1997). As Pettigrew (1997, p. 338) reflects: 'Human conduct is perpetually in a process of becoming. The overriding aim of the process analyst therefore is to catch this reality in flight.'

The processual framework developed by the author below is based on the assumption that companies continuously move in and out of many different states, often concurrently, during the history of one or a number of organisational change initiatives (see Dawson 1994). Although for analytical purposes it may prove useful to identify and group a number of tasks and decision-making activities, such as the search and assessment of options or implementation, these should not be treated as representing a series of sequential stages in the process of change (as with conventional stage models). The approach taken here is that organisations undergoing change comprise a number of dynamic states which interlock and overlap, and that processes associated with change should be analysed as they happen, so that their emergent character can be understood within the context in which they take place.

A central element under the proposed approach is the need to incorporate an analysis of the politics of managing change (Dawson 1996). On this count, management writers such as Stace and Dunphy (1994) can be criticised for ignoring the political processes associated with trade union and employee actions in response to management's decision to introduce change, whereas political writers such as Braverman (1974) can be criticised for treating management as an homogeneous political group. The position taken here is that an understanding of organisational politics should be central to any approach which seeks to explain change management. For example, the commitment of middle management to strategy implementation cannot be taken for granted (see Porter, Crampon & Smith 1976). As research has shown, variations in commitment can significantly influence the successful management of change (Guth & MacMillan 1989), particularly in cases where vested interests, differing between management levels and functions, do not align with strategic objectives (Wilkinson 1983). Buchanan and Badham conclude:

> In the domain of practical action, as we noted earlier, management is a contact sport. If you don't want to get bruised, don't play. There is little to be gained by complaining about the turf game, its players, its tricks, its strategies, its tactics and its potential damage. Criticism of the existence of organisational politics is likely to have as much impact as criticism of British weather ... The main argument of this book is that the change agent who is not politically skilled will fail. (Buchanan & Badham 1999, p. 231)

The second major concern of a processual approach is with the context in which change takes place. An historical perspective on both the internal and external organisational context is central to understanding the opportunities, constraints and organisationally defined routes to change (Kelly & Amburgey 1991, p. 610). As already noted, the coexistence of a number of competing histories of change can significantly shape ongoing change programs. In this sense, the contextual and historical dimension can both promote certain options and devalue others during the process of organisational change. Consequently under this framework, the contextual dimension is taken to refer to the past and present external and internal operating environments as well as to the influence of future projections and expectations on current operating practice.

External contextual factors are taken to include changes in competitors' strategies; the level of international competition; government legislation; changing social expectations; technological innovations; and changes in the level of business activity. Internal contextual factors are taken to include Leavitt's (1964) fourfold classification of human resources, administrative structures, technology and product or service, as well as an additional category labelled 'the history and culture of an organisation.' This latter category is used to incorporate both an historical perspective, which can take account of multiple histories of the context in which change is taking place, and an understanding of organisational culture. By so doing, the framework is able to accommodate the existence of a number of competing histories of the rational management of change (these organisational histories may be further refined, replaced and developed over time). The dominant or 'official version' of change may often reflect the political positioning of certain key individuals or groups within an organisation, rather than serving as a true representation of the actual implementation of change. As such, it may further act to shape, constrain and promote the direction and content of future change programs.

The third and final area of concern relates to the substance of change. The four main dimensions are:

1 the *scale and scope of change*, which may range along a continuum from small-scale discrete change to a more 'radical' large-scale transformation; a distinction can be made between change at the level of the unit, plant/branch, division and corporation

2 the *defining characteristics* of the change program, which refers both to the labels attached to change projects and the actual content of the change in question

3 the *time frame of change*, which can vary, and programs may evolve incrementally over a number of years only to be followed by a fairly rapid and specified period of implementation; thus, the longer-term nature of these changes can go unnoticed in studies that focus on only one critical period in the process of workplace change

4 the *perceived centrality of the change* to the survival of the organisation; if the transition is viewed as central to the continual operation and competitive position of the company, then it can have major implications for the timescale, resource support and overall employee commitment to change (see for example, Dawson 1994, pp. 104–22).

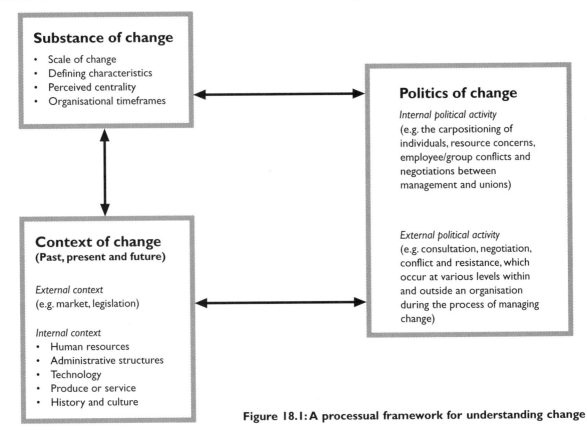

Figure 18.1: A processual framework for understanding change

Finally, it should be stressed that the members of the group of determinants categorised under the substance of change are not static, but rather change over time and overlap with contextual and political elements. For example, it is not uncommon for definitional confusion to surround the introduction of new management techniques and for the content of change to be redefined during the process of organisational adaptation. Moreover, knowledge of the substance of change and clarification of what the change means for a particular organisation can in themselves become political processes, influenced by external contextual views and the setting of internal agendas around the management of change. In this sense, there is a continual interplay between these three groups of determinants during the process of organisational change.

In short, the processual framework developed above (see figure 18.1) is concerned with understanding the political arenas in which decisions are made; histories recreated and strategies rationalised (politics); the enabling and constraining characteristics of change programs; the scale and type of change (substance); and the conditions under which change is taking place in relation to external elements, such as the business market environment and internal elements, including the history and culture of an organisation (context).

Practical guidelines on the management of change

One of the main conclusions that can be drawn from a processual perspective is that there can be no simple prescriptions for successfully managing change. What may prove successful in one context and in one time may not prove appropriate to comparable companies operating in different locations at some future point in time. Consequently, it would be neither appropriate nor feasible to produce 'tablets of stone' or exhaustive lists of the key ingredients to successful change. Nevertheless, there are some practical guidelines which can be drawn from this perspective. Perhaps one of the most important lessons that can be drawn is that managing large-scale change is about managing a non-linear dynamic process, which cannot be characterised as a rational series of decision-making activities and events. In other words, many of the routes taken by change cannot be predicted in advance as they unfold over time and comprise management omissions and revisions as well as unforeseen employee responses, technical problems and contingencies. This does not mean that planning is not important but, rather, that strategies need to be adaptive and flexible to accommodate the unforeseen. Furthermore, it is important to recognise that the management of organisational change is unlikely to be marked by a line of continual improvement from beginning to end. It is the failures and downsides that need to be managed, as well as the successes and early wins.

In recognising the importance of managing change as a complex process, and one that is political in nature, attention needs to be given to forming coalitions and developing networks of support. It is not unusual for radical change programs to experience a period in which there is an increase in agitation and complaints from employees and customers, a potential wavering of management commitment, and a possible loss of faith and growing uncertainty among outside stakeholders. Moreover, while it is clearly beneficial (although rarely achievable) to try to gain the support of all employees, some of the main obstacles which arise during processes of change are not due to an inability to gain total employee support but, rather, result from the lack of involvement of and/or poor communication with particular key groups (for example, supervisors, senior management, trade unions).

In a number of organisations studied over the years, communication has been central to bringing about a shift in employee attitudes towards change management. For example, in a case study of General Motors (Dawson 2000) conducted by the author the local management team set about improving employee relations prior to the introduction of change. They developed two major strands to their plan. The first centred on improving the work environment, whereby the shopfloor was transformed from a grey and greasy workplace to a newly painted and clean work environment. The second major thrust of the plan was based on improving the climate of industrial relations through the practice of greater communication between management and shop stewards. The central aim was to achieve full union involvement and cooperation, and to develop and maintain a relationship of trust between local management and union officials. At the outset, there was considerable conflict between the plant manager and the shop stewards. However, following the provision of accurate information and a more open management approach, there evolved a far more harmonious climate of employee relations. This set the context in which the successful management of change could more easily be achieved (Dawson 1994).

On the question of context, it is important to be aware of both the external business environment and the internal organisational context. For example, the values postulated by, and implicit in, the proposed change must be congruent with the values and assumptions that comprise the organisation's culture. Where there is conflict between the two, the change is likely to be resisted. The responsiveness of an organisation's culture to change can therefore be a crucial determinant of the process and outcomes of organisational change. Thus, the contextual dimension raises a host of issues which should be accommodated in the planning and management of change programs and highlights a general lesson — the need to be aware of and understand the context in which change is due to take place.

Questions concerning the substance of change raise a number of practical concerns over how to successfully manage organisational change. Two elements of particular importance centre on understanding what the change program is about (for example, what the main constituents of the new technology or management technique are) and also ensuring that employees who have to adopt to new working practices (the changing context) are adequately trained in the use of new equipment, techniques and/or procedures. Considerable time and attention should be given to the substance of change in terms of the technical, financial and human implications of change for the organisation. This includes the need to appraise technical requirements against existing techniques and technologies, and the development of appropriate implementation and training programs within the financial constraints set by the company. This should involve discussions and decisions on work organisation, on who are going to be the major implementers, and how the process is going to be managed.

Finally, it should be noted that, while it is possible to identify guidelines, there are no simple recipes for success. The management of organisational change is a political process, which cannot happen overnight, but takes time and will ultimately involve a range of political players who may shape the speed and direction of change at certain critical junctures during the process.

Conclusion

During the last few years those studying the area of change management have been bombarded by books that seek to offer simple recipes for the successful management of change in the never-ending search for competitive advantage. A number of popular accounts have been produced by leading business figures such as Geneen (Geneen with Moscow 1986) and Iacocca (Iacocca with Novak 1986), as well as the consultant 'guru' publications of writers such as Peters (1992), Waterman (Peters & Waterman 1982) and Kanter (1990). As Huczynski (1993) has pointed out in his book, Management gurus: what makes them and how to become one, successful gurus tend to share a common set of ideas which, while dressed differently, reproduce some fairly long-standing assumptions which support management. Given the demand for consultants and management gurus, these trends are set to continue. However, among the academic community, attention may focus on developing conceptual frames to help make sense of complex processes of change and to aid analyses of 'reality in flight'. The potential broadening of process type studies may refuel debates about the degree to which change processes are determined by the need for companies to adapt to new economic circumstances in order to compete and survive, and the extent to which individuals and groups shape the political process of organisational change. As the debates continue and new issues emerge, there will be a need to move beyond our conventional intellectual frames so that we can begin to appreciate the less clear and often muddied waters of change. Whatever the future of organisations, change is likely to remain a central concern during the early years of this new century.

References

Beckhard, R & Harris, RT (1987) *Organizational transitions: managing complex change* (2nd ed.) Reading, MA: Addison-Wesley.

Bedeian, AG (1980) *Organisations: theory and analysis.* Hinsdale Illinois: Dryden Press/Holt Rinehart and Winston.

Board, R de (1978) *The psychoanalysis of organisations. A psychoanalytic approach to behaviour in groups and organisations.* London: Tavistock.

Braverman, H (1974) *Labor and monopoly capital.* New York: Monthly Review Press.

Buchanan, D & Badham, R (1999) *Winning the turf game: power, politics, and organizational change.* London: Paul Chapman Publishing.

Burnes, B (1992) *Managing change: a strategic approach to organizational dynamics.* London: Pitman.

Burnes, B (2000) *Managing change: a strategic approach to organizational dynamics* (3rd ed.). London: Pitman.

Clutterbuck, D & Crainer, S (1990) *Makers of management. Men and women who changed the business world.* London: Macmillan.

Collins, D (1998) *Organizational change: sociological perspectives.* London: Routledge.

Dawson, P (1994) *Organizational change: a processual approach.* London: Paul Chapman Publishing.

Dawson, P (1996) *Technology and quality: change in the workplace.* London: International Thomson Business Press.

Dawson, P (2000) Multiple voices and the orchestration of a rational narrative in the pursuit of 'management objectives': the political process of plant-level change. *Technology Analysis and Strategic Management*, 12(1): 39–58.

Donaldson, L (1987) Strategy, structural adjustment to regain fit and performance: in defence of contingency theory. *Journal of Management Studies*, 24(2): 1–24.

Dunford, RW (1990) A reply to Dunphy and Stace. *Organization Studies*, 11(1): 131–4.

Dunphy, D (1981) *Organizational change by choice.* Sydney: McGraw-Hill.

Dunphy, D & Stace, D (1990) *Under new management: Australian organizations in transition.* Sydney: McGraw-Hill.

Eccles, T (1994) *Succeeding with change: implementing action-driven strategies.* London: McGraw-Hill.

French, W and Bell, C (1995) *Organizational development and change* (5th ed.). Minneapolis: West Publishing Company.

Geneen, H with Moscow, A (1986) *Managing.* London: Grafton Books.

Gray, LG & Starke, FA (1988) *Organizational behavior: concepts and applications* (4th ed.) Columbus: Merrill Publishing.

Guth, WD & MacMillan, C (1989) Strategy implementation versus middle management self-interest. In D Asch, and C Bowman (eds) *Readings in strategic management.* London: Macmillan.

Hammer, M & Champy, J (1993) *Re-engineering the corporation: a manifesto for business revolution.* New York: HarperBusiness.

Hatch, J (1997) *Organization theory.* Oxford: Oxford University Press.

Hellriegel, D, Slocum, J & Woodman, R (1995) *Organizational behavior* (7th ed.) New York: West Publishing Company.

Hobsbawn, EJ (1969) *Industry and empire.* Harmondsworth: Penguin.

Hofstede, G. (1980) *Cultures' consequences: international differences in work-related values.* London: Sage.

Hofstede, G. (1991) *Cultures and organizations: software of the mind.* Maidenhead: McGraw-Hill.

Huczynski, A (1993) *Management gurus: what makes them and how to become one.* London: Routledge.

Iacocca, L with Novak, W (1986) *Iacocca.* London: Bantam Books.

Kanter, RM (1990) *When giants learn to dance: mastering the challenges of strategy, management, and careers in the 1990s.* London: Unwin Hyman.

Kanter, RM, Stein, BA & Jick, TD (1992) *The challenge of organizational change: how companies experience it and leaders guide it.* New York: Free Press.

Kelly, D & Amburgey, TL (1991) Organizational inertia and momentum: a dynamic model of strategic change. *Academy of Management Journal*, 34(3): 591–612.

Kreitner, R & Kinicki, A (1992) *Organizational behavior* (2nd ed.) Homewood: Irwin.

Leavitt, HJ (1964) Applied organizational change in industry: structural, technical and human approaches. In WW Cooper, HJ Leavitt, and MW Shelly (eds) *New perspectives in organizations research.* New York: John Wiley.

Ledford, GE, Mohram, SA, Mohrman, AM & Lawler, EE (1990) The phenomenon of large-scale organizational change. In A Mohrman, SA Mohram, GE Ledford, TG Cummings and EE Lawler (eds) *Large-scale organizational change.* San Francisco: Jossey-Bass.

Lewin, K (1947) Frontiers in group dynamics. *Human Relations*, 1: 5–42.

Lewin, K (1951) *Field theory in social science.* New York: Harper & Row.

Mangham, I (1979) *The politics of organizational change.* Westport: Greenwood Press.

Peters, T (1992) *Liberation management: necessary disorganisation for nanosecond nineties.* Pan Books.

Peters, T & Waterman, RH (1982) *In search of excellence: lessons from America's best-run companies.* New York: Harper and Row.

Pettigrew, A (1985) *Awakening giant: continuity and change in ICI.* Oxford: Basil Blackwell.

Pettigrew, A (1990) Longitudinal field research on change: theory and practice. *Organization Science*, 1(3): 267–92.

Pettigrew, A (1997) What is a processual analysis? *Scandinavian Journal of Management*, 13(4): 337–48.

Pettigrew, AM (1973) *The politics of organizational decision-making.* London: Tavistock.

Pfeffer, J (1993) Understanding power in organizations. In C Mabey and B Mayon-White (eds) *Managing Change.* (2nd ed.): London. Paul Chapman Publishing.

Porter, LW, Crampon, WJ & Smith, FJ (1976) Organizational commitment and managerial turnover: a longitudinal study. *Organizational Behavior and Human Performance*, February: 87–98.

Quinn, JB (1980) *Strategies for change: logical incrementalism.* Homewood: Irwin.

Ropo, A, Eriksson, P & Hunt, J (1997) (eds) Special issue: reflections on conduction of processual research on management and organizations. *Scandinavian Journal of Management*, 13(4).

Stace, D & Dunphy, D (1994) *Beyond the boundaries: leading and re-creating the successful enterprise.* Sydney: McGraw-Hill.

Taylor, F (1911) *The principles of scientific management.* New York: Harper.

Van De Ven, A & Huber, GP (1990) Longitudinal field research methods for studying processes of organizational change. *Organization Science*, 1(3): 213–19.

Weisbord, MR (1988) *Productive workplaces: organizing and managing for dignity, meaning and community.* San Francisco: Jossey Bass.

Wilkinson, B (1983) *The shop floor politics of new technology.* London: Heinemann.

Willmott, H (1995) The odd couple? Re-engineering business processes, managing human resources. *New Technology, Work and Employment*, 10(2): 89–98.

Wilson, DC (1992) *A strategy of change. Concepts and controversies in the management of change.* London: Routledge.

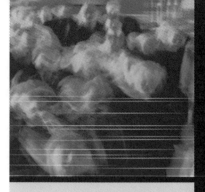

CHAPTER 19

Business networks: spanning boundaries and incorporating teams

by Ronel Erwee

Dept of Human Resource Management and Employment Relations, Faculty of Business, University of Southern Queensland, Toowoomba

Erwee@usq.edu.au

Introduction

Most management and organisational behaviour textbooks have extensive information about group dynamics, teamwork, conflict management and leadership. Despite the fact that team leaders and managers build systems and networks in all directions across levels and boundaries in organisations (Daft 1999; Yukl 1998), most of these textbooks pay insufficient attention to themes such as building networks and the role of teams within these networks.

Many international cooperative ventures by multinational enterprises and external interorganisational networks by small and medium enterprises have been established to improve Australian trade with organisations in the Asia–Pacific region. This trend emphasises the importance of research of inter- and intraorganisational networks in organisations that were expanding or emerging during the 1990s (Limerick & Cunnington 1993; Hastings 1993; Miles & Snow 1994; Lee, Tummala & Yam 1996; Naidu, Casusgil & Chan 1996; Tallman & Shenkar 1997; Hill & Jones 1998).

This chapter aims to link information from two streams of research, namely networks and teams. The chapter does not repeat research on teams that spans four decades with analysis on a group level in organisations. Instead, it emphasises research on networks that has emerged over the last decade, focusing on the meta or organisational level of analysis. Much of this research has focused on the interorganisational networks of multinational corporations but information on local and regional networks among small and medium-sized organisations is becoming more prevalent.

One of the challenging issues in relation to networks is that one cannot assume that teams in an organisation will spontaneously form networks that span boundaries or, conversely, that people belonging to a broad business network will evolve into teams. Other challenging issues are associated with how to map networks as well as discerning the stage of development of a network. Specific dilemmas that need attention in managing networks are dealing with interdependence; cooperation and competition in a network; and the development of trust between members. The practical implications for organisations, managers and employees in building competencies in managing networks will also be discussed. Exploratory research on cultural diversity in networks and how knowledge is managed by key actors in a network will be noted.

Defining teams and networks

This section starts by defining teams on a continuum from groups to high-performance teams.

It includes examples of types of networks to provide an overview of the diversity of networks as a concept.

Groups consist of two or more freely interacting individuals who share collective norms and goals and have a common identity. Teams are usually described as small numbers of people in an organisation with complementary skills who have:
- a common purpose
- integrated their efforts to reach performance goals
- developed an approach for problem solving and mutual accountability.

Teams fulfil individual and organisational functions to accomplish complex interdependent tasks. Self-managed teams are defined as workers in an organisation who are given administrative oversight for their task domains, and who could have cross-functional membership. High-performance teams are characterised by:
- participative leadership
- shared responsibility
- alignment on goals
- effective communication
- mutual trust
- focus on the future
- rapid response
- using all the diverse talents of members creatively (Kreitner & Kinicki 1998).

All these standard descriptions focus on teams operating within a company and do not extrapolate how the descriptions need to be adapted if these teams function in a broader business network that spans organisational boundaries.

Research into business networks, especially in international or relationship marketing, seldom clarifies the role of teams in a network, but tends to provide examples of the types of networks across organisations.

A simplistic form of a network is a *virtual organisation*, linking members by electronic means for the duration of a specific project to fulfil contractual obligations before dissolving to move on to other projects. An example of such a virtual organisation is Andersen Consulting with 40 000 consultants who operate independently, meet clients throughout the world and visit branch offices only intermittently. An extensive internal database helps the consultants pool knowledge when they cooperate on specific projects (Hill & Jones 1998).

A more complex form of network is that of a *boundary-spanning business network*, defined by Hastings (1993, p. 14) as:

> the implementation of a range of social, cultural and technological processes that result in a devolution of power and responsibility and the breaking down of organisational boundaries. This facilitates direct person-to-person connections, sharing of information and joint working (both within and between organisations) in order to pursue common objectives, solve problems and satisfy the expectations of internal and external stakeholders more effectively and rapidly.

An example of a boundary-spanning business network is the Australian company Technical and Computer Graphics (TCG). It was a highly interactive network of 200 people in 24 companies with revenue of $50 million in 1994. New product development followed a triangulation process that involved a three-cornered partnership between a TCG firm, a technology-based company outside TCG and a major customer. The TCG firm would have 5 to 10 professionals, and a project leader was elected from the three partner groups. Further internal and external alliances with other professionals were formed for the duration of the project. Leadership and entrepreneurship were rotated and principles of self-managed teams and a human investment philosophy were cornerstones of TCG (Miles & Snow 1994).

A further type, *the strategic network*, occurs when a long-term purposeful arrangement among distinct but related for-profit organisations is formed. This allows those companies in the network to gain or sustain competitive advantage vis-à-vis their competitors outside the network by optimising activity costs and minimising coordination costs (Jarillo 1993; Limerick & Cunnington 1993). The definition can also be applied if a company is a not-for-profit organisation (Hastings 1993; Lipnack and Stamps 1994). Networks may consist of equals or may have a dominant partner (Buttery & Buttery 1994).

McDonald's is an example of a for-profit strategic network that incorporates the key principles of vertically integrated networks with those that concentrate on a few things, while subcontracting the rest. McDonald's is the strategic hub in the network and exercises control over decisions in the value chain. The essence of McDonald's is its system of franchisees and their closely tied suppliers acting together. A further example is Toyota and Honda who purchase subsystems such as gearboxes from subcontractors to form a *keiretsu* of firms with successful interfirm dealings (Jarillo 1993).

Companies such as McDonald's or Toyota are facing similar pressures, namely the need to be efficient (to deliver products or services at lower costs) and the need to be flexible (to be innovative and do things differently). The two goals of vertical integration and subcontracting need not be mutually exclusive and a strategic network could be the appropriate organisational form to achieve both sets of goals. The norm for transactional exchanges is seen to be changing from competition and opportunism to a collaborative style based upon relationships rather than transactions in order to successfully link activities (Buttery & Buttery 1994; Jarillo 1993; Lipnack & Stamps 1994).

A *community network* is a group of organisations in a local area that operates as a network. For example, in the USA, the Baldwin Corridor Coalition consists of a steel manufacturing company, the union, educational and financial institutions, government, economic development agencies and the local community. These diverse organisations are playing specific roles to ensure that the community will be able to sustain itself in an uncertain economic environment (Chisholm 1998).

The assumption in these descriptions of networks is that a network is a loose collection of people, implying that a network could consist of 'groups' rather than 'teams'. However, the proposition is that, to form a boundary-spanning network, the principles of self-managed and high-performance teams need to be consciously implemented by members, leaders or managers in a network, to achieve a superior level of performance. A leader or members of a network will need to decide what type of team within that specific type of network will be optimal.

Network formation and maintenance: challenging issues

This section deals with dilemmas in discerning why networks are formed and how to map a network to discover linkages between members. It notes the debate on the states or stages in the process of forming and maintaining a network.

Managers or leaders create teams in organisations for specific purposes such as advisory, project, production or negotiation (action) tasks. In contrast, many conditions in the external environment in which a company operates stimulate the formation of networks as a *new* organisational form. The emphasis on knowledge management made possible by leading-edge computers and communications systems and the complexity of current business problems in a globalised world contribute to the pressure to form networks across organisational boundaries.

Additional reasons for forming networks include the following:
- generating economies of scope or scale for a company
- manipulating the competitive structure of the market or technological alliances
- gaining access to partners implementing technological change
- members jointly finding ways to reduce costs and improve the quality of products
- rapid knowledge dissemination and demand for high-quality products and services while controlling costs (Hastings 1993; Limerick & Cunnington 1993; Buttery & Buttery 1994; Chisholm 1998; Hill & Jones 1998).

Leaders or managers in an organisation may form alliances or build loose networks for a variety of strategic reasons. The proposition is that members of a team within that network will have to define an additional, related set of reasons to evolve into a high-performance team. The complexity of the context in which the networks operate means that members who try to form teams will have to:
- practise participative leadership
- share responsibility
- be aligned on goals

- communicate effectively
- develop mutual trust
- be focused on the future
- respond rapidly
- use all their diverse talents creatively.

Mapping a network

If members can consciously overcome the tenuous couplings in a network, they can strive to form high-performance teams within the network. They need tools to map the network in order to identify potential linkages between members. In many textbooks on management and organisational behaviour, relationships between people in a team are depicted by means of one or more of the following methods:
- sociometric analysis
- network diagrams
- linkages in neural networks.

In network literature, a *radar screen model* (Hastings 1993) captures the complexities of linkages between different types of networked organisations (see figure 19.1). A proposition is that all these tools need to be used in conjunction to map the boundary-spanning business network and the potential teams within the network.

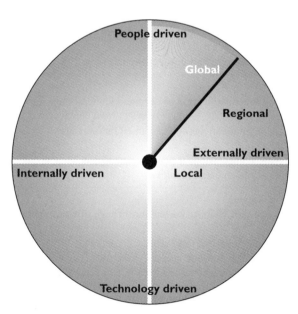

Figure 19.1: Dimensions of the new organisation — the radar screen model

Source: Hastings (1993:13)

An organisation could emphasise relationships within the organisation (internally driven) or shift to the other end of the continuum to its relationships with other organisations (externally driven — see figure 19.1). As shown on the vertical axis, the organisation could be concerned with the social processes between people or may prefer to give high priority to sophisticated information technology systems. The radar scanner rotates to establish whether the organisation has a primary focus on the local business environment, the region (for example, Asia–Pacific or Europe), or a global environment. These are not either/or dimensions, but indicate the preferences of an organisation and reflect its sense of identity.

In figure 19.1, the emphasis is on mapping the networks of a single organisation. Many companies in an industry or in a region tend to form networks to break through geographic or organisational boundaries. For example, Australian small business owner/managers view their direct, *industry* network (the supplier–buyer value chain) and their networks with local *government agencies* or *people* as their most important networks (Healy & Perry 1998).

Stages in the development of business networks and teams

Most management and organisational behaviour textbooks describe the stages of group development. These stages are mirrored in the network literature, supporting the proposition that knowledge of teams is crucial for developing business networks.

Batonda (1995) synthesised the debate about stages or states of network formation, and maintenance over time, into the five-stage model shown in table 19.1. The first stage usually revolves around the *search* for and evaluation of partners based on economic and social aspects with very little commitment or trust.

During the next stage, *relationship starting*, the new partners try to identify the intercompany as well as interpersonal dynamics. Based on these experiences and perceptions of each other's abilities, they will selectively enter into contracts. The immediate and long-term compatibility becomes important and the partners aim to define mutual goals.

Bonding must start at this stage and continue to be cultivated over time (Buttery & Buttery 1994).

Joint planning efforts emerge during the *relationship development* phase and partners are evaluating the relationship to verify if mutual obligations of performance and effectiveness are met. There is sufficient trust for a gradual increase in interdependence. Mutual benefits are enhanced as the partners strive to create value through a synergistic combination of their strengths. There is a clear commitment of resources and people to developing the business relationship. The boundaries between partners, and how permeable these boundaries are, need to be determined. Information exchange needs to be investigated to determine what is acceptable to all members (Batonda 1995; Buttery & Buttery 1994).

During the *maintenance* stage, operations and strategies are more closely integrated and institutionalised conflict resolution procedures have developed. Increased commitment is visible through long-term adaptations and adjustment through agreements, negotiations and the curbing of opportunistic behaviour. Mutual trust is manifest. Criticism is accepted and conflict is managed in such a way that the relationships are not threatened.

If the members decide to *terminate* the relationship, the decision is based on an analysis of the costs or benefits of continuing in the network. They jointly develop acceptable strategies to dissolve the relationship. Opportunistic behaviour at this late stage may lead to network breakdown. Despite this, certain bonds may be maintained after the break-up if the partners think that benefits have been appropriately distributed (Buttery & Buttery 1994).

However, recent research argues that network development does not follow a predetermined sequence; rather, it can be recursive and/or even 'skip' a stage (Batonda 1997). Chisholm (1998, p. 213) warns that the 'process of developing networked organisations is disorderly and nonlinear.'

Table 19.1: A network development stages/states model

Dimensions	Activities
Stage 1: Relationship searching processes	search and trail for potential exchange partners no commitment at this stage evaluation of potential exchange partners based on economic and social aspects
Stage 2: Relationship starting processes	identification [of] interfirm and interpersonal dynamics of network partners selective entry based on abilities and intermediate and long-term compatibility of partners determining and defining set of mutual goals and objectives
Stage 3: Relationship development processes (interfirm planning and expansion)	joint planning efforts evaluation process of relationship for identification of continued mutual obligation of performance and effectiveness increase of interdependence through enhancement of mutual benefits and attractiveness value creation through synergistic combination of partner's strengths commitment of resources and people to relationships
Stage 4: Relationship maintenance processes (interfirm adaptation and adjustments)	integration of operations and strategies increased commitment and recognition of mutual benefits through institutionalised conflict resolution processes long-term rewards based on mutual behaviour and trust internal monitoring systems based on behaviour and self control adaptations and adjustments through agreement, negotiation and self-control
Stage 5: Relationship termination processes	termination based on extent of mutual interest and cost benefit analysis of continuing in the network developing strategies to mutually dissolve the relationship

Source: Batonda (1995)

Dilemmas associated with the dynamics in networks

This section addresses dilemmas in relation to teams and networks, including interdependency, cooperation and conflict, and, especially, the violation of trust between partners in a network.

The dilemma of *interdependency* is discussed in relation to conflict management in most management and organisational behaviour texts as well as in the network literature.

Members of a network usually recognise that their competencies complement their potential partners' knowledge skills or expertise — this is described as domain overlap. There are similarities or complementarities between products, services, clients, modes of operating, territory and seasonal or time spectrums. Partners share their expertise or other valued resources within the network. This contributes to different types of interdependency that develop over time between members of a network:

- *Sequential interdependency* occurs when a company produces the first stage of a product, and a second partner completes the next phase in the sequence, before a third partner adds value to the product.
- *Pooled interdependency* occurs when most partners draw expertise from a central pool of knowledge or resources such as a business start-up facility and adds value back into the pool.
- *Reciprocal interdependency* assumes that a company and its partners will be learning from each other over a long period of time, but is also the most difficult interdependency to manage (Buttery & Buttery 1994; Hastings 1993).

One should remember that a local company might be so large (for example, BHP in Australia) that it is able to form internal networks across organisational boundaries to share resources. Managers in this situation have a particular mind-set or cognitive map; they see themselves and their units as autonomous, with distinct competencies, but choose to focus on the 'bigger picture' of the organisation and voluntarily look for collaborative ventures with other units in the company (Limerick & Cunnington 1993).

The second dilemma in networks is how the two pressures of *competition* and *cooperation* are reconciled (Jarillo 1993; Lipnack & Stamps 1993, Hastings 1993). Cooperation is usually associated with the ways in which a network's members work together to reach a goal such as maintaining market share or delivering a high-quality service. Competition is associated with unacceptable behaviour between members — for example, taking away market share from one another. The section on building TeamNets (Lipnack & Stamps 1993, p. 11) in this chapter discusses *co-opetition* strategies for integrating competition and cooperation.

One of the key factors influencing a company's decision to cooperate in a strategic network is economic efficiency, expressed as the point when the external cost of the transaction between the companies is lower than the internal cost of producing the product within a company. This focus on financial aspects implies that members have a specialised investment in the network. Consequently, transaction costs can be lowered even further if the members of the network trust each other and rely on each other to deliver the required service.

The third dilemma, *developing trust*, is an essential component in groups, teams and networks. Trust between business partners in a network can be defined as a willingness to rely on a partner in whose integrity and reliability one has confidence, as the trust has been earned and built up over time. Partners in a network have to be selected carefully — for example, by selecting partners with similar value systems. Network members adapt their business practices, specialise in a particular aspect of the business, trust each other, focus on the longer term and have an internal consistency to provide efficiency and flexibility (Jarillo 1993). Members of the network will be worse off if they behave opportunistically and put their partners at risk (Kimber 1996; Healy & Perry 1997; Williams 1998).

An example of developing trust is Benneton's careful selection of partners by choosing subcontractors from people known to the family in the immediate area. It still operates on the basis of trust, with 380 subcontractors and carefully selected agents that sell its products. Other factors to establishing trust in this company's case are that relationships between the partners are long-term, based on mutual respect and the building up of each other's reputations. If a subcontractor does not keep to quality standards over the longer term, it is eventually released from the network (Jarillo 1993).

Violation of trust in business networks

Conflict management and psychological contracts are discussed in most management and organisational behaviour textbooks. However, an issue that warrants inclusion is whether there is an emerging perception that trust has been violated in business relationships.

The concept of *violation* of the psychological contract refers to the perception that a partner has failed to fulfil one or more obligations in the psychological contract (Rousseau 1996; Morrison & Robinson 1997; Morgan & Hunt 1994). The development of violation is depicted as a process that has discernible decision points or 'a set of interceding judgements' (Morrison & Robinson 1997, p. 230). At the beginning of the process, the partners become aware of negative feelings and perceptions about their psychological contract. A decision point occurs where a perception arises that a promise has not been met. A partner may believe that an act or decision may be 'unfair'. Morrison and Robinson (1997) describe this as *reneging* (when a partner knowingly breaks a promise) or *incongruence* (when the partners have different understandings of a promise). This creates strong emotional experiences such as betrayal and anger (see figure 19.2).

Either incongruence or reneging may lead to a perceived unmet promise by creating a discrepancy between what a partner understood of what was promised and what was received. This discrepancy triggers a process of comparing how well the partners upheld their promises. A partner may then perceive a breach of contract based on a decision that this partner fulfilled all the obligations, but that the other partner did not reciprocate. In this state of mind, the aggrieved partner may still decide to renegotiate (Rousseau 1996) or feel that a violation of the psychological contract occurred. Morrison and Robinson (1997) then argue that further comparisons take place before the partners decide that the contract has been breached and that they have to make a decision whether to renegotiate or terminate the relationship.

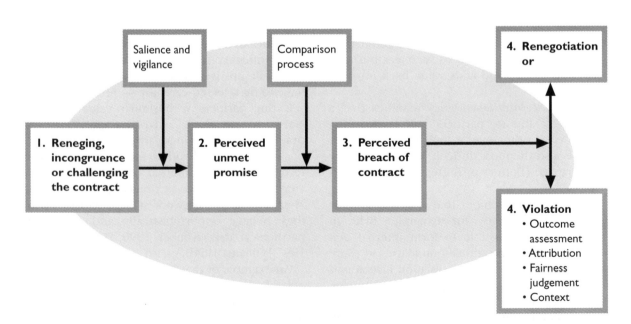

Figure 19.2: Renegotiation or violation of psychological contracts (adapted from Morrison & Robinson (1997) and Rousseau (1996))

Erwee and Perry (1999) studied the perceptions of violation of trust in partnerships between educational institutions and small and medium enterprises in the Asia-Pacific region. The reasons why a network was decaying were analysed by using the concepts of 'reneging', 'unmet promises' and 'perceived breach of contract'. The focus was on how trust was violated within a psychological contract, particularly by partners from different cultures. The psychic distance between partners of different cultures could contribute to diverging perceptions of the relationship.

In one of the cases, an Australian importer experienced a multitude of psychological contracts that were operational between different partners. The importer company had a psychological contact with its Malaysian supplier, but also with Australian merchants, and the latter had contracts with builders. Any unmet promises from the Malaysian supplier caused unmet promises between the Australian importer and merchants and between merchants and builders. There were *multiple* decision points in any one time period. For example, within a few weeks in July, the full cycle of incongruity — reneging — vigilance — unmet promise — breach — renegotiation had been experienced between the Australian importer and the Malaysian supplier. This full cycle was rapidly followed by a second, shorter cycle in September. This recursiveness helps explain why predetermined stages are difficult to discern in the life span of an international marketing network.

Members of a network should not only build trust but also guard against violations of trust resulting from making promises that cannot be met and against perceived breaches of contract. Restoring and protecting the capacity to form positive psychological contracts is essential to managing relationships between partners in a network.

Practical implications for managing networks and building TeamNets

Discussions of strategies to manage teams in most management and organisational behaviour textbooks need to be adapted to take account of the ways in which company structures are changing. For example, many Australian organisations are evolving into sustainable, networked organisations. Some of the key competencies of sustainable organisations are to:

- create 'communities of practice' (Limerick & Cunnington 1993) that cut across organisational boundaries
- be involved in ongoing dialogue to expand their intellectual capital
- be flexible and fluid
- often use intranet or electronic means of communication.

Limerick and Cunnington (1993) highlight a number of competencies essential for managers of networks. These competencies are related to certain strategies for forming 'TeamNets'. A TeamNet can be defined as a network of teams that crosses conventional organisational boundaries to harness the power of creative individuals and teams (Lipnack & Stamps 1993, p. 1994). This way of working emerged in Europe and occurs in both large and small companies, in economies as diverse as Denmark and Italy and in different industries, e.g. textiles and tourism.

TeamNets share certain principles of managing effective teams by combining two powerful business ideas:

- Teams consisting of small groups are formed to work with focus, motivation and skill to achieve shared goals.
- Networks of disparate teams are formed to work together based on a common purpose.

The aim of this section is to suggest practical implications for managing the relationship between partners in a network consisting of teams.

- The principles of forming TeamNets were applied in two Southern African examples (Erwee 1997; 1999). The Enterprising Women's Initiative (EWI) and the XYTeamNet (the name has been changed on request) were created. The EWI grew out of a number of organisations that have women entrepreneurs as members or that assist in the development of entrepreneurs. The XYTeamNet was an internal network of young managers of the various divisions of a high-technology company. The basic principles that Lipnack and Stamps (1993, p. 1994) formulated were applied in the South African examples, namely:

- having a unifying purpose
- having independent members
- building voluntary links
- using multiple leaders
- having interaction on many levels.

Establish a unifying purpose

Any potential TeamNet needs to find a purpose that can unify diverse teams or individuals. This vision must be so strong and compelling that it will help the members survive the future patches of strife or dissent inherent in such teams within networks that span boundaries. TeamNets have needs and common goals that become so explicit that they can be tested against real products or services.

Limerick and Cunnington (1993) confirm that competencies in defining the focus, as well as in building a unifying vision, are necessary. This clear purpose should benefit a critical mass of participants who will be able to stick to the TeamNet when it is threatened with collapse.

Identify independent members

A powerful myth exists that if one joins a network, one gives up one's independence. This myth usually causes subtle resistance among potential members and most members need much reassurance that their independence will be respected, and that no mergers, takeovers or dissolution will take place. A number of independent members should be invited to the first series of meetings. A few will withdraw as they may not be able to identify with the purpose, or may be threatened by other members, or may find the TeamNet principles too difficult to implement. Therefore, the choice of participants is crucial.

This strategy is related to the competencies of liberating network members, developing boundary roles and setting up the alliance carefully (Limerick & Cunnington 1993). Members of networks should be competent to take personal responsibility and to initiate and maintain contact, without having to obtain permission to proceed. Network members should be empowered to develop boundary roles, in order to become outward-looking and active external to their units or companies. Compatible and strong partners should be chosen carefully to complement each other's strengths in technology, information and decision systems, as well as in values and decision styles.

Create voluntary links

TeamNets usually cross geographical, organisational and professional boundaries. The TeamNets are not merely local area networks connected by fibre-optics, but groups that are 'working together apart' (Lipnack & Stamps, 1993, p. 43). The real connections between participants are the trust, respect and relationships they have to build up over time. The relationships need to shift from being intangible, unreal or fleeting to visible, strong and sustainable. As relationships take time to mature, every link that can be created can contribute to building the relationship. In the beginning, links have to be consciously created, but as trust develops these links become spontaneous and voluntary. The existing relationships between potential TeamNet members should be analysed. For example:
- Which members know each other?
- Who has worked together before?
- Who will resent the inclusion of particular members?
- How often do they come into contact?

Decisions need to be made on how trust can be built among the members and what strategies can be used to stimulate voluntary contact.

Recognise the power of multiple leaders

A network does have leaders, yet a specific individual does not carry all the leadership responsibilities. TeamNets usually consist of many powerful individuals who are well known for their expertise or who play significant roles in companies, industries or professions. These individuals are used to sole leadership and many starting TeamNets meetings can deteriorate into a battle for leadership. The partners need exceptional maturity to deal with the leadership pressures that can arise; they especially need the ability to share or rotate leadership between members or companies.

This strategy is related to the competencies of developing an appropriate mind-set and managing leadership diversity (Limerick & Cunnington 1993). The mind-set includes a new cognitive framework as well as a new set of values. The members of the network need to reconceptualise their companies as networks or value chains to enable them to challenge organisational boundaries. Partners need to be able to tolerate diverse values, differences and independence within a collaborative and harmonious culture. Collaborative individualism focuses on the autonomy of the individual who has the ability to tolerate the uncertainty of moving in and out of temporary teams while collaborating with others to achieve a goal.

Ensure connections on all levels

The myth that networks are flat structures with only horizontal connections needs to be dispelled. Lipnack and Stamps (1993, p. 51) note that a network has at least two levels: the level of the member parts and the level of the network whole. A TeamNet has at least three levels:
1 the individual members and their personal networks
2 the network of teams that make up the TeamNet
3 the larger systems of which the TeamNet is a part, e.g. professional bodies or other stakeholders in the business environment.

This strategy is related to the competency of developing communication systems (Limerick & Cunnington 1993). Transaction costs of networking are kept relatively low by the computer-assisted integration of systems between partners in a network. Partners should not only rely on high-technology communication systems, but also on personal communication with peers. All types of communication should be used to enhance the shared vision and core values of the network.

Partners should not assume that mutual trust alone would sustain the relationship through difficult periods. Clear legal contracts need to be negotiated, behavioural expectations need to be openly discussed and penalty clauses for reneging on commitments should be explored.

Lipnack and Stamps (1993, p. 38) caution that networks exist in the 'creative tension between competitive and cooperative tendencies, ever-shifting between the self-assertion of individuals and the integration required for the group as a whole.' The only way to test if Team-Nets can work in an environment is to risk experimenting with the principles.

Future directions: cultural diversity and key actors

There are a number of major gaps in the network literature that need further research before more practical guidelines can be developed. Two of these areas are the impact of cultural diversity in networks and the role of key actors in networks. The latter issue again relates to how knowledge is managed in the network.

Cultural diversity in teams and networks

Diversity within teams can include the dimensions of age, gender, race, culture of origin, sexual orientation and physical and intellectual disability. All teams and networks are diverse, but they do not necessarily recognise the extent of the diversity or have policies or practices to harness this diversity (Erwee & Innes 1998).

A network can have strong geographical (see the previous example of Benneton) or cultural components (Orthodox Jews in the diamond trade or emigrant Chinese in South-East Asia). In these cases, the psychic distance between the members in the network is low as they share basic belief systems, have similar traditions of doing business and may have other social connections such as language or family ties. Furthermore, different cultures employ different networking strategies or are more 'open' to networking. The history of relationships, or ties between groups within a culture, may facilitate or impede new entrants, especially from different cultures or groups.

Perry, Erwee and Tidwell (1999) explored the linkages between stages of network development and psychic distance in partner selection. The results suggested that cross-cultural business networks between Australians and

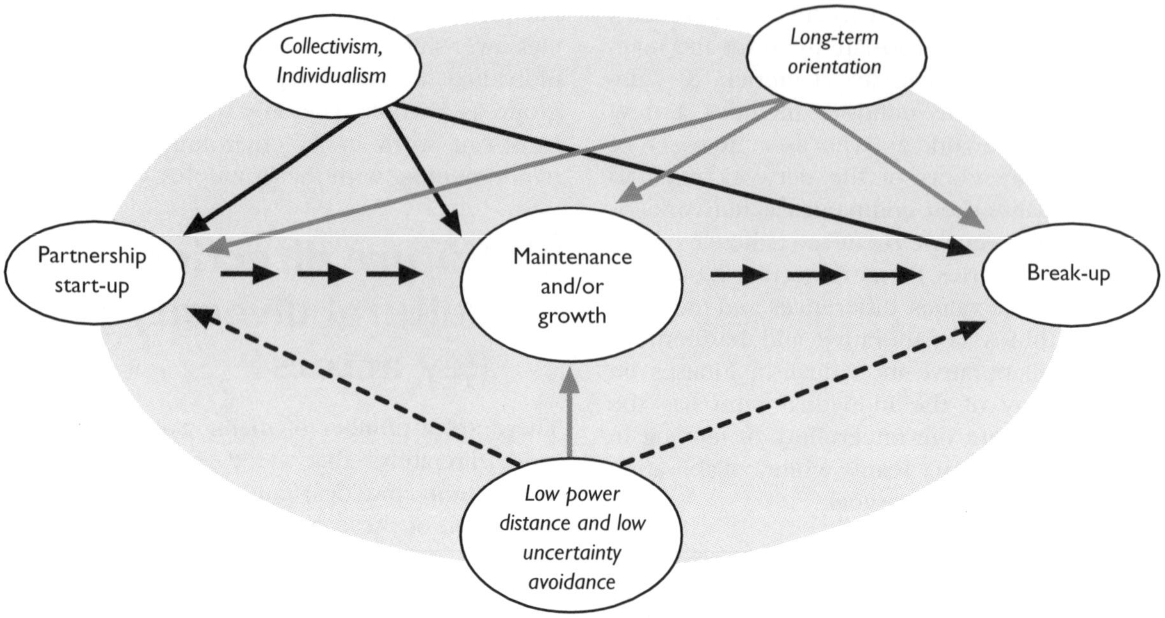

Figure 19.3: Complexity of Hofstede's dimensions of culture during the life of a network

Source: Perry, Erwee & Tidwell (1999)

Malaysians do not appear to develop through clearly defined, predictable stages. Their study showed that all dimensions of culture appeared to consistently influence a network's development. The complexity of dimensions is illustrated in figure 19.3.

This study showed that there was a gradual dissolution of partnerships in business networks over a decade and this contributed to an undermining of trust between the Australian and Malaysian partners. This would probably have a negative effect on future links with wider networks. It seems that personal and business networks are important for both partners (not only for Chinese Malaysians) but if these networks are not consciously linked or expanded jointly, very little basis for cross-cultural understanding is built.

Research suggests that, of all the Asian countries, Malaysia has the greatest psychic distance from Australia. However, in another exploratory study it was found that psychic distance is reduced by the international experience of network members who have previous contacts or experience in the overseas countries (Healy & Perry 1998). It appeared that psychic distance has only a moderate or weak impact on a business network between Australian companies with partners in the Asia–Pacific region.

The implications from these exploratory studies could be that partners should be aware of cultural differences and try to understand these differences between countries and teams within an organisation. However, this understanding should not blind cross-cultural TeamNets to the particular needs of individual persons in teams.

Leadership or key actors in networks

In most of the descriptions of teams or groups, formal and informal leaders are identified, whereas in self-managed teams leadership is shared or rotated. More exploratory research is needed to investigate the role of leaders or key actors during all the stages of network formation and maintenance.

Networks often start with chance encounters between individuals who can form the nucleus of each network and these 'key actors' are the driving forces in that network. The concept of *network embeddedness* indicates that a key actor can be embedded in a dyadic relationship or be part of a task force that has business relationships with other groups in the network (Williams 1998). They usually are known and trusted by all network members and can share information at critical times. The role that key actors play in managing the knowledge contained in the network needs further exploratory research.

An example of key actors in international agribusiness emerged from our case studies (Perry, Brown & Erwee, 1999). The European share-ownership of one Australian agribusiness company 'pushed' the company to become more international. It hired an export consultant who became the export manager and brought his networks with him. Therefore, this company did not have to establish new networks to enter overseas markets. The export manager illustrated the embeddedness of his networks by saying, 'I've worked in the pig industry in this part of the world over the past 11 years ... the pig industry is fairly incestuous really ... we seem to know whether we attract one another or we seem to, and we get fairly well known'(Perry, Brown & Erwee 1999, p. 4).

Arising from this case was the important role of the export manager as a 'knowledge information node'. This type of node has extensive knowledge of the complex international networks involved and actively uses this information to coordinate activities between the partners to gain competitive advantage. 'Without this node, the whole system would not work' (Perry, Brown & Erwee 1999, p. 6).

In a second case, the chief executive officer, business manager and five regional managers of the Australian subsidiary of an international company integrated information from their national and international networks. This core group of managers formed the Australian *knowledge integration node* that disseminated information nationally and internationally. Quarterly national meetings ensured that information was disseminated, but there was a high use of information technology daily. The core group has their own individual networks that they have built up regionally, nationally and internationally to assess trends. It was proposed that the role of key actors and knowledge information nodes in such networked organisations are critical to the establishment, development and control of international networks (Brown & Erwee 1999).

A further proposition is that the emerging research stream of knowledge management may be one of the mechanisms that could link the disciplines of team dynamics and network research. Davenport and Prusak (1998, p. 37) argue that 'knowledge markets' cluster around informal and formal networks within firms. Nonaka and Takeuchi (1995) identify knowledge practitioners, knowledge engineers and knowledge officers as part of the knowledge crew or team within a firm. A knowledge integrator node could be an additional role that a person engages in, one that is not bound to the hierarchy as the Nonaka and Takeuchi (1995) model implies. Knowledge integrator nodes could also be those actors who integrate aspects of the roles of the knowledge crew. Such actors could ensure that a knowledge spiral will be built by drawing out tacit knowledge from various sources and sharing this with other knowledge integrator nodes in the internal and external networks of the firm (Erwee & Brown 2000). Without the specific attempts to integrate explicit knowledge, build a knowledge system or create a knowledge spiral, the network will be less effective.

Conclusion

A major research gap in the literature is how the extensive knowledge of team dynamics can be integrated in the growing network research, to enhance the latter's practical application for managers.

Key challenges will be how to enable teams in an organisation to form networks that span boundaries within that organisation or industry, as well as how to ensure that teams can evolve within broad business networks. Networked organisations are not the only viable, sustainable organisations for the next decade, but there are many types and approaches to building business networks and developing boundary-spanning teams in a network. Tools for analysing relationships within teams, and those for mapping networks, need to be integrated into a set of complementary self-assessment strategies. Knowledge about group and team development needs to be utilised to enhance the emerging debate about stages or states in network development.

Network research could investigate the concept of violation of trust in business relationships to ensure the building of effective relationships over time. Some exploratory research has been conducted in Australia, but further in-depth research about the impact of cultural diversity in cross-national teams or networks is necessary. The training of managers should concentrate on the dynamics and complexity of cross-cultural relationships over the life span of a boundary-spanning team, and the need to bridge communication gaps within cross-cultural teams in business networks.

The practical implications for organisations, managers and employees are that they need to build competencies in managing networks. Key actors need to understand what is happening in the teams in their current network and be more deliberate in designing and developing the network and its teams. The role of the knowledge integrator node, who elicits, shares and manages knowledge within a team or a network, is a new area of investigation that should be explored. Key actors need to be continuously revising their development plans in an action learning way by using recent research to make their teams or networks more viable.

References

Batonda, G (1995) Development processes in Australian and Chinese networks. Paper presented at the Research Colloquium of the Australian Services Research Academy, Bond University, 9–10 December: 1–17.

Batonda, G (1997) Dynamics of China/Australia business networks. Paper presented at the Faculty of Business Research Colloquium, University of Southern Queensland, 28 October, pp. 1–10.

Brown, L & Erwee, R (1999) Key actors in networked international firms. *Proceedings of the ANZMAC Conference* on CD-ROM, Sydney 29 November to 1 December.

Buttery, E & Buttery, A (1994) *Business networks: – reaching markets with low-cost strategies.* Melbourne: Longman Business and Professional.

Chisholm, RF (1998) *Developing network organisations.* Reading Massachusetts: Addison-Wesley.

Daft, RL (1999) *Leadership: theory and practice.* The Dryden Press, Harcourt Brace College Publishers.

Davenport, TH & Prusak, L (1998) *Working knowledge: how organisations manage what they know.* Boston: Harvard Business School Press.

Erwee, R (1997) Human resource managers as TeamNet members. *People Dynamics*, February: 28–31.

Erwee, R (1999) *Building business networks.* Unit 55208 Study Book, University of Southern Queensland, Toowoomba.

Erwee, R & Brown, L (2000) Knowledge management in Australian agribusiness with international networks. Refereed paper accepted for presentation by the International Council for Small Business Conference. Brisbane, July.

Erwee, R & Innes, P (1998) Diversity management in Australian companies: compliance or conviction? *Proceedings of the Australian and New Zealand Academy of Management.* (CD-ROM) Adelaide, 6–9 December.

Erwee, R & Perry, C (1999) Violation of trust in cross-cultural networks. *Proceedings of the Academy of International Business South-East Asia Region Conference.* Melbourne, 8–10 July, pp. 41–65.

Hastings, C (1993) *The new organisation.* London: McGraw-Hill.

Healy, M & Perry, C (1997) Exploring perceptions of Australian small business owner/managers of typologies of international marketing networks. *Proceedings of the IMP-OZ Conference.* Sydney, 13–16 Feb.

Healy, M & Perry, C (1998) Focus groups in academic research. Paper delivered at the ANZMAC conference, University of Otago, Dunedin, 30 Nov–2 Dec: 911–16.

Hill, CWL & Jones, GR (1998) Strategic management: an integrated approach. Boston: Houghton Mifflin.

Jarillo, JC (1993) *Strategic networks: creating the borderless organisation.* Oxford: Butterworth Heinemann.

Kimber, D (1996) Sharing, giving and friendship — the forgotten factors of business relationships. Unpublished manuscript, RMIT Business, Melbourne, pp. 1–17.

Kreitner, R & Kinicki, A (1998) *Management and organizational behaviour* (4th ed.) Boston: Irwin McGraw-Hill.

Lee HYH, Tummala, VMR & Yam, RCM (1996) Global competitiveness framework for Hong Kong manufacturing industries. *Proceedings of the Pan-Pacific conference.* Chiba, Japan, May 28–31, pp. 44–46.

Limerick, D & Cunnington, B (1993) *Managing the new organisation: a blueprint for networks and strategic alliances.* San Francisco: Jossey-Bass.

Lipnack, J & Stamps, J (1993) *The TeamNet factor.* Essex Junction USA: Oliver Wight Publications.

Lipnack, J & Stamps, J (1994) *The age of the network: organising principles for the 21st century.* Essex Junction, USA: Oliver Wight Publications.

Miles, R & Snow, C (1994) The new network firm: a spherical structure built on a human investment philosophy. *Organisational Dynamics*, 5–18.

Morgan, RM & Hunt, SD (1994) The commitment-trust theory of relationship marketing. *Journal of Marketing*, 58: 20–38.

Morrison, EW & Robinson, SL (1997) When employees feel betrayed: a model of how psychological contract violation develops. *Academy of Management Journal*, 22(1): 226–56.

Naidu, GM, Casusgil, ST & Chan, AKK (1996) An integrative model for joint venture management in the People's Republic of China. *Proceedings of the Pan-Pacific conference*, Chiba, Japan, May 28–31, pp. 155–8.

Nonaka, I And Takeuchi, H (1995) *The knowledge-creating company; how Japanese companies create the dynamics of innovation.* New York: Oxford University Press.

Perry, C, Brown, L & Erwee, R (1999) Australian agribusiness firms in Asia: business relationships and intellectual property. *Proceedings of the ANZAM conference* Hobart, 3–5 December. (CD-ROM)

Perry, C, Erwee, R & Tidwell, P (1999) Forming and maintaining cross-cultural interorganisational networks. *Proceedings of the XV Pan-Pacific Conference*, Fiji, 1–3 June.

Rousseau, DM (1996) Changing the deal while keeping the people. *Academy of Management Executive*, 10(10): 50–59.

Tallman, SB & Shenkar, O (1997) A managerial decision model of international cooperative venture formation. In HV Wortzel and LW Wortzel (eds) *Strategic management in a global economy.* New York: Wiley.

Williams, T (1998) Interorganisational networks: strategic cooperation in different network types. *Academy of Management Proceedings '98*: BPS, pp. A1-A15.

Yukl, G (1998) *Leadership in organizations* (4th ed.) Prentice Hall.

index

adaptive learning 188
adding of value to organisations 70
advisory panels 66-7
age-stage theories 13
archetypes in leadership 176-81
assumption learning 188
attribute model 136, 137, 140
auditing, social capital of organisations 168-9

behaviour (organisational culture) 123
behavioural professionalism 145-6
boundary-spanners 204
boundary-spanning business network 225
burnout 205
business case, building a 67-8
business networks 224-36
  development stages 227-8
  violation of trust 230-1
business process re-engineering (BPR) 129-30

career anchors 12-13
career building
  how not to be successful 15
  implications for management 20-1
  principles for 21st century 17-21
  strategies 15-16
  taking responsibility for your own 12
career experiments 18
career implications for 2000 and beyond 7-8
career lattices 7
career mythologies 12-13
career options, maintaining 20
career theories 12-13
careers
  future directions 14-15
  trends affecting 14
celebration (team development rewards/recognition) 82
centralised networks 204
change
  and the psychological contract 42-3
  origins of 4-5
  see also organisational change
change management theory 118
chaos theory 117
collaborative organisational culture 106-7
collective learning 187
Collins' perspectives of the professions 136-7
communication 197
  affect on organisations 205-6
  gender and culture 201-2
  in organisations 203-4, 205

  mechanistic model 197-9
  new perspectives 200-3
  psychological model 199-200
communication climate 202-3
communication networks 204-5
community networks 226
competence-based management (CBM) 130
competition (networks) 229
complexity science 117
computer-mediated communication (CMC) 86
  conceptual understanding 87-9
  definition 87
  future research implications 92
  implications for managers 92-3
  see also e-mail
conflict
  at an institutional level 101-3
  between individuals 97-8
  within and between groups 98-9
  within individuals 98
  within the organisation-as-a-whole 99-101
  see also workplace conflict
Confucian culture values 51, 52
contingency change approach 217
continuance commitment 47
continuous learning, importance of 19
convergence (speech) 201
cooperation (networks) 229
cooperative effort, concept of 9
corporate identity 189
corporate restructuring, age of 4-5
cultural audits 66
cultural diversity 63
  in teams and networks 233-4
culture
  and communication 201-2
  as a control mechanism 126-7
  as fixed or variable quantity 124
  changing 125-6
  creation and transmittal of 124
  effect on organisations 125
  forms or meanings 122-4
  measuring 126
  nature of 122-5
  study and diagnosis 124-6
  see also organisational culture
culture change 129
  facets of organisational behaviour to be targeted 132
  implementation process 131-2
  problems to be encountered 132
culture school 121, 124
culture theorists 121-2
culture theory, strengths and weaknesses 127-8
decentralised networks 204
decision making, and teams 206

demonstrating organisational improvements 67
developing a knowledge base 189
differentiation (organisational culture) 89
direction (team development rewards/recognition) 82
discontinuity, be open to 17
displacement, idea of 96-7
divergence (speech) 201
diversity 61-2
  concept of 64-5
  conceptual models 62-3
diversity enlargement 65
diversity sensitivity through training 65-6
downsizing 5, 14, 53, 54, 170, 193
downward communication 203
Dunphy and Stace's situational or contingency approach 217
dynamic equilibrium versus far-from-equilibrium 118-19

e-mail 87-8, 198-9
  and organisational culture 91-2
  future research implications 92
education and development 14
employee-organisation relationship, identity in 35-44
employees
  and leadership 171-2
  and organisational commitment 52
  exchange relationship with organisation and superiors 40-1
employers, treated as temporary partner 18-19
employment process, and identity 39-40
employment relationships 69-70
empowerment 129
ending stage (team development) 80-1
execute now (pattern of leadership) 188, 193-4
executive, functions of 140-1
executive leadership, and strategic learning 187-9
extending the periphery 14
external rewards 29-30

far-from-equilibrium conditions 118
feminisation of the workforce 14
financial rewards, relationship to non-financial rewards 30
flexible forms of work 14
forming level (team development) 79
forms (organisational culture) 123
fourth-wave careers 14
fragmentation (organisational culture) 89
full-time department team 74

gatekeepers 204
gender and communication 201
globalisation 14
government agency networks 227
groups 225

Hall's perspectives of organisational theories 113-14
heroic archetype 17708
hotdesking 8
human resource theories 13

ideal professionalism 145
identity 35-6
   and employment process 39-40
   and psychological contract 42-3
   conceptual models 37-8
   in work organisations 38-9, 40-1
   motivation as part of 36
   subgroups and conflicts 41-2
   see also organisational identity
individual development
   and leadership 171-2
   and needs 78-9
   levels of 77-8
individual rewards, practical implications for organisations and managers 83-4
industry networks 227
information overload 200
information technology 14
initiating level (team development) 79
institutional model 113-14
integration (organisational culture) 89
interdependency (networks) 229
internal social capital of organisations 168
Internet 9
interpretive schemes 89-90
intrinsic motivation
   future directions 32-3
   harnessing power of 28-30
   how does it work? 26
   models 27-8
intrinsic motivators, what are they? 25-6
intrinsic rewards 29, 32
   relationship with non-financial rewards 29-30

Japan
   corporate restructuring 5
   manufacturing industry ascendency 4

keiretsu 226
key actors in networks 234-5
knowledge integration node 235
knowledge management 131

leadership 161-2, 174-6
   and management 164-8
   and strategic learning 185-7
   and the contemporary climate of work 170
   archetypes in 176-81
   as part of management 163
   'collective unconsciousness' of 182-3

differences from management 162, 164
impact on bottom line 169
in networks 234-5
integrating past and future 181-3
management as part of 163-4
overlap with management 162-3
leadership outcomes 169-70
implications for individual employees 171-2
implications for practice 170-1
leadership patterns 187-8, 192-4
leadership style, versus managership style 165-7
leadership theories, and managership 167-8
lean business unit 190, 192
learning, continuous 19
learning organisations 129
leveraging your experience 20
Lewin's planned change model 216-17
linear systems versus nonlinear systems 117-18

maintenance stage (networks) 228
management and leadership 162-4
   challenging issues 164-8
   traditional notions 164
management knowledge 141-2
   and moral order 142-4
   types of orientation 143-4
management professionalisation see professional management
management work 140-1
managerial action, basis of 111-19
managerial control 121
managerialism, and professional management 138-40
managers, perceptions of organisations 114-16
managership style
   relationship to extant leadership theories 167-8
   versus leadership style 165-7
managing diversity 61-2
   challenging issues 64-8
   conceptual models 62-4
   future directions 68-70
   legislation 69
   techniques 65-7
Martin's perspectives of culture 89, 91-2
mechanistic model of communication 197-9
media richness model 88
meta-messages
   in speech styles 200-1
   organisational consequences of 201
motivation 25
   and achievement of organisational goals 43-4
   as part of identity 36
   see also intrinsic motivation
motivational strategies 30-2
mutual investment employee-organisation relationship 43

network dynamic dilemmas 229-31
network embeddedness 234-5
networking, for career development 19
networks 224, 235-6
   cultural diversity in 233-4
   definition 224-6
   development stages 227-8
   formation of 226-7
   leadership in 234-5
   mapping 227
   practical management implications 231-3
   types of 225-6
   see also teams
non-financial rewards
   preferences for 31
   relationship to financial rewards 30
   relationship with intrinsic awards 29-30
nonlinear systems versus linear systems 117-18
normative commitment 47
normative dimension (managerial knowledge) 143, 144
norms 90
North American model of management 5

Odyssean hero and heroine 178-80
operating core 192
orchestrated learning (pattern of leadership) 187-8
   transition to, case study 192-5
orderly transition (pattern of leadership) 188, 192
organisation-employee relationship identity in 35-44
organisation theories 112-14
organisational change 211, 221-2
   conventional theories and models 215-17
   definition 211-13
   history 213
   practical management guidelines 220-1
   processual approach 217-20
   resisting 214-15
   triggers to 214
organisational citizenship 168, 170
organisational commitment
   and employees 52
   benefits of 48
   definition 47
   determinants 50
   employee strategies to improve 55-6
   in an era of restructuring 52-4
   in different cultures 50-2
   job types and level of 48-50
   management strategies to improve 54-5
organisational communication see communication
organisational culture 121-2
   and e-mail through Martin's perspectives 91-2

and technology adoption 89-92
change, implications for
  managers 131-2
future directions for study 128-31
nature of 122-5
scientific perspectives (Martin) 89
theories of 123
organisational effectiveness 113
organisational goals, achievement
  through motivation 43-4
organisational identity
  definition 189-90
  phases and nature of change 190-2
organisational learning 130, 187
organisational socialisation 205
organisations
  adoption of technology 88-9
  identity in 38-9, 40-1
  managers' perceptions of 114-16
outsourcing 14
overinvestment approach 43

part-time special team 74
participation 129
planned change models 216-17
political behaviour, and
  power 156-9
pooled interdependency 229
population ecology model 113
portfolio careers 7, 14, 20
post-heroic leadership 180
post-revisionist perspective
  (professions) 137
power 90
  and politics 156-9
  definitions 153-6
  sources of 156
power/control (professions) 137
practical orientation 144
pre-conceptual period
  (professions) 136
processes (organisational
  culture) 123
processual framework (organisational
  change) 217-20
professional management 135-6,
  147
  and managerialism 138-40
  challenging issues 140-1
  future directions 144-6
  orientation to knowledge and moral
    order 142-4
  tension between knowledge and
    practice 141-2
professional orientation 144
professions, Collins'
  perspectives 136-7
project teams 74
  and collective identity 39
  identity and conflicts 41-2
psychological contract, and
  identity 42-3
psychological model of
  communication 199-200

quasi-spot-contract approach 43

radar screen model 227
rational-contingency model 113
realist orientation 144

reciprocal interdependency 229
reinforcement (team development
  rewards/recognition) 82
relational geography 204
relationship development
  (networks) 228
relationship starting (networks) 227
resource-dependence model 114
restructuring 14, 170
  and organisational
    commitment 52-4
  Toowoomba Foundry, case
    study 185-95
revisionist perspective
  (professions) 137
reward/recognition methods
  matching with team
  development stages 81-2
reward systems
  for teams and individuals 74-7
  impact on team and organisational
    cultures 82-3
rewards, determining suitable for
  individuals and teams 77-83

Scott's concept of organisational
  effectiveness 113
self-designed apprenticeship 17
self-employment 19-20
self-reliance through travel 18
sequential interdependency 229
servant-leadership 181-2
shock treatment (pattern of
  leadership) 188, 193
situational change model 217
social capital of organisations
  auditing 168-9
social defence theory 103-4
social information processing
  model 88-9
social networks 204
social processes 168
sociotechnical systems, conflict
  in 95-107
solidifying level (team
  development) 79-80
speech styles, meta-messages
  in 200-1
strategic alliances 130-1
strategic learning
  and executive leadership 187-9
  Toowoomba Foundry 185-95
strategic networks 225-6
strategic orientation 144
stress 205
structuration approach to
  technology 90-1
structures of control 90
subgroups, identity and conflicts 41-2
support (team development rewards/
  recognition) 82
symbols 123
systems theory, emerging
  themes 116-18

team development levels 77-8, 79-81
  matching reward/recognition
    methods with 81-2
team rewards
  aligning with business goals 74-6

designing and implementing
  reward systems 76-7
practical implications for managers
  and organisations 83-4
TeamNets 231-2
  creating voluntary links 232
  ensuring connections on all
    levels 233
  identifying independent
    members 232
  recognising power of multiple
    leaders 232-3
  unifying purpose 232
teams
  and decision making 206
  cultural diversity in 234-5
  definition 224-5
  development stages 227-8
  types of 74
  see also project teams
technical professionalism 145
technology adoption
  and organisational culture 89-92
  reasons for 88-9
termination stage (networks) 228
theoretic dimension (managerial
  knowledge) 143, 144
Toowoomba Foundry (case
  study) 185-95
  background 186
  orderly transition to orchestrated
    learning 192-5
  phases and nature of identity
    change 190-2
total quality management (TQM) 129
transaction-cost model 114
transformational leadership 168
transformative capacity 90
transforming level (team
  development) 80
trust development
  (networks) 229-30
  and violation 230-1

underinvestment approach 43
unified performing level (team
  development) 80
upward communication 203-4
violation of trust, business
  networks 230-1
virtual leadership 180
virtual organisation 225
vocational fit theories 13

work
  contemporary climate of 170
  future of 3-9
  new world of 5-6
work arrangements, changing 7-8
work groups see teams
workforce, changing nature of 69
workplace conflict 95-6
  cost of 96
  idea of displacement 96-7
  implications for working
    with 105-7
  social defence theory 103-5
  systemic levels 97-103